The Sporting World of the Modern South

SPORT AND SOCIETY

Series Editors
Benjamin G. Rader
Randy Roberts

*A list of books in the series appears
at the end of this book.*

The Sporting World of
the Modern South

EDITED BY PATRICK B. MILLER

University of Illinois Press

URBANA AND CHICAGO

Library of Congress Cataloging-in-Publication Data
The sporting world of the modern South / edited by
Patrick B. Miller.
p.   cm. — (Sport and society)
Includes bibliographical references and index.
ISBN 0-252-02718-3 (cloth : alk. paper)
ISBN 0-252-07036-4 (paper : alk. paper)
1. Sports—Southern States—History.
2. Sports—Social aspects—Southern States—History.
I. Miller, Patrick B. II. Series.
GV584.S68S66   2002
306.4'83'0975—dc21   2001003997

For Leon F. Litwack

Contents

Acknowledgments

Before the era that has come to be called "postmodern," historians long played a prominent role in rendering, or creating, origin stories for whole cultures and nations. Scholars still do so today, of course, though most strive to be mindful that myth and memory loom large in the invention of tradition and the imagination of community. This cautionary impulse is particularly applicable to discussions of the New South or the modern South, where social change has occurred at a very fast rate and yet all sorts of legends linger—about the Confederacy, for instance, or a particular brand of honor. At the same time, whether owing to the linguistic turn of recent cultural theory or good, old-fashioned attention to historical irony and paradox, many scholars seek to grasp the deeper meanings of timeworn catchwords or deft phrasings. Fifty years ago, it might be remembered, white racial "moderates" in the South were sometimes praised and often vilified by their peers for proposing that institutional separation of the races should be made somewhat "more equal," even as they admonished civil rights activists to be patient about the desegregation of buses, lunchrooms, hotels, and restaurants or the extension of the right to vote.

Scholars today probably do not need to rely on friends and colleagues for reminders about irony and paradox in the relationship between "compassionate conservatism" and the execution rate in states such as Texas, for example, or in the realm of sport, about the connections between character formation and commercialism, valor in the athletic arena and ritualized violence. But good friends and colleagues do keep us from overgeneralizing about such matters as regional culture. The idea for this collection originated in just such an exchange. Several years ago I sent a draft of an essay on the development of southern intercollegiate sport to a friend, Robert Argen-bright, for his comments. Bob, who is an historical geographer as well as a son of the South, suggested that my phrase "year-round fine weather" might be excessive, even if it stood as only one explanation for an expansive regional culture conducted largely out-of-doors. A short time afterward, while I was attending a sport history conference in Alabama, an afternoon of ninety-five-degree heat swiftly followed by a thunderstorm and tornado warnings rein-forced Bob's point. I altered the phrase and have tried to follow his other insights since then.

Selecting articles for this collection was a simple task; there is an impres-sive array of scholarship on sport and culture. It was at the same time a difficult one; I wish that I could have included more. David Wiggins, Steve Riess, Paul Spickard, and Charles Martin have been constant sources of good ideas about editing and organizing the volume. All helped me shape the in-troductory comments. I am also grateful to Benjamin Rader and Elliot Gorn for their careful readings of the entire manuscript, their smart suggestions, and their support.

During the course of editing this book, I have enjoyed a wide-ranging correspondence with all of the respective authors, who were unfailing in tracking down fugitive citations, updating information from their original publications, or getting permission letters into the hands of the people in authority at the University of Illinois Press. A special thanks goes to Bud Ford at the University of Tennessee for supplying the cover photo. At the press, Theresa L. Sears and the production staff provided substantial help in pre-paring the text for publication; Matt Mitchell did a superlative job as our copy editor. Beyond that, Richard L. Wentworth displayed the same wisdom and patience regarding this volume that for many years have marked his substan-tial contributions to the historical profession. I have benefited from his guid-ance at every point.

Finally, I should say that the way I approach history—especially concern-ing the ironies and paradoxes that inform the story of the modern South—owes largely to the models set by my one-time advisor and now good friend, to whom this book is dedicated. His thoroughness as a scholar and his con-scientiousness as a teacher, his sense of humor as well as his sense of justice, have been inspirational in countless ways.

Introduction

PATRICK B. MILLER

When Huey P. Long endeavored to render the image of Louisiana more prominent in the consciousness of the nation and at the same time place his own stamp on the state university three-quarters of a century ago, he looked to the football field. Indeed, many of the stories emanating from Baton Rouge during that era shed considerable light on subtle but significant cultural processes and social practices that link sport to the shaping of the modern South. As governor and senator, Long was never shy about publicizing his wide-ranging visions and economic programs, but in seizing on sport as a measure of display, that most energetic and calculating of politicians believed he had tapped a particularly southern source of cultural pride. Between 1928 and 1935, Long threatened and cajoled coaches in an attempt to find the formula for winning football seasons and fame. He fired one coach then rehired him during the same weekend (at a salary approximately two or three times what the average faculty member at Louisiana State University could expect to earn). During those years he also dispatched the team manager to far-flung locales to recruit talent for the gridiron squad. At one point, he insisted on lodging several injured athletes in the governor's mansion, feeding them at his own dining table: two enormous meals a day, one athlete recounted, "'of turnip greens and cornbread and broiled steak and pineapple upside down cake.'" Another player was moved into the mansion weighing 240 pounds and departed several months later weighing around three hundred. Long also drew up strategies for the team, exhorted players before hard-fought contests, ran and up and down the sidelines bellowing encouragement, then participated fully in postgame celebrations.[1]

On one occasion, when a visit by a traveling circus threatened ticket sales for an evening football matchup, the governor reportedly invoked a long-forgotten law: before entering the state, each and every elephant and tiger would need to be dipped, Long affirmed, so as to prevent the spread of disease. The circus accordingly canceled its performance in Baton Rouge, and ticket sales for the game soared. Similarly, when Long decided to charter transportation to Nashville for the entire LSU student body for a gridiron confrontation with Vanderbilt, he was told that the Illinois Central Railroad could not reduce its fares for a special group. Long responded by advising the president of the railroad that the bridges over which the trains traveled in Louisiana were taxed at one hundred thousand dollars, but their value actually amounted to $4 million. He then asked simply if the railroad wanted to alter that arrangement. Long won this contest, and the fares were reduced.

Huey Long not only searched for the best players and coaches, but, as legend would have it, he also "kidnapped" the orchestra leader from a prestigious New Orleans hotel. The new director of the marching band, Castro Carazo, was charged with the task of assembling a group of 242 musicians (out of a student body numbering only eighteen hundred), though Long assured him that there would be enough scholarships to go around. Carazo would also help Huey compose "Every Man a King" and "Touchdown for LSU," and both songs were played everywhere the team traveled as signature political pieces during the Great Depression. Concerning those road trips, one chronicler declared: "'Huey's football shows could not be kept out of the newspapers, no matter how much the newspapers hated Huey.'" The spectacles included "'2,000 cadets, 200 musicians, 50 "purple jackets"—coeds in white pleats, blazers and 50 smiles—octets of dancing boy and girl cheer-leaders and 50 sponsors in a row. And the star of the troupe, Huey, swinging, roaring, hightailing it at the head of the march. He led his boys and girls down the main streets of the invaded towns, razzled-dazzled over the field between halves and remained, as usual, perilously close to the players during the game.'" With respect to important matters of athletic business at LSU, it can be said that the president of the university was sometimes present when Long made his decisions.[2]

As matters of fact and myth, all of this adds to our knowledge of the distinctive character and personality of Huey Long. But such tales also suggest something more. They tell us about the significance of sport in the mind of much of the South. Long's locker-room orations were said to dwell on "fighting hard" or other limns on traditional notions of manhood and valor. Yet by Huey's time, such considerations of toughness and courage were mingled with more modern impulses. Football schedules were meticulously arranged. Winning seasons generated handsome revenues, and such mid-winter sporting carnivals as the Sugar, Orange, and Cotton Bowls began to stand out not only as emblems of regional pride but also as tourist attractions, part of the fabric of what would become Sunbelt culture. Although Long's quixotic foray into the realm of intercollegiate athletics does not illuminate every aspect of sport in the South, his saga is highly revealing. The upwelling of feelings about athletic rivalries have helped mark the boundaries of a distinct regional identity. In similar fashion, the rituals and spectacles of sporting competition have often played into the values, ideals, and popular images of modern southern culture.

* * *

The stories that inform learned discussions of regional exceptionalism certainly do not begin with Huey Long. In fact, scholars of sport and culture as well as historians of the South have traced distinctive patterns of leisure and recreation back to the colonial era. There too they have found particular definitions of honor and manhood, often expressed in ritual combat. It was not long after the founding of the Jamestown colony in 1607 that a report linking sport to the emerging ethos first circulated. While hundreds of the first settlers were dying of hunger and disease, Captain John Smith complained to his English sponsors that for many newcomers, "'4 hours each day was spent in worke, the rest in pastimes and merry exercise.'" During the ensuing years, both the mercantile interests who sought control over capital and labor in the Chesapeake and the royal governments hoping to create a rational social and political order attempted to curtail fighting and gambling as well as such pastimes as horse racing and cockfighting. But they did so in vain. In a society that was overwhelmingly male and where unstable economic relations prevailed, fortunes might be lost and won in ferocious bouts of gambling. Participants and observers alike described the tumult in vivid terms, as blood ran and raucousness ruled. At the outset, to be sure, all of the North American colonies drawing settlers from England harbored what we have come to call a Puritan distrust of worldly matters and disdain for various "sensory" pleasures. Another Old World legacy, however, was a rich array of play, games, and sport. As Elliott Gorn reminds us, "Calvinist beliefs in original sin, predestination, and election manifested themselves at one time or another in all the colonies. Yet Virginia always seemed a little more at ease with the joys of the flesh than Massachusetts, and as time went on, economic circumstances, demography, and the environment tipped Virginia culture ever more toward the camp of traditional recreations."[3]

A distinct "southern ethic," which valued leisure, camaraderie, and a passion for the out-of-doors, may have emerged in contrast to the work ethic and asceticism embraced by Puritans and Yankees. Regional customs for the most part withstood challenges posed by Enlightenment rationalism and evangelical moralism concerning such matters as blood sports, although one can read many sermons condemning certain forms of brutality and barbarism. From the late eighteenth century down to our own time, the praying South would persist as an important counterpart to the fighting South.[4] From a different standpoint, southern sporting culture during the colonial and early national eras remained bound to considerations of class and status, gender and race. After years of poverty and plague, a robust masculine physicality stood as an ideal among a substantial portion of colonial southerners, and how that vitality was expressed marked off the different worlds of tidewater planter and up-country yeoman, as well as of masters and slaves. At one level, the gentry used leisure and display to identify themselves as members of an elite, and the breeding of fine horses, fox hunting, or the cultivation of sports such as fencing served their purposes splendidly. For those white southerners who labored long and hard, status gained through physical competition took rougher forms, though the point of their heavy drinking, gambling, and fighting was also to demonstrate an intense virility. Whether refined or rugged, sport formed a critical part of an expressly white male southern culture.

Among the witnesses to the diversity of manly sport in the South, perhaps none had a sharper eye than the transplanted northerner, Philip Vickers Fithian, a New Jerseyan, graduate of Princeton, and tutor to a prominent Virginia family. Several years before the American Revolution, Fithian commented in his journals on the conduct of a horse race held near the Richmond courthouse. Fithian detailed the heavy wagering between the owners of the horses as well as many side bets among the spectators. "'The Assembly was remarkably numerous; beyond my expectation and exceedingly polite in general,'" he noted. What stood out in his mind, he concluded, was that the race had reflected the values and standards of true gentlemen. In contrast, another of Fithian's journal entries elaborates on several "'fist battles'" that derived from what he called "'triffling and ridiculous'" causes and shocked him for all their brutality. There were no rules to be found here, Fithian declared, but rather "'every diabolical Stratagem for Mastery is allowed and practiced, of Bruising, Kicking, Scratching, Pinching, Biting, Butting, Tripping, Throtling, Gouging, Cursing, Dismembering, Howling, &c.'" Clearly, the sports of the gentry, such as horse racing, stood in a distant relation to the mayhem of the rough-and-tumble confrontations that so appalled Fithian. Even though members of the plantation elite and those who were denominated the "lower orders" might share the spectacle of a cockfight or a horse race on occasion, there remained substantial social distinctions. As Gorn points out, "in Virginia, and later in the other Southern colonies, great disparities of wealth and the racial chasm separating blacks from whites made an individual's social status a constant source of anxiety. Sports became one venue where these anxieties were played out."[5]

A number of historians have reminded us in recent years that the tidewater and backcountry South were, in many ways, very different places socially, economically, and culturally. David Hackett Fischer, for instance, has argued that the folkways brought from diverse parts of Britain to the Chesapeake or to the Appalachians helped shape distinctive regional subcultures during the antebellum era, and the values and beliefs embodied in those subcultures persisted into the modern era.[6] Yet even as such folkways became part of broader patterns of geographic and economic tradition and change over the course of several centuries, a larger story about white Southernness began to unfold during the years preceding the Civil War. What emerged as an important connection among "aristocrats," yeoman farmers, and backwoodsmen was the notion of honor. As Bertram Wyatt-Brown and others have discussed the concept, southern honor both reinforced social hierarchies and, in some measure, dissolved the differences among white southern males. In their sporting rituals, as well as other public displays of manhood and physical prowess, white males of the South competed within a sphere that served to distinguish between the status of gentleman and farmer. Critically, though, that domain remained off-limits to male slaves and free men of color, as well as to all women.

Southern honor, no matter how far back in the Celtic or Roman past one might trace the notion, was most sharply defined—and violently defended—within the specific historical contexts of chattel slavery and the cult of female domesticity. Manly character and manly courage were collocations that had long been used to mark the passage from childhood to adulthood in America. But during the nineteenth century such formulations increasingly stood in contrast to effeminacy, or what were broadly conceived of as the boundaries of women's proper place in society. At the same time, the pastimes and leisure activities of many southern males marked their status not only as slaveholders or overseers but as free white men. Defined in highly idealized terms such as virility and valor, that status derived, in fact, from their position of power over the enslaved as well as free people of color. The lessons in leadership that hunting, shooting, and wrestling were supposed to inculcate in the scions of the ruling race constituted one plank in a broader platform of social control. Significantly, as numerous slave narratives described in gruesome detail, assertions of manly honor on the part of bondsmen—in the protection of *their* families and homes, for instance, in statements about *their* dignity—were dealt with ruthlessly. Within this framework, the notion of southern honor, frequently demonstrated in acts of oppression as well as of physical prowess, fully expressed the shared authority of white patriarchy in the antebellum South.[7]

Ultimately, the social order was also bound to processes of economic development and urbanization. To the prevailing ideology of manliness, honor, and white supremacy, some new men of the Old South added a greater variety of athletic pursuits. Horse racing and field sports were still enormously popular throughout the region during the years preceding secession and rebellion. But especially in cities such as New Orleans, the staging of well-organized prize fights and pedestrian competitions, the first glimpses of sailing and rowing as measures of skill, strength, and speed, and the introduction of team sports—baseball and cricket foremost among them—all signaled changing patterns in southern athletic culture. Those innovations had not sunk deep roots before the Civil War brought a halt to most pastimes and leisure activities, but they offered a foretaste of later developments. What would occur in the postbellum South were changes in the structures and arrangements that connected sport to larger social forces as well as to new athletic customs and practices. Sometimes the new sports played in the New South, college football for instance, originated above the Mason-Dixon line. For their meanings, though, those athletic endeavors drew heavily on southern tradition.[8]

* * *

The essays compiled in this volume engage modern southern history from a variety of perspectives, employing a wide range of methodologies—from close readings of archival and manuscript sources to oral history, ethnography, and symbolic anthropology. Through such diverse lenses, the book examines not only the "facts" concerning the modern manifestations of a particularly rugged leisure ethic in the South but also the legends and lore surrounding the football gridiron or the NASCAR racetrack, interpreting the various ways sport has reflected and shaped the social, cultural, and political history of the region. Ultimately, this book uses sport to trace the notion of southern exceptionalism and regional distinctiveness through several historiographical dimensions and over the course of more than a century.

Collectively, these essays examine the ways that sport has evoked traditional assertions of southern honor, kindled images of an idealized antebellum past, and reinforced long-standing hierarchies of racial and gender privilege and subordination. At the same time, they show how athletic competition in the aftermath of the Civil War rapidly embraced the regulations and customs of modern sports such as professional baseball and intercollegiate football and how these new cultural institutions illustrated a "New South Creed." And from a different vantage, these essays also suggest the means by which leisure pursuits and passions that originated in the South now captivate fans throughout the nation, how Daytona or Charlotte, for instance, or Tuscaloosa and Tallahassee have become household words for sports-minded people, South and North.

More importantly still, a large number of the works assembled here reveal how sport became a mechanism that was used to challenge some of the prescriptions and proscriptions historically bound to gender and racial distinctions. This has been especially true with respect to the claims made by African Americans to equality and opportunity. Simply stated, race relations and the process of desegregation lie at the center of modern southern history. Though the ordeal of integration was slow and the final outcome never sure, mainstream southern sport was eventually forced to play by the standards and rules of truly "national" pastimes, which were being reshaped by the civil rights movement. Viewed from a different perspective, athletic competition—because it meant so much both to black and white southerners—contributed, at least in small measure, to racial reform in the mid-twentieth-century South.

Further, through their respective analyses of continuity and social change, as well as their attention to the significance of myths and symbols, these essays attempt to illuminate some of the paradoxes of modern southern sport. How does the solitary hunter, long a symbol of personal independence, deal with various regulatory agencies, as well as with a recent profusion, not of game, but of fences? How do long-standing notions of southern honor commingle with images of high-tech racing vehicles? How can the stellar achievements of African American athletes, male and female, be reconciled to the resilient image of W. J. Cash's "helluvafella" or the proverbial "good ol' boy" of white southern tradition?[9]

The volume is divided into three sections, roughly marking the development of southern sport over the last 150 years. The first section explores the transformation of southern sport "from ritual to record," from isolated episodes of local and regional competition to full-fledged participation in team sports and national pastimes. As they considered models for the creation of sporting programs and enterprises, and as they reckoned with changing class, gender, and race relations in the postbellum South, athletic innovators on college campuses and in the realm of professional sports offered various meanings for "modernity." The first essay, "The Manly, the Moral, and the Proficient," assesses the diverse contexts for the development of collegiate sport in the New South. One of these contexts involved traditional notions of manhood and honor, often elaborated as pronouncements on the building of character or devotion to the Lost Cause. Another involved new models of sport, frequently originating elsewhere though bound to emerging ideals, such as the urbanizing, industrializing impulses associated with the New South creed. This essay also introduces the cultural contest that emerged when evangelical Protestants inveighed against the rugged values and violence of intercollegiate football, and it profiles some of the ironies that would shadow college sport throughout the nation when players who bore scant resemblance to bona fide students were recruited to represent institutions of higher education on the gridiron. In the second essay, Robert Gudmestad delineates the rise and brief history of professional baseball in Richmond, Virginia, discussing in detail the mingling of Lost Cause and New South imagery in the shaping of postbellum athletic enterprise. In discussing the recruitment of players from one team and city to another across the Mason-Dixon line, this essay illuminates one of the rites of "reunion" that characterized the modernizing process. It also provides a telling reminder of the economic uncertainty that plagued even the most dedicated entrepreneurs during the Reconstruction era and beyond.

At the turn of the century, young men were finding in sport new outlets as tests for traditions of honor and physical prowess. For young college women, athletic competition offered the benefits of improved health and a particular kind of esprit on campus. This is the subject of Pamela Dean's essay, "'Dear Sisters' and 'Hated Rivals,'" which explores the challenges to conventional ideals of femininity in the invention of "basquette" at Sophie Newcomb College in New Orleans and in expansive recreational programs at North Carolina Normal and Industrial College. In adapting the rules of the increasingly popular sport of basketball to their own needs and values, or in taking to the road on their bicycles, the "New Women" of the New South hoped to redefine gender boundaries during the Progressive era. Although they needed to be careful about their initiatives, several notable educators promised not only to broaden participation on the playing fields but also to enlarge women's "sphere of influence" beyond. It was at this time that southern college football squads began to measure themselves against rivals from other parts of the nation. At first, the results were rather dismal for representatives of Dixie, as Andrew Doyle describes the early years of intersectional competition in "Turning the Tide." But by the 1920s, southern football had come of age. The turning point occurred in the successive appearances by the University of Alabama in the Rose Bowl and especially its upset victory over the University of Washington in 1926. Coach Wallace Wade's Alabama teams defended the honor of the South in a rather new mode of ritual combat. What is more, as Doyle shows, football also helped reconcile conservative standards and values, including the tenets of evangelical Protestantism, with the secular gospel of progress and innovation.

The essays in the second section, concerning race relations and southern sport, discuss African American culture as reflected in the athletic programs of Historically Black Colleges and Universities (HBCUs) and the desegregation of sport in the South during the civil rights movement. Critically, those who established athletics at HBCUs shared many of the same concerns about modernization and moral probity as their white counterparts at schools such as Trinity/Duke and the University of Alabama. Yet a more significant feature of the development of sport behind the veil of segregation was the enlistment of athletics in the cause of racial reform. "Muscular assimilationism" is the phrase that stands out from "'To Bring the Race Along Rapidly,'" a discussion of how sport was incorporated into the educational mission of HBCUs as a way for black collegians to participate in a national collegiate culture and to demonstrate the traits of character and courage that were said to derive from athletic competition. To be sure, African American competition in games and sports suffered from many restrictions, but as Rita Liberti explains in "'We Were Ladies, We Just Played Like Boys,'" a high level of play was matched by the pride and intensity of the athletes who competed for Bennett College between 1928 and 1942. The recollections of those players suggest the significance of oral history in telling the stories of athletic pioneers and illuminating the multiple and shifting roles expected of middle-class black women. At the same time, Liberti's sources from the educational establishment reinforce a number of the arguments made by Pamela Dean that femininity and propriety were fervently contested notions on black as well as white college campuses and that the ideal of competitive sport for women was ultimately a fragile one. Nevertheless, the women of Bennett, like those at Sophie Newcomb and North Carolina Normal and Industrial, set precedents that would be developed in later years.

Racial reform in southern athletics was a long and difficult process, as the following essays demonstrate. Although racial enlightenment on the part of white southern political, educational, and athletic authorities may have played some small role in the desegregation process, it was expediency, a quest for higher rankings in the polls, or for greater revenues, that helped alter race relations in Dixie. Charles H. Martin's "Integrating New Year's Day" advances this observation in its expansive assessment of the rise and fall of racial exclusion in southern college bowl games between 1935 and 1965. Discussing the Orange, Sugar, Cotton, and Sun Bowl contests of those years, Martin offers a case-by-case chronicle of the ways Jim Crow was challenged and how white southern officials gradually, grudgingly accommodated the participation of northern and western African American athletes in their respective midwinter carnivals. The negotiations beyond the playing field were no less dramatic than what occurred on the gridiron; historically, they were far more significant. But as Martin demonstrates, the process was an arduous one, and racial reformers did not consistently prevail until after the landmark civil rights victories—from the sit-in movement to the Voting Rights Act of the early- and mid-1960s.

Two contrasting scenarios are presented in the next essays dealing with sport and civil rights. Jack E. Davis, in "Baseball's Reluctant Challenge," reconsiders the influence of sport on changing racial relations and sounds a revisionist note by suggesting that celebratory accounts of baseball's role in the larger civil rights crusade have often been overblown. Specifically, in examining Florida's major league training sites and the controversies surrounding desegregation between 1961 and 1964, Davis finds few praiseworthy characters within baseball management and no white Floridian in authority who would oppose the exclusion of even the most famous black athletes from decent lodging and eating facilities. It was pressure from the North and the threat of huge financial losses—all of this occurring long after Jackie Robinson's entry into baseball—that facilitated the desegregation of spring training. Finally, Russell J. Henderson offers a minutely detailed examination of the means by which Mississippi State University traveled to the NCAA basketball tournament in 1963 to face integrated competition. "'Something More Than the Game Will Be Lost'" is an ironic title for a discussion of an episode teeming with ironies. The "unwritten law" of Mississippi sports meant that no team could participate, anywhere, at any time, against black athletes. But that stipulation necessarily denied successful programs participation in national competition, and there were people who wanted to make an exception in such cases. When MSU won a bid to the NCAA tournament in 1963, students protested the "law" not only with sit-ins on campus but also by hanging in effigy the strict segregationists in the state legislature who opposed the team's trip. And while the fate of segregation was the central theme of the debate, the hallowed notion of "southern honor" found expression when the basketball team slipped out of Starksville late one night to catch a plane for the tournament, and again when the state board of trustees effectively nullified the "unwritten law" by off-handedly refusing to prohibit mixed competition in the future. The significance of the event in Mississippi history—and of sport in the overall history of the civil rights movement—can be measured against two other occurrences during this time. Six months before MSU received the bid to play in the national tournament, James Meredith successfully desegregated Ole Miss, though it required five hundred federal marshals and five thousand army troops to help him accomplish the task. Three months after the NCAA contests, Medgar Evers was assassinated in the driveway of his home in Jackson. Despite the erasure of the "unwritten law," by 1963 the time had not yet arrived when African Americans could become a significant presence in integrated sport in the South or full participants in the political, economic, and social life of the region. And the resistance to their claims for equality and opportunity could be ruthlessly violent.

Discussing myths, symbols, and stereotypes in southern sport, the third part of the volume addresses the ways heroes and traditional notions of manly honor continue to shape a distinctive regional identity and how readily they have been reconciled to images of modernity. Significantly, the essay that leads off this section, Andrew Doyle's assessment of the iconic status of Alabama's Bear Bryant, makes a critical link between the cultural analyses that inform this part of the volume and the extension of the civil rights struggle to the playing fields of the traditionally white colleges and universities in the South. Bryant was a figure who embodied both the values of the agrarian past and some of the features of the "Bulldozer Revolution" that largely reshaped the economic landscape of the region in the aftermath of the Second World War. At the same time, he stood as a symbol for an embattled *white* South during the civil rights revolution. After examining many of the media characterizations of Bear Bryant during the years of athletic triumph in Tuscaloosa, Doyle steps back to mention that the University of Alabama was the seventh of the ten Southeastern Conference schools to desegregate the gridiron. He then ponders the effect Bryant might have had on race relations and the larger history of the South if the coach had chosen to use his considerable fame to advance the cause of desegregation.

While Doyle concludes by lamenting Bryant's relative inaction on matters of conscience and social change, Louis M. Kyriakoudes and Peter A. Coclanis offer a highly contrasting portrayal of the relationship between sport and regional culture. Their article on "Professional Wrestling and Southern Cultural Stereotypes" moves from the history of backwoods eye-gouging and hair-pulling matches to notions of wrestling as postmodern theater elaborated by the French theorist Roland Barthes. The heroes they examine, who enact the roles of hillbillies or drill instructors, by turns sadistic and patriotic—as well as the occasional steroidal transvestite—differ sharply from the image of Bear Bryant, who was widely perceived as a role model. Kyriakoudes and Coclanis tell us that, as of the mid-1990s, southerners comprised a large portion of the audience for professional wrestling and that a significant number of the wrestlers themselves claim southern origins. At the same time, they recognize that the enormous popularity of World Wrestling Federation extravaganzas on television may speak to the concept of "the Southernization of America," though they leave us to speculate as to how history texts a century from now will deal with the phenomena of the wrestlers Henry O. Godwinn (HOG), Phinneas I. Godwinn (PIG), and the cross-dressing Goldust.

The huge following of stock car racing on network and cable television further suggests that images of rough masculinity and a fascination with hazard and chance have transformed southern sporting rituals and spectacles into "national" pastimes. In "The King, the Young Prince, and the Last Confederate Soldier," Karyn Charles Rybacki and Donald Jay Rybacki explore the ways many Americans have been drawn to the motor speedways of Daytona and Darlington and trace the cultural significance and appeal of Dale Earnhardt, Cale Yarborough, the Allison brothers, and Richard Petty to their southern origins and the values their exploits are said to reveal. This essay stresses the cultural connection linking the idealized images of up-country yeomanry, the foot soldiers of the Confederacy, the moonshine runner, and the most popular drivers on the Winston Cup circuit, illuminating what a long, strange trip it has been from antebellum notions of southern honor to the oil-stained concrete of modern motor speedways. In the essay closing this volume, "Manhood, Memory, and White Men's Sports in the American South," Ted Ownby challenges the notion that there is a direct line between centuries-old customs and beliefs and today's sporting practices. Writing about the ironies embedded within modern hunting practices, stock car racing, and college football—all increasingly bound to rules and formal structures of authority—Ownby highlights the transformation of sport, with traditional southern meanings of manhood dramatically redefined "to fit contemporary needs." W. J. Cash's notion of the "helluvafella" may live on in myth or in the memory of some white male southerners, Ownby suggests, but fans and practitioners of sport in the South today are largely bound to modern economic practices and social mores. They observe, more or less, the legal limits of raising hell and thus necessarily stand not as rebels but as organization men.

Appraisals of continuity and change within southern sporting culture, such as Ownby's, clearly engage a growing scholarly literature seeking the meanings of Southernness at the outset of the twenty-first century. Some of those books and articles examine broad patterns of historical development with respect to the idea that there are different Souths, distinctive subregions and subcultures, while others engage the issue of cultural diffusion, either in terms of the "Americanization of southern culture" or the "Southernization of American culture."[10] From assessments of gender and race relations on the playing field to examinations of the many dimensions of tradition and innovation, the study of sport informs a broader discussion of regional exceptionalism and the particular features of modern southern identity. Whether along the bar rail or around the seminar table, any conversation about a "muscular South" is likely to prompt numerous responses. Perhaps the considerations of sport and regional culture found in this volume will also help raise some significant new questions.

Notes

1. Peter Finney, *The Fighting Tigers: Seventy-five Years of Louisiana Football* (Baton Rouge: Louisiana State University Press, 1968), 93–105 (quote on 103); T. Harry Williams, *Huey Long* (New York: Knopf, 1969), 503–12.

2. Finney, *Fighting Tigers,* 106–31 (quotes on 118).

3. Quote in Elliott Gorn and Warren Goldstein, *A Brief History of American Sports* (New York: Hill and Wang, 1993), 19. See also Jane Carson, *Colonial Virginians at Play* (Charlottesville: University Press of Virginia, 1965); Nancy Struna, *People of Prowess: Sport, Leisure, and Labor in Early Anglo-America* (Urbana: University of Illinois Press, 1996), 96–118; and Rhys Isaac, *The Transformation of Virginia: Community, Religion, and Authority* (Chapel Hill: University of North Carolina Press, 1982).

4. C. Vann Woodward, *American Counterpoint* (Boston: Little, Brown, 1971), 13–46; Ted Ownby, *Subduing Satan: Religion, Recreation, and Manhood in the Rural South, 1865–1920* (Chapel Hill: University of North Carolina Press, 1990).

5. Philip Vickers Fithian, *Journal and Letters,* ed. Hunter Dickinson Farish (Williamsburg, Va.: Colonial Williamsburg, 1943), 240–41; Gorn and Goldstein, *Brief History of American Sports,* 17–18. See also Timothy Breen, "Horses and Gentlemen: The Cult of Gambling among the Gentry of Virginia," *William and Mary Quarterly* 34 (1977): 239–57; and Elliott J. Gorn, "'Gouge and Bite, Pull Hair and Scratch': The Social Significance of Fighting in the Southern Backcountry," *American Historical Review* 90 (February 1985): 18–43.

6. See David Hackett Fischer, *Albion's Seed: Four British Folkways in America* (New York: Oxford University Press, 1989).

7. See Bertram Wyatt-Brown, *Southern Honor: Ethics and Behavior in the Old South* (New York: Oxford University Press, 1982); and Orlando Patterson, "The Code of Honor in the Old South," *Reviews in American History* 12 (March 1984): 24–30. For discussions of how slaves used the little leisure they found, see Peter Wood, *Black Majority: Negroes in Colonial South Carolina from 1670 through the Stono Rebellion* (New York: Norton, 1974); and David K. Wiggins, *Glory Bound: Black Athletes in a White America* (Syracuse, N.Y.: Syracuse University Press, 1997), 3–20.

8. Dale A. Somers, *The Rise of Sport in New Orleans, 1850–1900* (Baton Rouge: Louisiana State University Press, 1972), 19–81; Patricia Click, *The Spirit of the Times: Amusements in Nineteenth-Century Baltimore, Norfolk, and Richmond* (Charlottesville: University Press of Virginia, 1989).

9. Some contexts for this discussion are provided in Allen Guttmann, *From Ritual to Record: The Nature of Modern Sport* (New York: Columbia University Press, 1978).

10. See, for example, John Shelton Reed, *The Enduring South: Subcultural Persistence in Mass Society* (Chapel Hill: University of North Carolina Press, 1972); Raymond A. Mohl, ed., *Searching for the Sunbelt: Historical Perspectives on a Region* (Athens: University of Georgia Press, 1993); Peter Applebone, *Dixie Rising: How the South Is Shaping American Values, Politics, and Culture* (New York: Times Books, 1996); and James C. Cobb, *Redefining the American South: Mind and Identity in the Modern South* (Athens: University of Georgia Press, 1999).

PART 1

The Transformation of Southern Sport: Gender, Class, and Some Meanings of Modernity

1. The Manly, the Moral, and the Proficient: College Sport in the New South

PATRICK B. MILLER

Who are these youths with such athletic mastery and where did
they come from and who taught them to play such football?

They are the sons of men who fought in the charge of Pickett
and Pettigrew at Gettysburg; of men who laid down their arms
with Lee at Appomattox. As their fathers learned of themselves and
their leaders how to fight, so have these young men learned of
themselves and their leaders how to play football.

—Conversation between a prominent Virginian and Professor J. M.
  Bandry, Trinity College (later Duke University), ca. 1890

Say the defenders of [football], it develops *manhood of youth*. I
deny it unless by *manhood* they mean mere physical strength.

—John Singleton Mosby, writing in the aftermath of the death of
  the University of Virginia football player Archer Christian in
  1909

SURVEYING THE AMERICAN educational landscape toward the end of the
nineteenth century, various commentators assessed the development of collegiate athletics by geographical region. In contrast to their appraisals of the
relatively mature status of organized sport in the Northeast and what they
observed about the increasing experience and expertise of midwestern athletes as well as growing enthusiasm along the Pacific coast, those who took
note of the southern states at all simply asserted that they lagged far behind
in matters pertaining to the sporting spirit. "'Neither the general nor college
public at the South manifests much interest in athletics or gymnastics,'" the
United States Bureau of Education concluded in its *Bulletin* of 1885. In attempting to account for this particular anomaly, the bureau could only suggest that "'military drill is in vogue in many places'" throughout the region.[1]

The *Bulletin* was clear in its considerations: it was the white South that prompted such concern. Like other mainstream commentaries at the turn of the century, the *Bulletin* did not deal with the expansion of traditionally black colleges or the issue of race relations in the South; its omissions are thus as significant historically as its assertions concerning athletics and regional culture.[2] Within its narrow frame of reference, however, the Bureau of Education did touch on issues critical to the assessment of "southern exceptionalism" within the larger transformation of American society. Though it is true that the development of college sport in the white South followed a different pace and pattern than it did elsewhere, in fact, even as the bureau's *Bulletin* was being published, students on many southern campuses had begun to devote an increasing amount of their leisure hours to formal competition in a variety of athletic endeavors. Most notably pursuing long, exhausting baseball schedules against club and collegiate opponents, they also participated with a vengeance in the newly discovered, rough-and-tumble game of football. At the same time, many of their elders—educational authorities prominent among them—began to articulate a formal justification for athletics, praising sport for its contributions to the building of "manly" character and the strengthening of regional pride.

From a different vantage, it is noteworthy that the Bureau of Education ignored the numerous factors, geographic as well as economic, that actually *had* impeded the spread of athletics below the Mason-Dixon line during the first years of the postbellum period.[3] In its reference to "military drill," moreover, the bureau's report missed the connection that some observers would discern between the martial traditions characterizing the Old South and the virtues attributed to athletic competition. And ultimately, the *Bulletin* may have been written too soon to consider yet another, contrasting interpretation of the role of athletics in southern culture at the turn of the century: the important ways in which the rituals and spectacles of "modern" team sports resonated for those seeking to create a "New South."[4]

To chronicle the origins and development of southern college sports would be to address not only a broad range of social practices but also the values and ideals defining the region a century ago. First, intercollegiate athletic competition offers a case study in "cultural diffusion," the manner in which games imported from the North gained popularity in the South, or from a different perspective, the ways homegrown energy and enthusiasm found expression in "national" pastimes. Beyond that, the traits of hardihood and courage that were associated with the sport of football were lauded by many southern leaders in much the same terms employed by their northern counterparts. By the turn of the century, young men of both sections might thus be seen playing out a "ritual of reunion" on the college gridiron, the significance of the game widespread as well as firmly entrenched as an emblem of the strenuous life. Within a few short years, athletes from the South would join northerners on the "All-America" teams chosen annually by the coaches and journalists who stood as the arbiters of athletic culture in the United States.[5]

Cast within a slightly different context, athletic competition spoke to traditional notions of southern honor and at the same time to the "New South creed," especially as both ideals reinforced distinctions predicated on gender and race. Accentuating the particular fitness of the white southern male, games such as baseball and football, like the rugged physical pursuits of the antebellum era, stood out as demonstrations not merely of difference but of dominance. Yet with respect to continuities and innovations—an ongoing debate among historians of the postbellum South—the desire by students to increase their "proficiency" in technical terms, like the efforts of their coaches to organize games and athletic seasons, attested to increasingly "modern" sensibilities. Along with frequent evocations of football as a "scientific" sport, such developments reflected an ideology bound to the processes of urbanization and industrialization rather than an attempt to redeem an idealized agrarian past of "horses and gentlemen" or the legacy of the "Lost Cause." "As in so much else," one recent historian has concluded, "modern innovations [in sport] did not so much dilute Southern identity as give it new, sharper, focus."[6]

Finally, set against the backdrop of intraregional cultural rivalries, debate over the conduct of college games became implicated in broad-based discussions about the meanings of manliness and morality, as well as modernity. This occurred when New Southerners extolled sport as a carrier of the modern creed, while evangelical Protestants—joined by old warriors like John Singleton Mosby—inveighed against the excesses they believed were bound to the games played by a younger generation. That numerous colleges dropped football within a few years after its arrival in the South suggests that the gridiron was, at least at the outset, contested cultural territory. Ultimately, football prevailed. But when "pigskin fetish-worship" triumphed over religious pieties—a victory not completed until the 1920s—the new cult continued to embrace a paradox. Since that time, an exalted notion of manly sport has loomed large in shaping popular perceptions of a traditional white southern culture played out within the modernizing experience.

* * *

Congruent in many respects with field sports, horse racing, and other gentlemanly but strenuous pastimes, baseball—in its early versions—was first introduced to the region before the Civil War, becoming popular in the larger cities and on some college campuses.[7] Nonetheless, the conflagration of the 1860s was devastating to the educational institutions of the Old South and thus militated against the further organization of athletic competition until rather late in the century. Several state-supported colleges closed during Reconstruction, for lack of funds and as a strategy to suppress the educational aspirations of many freedmen; numerous other schools, whether affiliated with various Protestant denominations or publicly endowed, operated on the most meager of budgets. As a consequence, extracurricular activities that might involve the expense of equipment, travel, and lodging found little place in the programs of state legislators or educational leaders, just as such endeavors often might lie beyond the financial reach of many students.[8]

If the destruction of life and property during the Civil War created an enormous gap in the student traditions of the South, other factors inhibited the process by which new patterns of social and cultural exchange might replace, or augment, the old. The dearth of high schools and more formal systems of secondary instruction (such as those being established in the Northeast and Upper Midwest) severely limited the ways students might share their interest and expertise in athletics. College campuses of the South, moreover, were in many cases located farther from one another than those in New England or in states such as Ohio and Pennsylvania, and transportation networks were far less extensive than in other sections of the nation. And with fewer large cities in the South, the region lacked the concentrations of middle-class populations, which elsewhere had been instrumental in sponsoring the expansion of sporting activity.[9]

Against these impediments stood numerous incentives for southern youth to participate in games of strength and daring. An abundance of warm weather as well as the history and lore of the rigorous frontier experience were conducive in their own ways to the development of sports in the South. Southern commentators consistently stressed the prominence of outdoor life, the pleasure derived from trials of skill, boldness, and tenacity, and the need to maintain the ethos of aggressive white manhood as central to the perpetuation of a rugged regional culture.[10] According to the catalog of the University of the South (Sewanee), the institution had been established in 1858 to promote the "raw planter mentality," its founders arranging the academic calendar so as to allow the student time "to engage in the sports which make him a true Southern man, hunting, shooting, riding." In this instance, such pursuits were intended to lend themselves to the training of young men in the management of large plantations and their slaves. After the Civil War, southern elites could project onto other sports—especially those conceived in terms of certain "rules"—a similar means of training for social leadership and racial control.[11]

A richly textured tradition of southern honor that had long animated the region also facilitated the rise of intercollegiate athletics. Though the Bureau of Education in its *Bulletin* of 1885 had suggested that military drill could distract students from athletics, both the structure of organized sports and the sensibilities they were intended to inspire corresponded well with "a passion for the physical," a fascination with violence in formal as well as spontaneous manifestations, and antebellum military tradition.[12] Rough and romantic, like the martial valor representing the legend of the Lost Cause, athletic exploits thus could give young men a sense of exhilarating contest and conflict in battle. This was a shadow perhaps of what their fathers might have recalled from their exploits at Vicksburg and Gettysburg, but it was a deeper experience than marching on a parade ground might ever provide.

For some educators, moreover, college sports served to unite tidewater and up-country, metaphorically if not always politically, socially, and economically. As Professor John Spencer Bassett of Trinity College observed, athletic competition brought together the well-bred scion of an established family and the rough-hewn lad down from the hills to compete on the level surface of the baseball diamond or football field. The intensely masculine "bonding" of the sporting experience thus could ease tensions on campus by channeling, temporarily at least, distinctions of class into a shared endeavor. Once again, as in memories of combat, for white southern males dauntlessness and dash—represented in the bristly faced rebel and in Robert E. Lee, respectively —could, ideally, reinforce each other.[13]

Interpreted from a substantially different perspective, the "embrace of muscle" by southern college students not only appeared to "fit" the dominant culture of the old South; their games also sustained analogies to an emerging *new* southern mentality, following patterns originally deriving from the Northeast. To be sure, what occurred in Charlottesville or Chapel Hill did not compare in magnitude to the contests being orchestrated in New Haven or Cambridge, even by the turn of the century. Yet in admiration of the techniques and strategies of so-called scientific sport, southern college athletes emulated their northern counterparts when they could, and their increasing emphasis on organization and regulation, their desire to stage events with appropriate care, bespoke a changing games ideal in the South.[14]

With the structures of sport beginning to conform to models of commercial and industrial enterprise associated with the urban North, the rituals of competition acquired added significance. Representations of strength and energy thus came to share the sporting arena with more clearly recognizable limits to the play, just as the notion of manliness might be defined in terms of vigor and assertiveness yet also as the measure of discipline and self-control. Spatial and temporal boundaries imposed by the size of the field and the precision of the clock or stopwatch placed an emphasis on the coordination and timing of well-ordered teamwork. The rules of games, codified and published nationwide, likewise stressed increasingly "rational" processes, as opposed to spontaneous action. And an emerging hierarchy of authority headed by expert, professional coaches and trainers (often imported from outside the region) suggested efficient management along the lines of the factory system.[15] By the 1890s, furthermore, numerous southern schools had adopted distinctive emblems—colors, mascots, songs, cheers, and chants— and had inaugurated local rivalries as well as seasonal pageants surrounding big games. Still, as much as these symbols and spectacles reflected loyalty to a specific college and community, they also marked the assimilation of many institutions in the region to a national intercollegiate culture.

What appeared, then, at the end of the century as changing means and ends in athletics did not emerge suddenly as successors to venerated rites of passage or patterns of belief. Nor did "new" methods and standards necessarily intrude on the conventional imperatives of racial and gender solidarity. The cultivation of manly self-expression continued to serve a narrowly based system of social leadership both regionally and nationally. Thus, for the majority of white southern males, an idealized conception of sport, traditional evocations of honor, and emerging "modern" sensibilities formed a widely respected constellation of values and virtues, complementary discourses supporting the assertions of strenuous masculinity. And though this system of thought and action did not go unchallenged, it would ultimately prevail in defining a significant dimension of New South culture.

* * *

Although students participated in a wide range of muscular pursuits, until late in the century baseball had no rivals in popularity among organized collegiate sports. The running and jumping contests of "field days," part of the rites of spring at Washington College as early as 1872, remained informal affairs, bearing scant resemblance to the events performed by English university students or northeastern track and field squads. During the 1880s undergraduates at the University of North Carolina initiated a series of competitions, ranging from the one-hundred-yard dash and three-mile run to the long jump (with dumbbells in hand) and the "fat man's" race. A decade later, athletes at Alabama competed for a variety of cups and gold medals in intramural competition before they challenged Tulane to an intercollegiate meeting. And at the University of Georgia, a gangling senior named Ulrich Bonnell Phillips set the school record in the mile before hanging up his spiked shoes and undertaking graduate study in the history of the South. Yet track and field never enjoyed widespread popularity in the region until well after the turn of the century.[16] Likewise, crew attained only limited support in southern colleges. It may be noteworthy that Robert E. Lee, the president of Washington College in the late 1860s, was an appreciative spectator on some occasions, sitting on horseback to watch students row on the North River near Lexington. The trustees of Washington even provided four hundred dollars for the boat club. Yet elsewhere, aspiring oarsmen, like those at the University of Virginia, grew impatient as they suffered high-standing rocks below or low-hanging branches above their boats in order to practice their rowing. In most cases the athletes simply lost interest in the sport after a few seasons of hardship.[17]

Baseball, however, was played nearly everywhere. Known in some parts of the region before the Civil War and learned from Union occupation troops and carried to more remote parts of the South after the struggle, baseball grew in popularity in both town and country during the ensuing decades. Much in the manner of midwestern teams, college associations competed first against local squads and then against rivals from nearby schools. Such clubs as the Franklin, Dixie, Adelphian, and Champion could be found on the campus of the University of Georgia in the late 1860s; during the next decade the best players on campus were assembled as a "varsity" team and sent off to defend institutional honor against a variety of foes. Cadets from the Virginia Military Institute used their parade ground as a field in games against neighboring Washington College. In other parts of Virginia, undergraduates from the state university, Roanoke College, and the Polytechnic Institute participated in the sport regularly and formally in contests against other clubs and colleges. By the 1890s the game between the University of Virginia and the University of North Carolina weighed heavily as an interstate as well as an intercollegiate rivalry, its outcome stirring passions beyond the immediate campus communities. It was also during the last decade of the century that northern college teams first ventured into the South, and a few southern clubs traveled northward during the spring and summer. The southerners more than held their own. In fact, for the last two years of the century the Georgetown varsity team, composed largely of "semiprofessional" players from the Carolinas, was considered the unofficial college champion in baseball.[18]

If for many years baseball remained the most popular athletic activity at most southern colleges—drawing large numbers of fans and inspiring voluminous student newspaper reports and editorials—it may have been because the game was customarily learned at home in childhood and played at many levels. For numerous participants, it must have seemed a natural part of the maturation process, woven into the fabric of southern male custom and convention, a fitting pastime in its rhythms and routine for a largely agrarian culture. Significantly, football was conceived by undergraduates, their teachers, and other observers in contrasting terms: it carried physical prowess into a new realm of discipline and organization and thus embodied some of the features of modern higher education in the South. Ultimately, many perceived it as a "scientific" sport. Stated in different terms—and at the time, without irony—the pigskin game stood for progress. Football was a sport that was predominantly collegiate; it reinforced elite standards within an educational setting, yet at the same time it suggested the "egalitarian" element in the shared virile tradition of white southern sporting competition. It stood as a means of expressing or even inculcating the qualities of strength, endurance, and valor deemed highly honorable by generations of cultural commentators. Football highlighted specific individuals struggling in hand-to-hand combat along a moving line, anticipating—perhaps promising—the rush of life-threatening violence; it also brought together mass and mobility in the manner of an infantry charge; it rewarded bravery and, as it evolved, technique and strategy as well. Both in its form and in the public response to the spectacle, the sport embraced the "deep play" of hazard and chance, of numerous degrees of risk. Yet it also demanded considerable preparation and exalted the pushing, driving coordination of teamwork. Largely because it offered numerous "meanings" and expressed a formidable array of virtues and values, football grew substantially in its appeal for participants and spectators alike.

Football possessed enormous metaphorical value concerning the rites of passage toward southern manhood, and it clearly corresponded with the region's martial culture and tradition of blood sport. Yet no one denied that the game was imported from the North or that it somehow spoke to the "imperatives" of modernity. Indeed, students as well as professors articulated pride in the fact that football bound their often small and relatively impoverished institutions to a prestigious collegiate pastime. The first facts in the history of southern football often concern the ways the game was introduced, either by "Yankees" or natives returning from the North. At AddRan Christian University—now Texas Christian—two professors, one the son of the college president, returned from Michigan where they had been "bitten by the football bug." Soon much of the campus community had received instruction in the strange new sport. The great football tradition at Alabama began in a similar fashion when Bill Little returned to his home state after a year at Andover Academy, bringing with him canvas clothes, cleated shoes, and a pigskin. Meanwhile, officials at Transylvania College recruited an instructor from Yale to teach the "young natural athletes from mountains and blue grass" the rudiments of the sport.[19]

Among scores of other "football missionaries," Hugh and Thomas Bayne departed from Yale for New Orleans in the late 1880s to teach the game to students at Tulane, Thomas eventually laying out an athletic field, handling all the tickets, and serving as referee for home games. In the early period— some would recall it as the halcyon days—of early sporting competition, it was not always necessary for the new mentor to have been a former player; someone who had only been a bystander in the North might also be sufficiently knowledgeable, then energetic, in introducing the intricacies of the game to the unschooled youth of the South. Vernon L. Parrington was such an advisor. A Harvard graduate who joined the English department at the University of Oklahoma in the mid-1890s, Parrington guided the football team during its first seasons before moving on to a distinguished academic career as one of the foremost interpreters of American history and culture. As the resumés of the early coaches might suggest, the diffusion of the new system of play could take many forms.[20]

Despite the northern origins of the game, regional pride in football manifested itself in a number of ways. The clippings in college archives and the early, filiopietistic histories of southern educational institutions reveal contending assertions of priority concerning football competition. Long before intersectional rivalries developed, even before intrastate clashes marked the high point of a season, ardent alumni linked the first games of football to the coming-of-age of their alma maters. In similar fashion, civic boosters tied the development of the sport to the maturation of the New South. The earliest games were actually intramural rather than intercollegiate frays, however, resembling an Irish faction fight more than the modern version of football. The editors of the college magazine at the University of Virginia, for instance, declared that one afternoon in November 1870, members of the junior mathematics class, upon hearing that there would be no lecture, adjourned to the Lawn to initiate the South's first game of football. This would have meant that the Virginians had closely followed on the heels of the first eastern colleges, Rutgers and Princeton, which had engaged in a game like soccer in 1869. But the sport that the southern students claimed was football was described by other observers as "'a crowd of coatless youth engaged in what seemed . . . the insane sport of rushing together and trying to kick each other's hats off.'" Before the decade had ended, though, Virginia athletes had played one team of British citizens from Albemarle County and another squad from Washington and Lee, reportedly based on rules they had requested from Rutgers, Princeton, and Yale. Yet even with the northeastern regulations in hand, southern players sometimes modified the game to suit themselves; in 1872 no fewer than two hundred students participated at one time in a contest in

Charlottesville, while in Lexington, athletes from Washington and Lee and Virginia Military Institute argued whether fifty or only thirty-five men should be allowed on a side.[21]

It was not until the late 1880s that southern college teams became familiar with northeastern rules, then adequately organized to challenge cross-county or interstate rivals to a game they all understood. Within the context of increasing interregional competition, undergraduates at the University of Virginia learned harsh lessons about the sport from their neighbors in Maryland, Pennsylvania, and New Jersey. In 1888 the Cavaliers of Virginia—as they had come to be called—defeated two local high schools, but then they lost to Johns Hopkins. In 1889 they succumbed to more formidable teams from Lehigh and Navy after defeating Johns Hopkins. And the following year they began their season with humbling losses—62-0 to Pennsylvania and 115-0 to Princeton—before crushing less experienced foes from Randolph-Macon and Washington and Lee. Through the decade that nearly everywhere in the South was marked by depression and Populist upheaval, University of Virginia teams traveled widely and sometimes hired a coach for a few weeks or a season. And ultimately, the level of their play was good enough to post victories against both neighboring and distant rivals.[22]

Elsewhere in the state, however, football remained a more rustic affair. Students at up-country colleges such as Emory and Henry learned the game from the most recent rulebook they could obtain or from an enthusiastic professor educated in the North. Sometimes ardent and aspiring athletes practiced formations and plays invented at Yale, Princeton, or Pennsylvania; more often they devised their own systems or played without much method. One participant on the early teams of Virginia Polytechnic recalled that "there was no idea of team play; whoever got the ball—by luck—ran with it; no one knew anything about interference, and tho' we had a system of signals, it was a question of luck how each play went." Those most interested in the sport removed rocks from the field, then measured and traced a quadrangle, but even this would not always conquer difficult terrain. At Virginia Polytechnic, "the boundaries of the field were marked off with a plough, as also the 25-yard lines. The field was not as smooth as the bed of the new Blacksburg railroad, but ran up and down hill, with interesting little hollows which hid the play from spectators on the other side of the field."[23] In the attempt, at least, if not always in the outcome, southern college youth enthusiastically embraced modern college sport.

The same kind of social dynamic, between the rough and increasingly "rational," characterized the inauguration of intercollegiate sport in North Carolina. Students at Wake Forest had organized football clubs and engaged in intramural play as early as 1882; similarly untutored, their peers at the state university had been arranging inter-class games of football since 1883. Yet in 1888 the *Raleigh News and Observer* measured substantial changes in the sport since those first contests were staged, boasting that the twenty-nine-year-old John Franklin Crowell, a Yale graduate recently appointed president of Trinity College, had presided over "the first scientific game of football ever played" in the state. Before a crowd of six hundred, the small Methodist college—then located in the hills of Randolph County—defeated the University of North Carolina in Raleigh on Thanksgiving Day. Within the ensuing year students from the two institutions, joined by representatives from Baptist Wake Forest, established the North Carolina Intercollegiate Foot-Ball Association. An intense but short-lived rivalry had begun.[24]

That the first "match game" in the state took place not on the campus of one of the contending schools but in the capital city, and that it was scheduled for a national holiday, indicated the ways intercollegiate sport would develop in the South at the turn of the century. Attracting what was for the time a sizable collection of spectators, many of whom were not college students, the contest also suggested the larger appeal of football in the region. Significantly, the rivalries among Trinity, UNC, and Wake Forest revealed yet another dimension of athletic competition as it escalated throughout the New South. For the popularity of football, combined with intensifying school spirit, motivated many students to seek outside help in order to prepare their teams for upcoming contests. First the state university hired a Princeton player to demonstrate the finer points of the sport, then Wake Forest acquired the services of a former athlete from Lehigh. Both teams subsequently trounced Trinity, which continued to be led by sons of the South: Stonewall Jackson Durham and, later, his brother, Robert E. Lee Durham. Given the opportunity to win through innovation, most college students were loathe to rely on something so tenuous as tradition. Social history always works within certain limits, though it has its literary counterparts; sadly, however, such episodes as the failures of Jackson and Lee Durham never found their Faulkner.[25]

* * *

The presence of northern coaches on the sidelines of southern playing fields not only marked the assimilation of the South to a prominent national pastime; it also contributed substantially to the rationalization of sport throughout the region. At one level, the transformation of the game meant that coaches would appropriate a dominant role in the manly ritual of athletic struggle, introducing their players to new rules, to a carefully planned training pro-

gram, and to the latest formations and competitive tactics. Striking innovations, such as the V—the prelude to the flying wedge—captivated participants
and fascinated fans. They also clearly linked southern sport to the pounding,
pushing game that was attracting increasing notoriety elsewhere throughout the nation.[26]

By the mid-1890s, a growing number of schools were spending increasing
sums for the special skills of coaches and trainers. In 1894, for instance,
Vanderbilt began hiring recent graduates from Pennsylvania, Princeton, and
Harvard at salaries ranging from four hundred to eight hundred dollars for
a seasons's work. The majority of journeymen coaches traveled from school
to school for several years, earning enough money to initiate other careers.
But a few stayed in the game, transforming it through more persistent ex-
perimentation. Moving from jobs at several colleges in Ohio to Auburn and
Clemson during the 1890s and then to Georgia Tech in 1904, John Heisman
earned as much as two thousand dollars for his talents, drawing his income
from contributions by enthusiastic undergraduates and alumni and later in
his eminent career from the college treasury. In the ensuing decades he would
be joined by other experts in sport, who often became the best paid and most
prominent individuals associated with higher education, and its accouter-
ments, in the South.[27] Thus an increasing emphasis on victory, stimulated by
partisans on and beyond the campus setting and intensified by the regimens
and stratagems devised by a new elite of professional coaches, significantly
reshaped the games of youth. At the same time, paradoxically, athletic competition continued to be justified in terms consonant with traditional southern standards and ideals: character, honor, and courage.

College sport in the South, as elsewhere, originated among students, who
participated in the athletic enterprise variously as players, managers, cheer-
leaders, and fund-raisers. Yet they were often joined in their endeavors by
alumni and local boosters. And in some instances they found valuable allies
in professors such as Charles Herty of the University of Georgia and in college presidents like Trinity's John Franklin Crowell and George T. Winston,
who headed the University of North Carolina from 1891 to 1896. Beyond the
popularity of sport among most students, it was the influence exerted by
those who strove to fashion a muscular as well as a moral and intellectual
plan of education in the New Southern academy that facilitated the expansion of athletic competition in the South. For some educational authorities,
success on the gridiron translated into institutional prestige within the region and in the nation at large.

Just as significant as those parochial concerns was the philosophical ra-
tionale for sport, deriving from the ancient doctrine of civic republicanism

as well as considerations about the future of higher education. As Crowell strenuously argued, football not only destroyed "'the namby-pambyisms of caste'" by bringing "'everybody face to face to stand on his own merits,'" it also stood as the "'first among those sports in which the qualities of the soldier are capable of being developed.'"[28] Football taught significant lessons in life, the president of Trinity avowed. It developed "'virility, self-control, and daring courage of American youth.'"[29] For Crowell, football served to shape the education of the well-rounded and ambitious man, someone capable of leading a college, or a region, into the modern era.

Reinforcing as well as reflecting concerns about training in manly character, the apostles of sport linked the southern academy not only to the strength of the nation but also to the story of Western civilization. Thus George Winston declared in 1894 that "'It would not be dishonest to say that the greatest force in the university today contributing to sobriety, manliness, healthfulness and morality generally is athletics,'" asserting as well that sporting competition helped create the stuff of social progress. The greatest men of all countries were "'fine specimens of physical manhood,'" Winston avowed: Moses, Joshua, St. Paul, Martin Luther, Shakespeare, Goethe, Humboldt, Napoleon, Gladstone, Washington, and Webster; "'all were men of great physical power and endurance.'"[30] Echoing some of the sentiments expressed by Crowell and Winston but extending the argument in nationalist and racialist terms, Kemp Battle, the president and then historian of the University of North Carolina, would write in 1912: "A nation can not afford to lose its aggressive manliness, endurance, courage, restraint, the power to act surely and unfalteringly in an emergency. A man in football must learn to be cool headed while he is impetuous, to think and act on the instant. And if he has the making of a man in him he attains the blending of courage and courtesy, which distinguishes the strong man from the powerful brute."[31] Thus inscribing football in world history, binding the sport to the future of American higher education, and marking what for their era were forceful, if coded, racial distinctions, the academic promoters of athletics contributed substantially to the establishment of one of the pillars of New Southern identity and culture.

* * *

Apart from the lessons supposedly learned through athletic endeavors, considerable pageantry accompanied the play. And beyond the articles and orations speaking to notions of character and courage, a myriad of rituals and symbols reinforced for many southerners the intensity of the intercollegiate sporting experience. The anthems and totems of college athletic culture in the South took a variety of forms and projected a range of images, in some instances evoking a particular regional identity, in others reflecting students' desire to associate their games with those of more established institutions in the Northeast. The iconography of college sport, manifest in the waving of flags, the orchestration of chants and cheers, and the singing of inspiration-al songs, formed circles of significance around the actual sites of races or games, actively involving fans as well as participants in the intercollegiate sporting spectacle. The sights and sounds of boisterous athletics went beyond competitive exchange on the diamond or gridiron; those who watched be-came immersed in something like a sacrament against which a book, a lec-ture, or a laboratory experiment—among other academic offerings—often seemed to pale in comparison.[32]

Additionally, the anticipation created by the expanding newspaper cov-erage of sport at the turn of the century, the knowledge transmitted by the printing of illustrated programs, and the lore passed on from one student generation to another served to transform college culture, directing energy and interest away from classroom and chapel and toward the playing fields. Ultimately, it also bound campus to community in terms of shared emblems and experiences. And for the majority of Americans living in the age of mass media, the defining characteristics of a particular college or university have not resided in its curriculum or the honors accumulated by professors and graduates. Rather, the measure of a school in popular consciousness often rests on its athletic record against regional and intersectional rivals, and the host of signs and symbols that emphasize the distinctiveness of an institu-tion also advertise its involvement in a national pastime. Tellingly, even many of those who were entrusted with the academic mission of their schools learned to appreciate these facts. Or at least they became resigned to them.

The spectacle accompanying baseball and football games may have been communicated first through the colors of the uniforms worn by athletes and the pennants often carried by their fans. Undergraduates might make an historical reference when they invented athletic traditions, but numerous other factors were frequently involved. Georgetown collegians chose blue and gray for their colors to signify the division between students at the outset of the Civil War. At the University of Virginia, silver gray and cardinal red were intended to represent the glory of the Confederacy, dyed in the blood of the fallen. Popular for more than a decade, those colors eventually proved un-suitable for athletic uniforms, however, because the red dye tended to fade quickly. In 1888 one of the campus football heroes on his way to practice dropped by a meeting where the subject of replacement colors was being discussed. He was wearing a long, striped navy blue and orange kerchief around his neck, after the Oxford fashion. Devotion to the Lost Cause gave way to expediency that day, and orange and blue became Virginia's permanent colors.[33] Collegiate identity could be appropriated from other institutions that had already won laurels in sport, but in the South, as elsewhere, the image of a school would "necessarily" be cast in the most masculine of hues. That the University of Mississippi chose the blue of Yale and crimson of Harvard as school colors may have been due to the fact that the football coach first made the suggestion, perhaps in the hopes of emulating the athletic fame of the New England institutions. And when students at Davidson College applauded the choice of red and black as new colors, they were rendering an opinion on the best way to display their notions of manly pride: "a judicious change from pink and blue [had been] effected in 1895," the college historian has observed. Clearly, there was no simple means by which to select an emblem and maintain it over time.[34]

Like the choice of colors, the denomination of teams and mascots could become complicated matters, ultimately illuminating students' ambivalence concerning regional loyalties and their quest to become a part of a more expansive collegiate culture. In some places club names readily yielded to varsity titles. Before Washington College became Washington and Lee, and before the teams became the Generals, students played baseball as the "Shoo Flies," on several occasions challenging the University of Virginia's first club, the "Monticellos." After Yale had adopted a bulldog as a mascot in 1889, several schools throughout the nation followed the lead of the most famous football institution of the era. Among them was the University of Georgia, which disposed of its goat and acquired its own bulldog during the 1890s.[35]

In more practical terms, bulldogs were not only simpler to come by, they were also easier to maintain than some other mascots. Varsity teams at the University of Texas had been called the Longhorns as early as 1904; twelve years later, Texas partisans acquired a live steer, with horns measuring between seven and eight feet tip to tip. Shortly thereafter, someone suggested that the longhorn, christened Bevo, be branded with a large "T" as well as the score of the 1916 Texas victory over its arch rival Texas A&M. But before this could be accomplished, Bevo was discovered bearing the score of the 1915 A&M victory in the form of an eight-inch brand. Disfigured as he had become, Bevo also posed problems of another sort, costing eighteen dollars a month to feed, which was a sum many students believed to be excessive. Ultimately—again to juxtapose the pragmatic and the iconic—in 1920 Bevo was butchered and served as barbecue to more than one hundred guests, the majority of whom, appropriately, were "T-Men," the winners of varsity letters.[36] Bevo's immediate successor turned out to be no less controversial. His "lazy disposition and refusal to conform to standards of campus behavior," according to one report, meant that he would be kept from most games. Finally, during the Depression, Bevo II was officially prohibited from entering the football stadium, and due to the cost of his upkeep, his caretakers sent him back to the range.[37] Some traditions might prove difficult to invent.

As various critics would assert, athletic customs often seemed to reinforce the rather crudely democratic, often antiintellectual dimension of higher education in America. Yet at the same time, the emblems of school spirit could make powerful connections with history and community. Undergraduates at Louisiana State University, for example, nicknamed their team the Fighting Tigers, not simply because colleges were beginning to nominate ferocious animals as mascots, but because the Louisiana Tigers, composed of New Orleans Zouaves and Donaldsville Cannoneers, had been among the state's most distinguished fighting units during the Civil War. Students at other schools made choices almost as evocative, but sometimes they ran up against the resistance of their elders. After the First World War, undergraduates at Trinity College (soon to be renamed Duke University) also planned to name their athletic teams after a military squad—in this case a crack French Alpine Corps—indicating perhaps the prevalence of martial imagery in the thinking of many promoters of college sports. In this instance, however, the choice of Blue Devils as a nickname occasioned considerable upheaval among the trustees and more pious alumni of the Methodist institution throughout the 1920s. The controversy was not a major one, and in the end the students won out. But as was the case at Duke, college youth at several other schools in the more secular twentieth century resisted journalistic attempts to characterize their athletic heroes as "the Fighting Baptists" or "Fighting Parsons." Blasphemy aside, such appellations might seem altogether inappropriate, either from the vantage of the battered athlete or of the true believer in modern sport.[38]

With respect to songs, chants, and cheers, southern students joined in the tradition throughout the nation to boast of the prowess of their own teams and to denigrate their opponents' courage or ability. Often these followed a formula that did not speak to a specific regional or institutional distinctiveness and are remarkable principally for their banality: "Rah-Rah / White and Blue / Vive-la, Vive-la / N.C.U." Occasionally, however, an inspirational composition would assure students that they had much to be proud of or that they bore special responsibilities. In 1903 a campus poet at the University of Texas employed the words with which the president of the institution customarily closed his addresses. Thus was born "The Eyes of Texas Are Upon You." Other cheers evoked the special nature of a place, as when students at

Carson-Newman, emanating primarily from the hills of East Tennessee, boasted of their hard-scrabble heritage:

> Come out of the woods.
> Sandpaper your chin.
> We're wild, we're woolly
> We're rough like a saw.

The inventiveness of college students—South and North—added to the dynamic of the sporting contest; what they created to surround the field of play helped translate first impressions into memory and nostalgia.[39]

Distinctive colors, nicknames, mascots, songs, and cheers intensified the experience of a Saturday afternoon. Beyond the contest itself, even before the era when homecoming extravaganzas and precision marching bands added to the appeal of sporting events, other rituals contributed to an exciting atmosphere. From an early date, college baseball and football games in the South frequently became extended social occasions, offering to some a splendid opportunity for courtship, to others a fine setting for displays of prowess with a bottle. Belles and beaux mingled freely along the sidelines of the field, a custom explained by the absence of grandstands during the early years. And southern men were emphatic in their appreciation of female attendance at collegiate sporting events, believing that their guests lent dignity and at the same time a more festive air to the proceedings. Undergraduates at the University of Georgia addressed special invitations to the ladies of Athens, particularly the students of the Lucy Cobb School, while the president of Transylvania College praised the enthusiasm of women spectators for inducing the boys "to exert themselves more." Such acknowledgments, in suggesting some form of chivalry, also bespoke an exclusionary ideal of sport at the turn of the century, a marking of behavioral boundaries, a ranking of attitudes and actions. Simply stated, rough athletic contests measured substantial differences between the young men of the white South and those whom they were supposed to protect, or guide, or control.[40]

Even though women stood in close proximity to the field of play, and their presence contributed to the spectacle of college sport, social conventions isolated them in significant ways from the initiated: those who got dirty or bloody, who learned or displayed manly character, and who were expected to translate the lessons of a game into the talents of leadership. A writer for the *Tulane Collegian* illuminated the presumed gender roles in sports, asserting, "'With our fair friends near by we are inspired to be heroes in the base ball strife; particularly when said friends are in delightful ignorance of all rules, and applaud heartily with their daintily gloved hands bad and good plays alike.'" A hearty gentility in this circumstance nevertheless reflected attitudes and standards that extended throughout the culture, from the home to the workplace to the ballot box. Manliness was cast against notions of effeminacy, as a superior development of body and character. Implicitly, with regard to honor and courage, the masculine rituals of college sport also reinforced privilege and subordination predicated on the ideology of racial difference. Thus even without extensive written references, numerous prescriptions as well as proscriptions regarding racial and gender relations were dramatized in the athletic performances of white collegians in the postbellum South.[41]

Beyond the means by which white male prerogative was exercised both on and beyond the field of play, other dramatic performances help explain the influence of athletics in the New South. Several of the most important events on the collegiate calendar were inspired by athletic competition, while some of the most popular activities on campus were created to support the teams and stimulate school spirit. In these practices, southern institutions followed rituals developed elsewhere, adapting them to specific sports or rivalries. Bonfire rallies often preceded the big game of a season; the chiming of chapel bells followed if a victory had been gained. Vast parades and dancing in the streets threatened at times to overwhelm small towns and cities with celebrating youth, who carried "'torches, horns, bells, drums'" and launched "'fire-works and speeches'" to greet conquering heroes.[42] As a result of these developments, local custom flowed into what would become a national sporting culture, the similarities between collegiate festivals overshadowing their differences. First in the Northeast, but eventually throughout much of the country, athletic contests between college youth were scheduled in conjunction with other significant or symbolic events. Of these the most important was Thanksgiving Day. After the Civil War an official celebration of family and nation, Thanksgiving Thursday also marked the highlight of the football season at many colleges. A secular as well as a spiritual rite, it embraced one of the two principal college sports in the South, wrapping football in the flag and blessing it with a prayer.[43] Such an association would become more thoroughly elaborated as the twentieth century "progressed," with added layers of pageantry—and commercialism. Like the Fourth of July baseball game, Thanksgiving football glorified sport as a nationalist pastime and sanctified it as passion play.

Extremely adaptable, America's civil religion also accommodated regionalism and the reunion of distinct generations. Even before the turn of the century, regional rivalries enriched the intercollegiate athletic experience. These customarily resulted from the efforts of the players themselves or others among the undergraduate population. While Harvard fought Yale in "The Game," and California challenged Stanford annually in "The Big Game," what occurred when Texas struggled against Texas A&M, Georgia tackled Georgia Tech, or Alabama confronted the state Polytechnic school (later Auburn University) could be just as intense, and brutal. In the aftermath of an interdenominational athletic affray between Wake Forest and Trinity, one participant lamented: "'To be beaten by a rival sect, Christians though we both were, was more humiliating than to bite the dust before the pagan hordes of the constitutionally unchurched University! Queer that we church people love each other so.'"[44]

Often breeding considerable ill-will among regional foes, provoking the exchange of allegations about cheating, and increasing the tendency toward violence on the field, such rivalries intensified the meaning of southern athletic rituals. Over time, much more was at stake than the money that passed from the hands of one gambling undergraduate or alumnus to those of an another at the conclusion of a particular game. The care and tending of an individual's honor many southerners had long understood; through athletics, some believed, the prestige of an entire institution might similarly need to be protected.

Football in the South inspired emotional outpourings as well as demonstrations of physical toughness, perhaps no more than when Harvard played Yale, but certainly no less. Whether the offspring of Boston Brahmins, the younger generation of a rising midwestern middle class, heirs to Old South gentility, or the sons of backcountry yeomanry: as youth they seemed to many of their elders barbarians all. Yet southerners seemed to present extreme cases of aggression and violence, an exaggerated version of impulses and acts prevalent elsewhere in turn-of-the-century America. Sporting competition provoked numerous disputes among college students and partisan spectators: players attacked players, fans attacked players, and players attacked fans in the early days of southern football. On one occasion the athletic director of Alabama accosted a professor from the University of Georgia who was merely standing in for the principal athletic official of the school in Athens. For many years undergraduates at Washington and Lee and the cadets of Virginia Military Institute, two colleges located across the road from one another in Lexington, extended their athletic rivalries into street fighting.[45] This confirmed that sporting events meant much more than fluttering banners and boisterous yells and cheers. It tells us that one person's memory of halcyon days coincided precisely with another's hellacious experience. Ultimately, it suggests that football was not in every instance a thoroughly modern pastime, or perhaps that modern civilization would have to come to terms with the brawl.

Among the many legends and rough romances associated with southern college sport was that of Harold Ketron, the feisty player from Georgia who not only pulled opponents' hair but also spit tobacco juice in their faces. Another story concerns Texas Christian University's Edwin "Cowboy" Bull who, playing his first game away from home, had to be persuaded not to carry a pistol onto the field against the state university in Austin. And while the tale has many versions, all attempt to illuminate something central to southern culture: Standing at one end of the field is a Tennessee mountain man, clad in a green frock coat and a four gallon hat, bewhiskered and full of sour mash. At a critical point in the game, he loudly warns the visiting team that the first of them who "crosses that line will get a bullet in his carcass."[46] Possessing a rugged charm, these stories also occasioned a certain alarm about the exaltation of body over mind and the valorization of belligerence.

Indeed, the relationship among notions of rugged masculinity and violence contributed substantially to the early rendering of the history of southern athletic traditions. By adhering all too carefully to the rhetoric lauding sports as an expression of manly aggression, students sometimes violated both the customary and more rigidly legislated distinctions between football and battle. And by enlisting outsiders to help in the struggle, they consciously withdrew athletics from the educational setting that some commentators believed it was supposed to enhance. The speed with which southern colleges adopted new strategies to gain advantage over their rivals—the use of "tramp" athletes and "trick" plays, for instance—jeopardized the exalted status of football. To some extent, this was a natural and more honest approach to athletics than the rather arbitrary, often hypocritical notion of amateurism that would thicken the rulebooks of college sports in later years. Yet set against heavily endowed notions of honor, "modern" athletic practices created their own hypocrisies. Such practices also set up some very dangerous situations.

Even before the turn of the century, it became evident that in many instances the young men of the South were competing against far more mature athletes and that a few of their strongest adversaries were not even students. The most telling incident occurred during a game between Georgia and Georgia Tech, in 1893 a recently conceived rivalry, but already intense. Shortly before the game began, rumors surfaced that several of the athletes on both rosters could not be found in the academic records of the competing institutions. During the contest those suspicions were confirmed. An unfamiliar player, identified only as "Wood," dominated play for Georgia Tech. Described as "invincible" by one observer, he dragged Georgia tacklers up and down the field, literally fighting his way to three Tech touchdowns.

Toward the end of the game Georgia fans grew surly, first yelling at the referee, then striking out at Wood. According to one report, a large stone hit him in the head, opening a gash three inches long. Wood's response was to plaster the face of a Georgia player with a large handful of blood and gore. Once the game had ended, Georgia Tech players sprinted from the field amid a hailstorm of bricks, stones, and other projectiles; Wood reportedly walked off, went to his hotel room, and stitched up his own wound.[47]

This account derives from a presidential campaign biography written in 1919. Allowing for much exaggeration therefore, the story is nevertheless instructive. In 1893 Leonard Wood was a thirty-three-year-old army surgeon stationed near Atlanta. He had already helped pursue Geronimo through the Arizona–New Mexico border territory, and even before he launched his career as a muscular imperialist in Cuba and the Philippines, he had been described as "a splendid type of American manhood . . . as fine a specimen of physical strength and endurance as could easily be found." For all its hyperbole, the biography suggests that if it was good to be a military hero when running for president, it was even better to be a football hero too. As for southern culture, Wood's participation in the Georgia–Georgia Tech game provided an ironic twist to the discussion of the relationship between athletics and a distinctive martial spirit. Not only did his appearance illustrate the proximity of numerous army camps to the colleges of the region; it also suggested that few team captains or coaches could resist the temptation of enlisting soldiers or veterans to augment their own forces in important athletic conflicts.[48]

* * *

Though what occurred that afternoon in the autumn of 1893 represents tendencies that were not confined to the region, the event illuminates several issues that were particularly vexing to educators and athletic reformers in the southern states. The use of professional players, called "ringers" or "tramp athletes"—proficient in the sport if not by many reckonings "manly" or "moral"—opened up bidding wars among rival teams and kindled ill-will wherever it was detected. It also signified an increasing distinction between students and the athletes who would represent them in sporting competition. Alarmed professors and college presidents first addressed the problem of corruption. A few critics among them argued for the eradication of off-campus competition. Many more interested officials seemed to be persuaded that they could regulate sports by establishing committees to supervise student athletic associations and by drafting eligibility rules for participation in sports. During the mid-1890s faculty members at numerous institutions agreed to form regional conferences to set the standards by which athletic enterprise would be governed in the future. At the forefront of that movement was William L. Dudley of Vanderbilt University, who was instrumental in creating the Southern Inter-Collegiate Athletic Association. A decade later, college presidents came together to organize what would become the National Collegiate Athletic Association. Like the federal regulation of Wall Street financiers and corporate trusts, this was a "Progressive reform" in intent, structure, and ineffectiveness. Various southern college conferences hoped to mediate the increasingly antagonistic relationship between a growing athletic establishment and long-standing educational ideals. Yet as loud as they sounded in their pronouncements about so many assaults on the morality of sport, athletic reformers were ultimately modest in their accomplishments.[49]

If the corruption of sport troubled many commentators around the turn of the century, an even greater number inveighed against the "Football Moloch," devourer of young athletes. Some critics cited medical studies about the injuries the game produced; others pointed to newspaper photographs showing mangled football warriors. And when they described instances more horrible even than "broken membranes and bones, dislocated joints and bruised bodies," still other reformers used the term "manslaughter." One of the earliest deaths on the gridiron occurred on November 30, 1894, when Georgetown's George Bahen suffered a broken back during a rough contest against a local club. Since threats of intentional hitting had circulated before the match, and because the coroner believed that the fatal injury had been the result of a kick from behind, school officials suspended football for two years. During the decade following the revival of the game, yet another Georgetown player lost his life on the field. "The bloodshed had been altogether out of proportion to the athletic benefit," concluded the head of the university, who proceeded to banish the sport yet again.[50]

Most of the deaths and major injuries counted up by the critics of the game could be traced to secondary school matches or sandlot games. Occasionally, however, a football fatality in a major contest drew enormous publicity, focussing attention on the seeming ruthlessness of the sport. In 1897, Georgia's star fullback, Richard Vonalbade "Von" Gammon, missed tackling a University of Virginia runner and fell heavily on his head, his chin striking the ground first. Massed around the play, the majority of the two teams ended up falling on him. He was removed from the field semiconscious and taken to a hospital, where he died the next morning. As in several other instances, the popularity of the athlete and the circumstances surrounding his death immediately fired up the debate over football violence. In the aftermath of

Von Gammon's death, some observers predicted the end of the game in Georgia. The editor of the *Athens Banner* called football "an outrage which should have been stamped out long ago," and the state legislatures of Georgia and Virginia drafted bills outlawing the sport. But two letters to Atlanta newspapers appeared to save the game of football for the youth of the South. The first, written by Charles Herty, one of the most prominent members of the Georgia faculty and the patron of sport at the college, not only defended football but also urged lawmakers to make provisions for better training and conditioning facilities for athletes. The second, solicited by Herty from Von Gammon's mother, was an impassioned plea that her son's death "not be used to defeat the most cherished object of his life." In response, the governor of Georgia pocketed the bill.[51] Changes in the rules governing the sport, which reduced the risk of serious injury, along with persistent calls after the turn of the century for a reinvigorated college youth, meant that such legislation was never again considered in the South.

Still, some individuals condemned football for its violence. One in particular, John Singleton Mosby, fulminated against such analogies as those advanced by Crowell, who had likened football players to the "sons of men who fought in the charge of Pickett and Pettigrew." Mosby disputed assertions that "many a soldier [who] charged up that memorable hill at Santiago had been developed in courage, manhood, and nerve on the football fields of American colleges," just as he denied any resemblance between football and the martial traditions of the Old South.[52] For his part, Mosby had demonstrated considerable manly assertiveness before the Civil War, having been expelled from the University of Virginia for shooting another student over what may have been a point of honor. In later years he was held in high esteem in the region for his exploits as a Confederate guerrilla leader during the war. To Mosby, who wrote in the aftermath of the death of the Virginia football player, Archer Christian, the sport would best be "banished" from the university. "I do not think football should be tolerated where the youth of the country are supposed to be sent to be taught literature, science, & humanity." Then he asserted, mixing metaphors with a vengeance, "that cock-fighting is unlawful in Virginia: Why should better care be taken of a game chicken than a school boy?" "Football is only a polite term for prize fighting," he continued. It marked "a renaissance of the worst days of the Caesars."[53]

Mosby, "the Gray Ghost" of Confederate lore, went on to reject the notion that athletic training prepared men for battle, arguing that Stonewall Jackson's men "won their victories without any such nursing." He then declared that athletes belonged to a class "invincible in peace and invisible in war." During "our war," he observed, "I often wondered what had become of the bullies and bruisers I had known." Ultimately underscoring his belief that football stood in contrast to ancient traditions and as a testament to modern evils, Mosby concluded that "it is notorious that foot-ball teams are largely composed of professional mercenaries who are hired to advertise colleges. Gate money is the valuable consideration. There is no sentiment of romance or chivalry about them. The swords of the old Knights are rust."[54]

* * *

No less resistant to the transformation of manly pastimes and far more influential than "old Knights" such as Mosby were evangelical religious leaders, whose problems with college sport concerned the profound moral issues it raised. Many prominent Baptists sat on the boards of trustees of institutions like Wake Forest; Methodist piety likewise guided the development of Trinity, Vanderbilt, and Emory. Other Protestant conservatives exerted their influence through the pages of the religious press. To a considerable extent, ministers throughout the South took pride in the progress of denominational colleges, especially as the means of propagating the true faith. Thus the *Raleigh Christian Advocate,* the organ of the North Carolina Conference of the Methodist Episcopal Church, South, regularly carried "notes from Trinity College" during the early expansion of the institution and its move to Durham. For several years, it boasted of the accomplishments of John Crowell, the school's new president, especially when he expanded the academic program. Increasingly during the early 1890s, however, the journal became vehement in its criticism of the athletic policies at Trinity.[55]

The controversy in North Carolina was charged with dramatic elements, wherein the pious discerned paganism in some of the activities that others saw—in ideal form—as emblems of a progressive model of education. Matching F. L. Reid, the editor of the *Christian Advocate,* against President Crowell (and the Duke family), the conflict surrounding sports measured the reactions of evangelical authorities to the secularizing tendencies at Trinity and other colleges of the New South, reflected in such innovations as intercollegiate football. Reid, a trustee of the college, was upset about the intrusions of outside influences on the moral life of undergraduates. Accordingly, the *Christian Advocate* periodically bombarded its readers with indictments of college sport, carefully distinguishing, however, between the pernicious aspects of off-campus competitions and the benefits of vigorous athletics pursued close to home.

Arguing that contests between colleges, often taking place in cities such as Raleigh and Richmond, "tend[ed] to evil," Reid not only enumerated the charges against "match games" and what attended them. He also noted the efforts of other Christian educators and reformers, who took up the standard against "athletic enthusiasm." Specifically, he praised the stance taken by W. A. Candler, the president of Emory. "Inter-collegiate games bring needless expense," Candler wrote in the *Wesleyan Advocate*. They "provoke gambling and other immoralities; waste time; and arouse states of excitement absolutely subversive of habits of study. . . . [E]very proper end of college life is hindered by them, and no good purpose is promoted by them. Emory, therefore, forbids them." Authorities at Davidson, as well as Emory and Henry College, likewise enacted prohibitions against college sport, joining the campaign against urban vice and extending the evangelical crusade against the violence that prevailed in the manly traditions of the region. As one historian has asserted concerning similar controversies, the praying South had finally taken on the fighting South.[56]

To highlight the evils attending collegiate sporting rituals, the *Christian Advocate* published a diatribe in 1893 that had first appeared in a New York Methodist journal. In "The Morals of Intercollegiate Games," the Reverend C. H. Payne labored to condemn the "football craze," seizing on analogies to Spanish bullfights, the gladiatorial arena of Rome, and "the criminal class in general" to make his point about the barbarities of the sport. The violence of the game was but one of its evils, Payne contended. Good old-fashioned Christian intolerance, he argued at length, should also extend to the ways athletic enthusiasm hindered study and encouraged gambling, as well as to the "demoralizing effects" of "modern intercollegiate games." Sporting spectacles had fostered conduct "disgraceful in the extreme . . . wild revels, bacchanalian songs, and delirious shouts . . . enough to make a stout heart quake." A post-Thanksgiving game "orgy" in New York City, Payne observed, had made the night "hideous." For further effect, he quoted a former army officer's condemnation of college youth "'drinking recklessly, acting the part of roughs and rowdies, seizing and insulting women in the streets, passing the night in houses of prostitution, and all this as representatives of our higher seats of learning.'" Clearly, manhood was imperiled, Payne concluded, frightened about the fate of Christian colleges and the betrayal of "Christo et ecclesiae." Just as apprehensive, F. L. Reid endorsed those views and added that, if its youth turned from the path of righteousness to riot, he also feared for the South.[57]

The *Christian Advocate* kept up its campaign throughout 1893, reflecting the opinions of the North Carolina conferences of the Methodist Episcopal church that football was "a source of evil, and of no little evil, and ought to be stopped." Finally, in 1894 evangelical crusaders forced the resignation of Trinity's ambitious president Crowell and abolished intercollegiate football.

Crowell's successor at the Methodist institution, the Reverend John Carlisle Kilgo, maintained the ban throughout his tenure, and it was not until 1920 that the intercollegiate game was permitted to resume in the precincts of Durham that would soon become Duke University.[58]

* * *

The enormous tension and turmoil characterizing the Methodist crusade in North Carolina suggest that the modernization of southern sport and society was not a simple endeavor. Southern evangelicals made clear that there were contests other than football and baseball that could be aggressively pursued. Steadfast in their own pieties against the athletic pieties advanced by men like Crowell and Winston, they offered a competing discourse on the meaning of expressive masculinity in the postbellum South. Beyond the widely held view that athletics came into conflict with academics, many religious leaders argued that sports created an enormous rift between the "manly" and the "moral." A traditional notion of southern honor had been extended and reinforced with the advent of intercollegiate sports, and it had flourished in most respects even as numerous innovations had rendered athletic competition more modern in form and structure. Yet, for evangelicals, the game appeared to subvert their ideal concerning the matter and manner of gaining manhood and fame. Or perhaps, from the vantage of a later era, the boundaries between energy and excess had been vaguely defined all along. Ultimately, the reaction to football illuminated the complex processes of social change, the contrary tendencies woven into the fabric of late nineteenth- and early twentieth-century southern history. That the successes of evangelical reformers were mostly local and temporary should not obscure the influence exerted by the leaders of the praying white South, the widespread and deeply rooted convictions they have long represented.[59]

Still, sport won out. The transformation of an elite endeavor, which was also vastly popular, into a spectacle uniting audience and performers ultimately occurred more slowly in the South than in the North, but it followed the same broad outlines. After 1906, when a football player from Vanderbilt was selected to Walter Camp's All-America squad, an increasing number of southern athletes—and their teams—would gain national prominence. They would begin to play in the Rose Bowl during the 1920s and became household names throughout the land thereafter.[60] For youth, South and North, sport represented an important means to manliness, an expressive activity that was emotionally and physically charged. It was at the same time a utilitarian undertaking, a training ground for the development of character and self-control in the modernizing social order. Here was an impressively powerful testament to tradition but also to innovation: a new means of extending old ideals concerning individual growth and certain social relations, based on gender and racial hierarchies. During and after the Spanish-American-Cuban-Philippine war, when the tenets of the strenuous life were translated into a more muscular imperialism, athletic competition was enlisted in the service of larger goals as part of a national creed. Yet even then, and down to our own time, the rugged rituals of football could be perceived as the embodiment of distinctive customs and traditions, popularly identified with both white southern honor and a highly self-conscious masculinity.[61]

Notes

An earlier version of this essay appeared in *Journal of Sport History* 24 (Fall 1997): 285–316.

1. See, for example, Walter Camp, "California Athletics," *Harper's Weekly* 37 (February 25, 1893): 191; Henry Sheldon, *Student Life and Customs* (New York: D. Appleton, 1901). The *Bulletin* of the Bureau of Education is quoted in Bruce A. Corrie, *The Atlantic Coast Conference, 1953–1978* (Durham, N.C.: Carolina Academic Press, 1978), 11.

2. An exception can be found in J. Breckinridge Robertson, "Foot Ball in the South," *The Southern Magazine* 3 (January 1894): 632. In mentioning that some southern athletes had ventured to northern colleges, Robertson snidely observes that "The darker side of Southern life seems also to be blossoming out athletically in [William Henry] Lewis of Harvard." For the purposes of this essay, it should be understood that all references are to the white South or to the white New South. By the 1890s, black southerners were barred from competing against white southern youth in such games as baseball. And within the context of prevailing cultural considerations, white commentary omitted the African American presence from discussions of the values exemplified or inculcated by athletic competition. These facts should direct our attention to parallel developments and modes of interpretation. African American students and educators at colleges and universities such as Livingstone, Biddle, Talladega, Tuskegee, Fisk, and Howard established their own athletic agendas. Ever since the 1880s, this has been a history enormously rich in fact and lore. Just as significantly, it is important to understand that the ideal of white southern manhood was constructed *against* the conception of the slave and freedman, that within the mainstream culture such notions as character, honor, and courage loudly implied what were conceived as their opposites: docility, servility, and lack of control. Whiteness thus was not only cast apart from but above blackness in these formulations, although it was not until the early twentieth century that emphatically racialist readings of sport made their way into print. I have attempted to address this topic from several perspectives in *The Playing Fields of American Culture: Athletics and Higher Education, 1850–1945* (New York: Oxford University Press, forthcoming). For a brief assessment of the racial nuances within southern sport, see Edward Ayers, *The Promise of the New South: Life after Reconstruction* (New York: Oxford University Press, 1992), 312–13. See also Joel Williamson, *The Crucible of Race: Black-White Relations in the American South since Emancipation* (New

York: Oxford University Press, 1984). For an examination of one dimension of the black experience in southern sport, see Patrick B. Miller, "To 'Bring the Race Along Rapidly': Sport, Student Culture, and Educational Mission at Historically Black Colleges during the Interwar Years," in this volume.

3. See Robertson, "Foot Ball in the South," 631–32.

4. Concerning "ritual" and "spectacle," I have tended toward the looser definitions of vernacular usage, though my arguments also depend on the more technical meanings of the terms devised principally by cultural anthropologists. See Clifford Geertz, *The Interpretation of Cultures* (New York: Basic Books, 1973), chaps. 1, 8, and 15; John MacAloon, ed. *Rite, Drama, Festival, Spectacle: Rehearsals toward a Theory of Cultural Performance* (Philadelphia: Institute for the Study of Human Issues, 1984); and Victor Turner, *The Ritual Process: Structure and Anti-Structure* (Ithaca, N.Y.: Cornell University Press, 1969). See also Eric Hobsbawm and Terence Ranger, eds., *The Invention of Tradition* (Cambridge: Cambridge University Press, 1983), esp. 263–308. Here, I am suggesting—along with Edward Ayers—that "the integration of the South into the economy and mass culture of the nation" could be expressed through an elaborate system of rituals and symbols identified with sport. See Ayers, *Promise of the New South,* 311–16.

5. For notions of masculinity, the strenuous life, and the emerging ideology of sport, see Elliott J. Gorn and Warren Goldstein, *A Brief History of American Sports* (New York: Hill and Wang, 1993), 47–149; and Miller, *Playing Fields of American Culture.* Regarding the "rituals of reunion," I am taking a cue from the impressive study by Nina Silber, *The Romance of Reunion: Northerners and the South, 1865–1900* (Chapel Hill: University of North Carolina Press, 1993).

6. Ayers, *Promise of the New South,* 315. See also T. H. Breen, "Horses and Gentlemen: The Cultural Significance of Gambling among the Gentry of Virginia," *William and Mary Quarterly* 34 (April 1977): 329–47; Bertram Wyatt-Brown, *Southern Honor: Ethics and Behavior in the Old South* (New York: Oxford University Press, 1982), esp. chap. 2; Elliott J. Gorn, "'Gouge and Bite, Pull Hair and Scratch': The Social Significance of Fighting in the Southern Backcountry," *American Historical Review* 90 (February 1985): 18–43; Dickson Bruce, *Violence and Culture in the Antebellum South* (Austin: University of Texas Press, 1979); and Edward Ayers, *Vengeance and Justice: Crime and Punishment in the Nineteenth-Century South* (New York: Oxford University Press, 1984). On postbellum southern culture, see Ayers, *Promise of the New South;* Paul Gaston, *The New South Creed: A Study in Southern Mythmaking* (Baton Rouge: Louisiana State University Press, 1976); Gaines Foster, *Ghosts of the Confederacy: Defeat, the Lost Cause, and the Emergence of the New South, 1865 to 1913* (New York: Oxford University Press, 1987); and Don H. Doyle, *New Men, New Cities, New South: Atlanta, Nashville, Charleston, Mobile, 1860–1910* (Chapel Hill: University of North Carolina Press, 1990).

7. See Dale Somers, *The Rise of Sport in New Orleans, 1850–1900* (Baton Rouge: Louisiana State University Press, 1972), 49–51, 74–78. The obvious contrast would be to cockfighting, the brutal wrestling matches, and the duelling of antebellum culture across the classes. Increasingly, a positive value would be placed on male assertiveness balanced by self-discipline. See Gorn, "'Gouge and Bite, Pull Hair and Scratch,'" and the comments of late nineteenth-century southern educators on the value of sport.

8. See, for instance, Kemp P. Battle, *History of the University of North Carolina,* 2 vols.

(Raleigh, N.C.: Edwards and Broughton Printing Co., 1907); Philip A. Bruce, *History of the University of Virginia, 1819–1919*, 5 vols. (New York: MacMillan, 1920–22); and Joseph Steter, "In Search of Direction: Southern Higher Education after the Civil War," *History of Education Quarterly* 25 (Fall 1985): 341–67.

9. On the relationship of urban development to the expansion of sport, see Melvin L. Adelman, *A Sporting Time: New York City and the Rise of Modern Athletics, 1820–1870* (Urbana: University of Illinois Press, 1986); and Steven A. Riess, *City Games: The Evolution of American Urban Society and the Rise of Sports* (Urbana: University of Illinois Press, 1989).

10. To a significant extent, the standards and ideals represented in the southern sporting creed contrasted substantially with the set of concerns that animated northern muscular moralists of the mid-to-late nineteenth century. Fretful about the effects of city life on the health and character of young men of commerce, an increasing number of northeastern reformers were equally apprehensive about the sedentary, contemplative existence they presumed that college students were leading. Arguing from the lessons of classical antiquity as well as the legacy of the Revolutionary and early republican generations, elite reformers sought to restore to gentility its tradition of virility, just as they hoped to combat the maladies of modern civilization. To them, gymnastics and athletics offered a means of reconciling muscles and morals, of training young men in self-control and for social service, and ultimately of restoring a salutary balance to both individual and social development. On the masculine crisis in the North, see, for example, David Pugh, *Sons of Liberty: The Masculine Mind in Nineteenth-Century America* (Westport, Conn.: Greenwood Press, 1983); E. Anthony Rotundo, *American Manhood: Transformations in Masculinity from the Revolution to the Modern Era* (New York: Basic Books, 1993); E. Anthony Rotundo, "Body and Soul: Changing Ideals of American Middle-Class Manhood, 1770–1920," *Journal of Social History* 16 (Summer 1983): 28–33; Elliott J. Gorn, *The Manly Art: Bare-Knuckle Prize Fighting in America* (Ithaca, N.Y.: Cornell University Press, 1986), esp. chap. 6; and Gorn and Goldstein, *Brief History of American Sports*, chaps. 2 and 3. See also Orlando Patterson, "The Code of Honor in the Old South" (review of Wyatt-Brown, *Southern Honor*), *Reviews in American History* 12 (March 1984): 24. Nina Silber brilliantly demonstrates the connection between northern anxieties and perceptions of southern masculinity in *The Romance of Reunion*.

11. See Wyatt-Brown, *Southern Honor*, 94, 96–97, 165.

12. See Ted Ownby, *Subduing Satan: Religion, Recreation, and Manhood in the Rural South, 1865–1920* (Chapel Hill: University of North Carolina Press, 1990), for an excellent analysis of southern manhood "out-of-doors."

13. For an important assessment of sport in the South, see Jim L. Sumner, "John Franklin Crowell, Methodism, and the Football Controversy at Trinity College, 1887–1894," *Journal of Sport History* 17 (Spring 1990): 5–20. The reference to Bassett is on p. 15.

14. For the cultural and social history of early college sport in the North, see Michael Oriard, *Reading Football: How the Popular Press Created an American Spectacle* (Chapel Hill: University of North Carolina Press, 1993); and Ronald A. Smith, *Sports and Freedom: The Rise of Big-Time College Athletics* (New York: Oxford University Press, 1988).

15. The key text on the "rationalization" of sport is Allen Guttmann, *From Ritual to Record: The Nature of Modern Sports* (New York: Columbia University Press, 1978). It

should be noted, though, that Guttmann is not persuaded by Marxist or neo-Marxist analogies of sport to the means of production. See also Donald J. Mrozek, *Sport and American Mentality, 1880–1910* (Knoxville: University of Tennessee Press, 1983), esp. chaps. 2 and 3.

16. Tom Scott, "A History of Intercollegiate Athletics at the University of North Carolina" (D.Ed. dissertation, Columbia University, 1955), 59, 87; Edgar S. Kiracofe, "An Historical Study of Athletics and Physical Education in the Standard Four Year Colleges of Virginia" (Ph.D. dissertation, University of Virginia, 1932), 22; John H. Roper, *U. B. Phillips: A Southern Mind* (Macon, Ga.: Mercer University Press, 1984), 17.

17. While tennis captivated the undergraduates at Tulane, and gymnastic exercises found about the same number of partisans and practioners as running and rowing, those activities played a negligible role in the development of athletics in the postbellum South. See Ollinger Crenshaw, *General Lee's College: The Rise and Growth of Washington and Lee University* (New York: Random House, 1969), 213; Crew folder, 1876 to 1900, Georgetown University Archives, Washington, D.C.; and John S. Patton, Sallie J. Doswell, and Lewis D. Crenshaw, *Jefferson's University: Glimpses of the Past and Present of the University of Virginia* (Charlottesville, Va.: Michie Co., 1915), 67.

18. See the "Baseball" entry by John E. DiMeglio in Charles Reagan Wilson and William Ferris, eds., *Encyclopedia of Southern Culture* (Chapel Hill: University of North Carolina Press, 1989), 1210–11; Somers, *Rise of Sport in New Orleans*, 49–51; E. Merton Coulter, *College Life in the Old South* (Athens: University of Georgia Press, 1951), 268. See also W. K. Woolery, *Bethany Years: The Story of Old Bethany from Her Founding Years through a Century of Trial and Triumph* (Huntington, W.Va.: Standard Printing and Publishing Co., 1941), 217; Jerome A. Moore, *Texas Christian University: A Hundred Years of History* (Fort Worth: Texas Christian University Press, 1974), 22–23; Bruce, *History of the University of Virginia*, 4:133–37.

19. Moore, *Texas Christian University*, 211; James B. Sellers, *History of the University of Alabama, 1818–1902* (University: University of Alabama Press, 1953), 524; John D. Wright, *Transylvania: Tudor to the West* (Lexington: University Press of Kentucky, 1975), 306. For an expansive treatment of the development of the sport in the region, see Lorenzo (Fuzzy) Woodruff, *A History of Southern Football, 1890–1928* (Atlanta: Walter W. Brown Publishing, 1928).

20. When such personal advice was not readily available, college students sought assistance by writing to friends or acquaintances in the Northeast and, later in the century, by consulting the rule book published by the Spalding Company. See John P. Dyer, *Tulane: The Biography of a University, 1834–1965* (New York: Harper and Row, 1966), 165; Jonas Vilas et al., *The University of Missouri: A Centennial History* (Columbia: University of Missouri Press, 1939), 260; Edwin Mims, *History of Vanderbilt University* (Nashville, Tenn.: Vanderbilt University Press, 1946), 276; Richard Hofstadter, *The Progressive Historians: Turner, Beard, Parrington* (New York: Knopf, 1968), 371–72; and Patton et al., *Jefferson's University*, 69.

21. Bruce, *History of the University of Virginia*, 4:140. A similar appraisal of southerners' first attempts at the sport appeared in the *New Orleans Picayune* in 1893, concerning a contest between Tulane and the University of Mississippi: "'All that was visible from the benches were twenty-two long-haired and unkempt youths rushing wildly to a com-

mon center, animated by an insane desire to make pemmican of each other'" (quoted in Somers, *Rise of Sport in New Orleans*, 258). If the Virginians' claim to the South's first game of football remains problematic, perhaps that of the Kentuckians was better founded. On April 9, 1880, Centre College competed against Transylvania in a cow pasture, the players, fifteen of them to a side, wearing heavy shoes and padded apparel. Although that much is clear and impressive, the rest of the story is in dispute. Since one member of the Transylvania team had immigrated from Australia, the game may have been played according to the custom of that country; certainly the Centre College players were confused, protesting afterward that they had been deliberately sent the wrong set of rules and the wrong size of football with which to practice for the big match. See Wright, *Transylvania*, 302.

22. Bruce, *History of the University of Virginia*, 4:143; Kiracofe, "Historical Study of Athletics," 19.

23. George J. Stevenson, *Increase in Excellence: A History of Emory and Henry College* (New York: Appleton-Century-Crofts, 1963), 192; Robert E. Wilder, *Gridiron Glory Days: Football at Mercer, 1892–1942* (Macon, Ga.: Mercer University Press, 1982), 2–17; Duncan L. Kinnear, *The First 100 Years: A History of Virginia Polytecnic Institute and State University* (Blacksburg: Virginia Polytechnic Institute Educational Foundation, 1972), 152.

24. "History of Football, Trinity College, 1888–1891" and "Trinity College Athletic Association," in Duke University Archives, Durham, N.C.; Scott, "History of Intercollegiate Athletics at the University of North Carolina," 67; Glenn E. (Ted) Mann, *A Story of Glory: Duke University Football* (Greenville, S.C.: Doorway Publishers, 1985), 46–51. An especially thorough treatment is Jim L. Sumner, "The North Carolina Inter-Collegiate Foot-Ball Association: The Beginnings of College Football in North Carolina," *The North Carolina Historical Review* 45 (July 1988): 263–86.

25. John Franklin Crowell, *Personal Recollections of Trinity College* (Durham, N.C.: n.p., 1939), 45–46 (manuscript in Duke University Archives, Durham, N.C.); Mann, *Story of Glory*, 50–55; Sumner, "North Carolina Inter-Collegiate Foot-Ball Association."

26. On the role of the coach, see esp. Smith, *Sports and Freedom*, 147–64.

27. John F. Stegeman, *The Ghosts of Herty Field: Early Days on a Southern Gridiron* (Athens: University of Georgia Press, 1966), 69–70. See also Paul Conkin, *Gone with the Ivy: A Biography of Vanderbilt University* (Knoxville: University of Tennessee Press, 1985), 135–41; and Wiley Umphlett, *Creating the Big Game: John W. Heisman and the Invention of American Football* (Westport, Conn.: Greenwood Press, 1992).

28. Stegeman, *Ghosts of Herty Field*, 2–3; Crowell quoted in Sumner, "John Franklin Crowell," 8.

29. Crowell quoted in Sumner, "North Carolina Inter-Collegiate Foot-Ball Association," 267.

30. Winston quoted in Battle, *History of the University of North Carolina*, 2:510, and *Raleigh Christian Advocate*, March 22, 1893. With regard to Winston's mingling of references to military and religious figures, an instructive text is Robert J. Higgs, *God in the Stadium: Sports and Religion in America* (Lexington: University Press of Kentucky, 1995).

31. Battle, *History of the University of North Carolina*, 2:549.

32. One of the best discussions of symbols and school sports is in James Anthony Mangan, *Athletics in the Victorian and Edwardian Public School: The Emergence and Consolidation of an Educational Ideology* (Cambridge: Cambridge University Press, 1981), 142–

43. See also Frederick Rudolph, *The American College and University: A History* (New York: Vintage Books, 1962), 386: "From identifying an institution with a color to identifying it with a football team was a very short step, and before long very many Americans were acting as if *the* purpose of an American college or university were to field a football team." See also Miller, *Playing Fields of American Culture*, chap. 2; and Benjamin G. Rader, *American Sports: From the Age of Folk Games to the Age of Televised Sports* (Englewood Cliffs, N.J.: Prentice Hall, 1990), 101–6.

33. *New York Times,* October 12, 1932; Patton et al., *Jefferson's University,* 75.

34. Allen Cabaniss, *A History of the University of Mississippi* (Hattiesburg: University Press of Mississippi, 1971), 116; Mary D. Beaty, *A History of Davidson College* (Davidson, N.C.: Briarpatch Press, 1988), 190.

35. Crenshaw, *General Lee's College,* 215; Stegeman, *Ghosts of Herty Field,* 8.

36. Regarding Bevo, see Margaret C. Berry, "Student Life and Customs, 1883–1933, at the University of Texas" (Ph.D. dissertation, Columbia University, 1965), 130–36. It is noteworthy as well that the university's finest women athletes were invited to the feast. The participation of southern college women in sport has received scant attention in the historical literature. Ayers, in *The Promise of the New South,* 316, makes an initial foray, though the most impressive work to date is Pamela Dean, "'Dear Sisters' and 'Hated Rivals': Athletics and Gender at Two New South Women's Colleges, 1893–1920," in this volume. See also Pamela Grundy, "From Amazons to Glamazons: The Rise and Fall of North Carolina Women's Basketball, 1920–1960," *Journal of American History* 87 (June 2000): 112–46.

37. Berry, "Student Life and Customs," 135–36. For more on Texas football, see Lou Maysel, *Here Come the Longhorns* (Fort Worth, Tex.: Stadium Publishing Co., 1978); Kern Tips, *Football—Texas Style* (Garden City, N.Y.: Doubleday, 1964); John D. Forsyth, *The Aggies and the 'Horns* (Austin: Texas Monthly Press, 1981). For an examination of football at the University of Texas during the Depression, see James W. Pohl, "The Bible Decade and the Origin of National Athletic Prominence," *Southwestern Historical Quarterly* 85 (October 1982): 299–320.

38. Peter Finney, *Fighting Tigers II: L.S.U. Football, 1893–1980* (Baton Rouge: Louisiana State University Press, 1980), 12; William H. Lander, "How the Blue Devils Got Their Name," *Duke Alumni Register,* October 1964.

39. Berry, "Student Life and Customs," 168; Sumner, "North Carolina Inter-Collegiate Foot-Ball Association," 267; Isaac Newton Carr, *History of Carson-Newman College* (Jefferson City, Tenn.: Carson-Newman College, 1959), 262. The excitement and pageantry suffusing southern college sport depended as much on the armies of auxiliaries as they did on the feats of the leading athletes; cavorting and yelling cheerleaders combined with the first pep bands to add fun and frivolity to the drama of athletic conflict, filling the gaps between intense moments during the sporting duels on the gridiron, diamond, and track. Cheerleaders such as Duke's Wesley Frank Craven, who later became a prominent historian, were big men on campus, just a step below the athletes themselves in the hierarchy of popularity and influence. See *The Chanticleer* (Duke University Yearbook) 1926, 54.

40. Stegeman, *Ghosts of Herty Field,* 5; Wright, *Transylvania,* 302; Crenshaw, *General Lee's College,* 215. If women were perceived in some ways as marginal to the athletic extrava-

ganza, the inspiration provided by alcohol often played a major role in the experience, both during the period of local option in the South and the era of national prohibition. Spirits were prohibited at denominational colleges, but elsewhere they were a popular part of the Saturday afternoon and evening rites, especially in the cities where many intercollegiate contests were staged. One athletic tradition holds that during the late nineteenth century, Georgia players and fans alike raced away from the football field toward the Broad Street Dispensary in order to make purchases of liquor before sundown, the time when state law mandated such establishments be closed. Though such habits extended the euphoria of a day at play, they also provoked the wrath of the pious. Before long, moral reformers in the South would include drinking in the litany of abuses they associated with college sports, though their attempts to dry up masculine rituals would prove largely unsuccessful.

41. *Tulane Collegian,* quoted in Somers, *Rise of Sport in New Orleans,* 249. Concerning the issues of gender and sport (specifically the meanings attached to various modes of "play"), see Dean, "'Dear Sisters' and 'Hated Rivals.'" On the diverse ways white supremacy was cast (though not including sport), see Williamson, *Crucible of Race;* and Glenda Elizabeth Gilmore, *Gender and Jim Crow: Women and the Politics of White Supremacy in North Carolina, 1896–1920* (Chapel Hill: University of North Carolina Press, 1996). On the ideology of sport and race relations, see Miller, *Playing Fields of American Sport,* chaps. 7 and 8. For Jim Crow on the college gridiron, see Charles H. Martin, "Racial Change and 'Big-Time' College Football in Georgia: The Age of Segregation, 1892–1957," *Georgia Historical Quarterly* 80 (Fall 1996): 532–62.

42. *Wake Forest Student,* quoted in Sumner, "North Carolina Inter-Collegiate Foot-Ball Association," 280.

43. See, for example, Sumner, "North Carolina Inter-Collegiate Foot-Ball Association," 269, 283. Thomas Wolfe describes the intense rivalry between two fictional colleges, Pine Rock Baptist College of Old Catawba and Monroe and Madison College of Virginia: "The game on Thanksgiving Day was sanctified by almost every element of tradition and age that could give it color." See *The Web and the Rock* (New York: Harper and Brothers, 1939), 177–79. See also the detailed analysis in Oriard, *Reading Football,* 89–101.

44. R. L Durham, "The Beginning of Football at Trinity," quoted in Sumner, "North Carolina Inter-Collegiate Foot-Ball Association," 276.

45. Stegeman, *Ghosts of Herty Field,* 66, 88; Crenshaw, *General Lee's College,* 217.

46. Stegeman, *Ghosts of Herty Field,* 105; Moore, *Texas Christian University,* 213.

47. Joseph Hamblen Sears, *The Career of Leonard Wood* (New York: D. Appleton and Co., 1919), 58; Stegeman, *Ghosts of Herty Field,* 17–19.

48. Stegeman, *Ghosts of Herty Field,* 51.

49. See Corrie, *Atlantic Coast Conference,* 11–13; Mims, *History of Vanderbilt University,* 279–81; Conkin, *Gone with the Ivy,* 136–40; *Handbook of the Southern Inter-Collegiate Athletic Association,* 1905; Ronald Smith, "Preludes to the NCAA: Early Failures of Faculty Intercollegiate Athletic Control," *Research Quarterly for Exercise and Sport* 54 (1983): 372–82. Still, as late as 1916, after many reforms had been undertaken elsewhere, the football coach at Virginia Polytechnic Institute, J. E. Ingersoll, described "the great number of professionals and ineligibles on the teams here in the South," calculating that every college would have to acknowledge at least one tramp athlete. Writing to a northern cor-

respondent, Ingersoll noted that the ringers he observed usually lived in hotels and never even pretended to attend classes. Wearing "the most variegated collection of college insignia on their sweaters," they traveled from school to school, he declared, concluding that the ethics of sport in the South seemed "less developed and advanced" than in other regions. See Howard Savage, Harold W. Bentley, John T. McGovern, and Dean F. Smiley, *American College Athletics* (New York: Carnegie Endowment for the Advancement of Teaching, 1929), 28; J. E. Ingersoll to Walter Camp, October 30, 1916, Walter Camp Correspondence, box 15—Ingersoll, Yale University Archives, New Haven, Conn. See also Carr, *History of Carson-Newman College,* 266; Moore, *Texas Christian University,* 213; and Finney, *Fighting Tigers II,* 30.

50. Miscellaneous athletic material, Football folder, 1888–1896, and clipping, January 1912, Georgetown University Archives, Washington, D.C.; Joseph Durkin, *Georgetown: The Middle Years* (Washington, D.C.: Georgetown University Press, 1963), 228; Professor R. H. Dabney, letter to *Richmond Times Dispatch,* December 4, 1909, Lowell Papers, 1909–1914, folder 88, Football Rules, Harvard University Archives, Cambridge, Mass.

51. Roland J. Mulford, *A History of the Lawrenceville School, 1810–1935* (Princeton, N.J.: Princeton University Press, 1935), 285; Stegeman, *Ghosts of Herty Field,* 40–43. See also Crenshaw, *General Lee's College,* 219.

52. John S. Mosby, letter to Thomas Pinckney Bryan, December 7, 1909, Betty Cocke Collection, University of Virginia Archives, Charlottesville. I am indebted to Gaines Foster for sending me a copy of this document and stressing its significance to my discussion. See also Kevin H. Siepel, *Rebel: The Life and Times of John Singleton Mosby* (New York: Da Capo Press, 1997), 285–90.

53. Mosby, letter to Bryan. For an extensive discussion of the episode to which Mosby was responding, see John S. Watterson, "The Death of Archer Christian: College Presidents and the Reform of College Football," *Journal of Sport History* 22 (Summer 1995): 149–67.

54. Mosby, letter to Bryan.

55. *Raleigh Christian Advocate,* February 17 and July 13, 1892, July 12, 1893. The periodical supported antidrinking and antigambling crusades generally; it recommended not merely the restriction but the outright suppression of dancing on campus, and it fulminated against violations of the Sabbath, especially when the riding of bicycles was involved. Editorially, the North Carolina religious journal seemed rather ambivalent on the subject of tobacco. And it was much less censorious of the "barbarous custom" of lynching than it was in its observations concerning intercollegiate sports. See also Sumner, "John Franklin Crowell," 12–17.

56. *Raleigh Christian Advocate,* March 30, 1892. See Frederick Bode, *Protestantism and the New South: North Carolina Baptists and Methodists in Political Crisis (1894–1903)* (Charlottesville: University Press of Virginia, 1975). The key text for this entire discussion is Ownby, *Subduing Satan.* He observes: "Where evangelicalism demanded self-control, humility in manner, and harmony in personal relations, Southern honor demanded self-assertiveness, aggressiveness, and competitiveness. Where home life was generally quiet and peaceful, male culture was often loud and exciting" (12).

57. *Raleigh Christian Advocate,* January 11, 1893.

58. *Raleigh Christian Advocate,* January 25, March 1, March 22, and December 20, 1893,

January 31, 1894; Crowell, *Personal Recollections of Trinity College,* 45–46. See also Paul Neff Garber, *John Carlisle Kilgo* (Durham, N.C.: Duke University Press, 1937), 157–58. For similar conflicts at other colleges, see George Washington Paschal, *History of Wake Forest College,* 2 vols. (Wake Forest, N.C.: Wake Forest College, 1935–43), 2:311–13; Stevenson, *Increase in Excellence,* 191; Henry Morton Bullock, *A History of Emory University* (Nashville, Tenn.: Parthenon Press, 1936), 273–75; and Francis B. Dedmond, *Catawba: The Story of a College* (Boone, N.C.: Arromondt House, 1989), 93–95. See also Sumner, "North Carolina Inter-Collegiate Foot-Ball Association," 284; Sumner, "John Franklin Crowell," 17–20; Mann, *Story of Glory,* 50–55.

59. For an interesting treatment of "domesticated violence," see Pete Daniel, *Standing at the Crossroads: Southern Life in the Twentieth Century* (New York: Hill and Wang, 1986), 172–79. See also Ownby, *Subduing Satan,* 211–12: "And most churches have come to a shaky truce with some masculine institutions such as the football game and stock-car race. In many areas of the South, both of these events still begin with prayer that asks for safety, fair play, and a brief consideration of matters more important than sport."

60. On the first southern All-Americans, see Mrozek, *Sport and American Mentality,* 181. For developments of a later era, see Andrew Doyle, "Turning the Tide: College Football and Southern Progressivism," in this volume.

61. "Indeed," two historians of the region conclude, "pride in the strength of sectional football teams took its place along with pride in the valor of the Confederate army as a major source of Southern chauvinism." Francis Butler Simkins and Charles Roland, *A History of the South* (New York: Knopf, 1972).

2. Baseball, the Lost Cause, and the New South in Richmond, Virginia

ROBERT GUDMESTAD

ON SEPTEMBER 4, 1883, Charles F. Johnston took down the Confederate battle flag that hung in the window of his store on Main Street. Johnston, a veteran of the Army of Northern Virginia, sold newspapers, musical instruments, "fancy articles," stereoscopic views, and even season tickets for Richmond's professional baseball team. He needed to use the flag, since he and his fellow members of the Robert E. Lee Camp, number 1, were marching to the fairgrounds that day. The Lee Camp was a local veterans' organization that was open to all men who had fought for the South. That afternoon almost three thousand spectators watched Johnston and his army buddies file past in old Confederate uniforms that were too tight. Later, they saw "knights" on horseback use lances to capture rings balanced on the top of poles, cheered at horse races, and watched veterans shoot pigeons and glass balls. The daylong celebration closed with a grand ball in the evening. Such commemorations recalled memories of earlier days, inviting the citizens of Richmond to publicly honor the memory of the men who fought for the Confederacy. This celebration, however, incorporated an element foreign to antebellum southern society and the Confederate war effort: baseball. The Union veterans of the Phil Kearny club, a part of the Grand Army of the Republic that hallowed the sacrifices of northern soldiers, played a baseball game with the Lee Camp veterans. In sweet revenge for the war's outcome, the southerners won 6-4. In a later contest, members of the Richmond Virginias, the team for which Johnston sold tickets and was the "official" scorer, tangled with a club from Manchester, Virginia.[1]

In many ways, the Richmond, Virginia, baseball team became representative of the city during the first half of the 1880s. The club served as a tangible

1883 Richmond, Va., team. (Baseball Hall of Fame Library, Cooperstown, N.Y.)

link to the Civil War, not yet two decades distant, since many of the men who formed the Virginia Base-Ball Association had fought in the war. Baseball in Richmond fit neatly with romantic conceptions of war that began to emerge simultaneously with the Lost Cause. Those who directed the club used the game to promote the culture of the Confederacy, while the team itself became a visible reminder of the recent conflict.[2] The club's owners simultaneously embodied many values of the New South and of the nation's growing middle class. They represented a thriving professional class that stressed uniformity, standard business practices, and the need for experts to make difficult decisions in a competitive business. In a state that recently rebelled against national authority, management tried to integrate the team into a national system.[3] The members of the Virginia Base-Ball Association also recognized the demands of the working class for entertainment. A growing population of city dwellers who craved excitement was a natural audience for the team's games. The increasingly repetitive and boring labor in the Richmond factories meant that urban laborers desired more stimulating forms of amusement that distracted them from the cares of everyday life. Baseball in Richmond became one way to reconcile these differences.[4]

As it did in most of the South, the appearance of baseball in Virginia's capital coincided with the Civil War. Henry Chadwick, an Englishman who did much to promote the game during its infancy, tried to introduce team sports to Richmond in the 1850s. He failed, but when he returned after the war he noticed that the people of Richmond were now excited about baseball. The Civil War provided opportunities for southerners to learn the game, either when confined in prison camps or while guarding northern prisoners of war, and they continued to play the game when they returned home. Within a year of Appomattox, Alexander G. Babcock established a team. He probably learned to play the game during his service in the Confederate artillery. The sport quickly grew in popularity and became the favorite recreation of young men. By the 1880s there were more than a dozen clubs in the city, with teams organized along neighborhood, ethnic, or occupational lines.[5]

One of Richmond's young enthusiasts was Henry C. Boschen, a local shoe manufacturer. Local legend has it that Boschen, advised by his doctor to get some exercise, secured a bat and a ball and went to a vacant lot. He hit the ball, retrieved it, and hit it again. Soon growing weary of his solitary exertions, Boschen organized the Pacific Baseball Club in 1875 and served as its first president. He then formed a team from the workers in his factory, and when he spotted a promising young player, Boschen offered the man a job in exchange for a chance to play ball.[6] In this fashion, he located four players who would eventually have solid careers in the major leagues. The best, Charley Ferguson, played on Boschen's team before the Philadelphia Athletics of the National League purchased his services. He was one of the best pitchers of his day who could, and did, play any position. His promising career lasted only five years before he died of typhoid fever at the age of twenty-five.[7] Billy Nash was an adequate hitter but an excellent fielder with a strong arm. Originally a shortstop, he switched to third base when the first baseman complained that the velocity of the youngster's throws left his hands sore. Nash played eleven years with the National League's Boston Beaneaters, where he became captain and helped his team win the pennant three times. Eddie Glenn was a speedy outfielder who went on to play for three years in the major leagues before dying from an injury sustained during a collision on the basepaths. Christopher "Pop" Tate, a Richmond native like Nash and Glenn, was the team's catcher. He once threw out five runners at second base and went on to join Nash in Boston.[8]

By 1881 Boschen and his team, known as the "Richmonds," were playing strong amateur teams and major league clubs. The game they played was different from modern baseball, although the basic rules were the same. Pitchers delivered the ball on the run from the pitcher's box, a five-and-a-half foot long rectangle. They could only throw sidearm, and pitches above the shoulders were balks and automatically walked the batter. Hitters called for either a high or low strike, and seven pitches outside of the proper zone led to a walk. Catchers stood from six to fifty feet behind home plate and caught the ball after it bounced if there were no men on base. They were the only players to wear gloves, which were made of stiff leather with the fingers cut off at the joints. As a result, fielders commonly suffered from split fingers or broken hands. Substitutions, though, were rare, so an injured player stayed in the game even if, as happened to one hometown player, "the blood was continually dropping from his hand." A coin toss determined which team batted first, while a bell summoned the other squad to the field.[9] The Richmonds played at the Richmond Base-Ball Park, located at the corner of Clay and Lombardy Streets, opposite the Richmond, Fredericksburg, and Potomac Railroad yards. The facility eventually had a "beautiful grand stand with two private boxes on each end . . . expressly for the ladies." Although Boschen charged admission to his team's games, apparently much of the money for the club's operations came out of his own pocket.[10]

Boschen directed the Richmonds until June 1883, when a "number of gentlemen" organized a joint stock company called the Virginia Base-Ball Association. All ten of Boschen's players signed contracts to play for the association. Apparently the wholesale exodus caught the shoe manufacturer by surprise: he published a statement in the local papers angrily complaining of how "the nine" were "suddenly taken from me." Boschen indicated his desire to build up another team and respectfully asked the citizens to continue to patronize his games even though the quality of play would not be as high.[11] The men who organized the Virginia Base-Ball Association were mainly wealthy professionals. William C. Seddon, the association's president, operated a wholesale grocery and expanded his business in 1881 to include speculation as a stockbroker. Most Richmond residents knew Seddon as the son of James A. Seddon, the former Confederate secretary of war. William and James were closely identified, with the father using his influence to help his son's fledgling business after the war. Known as a man of "sterling integrity and rare ability," the younger Seddon was also wealthy, claiming a personal income of twenty-four hundred dollars, while his company was worth five thousand dollars. He grew up in Sabot Hill, a twenty-six-room plantation twenty miles outside of Richmond on the James River, and the family owned a sugar plantation in Louisiana.[12] The association's officers and board members did not come from backgrounds as privileged as Seddon's, but most were affluent businessmen, socially prominent, and from the white-collar class. They were, most agreed, "best people of all classes." Frank D. Steger and

Thomas L. Alfriend, the secretary and treasurer, respectively, sold insurance. A pork packer, a railroad and machinist supplier, an attorney, three merchants, and a stockbroker also sat on the board. Only Charles H. Epps, the captain of the police force and a former janitor at City Hall, was not securely ensconced in the professional class.[13]

Not only were the members of the Virginia Base-Ball Association respected civic leaders, they were closely connected to the memory of the Confederacy. Seddon, although he was too young to enlist, was linked to the war effort through his father's service. Eight of the eighteen men who served as officers or directors of the Virginia Base-Ball Association had worn a Confederate uniform, as had the team's official scorer. Charles H. Epps, for instance, enlisted within a week of the firing upon Fort Sumter, served as color bearer for the Richmond Light Infantry Blues, and was left for dead on the field of Hatcher's Run in 1865. George A. Smith was a second lieutenant in the president's guards and accompanied President Jefferson Davis in the closing days of the Confederacy.[14] Not only did these men fight in the war, they also kept its memory alive by joining veterans' organizations. At least five officers or directors of the Virginia Base-Ball Association enrolled in the Lee Camp, organized only two months before the formation of the association. Charles R. Skinker, who helped quell the John Brown "insurrection" at Harpers Ferry and enlisted within two weeks of the firing upon Fort Sumter, was frequently elected as president of the F Company Association of the First Virginia Infantry. Peyton Wise, known as "General" because of his postbellum commission in the Virginia State Line, went on to chair arrangements for the United Confederate Veterans' reunion in 1896 and was one of the organizers of the Jefferson Davis monument association. Such men were typical of the veterans of their day. During the 1880s and 1890s, large numbers of Civil War veterans in the South and North joined organizations such as the United Confederate Veterans or the Grand Army of the Republic. Such societies led the efforts to erect monuments on battlefields and town squares and planned reunions that commemorated both armies.[15]

In stark contrast to the management of the team under Boschen, the ex-Confederates used the Virginias baseball team to promote the memory of southerners who fought in the war. Besides the game during the celebration at the fairgrounds, the Virginias played a benefit contest with a local amateur team to raise money for the Lee Camp soldiers' home. Beverly R. Wellford Jr. helped make the arrangements, since he sat on the board of directors for both the home and the Virginias. Like the home it was building, the Lee Camp provided a place of refuge from the bitter effects of the war. Furthermore, just as the soldiers' home paid homage to the sacrifices of those who had fought for the Confederacy, the bodies of the veterans themselves were visible reminders of the war. Skinker lost the lower portion of his left leg at Hatcher's Run in 1865, while Smith had his left arm blown off at Fredericksburg. When these men attended the games and sat together, the absence of their limbs spoke volumes.[16] Wise became something of an official spokesman for the team, reaffirming the visibility and authority of Confederate leadership in the city. No doubt he wore his uniform for occasions such as the presentation of a gold watch and chain to Glenn in recognition of the speedy left fielder's outstanding play. After the club joined the American Association in 1884, Wise headed up the solicitation committee in charge of encouraging more people to buy stock. It was common throughout the South to use a Confederate general's blessing to raise stock subscriptions. Spectators at the games were reminded of the service of veterans in another way when the Stonewall Band from Staunton played before some of the contests. The twenty-member band entered the northeast corner of the stadium and marched to the grandstand. Such a ceremony had several meanings. It was a tangible reminder of the men who fought in the war, it paid homage to the Confederate dead, and it brought more people to the ballpark to see the popular band. In short, it was difficult not to remember the Confederacy when attending a Virginias game.[17]

It was in part the team's identification with the Confederacy that made the Virginias so widely accepted in the city. Baseball became amazingly popular after the Civil War throughout the country partly because it validated the experience of that conflict. The game allowed veterans to assert their wartime experience as good while encouraging younger fans to praise their accomplishments. Like the military, players wore uniforms, engaged in physical training, and developed a sense of cohesiveness as a unit. The game, like war, demanded precision, organization, and teamwork to defeat the enemy. It also promoted values essential to traditional notions of masculinity, such as courage, initiative, self-control, and competitive drive. All of the rituals employed by the Virginia Base-Ball Association strengthened the feelings of social solidarity, deference to leadership, and homage to the common soldier. Confederate veterans controlled the team and used it as a vehicle to promote the memory of the war and the celebration of veterans' sacrifices while simultaneously pursuing sectional reconciliation rather than confrontation. The celebration at the fairgrounds included a ballgame with federal veterans, in contrast to the attitudes of a Richmond team in 1866. The earlier club refused to play the city's Union team, composed of businessmen and federal officials. Furthermore, instead of seeking membership in a league composed of Virginia teams or southern teams, the Virginias sought to join leagues dominated by northern teams. Even before it played clubs from around the United States, the team hired "foreign players" from everywhere but the South. By the beginning of the 1885 season, only three players were born or had grown up south of the Mason-Dixon line, a stark contrast from only two seasons earlier, when the entire team was from the Richmond area. Ironically, the father of one of the new players had died in Andersonville Prison in 1863.[18]

Even though the leadership of the Virginias was closely tied to the Confederacy, they were also keen businessmen, judging from the reports of R. G. Dun and Company. Seddon was "a young man of excellent char[acter] & bus[iness] habits," who, according to Dun's Richmond correspondent, ran a "First class house." The correspondent universally praised the character and business acumen of the officers and board members. For instance, he described Alfriend, who would later become president of the association, as an honorable man of "integrity & character" and John L. Schoolcraft as a "man of fair bus[iness] qualifications, good char[acter], steady habits, and deemed honest." Skinker combined with his partners to do a large and safe business. They were "men of Excel[lent] bus[iness] qualifications." The general assessment was that the board members were honest and reliable businessmen who enjoyed the respect and trust of the community.[19] They were "some of the best men—that is if the best men are those who have comfortable bank accounts." Even the *Sporting Life,* a weekly paper with a national circulation, noted that the Virginia club was "supposed to be well heeled financially." These astute businessmen believed in the possibilities of baseball and considered it a sound investment.[20]

Once management acquired the team, it immediately set out to improve the quality of the club through organization. One of its first actions was the construction of the Virginia Base-Ball Park. In good bureaucratic fashion, the stockholders appointed a three-man committee to "secure suitable grounds" for the team's new playing field. Within two weeks, the association purchased a lot and put up the fence. Construction of the grandstands soon followed. Located just outside the city limits and across the street from the old site of Richmond College, the former pasture was stony, rough, and uneven.[21] It was prone to dust storms that choked the players, drove dirt into spectators' faces, and occasionally delayed games. Low spots in the infield caused the ball to bounce erratically, a condition worsened by the fact that the fielders played their positions barehanded. The park was so large—485 feet on a side—that wealthy fans parked their carriages along the outfield fence, forcing players to thread their way through horses and buggies in order to track down a well-hit ball. Since it was nearly impossible to knock the ball over the fence, outfielders ran long distances "hunting the sphere in all directions." One visiting player was credited with a home run after the Virginias' outfielders lost the ball in high grass.[22]

Although primitive by modern standards, Richmond residents eagerly paid a quarter to see games in this "beautiful" park that had "first-class, comfortable seats for ladies as well as gentlemen." To get to the grounds, most spectators took a streetcar to the end of Broad Street, where they boarded a horse-drawn omnibus that whisked them to the gate. An awning shielded spectators in the grandstand from the unrelenting summer sun, making this section worth the extra fifteen-cent admission price. Ladies and their escorts sat in a reserved portion of the western end of the grandstand, presumably to protect them from those in the general admission section, who engaged in such vulgar habits as spitting, drinking, and cursing. While ladies received a cooler of ice water on hot days, the men went beneath the grandstand to buy beer and whiskey. Truly devoted patrons bought scorecards for the games, and those who preferred comfort rented seat cushions. Spectators who could not afford to pay the extra price to sit in the grandstand were relegated to the general admission sections along the first and third base lines. Attendance at the park, including African Americans, who had their own area, swelled to three thousand on holidays or when a well-known opponent came to town.[23]

To help put fans in the new ballpark, the association used creative methods to promote the club and raise money for operations. A "Band Wagon," probably a small band in the back of a horse-drawn wagon, rolled through Richmond on game days to remind people of the day's game. The team also played benefit contests with local amateur clubs. During an Independence Day moonlight excursion on a steamer patrons could enjoy music, dancing, and refreshments while getting to meet the players. Prior to some contests, players competed in throwing matches and running contests.[24] These promotions by the association helped to finance the club, since the sales of stock only covered the initial expenses of the team. The twenty-five-cent admission price boosted attendance but limited revenue; even top-notch competition brought in gate receipts of only five hundred dollars. Guarantees for visiting teams, league dues, equipment, and traveling expenses all cut into the profit margin. By far the biggest expenditure was player salaries, which, on a national basis, doubled during the decade. At a time when an average laborer took home thirty dollars a month, members of the 1885 Virginias team made up to six times that amount.[25]

An even better way to ensure high attendance was competition with worthy opponents. As a temporary measure for the remainder of the 1883 season, the association notified baseball fans that it was making arrangements to "play match games with professional clubs from the North and West" in

an effort to bring in opponents of higher caliber. Seddon scouted out opponents during his trips to sign players and then used the telegraph to arrange
games. It was a haphazard system and one that sometimes hindered the club's
ability to draw large numbers of fans because of the unknown quality of the
visitors. The Philadelphia Southwarks, for example, agreed to play three
games with the Virginias in August. When they arrived in town it became
apparent the team was full of "scrub-players," so management called off the
games. Likewise, when "Our Boys" of Baltimore proved to be inferior, Seddon told the fans "that if they did not wish to witness the game under such
circumstances, their money would be refunded," and he promptly canceled
the next day's game.[26]

A better solution to the problem of finding quality opponents was joining a league, where a screening process took place. Seddon traveled to Philadelphia in September 1883 and met with delegates and proxies from eleven
other cities across the country. Eight of these clubs ultimately gained entry
to the Union Association, one of three major leagues that operated the next
year. Richmond joined with seven other teams, including some from the
erstwhile Inter-State Association, to form the Eastern League of Professional Base-Ball Clubs. In it, the Virginias played games with teams from Baltimore, Wilmington, Brooklyn, Trenton, Harrisburg, Reading, and Allentown.[27]
Joining a league went a long way toward ensuring the quality and uniformity of baseball in Richmond. Annual dues were one hundred dollars, enough
to discourage all but the serious teams. League teams adopted the reserve rule,
a clause that bound players to one team until that team gave the player his
release, either outright or through a trade. Players, therefore, could not jump
from club to club in an effort to increase their salaries. The rule created continuity within a team by keeping players attached to it but also reduced the
players to an untenable bargaining position when it came time to renegoti-
ate salaries. League play also brought a semblance of order to a haphazard
scheduling system. Now the team had a schedule two months before the first
pitch was thrown; fans knew exactly when the games would be played and
could plan accordingly. Joining a league was management's attempt to bring
order and predictability to the chaotic world of baseball and was something
they had in common with club owners across the country.[28]

Later in 1884 the club jumped to the American Association, and Richmond
was the first city in the former Confederacy to have a major league baseball
franchise.[29] Joining a major league brought a measure of prestige to the city,
since the club could now measure itself against the best teams in the country. Even before the Virginias entered a league, the *Richmond Daily Whig*
proudly informed fans that the Baltimore papers "speak of the Richmond

Base-Ball Club as being the strongest in America outside of the [National] League and American Associations." Success on the diamond led to bragging rights for the city. The *Richmond Daily Dispatch* reprinted a backhanded compliment by a Toledo paper that noted that the team does not "present an especially fine appearance upon the field, but if they do not look like hay-makers, their play is such as to put them in the first rank of base-ballists. Everybody was agreeably surprised." The papers only printed the positive assessments of the team rather than relaying the negative descriptions. Competition with teams from the North and Midwest helped the city shed some of its insularity. Just as the club eventually traveled to nine other states, players from across the country took the field in Richmond. The team exemplified the New South creed of progress coming from a small group of merchants, industrialists, and planters who were not hesitant to seek ties with the North.[30]

Management proved adept at running the business aspects of the club but recognized the need for a baseball expert to assemble and direct the team. To that end, the members of the association sought out an experienced base-ball man who could make decisions in matters they knew nothing about. In October 1883, Ted Sullivan, who had guided the St. Louis Browns of the American Association to a second-place finish in 1883, agreed to manage the team for the 1884 season. About a month before the 1884 season started, how-ever, Sullivan reneged on his contract. The St. Louis Maroons of the Union Association offered him one thousand dollars more than he could earn with the Virginias and also gave him the opportunity to manage a team that would compete with his former boss, a man Sullivan loathed. He refused to report to Richmond and, forgetting how the Richmond players abandoned Boschen, the *Dispatch* complained that "Ted is like all the rest. It is not so much his word as somebody else's money that controls him!" When Sullivan stayed in St. Louis, the team brought in Myron S. Allen, who had managed the King-ston Leaders of the Eastern League. He lasted less than a month. Failure to find an adequate manager would bedevil the team in 1884, as it left ultimate direction to Seddon and Felix Moses, the association's secretary who became the team's manager by default.[31]

Seddon conducted a frantic search for new talent and signed several men from northern cities. Moses did not settle on a consistent lineup and fre-quently used players who lasted for only a few weeks. Twenty-one new play-ers joined the team, and twenty-eight different men wore a Virginias uniform for the 1884 exhibition, Eastern League, and American Association seasons, a total of 130 games. This high turnover rate brought instability to the team and weakened its performance.[32] Seddon was even willing to sign Ed and Bill Dugan, two brothers who earned a notorious reputation in Richmond when their team had played the Virginias the year before. They drew much criticism in the local press for their "kicking," or complaining, about the umpire's calls. The most egregious mistake, however, was signing Frank S. "Terry" Larkin, an infielder with a questionable past. He had played on at least six other clubs before joining the Virginias. One day in 1883 Larkin first tried to kill his wife, then a policeman, and finally himself. His antics earned him six months in the penitentiary but did not cure his alcoholism. Once Larkin joined the Virginias, he performed adequately at second base for the team but went unaccounted for ten days in August. Such was the quality of players brought in by a wholesale grocer and a fertilizer salesman.[33]

The difficulty in securing talented players meant that the decision to join the American Association was a disastrous one. Richmond stumbled to a tenth-place finish in the thirteen-team league. Observers in other cities commented on the poor play of the Virginias, noting that "there is some good material in the Virginians [sic], but it needs bringing out badly."[34] While a contemporary publication claimed that "the new comers made a very good record," the numbers told otherwise. The Virginias' 12-30 record translated to a pitiful .286 winning percentage, at a time when talent in the league was down because too many teams competed in too many leagues. Moreover, the Virginias batted poorly and fielded worse. They finished last in most errors per game and tenth in batting, and their hurlers allowed more runs per game than any other staff. The best that can be said for the team is that it did better than Washington, the team it replaced. Not surprisingly, the association dropped Richmond from the league during the winter meeting.[35] Not only was the club an embarrassment on the field, but having to take the train to New York, Columbus, Louisville, St. Louis, Cincinnati, Baltimore, Philadelphia, Toledo, Brooklyn, Pittsburgh, and Indianapolis drained the association's treasury.

Management, however, did not dwell on its mistakes but took steps to fix the team's problems. Seddon resigned as president, probably by the mutual consent of him and the board. Most likely the directors wanted Seddon out because of his questionable decisions, but he had also married the daughter of a leading New Orleans merchant and moved to Louisiana. Richmond joined the "new" Eastern League, playing teams in Norfolk, Washington, Baltimore, Trenton, Lancaster, Newark, and Jersey City. After the disastrous 1884 season the club hoped to cut down on travel expenses by playing teams closer to home. The most important change came even before the team stowed its gear for the winter, when it began looking for "a first class manager," which was, according to *Sporting Life,* "something that it has been in need of the past season." Management learned from its mistakes and knew that it had to import an expert to oversee the team or it would repeat the ruinous 1884 season.[36]

Joseph Simmons agreed to guide the Virginias, and the board of directors gave him full control of the team. Simmons, who had managed the Wilmington Quicksteps to the pennant in the 1884 Eastern League, immediately cleaned house. He retained only four players from among those that finished the regular season and brought in a variety of players to fill the rest of the positions. In marked contrast to the previous year, the Virginias did not make a roster change until after the eighty-third game.[37] A surprisingly good player was George W. Latham, nicknamed "Jumbo" because he packed 250 pounds onto his five-foot, eight-inch frame and "Juice" because of his "extensive and inelegant vocabulary" that infuriated opponents. Although opposition players and fans taunted Latham as being washed up, he proved to be a good player who was a superb coach on the field.[38] Simmons also signed Samuel J. Kimber, who lacked control of both his temper and his pitches. While playing for the National League's Brooklyn Dodgers, Kimber pitched ten no-hit innings, but in a Virginias uniform hit two batters in the head in one game, causing one to quit the contest and leaving the other unconscious for fifteen minutes. The patience of Simmons paid off, as the erratic Kimber posted an earned run average of 1.52 for the year, sixth best in the league.[39]

The team opened the 1885 exhibition season by taking two of three games from the Providence Grays, champions of the National League in 1884 and winners of the first fully sanctioned World Series. The Virginias started quickly and amassed a 23-5 record by June 12. When the club returned to Richmond that day, a crowd of five hundred and Voelker's brass band greeted them at the train station. Team members climbed into two wagons built by the Lange Brothers especially for "base-ball transportation purposes," which were adorned with banners that read, "We Have Met the Enemy and They Are Ours" and "A Clean Sweep from Jersey City to Home-Plate." Twelve brooms, one for each player and the manager, jutted out from the wagons, while evergreens, flags, and streamers fluttered in the breeze. The crowd trailed behind the team as it rode across town to Manning's restaurant. In the short ceremony that preceded lunch, each player received "a handsome and nicely-arranged bouquet" of flowers. The next day, six humorous sketches depicting the fine art of "base-ball" graced the front page of the *Richmond Daily Dispatch*.[40] Simmons's ability to assemble a quality team is apparent upon examination of the club's record in the Eastern League. Richmond consistently won games and finished the year with sixty-five wins and twenty-six losses, a .691 winning percentage. The team was second in fielding percentage and batting average. It was certainly an impressive achievement, much better than their performances in the 1884 Eastern League and American Association.[41]

Even as the Virginias competed on the diamond, they played an important role in introducing to Richmond the practices of the emerging middle class and the values of the New South. Baseball acquainted fans with the growing emphasis on standardized business practices. Regular procedures, such as the official rain-out policy, became widely known. Even though there was "plenty of indignation" among fans who wanted their money back when a game was canceled, the posting of placards at the park effectively insulated the association from having to give out refunds. In a similar fashion, spring "practice" introduced the idea that teamwork, self-sacrifice, discipline, and the development of corporate values did not just happen but had to be cultivated. Before the 1884 season, practices were "largely attended" by curious spectators, and the general consensus was that the training put the Virginias "in excellent trim."[42] People also learned the importance of rules within an organization. When the manager disciplined players for violating a team rule, such as the time Simmons suspended Charlie Householder for staying out too late and fined Bill Greenwood for heavy drinking, fans learned about the necessity to adhere to standard policies. People learned the lessons of management so well that when the Newark team forfeited its game with the Virginias because the manager could not locate all of his players, the paper commented that the incident "goes for nothing, merely showing bad management." Such negligence on the part of the Virginias was unthinkable.[43]

Fans of the national game understood and accepted the way baseball incorporated a scientific worldview, appreciated rationality, and accentuated cooperation within groups to attain competitive ends. Individual players were accountable for their actions while trying to succeed in a group setting. People eagerly followed the results of the team but also wanted specific information on the performance of each player. As the game increased in popularity, both of the city's major dailies gave a detailed and fairly complex rendering of the previous day's games, complete with notations for bases on balls, first base on errors, strike outs, doubles, triples, home runs, and earned runs. Fans loved the order and efficiency of the game, so statistics became the standard measure of performance. Furthermore, such statistics must be precise. When the *Dispatch*'s correspondent questioned the accuracy of the "so-called 'official' scorer" of the Virginias, he "positively refused" to release the record. Baseball, especially when played by professionals, reproduced many of the character traits required by industrial capitalism.[44]

Uniformity was another value that came to be championed. A photo of the Richmond club taken in 1881 for the Yorktown Centennial Celebration shows a motley collection of players. Some of them have no discernible uniforms, while others have the letter R crudely drawn or sewn onto their shirts.

Their hats do not match, either. By 1883, however, uniforms became emblematic of being a good team. The *Dispatch* commented on the appearance of a "so called" professional team from Washington, D.C., one that lost two games to the Richmond club by the combined score of 49-8. "The appearance of the visitors plainly indicated that instead of being a professional nine (as was claimed for them) . . . they were the most indiffrent [*sic*] kind of amateurs. Their uniforms, in which there was an entire lack of *uniformity* (some being white, others gray, and others still different shades—representing, in fact, all the recognized colors), told as much." The clear lesson was that a team that did not pride itself on its appearance was likely to play poorly. One of the first actions of the Virginia Base-Ball Association was purchasing fancy uniforms that made them look like the National League teams they played in exhibition games. All agreed that the Virginias presented a "splendid appearance on the field." Uniformity, symbolized by the presence of uniforms, was now a value to be esteemed and pursued.[45]

Just as baseball introduced many of the values of the New South to Richmond's citizens, it also enabled industrial laborers to adapt to the new urban milieu. The game was a soothing way of recalling traditional patterns of life that smoothed out some of the differences in society. America changed drastically in the late nineteenth century with the movement toward industrial capitalism, rationalization, and bureaucratic methods. Such marked changes led many individuals to perceive a sense of disorder in society. Baseball was one method of coping with these changes. It blended many rural traits—open space, warm weather, and a grass field—with the urban setting. Fans in Richmond used baseball as a means of identification with one another, a way to establish rituals of mutual dependence in an increasingly fragmented society. Just as identification in Confederate veterans' organizations provided a shelter from the growing confusion of industrial society, so too did identification with the Virginias. True fans shared a common (and exclusive) vocabulary of terms like "flys [*sic*], fouls, base-hits, put-outs, spheres, sent-to-earth, daisy grass-cutters." Instead of celebrating the Fourth of July with pageants and military parades, as in antebellum days, "base-ball and private pic-nics" drew people together. "Base-Ball," the local paper concluded, was the "common plane upon which this democracy could meet, shake hands, and readjust the business difficulties of the city." The sport became a common denominator through which fans from all stations of life could meet and share a mutual interest.[46]

Richmond residents identified so much with baseball that passion for the game was raised to a "fever-heat." One publication found it "Strange how a furore [*sic*] will take hold of an entire city," while another marveled at how the town "has gone wild, and nothing can be heard but base ball." People flocked to see the Virginias. Although figures for attendance are limited, the team averaged more fans under the association's leadership than under Boschen's. Attendance of one thousand at a Richmonds game was considered outstanding. By contrast, the Virginias averaged just over one thousand spectators a game at the Virginia Base-Ball Park throughout the 1883, 1884, and 1885 seasons and drew two thousand fans or more on thirteen occasions.[47] When the team took to the road, large crowds assembled at various sites around the city to learn the scores of the games as they came over the telegraph wires. The Richmond Theater exploited the excitement for baseball by creating a minstrel show about "the cunning base stealers, artistic muffers, impartial umpires, [and] chronic kickers." Residents of the capital city were so smitten with baseball that even some of the town's ministers attended the games, despite general misgivings among clergy about the corrupting effects of organized sport. They probably objected to the large amount of gambling that took place on the games. Supposedly over three thousand dollars changed hands when the Virginias lost to the Ross Club of Pennsylvania, leading to a huge public outcry.[48]

Excitement for the team translated into increased profits for local merchants. Newspapers benefited from increased advertising revenue, local print shops kept busy printing posters and scorecards, and cigar dealers sold more of their products on game days. It was obvious that a "good game of ball attracts not only our own citizens, but outsiders as well." County merchants arranged to stay an extra day in the city to watch a game.[49] Andrew Krouse and W. J. Manning capitalized on the team's success as well. In an early version of a sports bar, Manning posted inning-by-inning reports of away games on a blackboard in his billiard hall. The hundreds of "enthusiastic" people "anxiously awaiting" the scores of the games blocked Broad Street when they could not cram into the building. Fans became so intent on getting up-to-the-minute scores that some accused Manning of withholding reports so that he could bet on the results of the games. Andrew Krouse posted the "correct score, by innings . . . with 'struck outs,' base hits, and errors," on a bulletin board outside his restaurant.[50]

Audiences at the Virginias' games were primarily from the working class, mainly because the ballpark was one attraction that laborers could afford. The twenty-five-cent admission price compared favorably with other amusements. Games with better opponents, though, brought "ladies, profession[al] men, merchants, mechanics, and others" to the ballpark. Richmond crowds were an unruly bunch, if the word of the *Wilmington Sunday Critic* is to be trusted. That paper, living up to its name, described Virginia fans as "'beyond description for rowdyism.'" It noted that visiting teams had to endure "'the vilest abuse from all classes.'" At a time when cheering, booing, and whistling were being relegated to saloons, burlesque, and sporting events, the behavior of the fans is not surprising. It was one of the few remaining places where they could freely express themselves. While Richmond crowds sometimes cheered the good plays of visiting clubs, they gained a reputation for being obnoxious.[51] Not only did the crowds jeer opponents, they taunted the Virginias, as well. They laughed at Jim Powell, a Richmond native and the team's captain, when he struck out. The ridicule was so intense that when Powell came to bat a second time and hit the ball to the fence, he taunted the crowd by allowing himself to be tagged out as he strolled to second base. Richmond crowds jeered Kimber so badly the manager sent police into the stands to restore order. Fans were obnoxious when cheering players, as well. A favorite means of expression was tossing rented seat cushions in the air, a practice so common that the papers feared for the safety of ladies at the games and called for the police to arrest the culprits. The fans were venting frustration from the increased tedium of urban life and the doldrums of daily toil. They took advantage of the sense of increased anonymity at the park to let off steam.[52]

Richmond fans' greatest outbursts of hooliganism, however, were reserved for the umpires. In this they were not alone, as umpires became "a convenient target" for the irritations and frustrations of the working-class crowds. Since only one umpire worked the game, he frequently had poor views of close plays, resulting in many questionable calls. The crowds at the Virginia Base-Ball Park "manifested their displeasure" at his calls with "howls, hoots, and hisses." When a ball struck an umpire and injured him, the spectators, "instead of sympathizing with him, laughed at his mishaps." Once the game continued, the attempts of an officer of the Virginia Base-Ball Association to quiet the crowd only made the fans rowdier.[53] Another time, Richmond fans berated an American Association umpire so mercilessly that he "very foolishly faced the whole crowd" and tried to single out the worst of the hecklers. His actions exacerbated the situation, and had "it not been for the prompt exercise of the police authority in silencing the crowd it is hard to say what might have ensued." The crowds were so bad that the team's manager wrote a letter to the editor asking patrons to stop "hooting and hissing" the decisions of the umpire. Such incidents occurred only after the team went professional and entered a league, suggesting that fans took the game more seriously once the Virginias signaled their intentions to play a better brand of ball. As the game passed from an amateur amusement to a professional business, the spectators took the liberty to engage in behavior that stretched the bounds of decency.[54]

African Americans were part of these uproarious crowds. During the 1880s segregation was the general rule in the city, although such arrangements had not yet been legally codified. African Americans who attended games probably did not sit in the grandstand but stood alongside the fence instead. These "colored spectators" made their presence known at the games because they would "always hurrah for the visiting club. They yell with delight when the home club gets a set-back." Such behavior was not "in good spirit." A tantalizing clue to the behavior of African Americans is found in a description of a game at Boschen's park, where "the colored part of the crowd yesterday cheered the home-boys on every good play." Such behavior was "quite different" from games at the Virginia Base-Ball Park. It is quite possible that African Americans were responding to the tangible and visible links of the Virginias to the Confederacy. Forms of covert resistance, like refusal to yield to whites on the sidewalk or cheering for the opposing team, were ways in which African Americans asserted their claims to equal civil and political rights. It was one way to declare their humanity while registering their disagreement with those groups they opposed.[55]

While African Americans might have been able to watch games in the Virginia Base-Ball Park, they were certainly not welcome to play. There were at least two baseball teams in Richmond composed entirely of blacks, one of which played "colored" teams from other cities, and the city council authorized the purchase of bats and balls for the "colored poor-house." A game between one of these clubs and the Virginias, or any other white team, was unthinkable. With Richmond swiftly moving toward a more segregated society, African Americans were not welcomed as participants in the all-white, all-male domain of the baseball diamond, something made perfectly clear in October 1884. The Toledo club of the American Association was set to close out its season in Richmond with a three-game series against the Virginias. One of the better players on the team was Moses Fleetwood Walker, the first African American to play in the major leagues. About a week before the series, Charlie Morton, Toledo's manager, received a letter that warned him not to "put up Walker, the negro catcher." The letter said that seventy-five "determined men" had sworn to "mob Walker if he comes on the ground in a [baseball] suit." While its author hoped there would be no trouble, the letter promised "much bloodshed" if the manager did not pay heed. The Richmond correspondent for *Sporting Life* recognized none of the four names signed to the letter. Walker did not play in Richmond because a rib injury in July led to his release. Enthusiasm for baseball was not allowed to cross the color line. In 1889 city leaders asked the Detroit Club of the National League to cancel its games with the Cuban Giants, an African American team. The locals did not want "colored and white clubs to play there [Richmond] against each other."[56]

Even though the ballpark provided a refuge for fans, and the Virginias had a first-rate club in 1885, the association ran into financial difficulties in July of that year. Success on the field led to a noticeable drop-off in attendance, making the team a victim of its own success. One resident noted that the club was "vastly too strong for the other clubs" in the Eastern League, so fans stay home because they "take it for granted that the club will win easily and there is no use in going out" to the games. If the combination of low revenue and high player salaries was not enough to bring the team to financial ruin, the actions of Thomas Carpenter were. Carpenter, the club's secretary/treasurer, cleaned out the safe and fled to Canada. He took what little cash the club had, and his theft exposed the critical state of the club's finances. The crisis forced the association to sell the team's two best players, Nash and Johnston, to the Boston Beaneaters of the National League just as the club left for its final road trip of the year. They were the main offensive weapons of the Virginias. In the first game after the transaction, Washington no-hit Richmond and then went on to sweep the three-game series. Eight games ahead of Washington when the pair were shipped off, the Virginias suddenly looked vulnerable. A local resident reflected popular sentiment when he confided to a friend that he was "beginning to fear that after all the Virginias will loose [sic] the pennant."[57] His fears were realized. A "weakened" and "disheartened" club saw its lead over Washington evaporate, and the Nationals ultimately captured the Eastern League pennant. When a committee of the players went to Alfriend's house demanding payment of the team's salaries from the previous month, he claimed the association did not have the money. Alfriend surrendered the treasury, and each player received $7.50. The team withdrew from management's control in order to finish the season on its own. A "right much demoralized" club played one more game, losing to Bridgeport before disbanding on September 19, 1885.[58]

Baseball clubs folded with regularity in the 1880s, and so it is not surprising that the Virginias did not last. The team, after all, was invited to join the American Association only because the Washington Nationals failed and clubs from Jersey City, Atlantic City, Lancaster, and Norfolk bowed out of the 1885 Eastern League because of financial difficulties. In the case of the Virginias, the club's president bitterly pointed out that "the public had themselves to blame" for the team's demise. He explained that people asked, "'who wants to see a one-sided game? We know who will win without going to the grounds.'" The game had lost its appeal in Richmond because it ceased to be unpredictable. Going to see the Virginias play was no longer entertaining

for the working class because they assumed the outcome was a foregone conclusion. The sport had lost its excitement. Attending a baseball game now
became a monotonous event, too much like the tedious work the spectators
wanted to leave behind. Although fans stopped coming to the park, they
closely scrutinized the treatment the players had gotten. Most of the team
members did not have enough money to pay their hotel boarding bills or buy
train tickets, but they eventually managed to drift to other cities and play for
other ball clubs. As Simmons tried to leave town, he was arrested for an un-
paid debt of forty-eight dollars for the printing of scorecards. The hardheaded
business decision of the association to withhold player salaries did not sit well
with Richmond citizens. One resident felt the club should have paid the players "instead of throwing them out in the cold at this stage of the season." It
was a desultory end to a promising year.[59]

Less than five years after the Virginias folded, a statue of Robert E. Lee was
erected at the edge of Richmond's city limits. The Lee Camp took the lead
in arranging the dedication ceremonies and asked citizens to drag the statue
from the railroad depot to its pedestal. This ritual deliberately mimicked the
method used to move the statue of George Washington from the waterfront
to its site next to the state capitol. Nearly nine thousand people took a turn
at the ropes that pulled Lee's statue. Marshals who led the citizens in their
efforts included Smith and Epps, both of whom squeezed into their uniforms
and both of whom had served on the board of directors for the Virginias.
Once the statue was in place, one hundred thousand spectators witnessed the
dramatic unveiling and the four-mile-long parade that preceded it. Marching in this procession were Smith, Epps, Alfriend, Wise, and Skinker. The
latter drew special notice for being able to keep up with his old unit despite
using crutches. All of these men had been closely affiliated with the Virginias and doubtless realized that the new statue stood on the site of the central
gate of the Virginia Base-Ball Park. It is somehow fitting that a monument
to the Lost Cause stands on the site of the old park, since the Richmond Virginias helped simultaneously to promote the New South and the culture of
the Confederacy.

Notes

This chapter is reprinted, with minor editorial changes, from the *Virginia Magazine of History and Biography* 106 (Summer 1998): 267–300, with the permission of the Virginia Historical Society.

1. *Richmond Daily Dispatch,* September 5, 1883; *Richmond Daily Whig,* September 5, 1883.
For information on the Robert E. Lee Camp, number 1, and veterans' celebrations, see

Gaines M. Foster, *Ghosts of the Confederacy: Defeat, the Lost Cause, and the Emergence of the New South, 1865–1913* (New York: Oxford University Press, 1987), 93–95, 100–101, 107–8, 112, 137–40 (quotation on 94). It was common to display battle flags in such parades. Johnston's background is found in *Richmond Daily Dispatch*, September 14, 1883; *Richmond Daily Whig*, October 18, 1883; J. H. Chataigne, comp., *Chataigne's Directory of Richmond, Virginia, 1882–1883* (Richmond: n.p., 1883), 228; and Jane B. Hewett, ed., *The Roster of Confederate Soldiers, 1861–1865*, 16 vols. (Wilmington, N.C.: Broadfoot Publishing Co., 1995), 8:504. The standard work on the Grand Army of the Republic is Stuart McConnell, *Glorious Contentment: The Grand Army of the Republic, 1865–1900* (Chapel Hill: University of North Carolina Press, 1992).

2. Foster, *Ghosts of the Confederacy;* Charles Reagan Wilson, *Baptized in Blood: The Religion of the Lost Cause, 1865–1920* (Athens: University of Georgia Press, 1980); William B. Hesseltine, *Confederate Leaders in the New South* (Baton Rouge: Louisiana State University Press, 1950).

3. *Richmond Daily Dispatch*, August 2, 1883. For the New South, see C. Vann Woodward, *Origins of the New South, 1877–1913*, (Baton Rouge: Louisiana State University Press, 1951); Edward C. Ayers, *The Promise of the New South: Life after Reconstruction* (New York: Oxford University Press, 1992); Paul M. Gaston, *The New South Creed: A Study in Southern Mythmaking* (New York: Knopf, 1970); Don H. Doyle, *New Men, New Cities, New South: Atlanta, Nashville, Charleston, Mobile, 1860–1910* (Chapel Hill: University of North Carolina Press, 1990); and James Tice Moore, "Redeemers Reconsidered: Change and Continuity in the Democratic South," *Journal of Southern History* (hereafter *JSH*) 44 (1978): 357–78. One explanation of why baseball was not popular in the South before 1861 is that it did not fit into the southern code of honor. Kenneth S. Greenberg, *Honor and Slavery: Lies, Duels, Noses, Masks, Dressing as a Woman, Gifts, Strangers, Humanitarianism, Death, Slave Rebellions, the Proslavery Argument, Baseball, Hunting, and Gambling in the Old South* (Princeton, N.J.: Princeton University Press, 1996), 115–25.

4. Industrial growth and the rise of the middle class is documented in Robert Wiebe, *The Search for Order, 1877–1920* (New York: Hill and Wang, 1967), esp. 111–63. Robert F. Burk, *Never Just a Game: Players, Owners, and American Baseball to 1920* (Chapel Hill: University of North Carolina Press, 1994), and John Rickards Betts, "The Technological Revolution and the Rise of Sports, 1850–1900," *Mississippi Valley Historical Review* 40 (1953): 231–56, discuss the interaction of baseball and industrialism, but not for the South. John F. Kasson, *Amusing the Million: Coney Island at the Turn of the Century* (New York: Hill and Wang, 1978), and Gunther Barth, *City People: The Rise of Modern City Culture in Nineteenth-Century America* (New York: Oxford University Press 1980), 148–91, introduce the idea of amusement for a working-class audience.

5. Ayers, *Promise of the New South*, 310–11; Henry Chadwick, "Baseball in the South," in *Sports Organized, 1880–1900*, ed. Gerald R. Gems, vol. 5 of *Sports in North America: A Documentary History*, ed. George B. Kirsch, 5 vols. (Gulf Breeze, Fla.: Academic International Press, 1996), 114. For information on Chadwick, see Charles C. Alexander, *Our Game: An American Baseball History* (New York: Oxford University Press, 1991), 10–13. Bernard Henley, "The Early Years of Baseball in Richmond," *Richmond Quarterly* 1 (1978): 48; *Richmond Daily Dispatch*, July 19, 1867, and May 1, 1875; Michael B. Chesson, *Richmond after the War, 1865–1890* (Richmond: Virginia State Library, 1981), 82; Walter S. Griggs Jr., "From

the Lads of Sheep Hill to the Braves of the Diamond: The Story of Professional Baseball in Richmond," typescript in National Baseball Hall of Fame, Cooperstown, N.Y. (hereafter Cooperstown), 1–21. Babcock's record of service is in Hewett, ed., *Roster of Confederate Soldiers*, 1:280. Union guards playing baseball in northern prison camps is documented in George B. Kirsch, "Bats, Balls, and Bullets: Baseball and the Civil War," *Civil War Times Illustrated* 37 (1998): 30–37. Louis A. Brown, *The Salisbury Prison: A Case Study of Confederate Military Prisons, 1861–1865* (Wendell, N.C.: Avera Press, 1980), 136–37, establishes that northern prisoners of war played the game as early as 1862.

6. Chataigne, comp., *Chataigne's Directory of Richmond, Virginia, 1882–1883*, 121; *Richmond Daily Dispatch*, October 22, 1898; *Richmond Times*, October 22, 1898; G. Watson James, "It's 'Batter Up!' Time on the City's Sandlots," *Richmond Times-Dispatch*, March 31, 1935, magazine section, 5–6; A. Woolner Calisch, "The Birth of Baseball in Richmond," *Richmond Times-Dispatch*, September 19, 1935, magazine section, 2–3. Businesses in the nineteenth century commonly sponsored baseball teams. Examples are found in Burk, *Never Just a Game*, 51; Steven M. Gelber, "'Their Hands Are All Out Playing': Business and Amateur Baseball, 1845–1917," *Journal of Sport History* 11 (1984): 22–25; Jacquelyn Dowd Hall, James Leludis, Robert Korstad, LuAnn Jones, and Christopher B. Daly, *Like a Family: The Making of a Southern Cotton Mill World* (Chapel Hill: University of North Carolina Press, 1987), 135–36; and Thomas K. Perry, *Textile League Baseball: South Carolina's Mill Teams, 1880–1955* (Jefferson, N.C.: McFarland and Co., 1993).

7. Information on Ferguson and all the other players mentioned in this study is found in the Lee Allen Notebooks and Vertical Files, Cooperstown; Index Cards, Swales Baseball Collection, New York Public Library, New York, (hereafter NYPL); Jeanine Bucek et al., eds., *Baseball Encyclopedia*, 10th rev. ed. (New York: MacMillan, 1996); and Marshall D. Wright, *Nineteenth-Century Baseball: Year-by-Year Statistics of Major League Teams, 1871–1900* (Jefferson, N.C.: McFarland and Co., 1996). For additional information on Ferguson, see Harry Clay Palmer, J. A. Fynes, Frank Richter, and W. I. Harris, *Athletic Sports in American, England, and Australia* (Philadelphia: Hubbard Bros., 1889), 115; Hiram T. Askew, "Charley Ferguson: A Baseball Star to Remember," *Richmond Quarterly* 5 (1983): 50–51; Allison Danzig and Joe Reichler, *The History of Baseball: Its Great Players, Teams, and Managers* (Englewood Cliffs, N.J.: Prentice-Hall, 1959), 178; and Robert L. Tiemann and Mark Rucker, eds., *Nineteenth-Century Stars* (Kansas City, Mo.: Society for American Baseball Research, 1989), 42. While with Philadelphia, Ferguson pitched complete game shutouts on successive days, the first a three-hitter and then a no-hitter. The next year he pitched both games of a doubleheader and only gave up one run in each.

8. For more information on Nash, see Hiram T. Askew, "Billy Nash: First Richmond Baseball Great," *Richmond Quarterly* 3 (1981): 34–36; Dan Abramson, "When Richmond Was in the Major Leagues," *Richmond Surroundings* 15 (1992): 48; George V. Tuohey, *A History of the Boston Baseball Club* (Boston: M. F. Quinn, 1897), 222–23; David Nemec, *The Beer and Whiskey League: The Illustrated History of the American Association—Baseball's Renegade Major League* (New York: Lyons and Burford, 1994), 61; David Quentin Voigt, *From Gentleman's Sport to the Commissioner System*, vol. 1 of *American Baseball* (Norman: University of Oklahoma Press, 1966), 243, 262, 276; and Harold Seymour, *The Early Years*, vol. 1 of *Baseball* (New York: Oxford University Press, 1960), 280, 297. After the Virginias played in St. Louis, the local paper described Nash as a "brilliant" third baseman "who is

also one of the best batsmen in the entire profession." *St. Louis Post-Dispatch,* September 19, 1884. Glenn died in Richmond in 1892 at the age of thirty-one. *Richmond Daily Dispatch,* February 11, 1892; *Richmond Times,* February 11, 1892; *Richmond State,* February 10, 1892. Tate was a rarity, a left-handed catcher. For evidence of his prowess, see *Richmond Daily Dispatch,* June 13, 1885.

9. See *Richmond Daily Dispatch,* May 4, June 4, and July 6, 1880, July 22, August 12, and October 19, 1881, for examples of games with other clubs. The rules are found in Nemec, *Beer and Whiskey League,* 28–29; Voigt, *From Gentleman's Sport to the Commissioner System,* 205–9; Seymour, *Early Years,* 176–81; Joseph Durso, *Baseball and the American Dream* (St. Louis: Sporting News, 1986), 32; and Alexander, *Our Game,* 45–46. *Richmond Daily Whig,* June 19, 1884 (quotation); *Richmond Daily Dispatch,* July 5, 1885.

10. *Richmond Daily Dispatch,* May 22, 1881, April 7, 22, and 27 (quotation), 1883; Michael Benson, *Ballparks of North America: A Comprehensive Historical Reference to Baseball Grounds, Yards, and Stadiums, 1845 to Present* (Jefferson, N.C.: McFarland and Co., 1989), 330.

11. *Richmond Daily Dispatch,* June 21, 1883 (quotation); *Richmond Daily Whig,* June 21, 1883; Robert L. Scribner, "Two Out and—?: The Richmond 'Virginians' Need Not Feel Unfamiliar within the International League. They Have Been There Twice Before," *Virginia Cavalcade* 4 (1954): 18–22. Boschen's reaction is in *Richmond Daily Dispatch,* June 22, 1883; and *Richmond Daily Whig,* June 25, 1883. He did scrape together a new team and continued to play through 1885, even adopting some of the Virginias' tactics: new uniforms, an expanded ballpark, membership in the Union League as an alliance club, and players from other cities. *Richmond Daily Dispatch,* June 27, 1883, March 27 and April 30, 1884; *Sporting Life,* March 19 and 26, 1884. After 1885, Boschen does not appear in any more accounts about baseball in Richmond, although he lived until 1898.

12. The officers of the association are listed in *Richmond Daily Dispatch,* June 21, 1883. The information on Seddon and his business operations comes from the various Richmond city directories of this period. A. J. Reach, ed., *Reach's Official American Association Base Ball Guide for 1884* (Philadelphia: A. J. Reach and Co., 1884), 23 (quotation); Personal Property Tax Book for Richmond, 1883 (manuscript), Library of Virginia, Richmond (hereafter LiVi); Roy Watson Curry, "James A. Seddon, a Southern Prototype," *Virginia Magazine of History and Biography* (hereafter *VMHB*) 63 (1955): 122–50; Gerard Francis John O'Brien, "James A. Seddon, Statesman of the Old South" (Ph.D. dissertation, University of Maryland, 1963).

13. *Richmond Daily Dispatch,* August 24, 1883. The information on occupations is from the various city directories of the period.

14. The list of officers and members of the board of directors is compiled from various newspaper and secondary accounts. Those who served in the Confederate military and their relation to the association are as follows: Thomas L. Alfriend (treasurer 1883–84, president 1885), W. M. Cary (director), Charles H. Epps (vice president), S. A. Ellison (director), Charles F. Johnston (scorer), Charles R. Skinker (director), George A. Smith (director), Beverly Randolph Wellford Jr. (director), and Peyton Wise (director). The records of service are in Hewett, ed., *Roster of Confederate Soldiers,* 1:100, 3:279, 5:345, 5:320, 8:504, 14:162, 14:218, 16:106, and 16:430. These men seem to be typical of those who joined organizations such as United Confederate Veterans after the war. Foster, *Ghosts of the Confederacy,* 109–12; Ayers, *Promise*

of the New South, 333–34. The *Confederate Military History Extended Edition* (hereafter *CMHEE*), 10 vols. (1899; reprint, Wilmington, N.C.: Broadfoot Publishing Co., 1987), has information on Epps (4:859–60) and Smith (4:1171–72).

15. Skinker's exploits are found in *Southern Historical Society Papers* (hereafter *SHSP*) 2 (1875): 317, 22 (1894): 285; *CMHEE*, 4:1170–71; Chataigne, comp., *Chataigne's Directory of Richmond, Viriginia, 1882–1883,* 30; and J. H. Chataigne, comp., *Chataigne's Directory of Richmond, Virginia, 1885* (Richmond: n.p., 1885), 81. Wise is noted in *SHSP* 25 (1897): 14; *CMHEE* 4:1280–81; and *Confederate Veteran* 5 (May 1897): 206. Alfriend, Epps, and Smith were the other three members of the Lee Camp. *SHSP* 17 (1889): 275–78. The scorer, Johnston, was also a member. For more evidence of the emphasis on sectional reconciliation among Civil War veterans, see Foster, *Ghosts of the Confederacy,* 67–70, 112–14; Wilson, *Baptized in Blood,* 28–32; and McConnell, *Glorious Contentment,* 185–93.

16. The veterans' home is described in Foster, *Ghosts of the Confederacy,* 93; *Richmond Daily Dispatch,* April 26 and 27, 1884. Wellford is noted in *SHSP* 20 (1892): 323; Skinker in *CMHEE* 4:1170; and Smith in *CMHEE* 4:1172.

17. See *Richmond Daily Dispatch,* August 3, 1884; and *Richmond Daily Whig,* September 20, 1884, for information on Wise. Gaston, *New South Creed,* 184. *Richmond Daily Dispatch,* August 11, 1885.

18. David Lamoreaux, "Baseball in the Late Nineteenth Century: The Source of Its Appeal," *Journal of Popular Culture* 11 (1977): 597–613; Michael S. Kimmel, "Baseball and the Reconstitution of American Masculinity," in *Cooperstown Symposium on Baseball and American Culture [1989],* ed. Alvin L. Hall (Westport, Conn.: Meckler, 1991), 292; Wilson, *Baptized in Blood,* 37–38; Foster, *Ghosts of the Confederacy,* 79–103, 137–43; Gaston, *New South Creed,* 167–77; Hesseltine, *Confederate Leaders,* 93–147. See *Richmond Daily Dispatch,* September 5, 1883, for the game with Union veterans; George B. Kirsch, *The Creation of American Team Sports: Baseball and Cricket, 1838–1872* (Urbana: University of Illinois Press, 1989), 209, for the snub by the Richmond team. *Richmond Daily Dispatch,* April 7, 1883 (quotation). The 1885 roster is found in *Richmond Daily Dispatch,* March 8, 1885. All three players—Glenn, Tate, and Nash—were Richmond natives. The player whose father died at Andersonville was Dick Johnston, who joined the team in 1884. Lee Allen Notebooks and Vertical Files, Cooperstown. According to *Richmond Daily Dispatch,* August 18, 1885, Richmond contemplated joining the Southern League for the 1886 season, but the team folded before that time. Bill O'Neal, *The Southern League: Baseball in Dixie, 1885–1994* (Austin, Tex.: Eakin Press, 1994), chronicles that league.

19. E. R. Chesterman, "Ball in Other Days" *Richmond Daily Dispatch,* September 16, 1894, 1. The members of the board of directors were Valentine H. Hechler Jr., Felix I. Moses, Otho O. Owens, John L. Schoolcraft, Charles K. Skinker, George A. Smith, Charles E. Straus, Simon Sycle, and Beverly Randolph Wellford Jr. Their occupations, along with those of the officers, were compiled from the various city directories of the period. Virginia vol. 43, 503 (first quotation); Virginia vol. 44, 212 (second quotation); Virginia vol. 45, 277 (third quotation), Virginia vol. 43, 23 (fifth quotation), R. G. Dun and Co. Collection, Baker Library, Harvard University Graduate School of Business Administration, Boston, Mass.

20. *Richmond Daily Dispatch,* August 2, 1883 (first quotation); *Sporting Life,* August 13, 1884 (second quotation).

21. *Richmond Daily Dispatch,* June 21, 24, and 27, 1883; *Richmond Daily Whig,* June 21,

1883; Map of Richmond, 1889 (manuscript), LiVi; Benson, *Ballparks of North America,* 330–31; Chataigne, comp., *Chataigne's Directory of Richmond, Virginia, 1885,* 420; James, "It's 'Batter Up!' Time," 6.

22. *Richmond Daily Dispatch,* June 30, 1884, May 15 and June 16, 1885 (dust); July 25, 1883, May 15, 1884 (infield); April 25, 1884 (size); May 24, July 5, and August 31, 1884 (carriages); March 25, 1884 (quotation); August 3, 1884 (high grass).

23. *Richmond Daily Dispatch,* September 25, 1884; and *Richmond Daily Whig,* September 26, 1884, contain information on transportation. The park is described in James, "It's 'Batter Up!' Time," 6. For specifics, see *Richmond Daily Whig,* July 11, 1883, June 21, and July 7, 1884; *Richmond Daily Dispatch,* April 20 (African American spectators), July 2 (costs), and July 5, 1884 (grandstand), April 7, 1885 (seat cushions). The park was typical of its day. See Alexander, *Our Game,* 46–49; Seymour, *Early Years,* 193–206; Nemec, *Beer and Whiskey League,* 25–28; and Philip J. Lowry, *Green Cathedrals: The Ultimate Celebration of All 273 Major League and Negro League Ballparks Past and Present* (Reading, Mass.: Addison-Wesley Publishing Co., 1992).

24. *Richmond Daily Whig,* September 18 and July 21, 1883; *Richmond Daily Dispatch,* September 9, 1883, June 27, 1884, and August 1, 1885.

25. *Richmond Daily Dispatch,* September 18, 1885; Chesterman, "Ball in Other Days," 1. National wage information is from J. Scott Gross, "Wilmington Quicksteps—Glory to Oblivion," *Baseball Research Journal* 15 (1986): 50; and Alexander, *Our Game,* 45.

26. *Richmond Daily Dispatch,* June 21, 1883 (first quotation), and March 18, 1884; *Richmond Daily Whig,* August 7 (second quotation), and August 11 (third quotation), 1883. See *Richmond Daily Dispatch,* October 9, 1883, and *Richmond Daily Whig,* October 10, 1883.

27. *Richmond Daily Dispatch,* September 14 and October 21, 1883, January 6 and April 18, 1884; *Sporting Life,* September 7, 1883, and January 9, 1884; Albert G. Spalding, ed., *Spalding's Official Base Ball Guide and Official League Book for 1884* (Chicago: A. G. Spalding Co., 1884), 68–69; Reach, ed., *Base Ball Guide for 1884,* 22–23; Joshua B. Orenstein, "The Union Association of 1884: A Glorious Failure," *Baseball Research Journal* 19 (1990): 3–5; Alexander, *Our Game,* 38; Seymour, *Early Years,* 148–51; Voigt, *From Gentleman's Sport to the Commissioner System,* 130–36. Chicago, Philadelphia, Baltimore, Washington, St. Louis, New York, Pittsburgh, Hartford, Brooklyn, Milwaukee, and Indianapolis formed the Union League. The other two major leagues were the American Association and the National League. The Eastern League is the ancestor of the International League, the current home of the Richmond Braves and the oldest active minor league. *International League of Professional Baseball Clubs, 1983 Record Book,* 47th rev. ed. (n.p., 1983), 1; Neil J. Sullivan, *The Minors: The Struggle and the Triumph of Baseball's Poor Relation from 1876 to the Present* (New York: St. Martin's Press, 1990), 20.

28. *Richmond Daily Dispatch,* January 6 and March 18, 1884; Reach, ed., *Base Ball Guide for 1884,* 23; Seymour, *Early Years,* 151. The Eastern League schedule is in *Richmond Daily Dispatch,* March 18, 1884. Burk, *Never Just a Game,* 82–85, characterizes the formation of leagues and the reserve rule as a "search for order," borrowing Wiebe's famous phrase. The reserve rule lasted until 1975, when a labor arbitration panel struck it down. Its demise led to free agency and higher player salaries. David Quentin Voigt, *From Postwar Expansion to the Electronic Age,* vol. 3 of *American Baseball* (University Park: Pennsylvania State University Press, 1983), 161, 211–14.

29. For information on the American Association, see *Richmond Daily Dispatch*, August 5, 1884; Nemec, *Beer and Whiskey League;* Alexander, *Our Game*, 35–40; Burk, *Never Just a Game*, 69–74; Seymour, *Early Years*, 137–47; Voigt, *From Gentleman's Sport to the Commissioner's System*, 122–28; and David Pietrusza, *Major Leagues: The Formation, Sometimes Absorption and Mostly Inevitable Demise of 18 Professional Baseball Organizations, 1871 to Present* (Jefferson, N.C.: McFarland and Co., 1991), 61–79.

30. *Richmond Daily Whig*, April 30, 1883 (first quotation); *Richmond Daily Dispatch*, September 30, 1884 (second quotation). For accounts criticizing the Virginias that were not reprinted, see *New York Times*, September 9, 1884; *Louisville Courier-Journal*, September 13 and October 11, 1884; and *Washington Post*, August 25, 1885. Gaston, *New South Creed*, 219.

31. *Richmond Daily Dispatch*, April 2 and 13, 1884; *Richmond Daily Whig*, July 1, 4, 7, and 18, 1884. Sullivan returned to Richmond to play three games for the Virginias, as shortstop and pitcher. The July 4, 1884, *Richmond Daily Whig* petulantly noted that "neither in the field nor at the bat did he display any particular ability." There is more information on Sullivan, who was replaced as manager in St. Louis by Charlie Comiskey, in Tiemann and Rucker, eds., *Nineteenth-Century Stars*, 120; Theodore Sullivan file, Lee Allen Notebooks and Vertical Files, Cooperstown; Bucek et al., eds., *Baseball Encyclopedia*, 178, 184, 710, 1645. He is said to have coined the word "fan," short for fanatic. The notice of Allen as manager is found in *Richmond Daily Dispatch*, April 2, 1884, while information on him is found in Bucek et al., eds., *Baseball Encyclopedia*, 730. Moses is named as manager in all the official records, and he accompanied Seddon to Eastern League functions. See Bucek et al., eds., *Baseball Encyclopedia*, 183, 704; Reach, ed., *Base Ball Guide for 1884*, 23, 111; and *Richmond Daily Dispatch*, July 18, 1884. Further information on him is found in Chataigne, comp., *Chataigne's Directory of Richmond, Virginia, 1882–1883*, 269; *International League Record Book*, 7.

32. The information on the players is taken from the various newspaper accounts during the season. Those players added to the team during the 1884 Eastern League season were Myron S. Allen (who played two games as player/manager), John A. Doyle, Edward J. Dugan, William H. Dugan, Richard F. Johnston, Frank S. "Terry" Larkin, Marshall J. Quinton, William G. Schenk, W. E. Stratton, Theodore P. Sullivan (who played three games as a player/manager), Washington J. Williams, and men named Devine, Hardie, Hetcher, and Shay. Those who joined the club during the stint in the American Association were Wesley Curry, Walter H. Goldsby, John Hanna, Michael R. Mansell, Peter J. Meegan, and Andy Swan. They joined Edward L. Ford, Edward C. Glenn, Paul Latouche, Henry W. Morgan, William M. Nash, James E. Powell, and William B. Smiley, who were holdovers from 1883. Those players not from Richmond boarded in the St. James Hotel.

33. The Dugans' behavior is described in *Richmond Daily Dispatch*, September 16, 1883. They were the first brother pitcher-catcher combination in major league history. After the Washington Nationals released Larkin, he came home drunk and shot his wife in the mouth. Mistakenly thinking he killed the woman, Larkin cut his throat with a razor in an unsuccessful suicide attempt. When a policeman arrived on the scene, Larkin fired two shots at the officer and wounded him. While in the hospital recovering, Larkin thought his wife would die of her wounds, so he again tried to kill himself by jumping off his bed and bashing his head against a steam register. Police had to restrain him while doctors

strapped him into his hospital bed to prevent any other outbursts. "For God's sake," Larkin begged, "hit me in the head and put an end to my suffering." After his release by the Virginias, Larkin was arrested for drunkenness in Brooklyn and eventually killed himself in 1894. Index Cards, Swales Baseball Collection, NYPL; Lee Allen Notebooks and Vertical Files, Cooperstown; Wright, *Nineteenth-Century Baseball,* 43, 47–48, 53, 58, 64, 119; Bucek et al., eds., *Baseball Encyclopedia,* 1253; Bill James, *The Bill James Historical Baseball Abstract* (New York: Villard Books, 1986), 37; Nemec, *Beer and Whiskey League,* 47, 52; *Washington Post,* April 29, 1883; *Sporting Life,* August 6, 1883, and October 22, 1884; *Richmond Daily Dispatch,* June 3, 1884. For a Richmond fan's allegations concerning Larkin's problems with "muddy" water (i.e. alcohol) and the player's response, see *Sporting Life,* February 11 and 18, 1885.

34. *Louisville Courier-Journal,* September 13, 1884. See also *New York Times,* August 9, 1884; *New York Tribune,* September 13, 1884; and *Louisville Courier-Journal,* October 11, 1884.

35. *Richmond Daily Whig,* August 11, 1884 (first quotation); *Richmond Daily Dispatch,* August 5 and 9 (second quotation), 1884; *Sporting Life,* August 20, 1884. The statistics are from Bucek et al., eds., *Baseball Encyclopedia,* 183–84; *Richmond Daily Dispatch,* October 21, 1884; and Albert G. Spalding, ed., *Base Ball Guide for 1885* (Chicago: A. G. Spalding and Brothers, 1885), 31, 36–54 (quotation on 36). For the record, the Virginias surrendered 7 runs per game, committed 6.7 errors per game, and batted .220 as a team. In Seddon's and Moses's defense, Richmond had less capital stock with which to work than did the other teams in the American Association. Nemec, *Beer and Whiskey League,* 5, 72; A. J. Reach, ed., *Reach's Official American Association Base Ball Guide for 1885* (Philadelphia: A. J. Reach and Co., 1885), 11, 73–74. The financial strain is noted in *Sporting Life,* August 13, 1884.

36. "Genealogy: The Bruce Family," *VMHB* 11 (1904): 443; *Richmond Daily Dispatch,* March 8, 1885; *Sporting Life,* October 21, 1884 (quotation). The "old" Eastern League became the New York State League; *International League Record Book,* 1.

37. *Sporting Life,* December 31, 1884, and January 14, 1885; Gross, "Wilmington Quicksteps," 49–51. After clinching the Eastern League crown, the Quicksteps jumped to the Union Association and posted a 2-16 record under Simmons's guidance. The .111 percentage was the worst ever in major league baseball history; Bucek et al., eds., *Baseball Encyclopedia,* 186. Simmons kept Nash, Glenn, Johnston, and "Steady" Pete Meegan, but the latter refused to sign with the team for one thousand dollars. *Sporting Life,* May 20, 1885. The information about the roster changes is compiled from the box scores of the *Richmond Daily Dispatch* and the *Richmond Daily Whig.*

38. *Sporting Life,* August 22, 1885 (quotation). More on Latham is found in Nemec, *Beer and Whiskey League,* 31–32, 40–41, 50. *Sporting Life,* September 8, 1885, has the taunts, while the coaching is in *Richmond Daily Dispatch,* March 24, 1885; and *Richmond Daily Whig,* April 10, 1885.

39. Information on both players is in Lee Allen Notebook and Vertical Files, Cooperstown; Swales Baseball Collection, NYPL; Bucek et al., eds., *Baseball Encyclopedia;* Wright, *Nineteenth-Century Baseball;* and Nemec, *Beer and Whiskey League.* For more on Latham, see *Richmond Daily Dispatch,* July 21, March 24, and April 6, 1885; and *Sporting Life,* June 24 and July 22 (quotation), 1885. Kimber's lack of control is found in *Richmond Daily Whig,* June 17, 1885; his hot temper is noted in *Richmond Daily Dispatch,* September 19, 1885; and

his ERA is calculated from *Sporting Life,* August 19, 1885. The team was Nash, Tate, Latham, Kimber, John Corcoran, William Greenwood, William Higgins, Charles Householder, Richard Johnston, and Harry "Shadow" Pyle.

40. Information on the Grays is from *Richmond Daily Dispatch,* April 4–8, 1885; Seymour, *Early Years,* 185–86; and Voigt, *From Gentleman's Sport to the Commissioner's System,* 109. The team's record is compiled from newspaper accounts. *Richmond Daily Dispatch,* June 12 and 13, 1885; and *Richmond Daily Whig,* June 12 and 13, 1885, have the story of the team's arrival. The humorous sketches are on the front page of the *Richmond Daily Dispatch,* June 13, 1885. Players of the opposing team commonly rode from their hotel to the ballpark in wagons, as there were no dressing facilities for visiting clubs at the park. During such trips, fans of the home team often hurled taunts or even objects such as rotten vegetables at the visiting squad. Alexander, *Our Game,* 46; Seymour, *Early Years,* 204–6.

41. The team's record is from the Eastern League standings in *Richmond Daily Dispatch,* September 16, 1885, plus one more game. *Sporting Life,* November 4, 1885, has the team statistics and individual player performances for the 1885 Eastern League season. The Virginias' numbers were .909 fielding average and .353 batting average. They could make a claim to being the best fielding team, as the first-place club played only eighteen games in the league.

42. *Richmond Daily Dispatch,* July 2, 1884 (first quotation). Practice is noted in *Richmond Daily Dispatch,* March 23 and 27 (second quotation), 1884, March 24 and 27, 1885; and *Richmond Daily Whig,* April 5, 1884 (third quotation). Barth, *City People,* 148–91; Lamoreaux, "Baseball in the Late Nineteenth Century," 597–602; S. W. Pope, *Patriotic Games: Sporting Traditions in the American Imagination, 1876–1926* (New York: Oxford University Press, 1997); Allen Guttman, *From Ritual to Record: The Nature of Modern Sport* (New York: Columbia University Press, 1978).

43. *Sporting Life,* July 29, 1885, recounts Simmons's confrontation with Charlie Householder and Bill Greenwood. See *Richmond Daily Dispatch,* May 31, July 1, 5, and 22, 1885, for more examples of Simmons disciplining players. *Richmond Daily Whig,* July 1, 1885 (quotation); Gaston, *New South Creed,* 167–77. For further information on the ways the middle class was able to inculcate its values, see Olivier Zunz, *Making America Corporate, 1870–1920* (Chicago: University of Chicago Press, 1990).

44. The *Dispatch* increased its coverage of baseball in part because of a letter to the editor. *Richmond Daily Dispatch,* May 26, 1883. For a progression of the coverage of the games, see *Richmond Daily Whig,* May 4, 23, and July 24, 1883. *Richmond Daily Dispatch,* May 21, 1884 (quote). For another incident of the scorer being sensitive to criticism, see *Richmond Daily Whig,* July 3, 1885. Steven M. Gelber, "Working at Playing: The Culture of the Workplace and the Rise of Baseball," *Journal of Social History* 16 (1983): 3–20; Gelber, "'Their Hands Are All Out Playing,'" 5–27; Kimmel, "Baseball and the Reconstitution of American Masculinity," 281–97.

45. The team picture is located in Photograph Collection, Cooperstown, and is incorrectly dated as 1883. *Richmond Daily Dispatch,* June 5 (first quotation), 6, and 24, 1883 (second quotation).

46. Guttman, *From Ritual to Record;* Foster, *Ghosts of the Confederacy,* 79–80; *Richmond Daily Whig,* July 7, 1885 (second quotation); *Richmond Daily Dispatch,* August 2, 1883 (first and third quotations). Kimmel, "Baseball and the Reconstitution of American Mascu-

linity," 293, argues that baseball supporters claimed the game was democratic when it really was not. See Ted Ownby, *Subduing Satan: Religion, Recreation, and Manhood in the Rural South, 1865–1920* (Chapel Hill: University of North Carolina Press, 1990), for an explanation of the appeal of rural recreation and one that could help explain baseball's allure.

47. *Richmond Daily Dispatch,* July 10, 1883 (first quotation); *Richmond Daily Whig,* April 2, 1884 (second quotation); *Sporting Life,* September 17, 1884 (third quotation). Few of the Richmonds' games had attendance figures. See *Richmond Daily Dispatch,* April 14 and 15, 1883, for example. Ninety-four of the Virginias' 161 home games had attendance figures, with a total of 95,600 spectators attending those contests. The attendance figures are from the local papers. If more than one figure was given, the lower one was used.

48. *Richmond Daily Whig,* April 3, 1884 (quotation). The term "muffers" refers to players who made fielding errors, while "kickers" denotes players who argued with the umpire's decisions. *Richmond Daily Dispatch,* August 2 (ministers) and 24 (telegraphs), 1883. Incidents of gambling can be found in *Richmond Daily Dispatch,* August 2, 1883, June 18, 1885; and *Richmond Daily Whig,* June 2 and August 2, 1883, April 3, May 26, and June 16, 1884. The entire Virginias team signed an affidavit that they did not throw the game. For more on the intersection of morality and sport, see William J. Baker, "Disputed Diamonds: YMCA Debate over Baseball," *Journal of Sport History* 19 (1992): 257–62.

49. Virginias Base Ball poster, Valentine Museum, Richmond, Virginia, as reproduced in Ben W. Blake, "Uncovering a Diamond: A Major League Club on Park Avenue," *Richmond Times-Dispatch,* August 9, 1981, B-2; *Richmond Daily Dispatch,* July 25, 1883 (quotation), and September 25, 1884.

50. *Sporting Life,* August 20, 1884 (first quotation); *Richmond Daily Dispatch,* May 1, 1885; *Richmond Daily Whig,* June 25, 1885; *Richmond Daily Dispatch,* May 30, 1884 (second quotation).

51. Patricia C. Click, *The Spirit of the Times: Amusements in Nineteenth-Century Baltimore, Norfolk, and Richmond* (Charlottesville: University Press of Virginia, 1989), 95–96; Seymour, *Early Years,* 76; *Richmond Daily Dispatch,* May 18, 1884 (quotation). *Wilmington Sunday Critic* quoted in *Richmond Daily Dispatch,* May 30, 1884. John Kasson, *Rudeness and Civility: Manners in Nineteenth-Century Urban America* (New York: Hill and Wang, 1990), 239–51, describes the changing codes of conduct. For examples of Richmond crowds cheering the good plays of the other team, see *Richmond Daily Dispatch,* May 25 and June 17, 1884.

52. See *Richmond Daily Dispatch,* October 9, 1884, for the antics of Powell, and *Richmond Daily Whig,* September 18, 1885, for Kimber's troubles. *Richmond Daily Dispatch,* April 7, 1885, and *Richmond Daily Whig,* July 7, 1885, describe two of the many incidents with seat cushions. Kasson, *Amusing the Million,* discusses urban workers' desire for amusement.

53. Barth, *City People,* 173 (first quotation); Alexander, *Our Game,* 47; *Richmond Daily Dispatch,* April 20, 1884 (second quotation).

54. *Richmond Daily Dispatch,* October 14, 1884 (first quotation), and August 13, 1885 (second quotation). For more examples of bad behavior by Richmond audiences, see *Richmond Daily Whig,* July 9, 1884; *Richmond Daily Dispatch,* April 17, July 9 and 10, August 31, and October 10, 1884, and July 9, 1885. Richmond fans were not alone in their rowdyism. During a game with the Nationals in Washington, a spectator assaulted the um-

pire. The Virginias "went to the rescue of the umpire and released him from his assailant." *Washington Post,* May 10, 1885.

55. *Richmond Daily Dispatch,* April 20, 1884 (quotations about the Virginias' game), and May 1, 1884 (quotations about Boschen's game); Jane Dailey, "Deference and Violence in the Postbellum Urban South: Manners and Massacres in Danville, Virginia," *JSH* 53 (1997): 555–57; Chesson, *Richmond after the War,* 101–2, 160–61, 191–96; C. Vann Woodward, *The Strange Career of Jim Crow,* 3d rev. ed. (New York: Oxford University Press, 1974), 31–65; Howard N. Rabinowitz, *Race Relations in the Urban South, 1865–1890* (New York: Oxford University Press, 1978), 189; Charles E. Wynes, *Race Relations in Virginia, 1870–1902* (Charlottesville: University Press of Virginia, 1961), 79–88.

56. *Richmond Daily Dispatch,* July 15, 1880, May 22, 1881 (African American teams), and September 2, 1884 (poor house); *Sporting Life,* September 24, 1884; David W. Zang, *Fleet Walker's Divided Heart: The Life of Baseball's First Black Major Leaguer* (Lincoln: University of Nebraska Press, 1995), 42; Robert Peterson, *Only the Ball Was White: A History of Legendary Black Players and All-Black Professional Teams* (Englewood Cliffs, N.J.: Prentice Hall, 1970), 23–24 (quotations); Seymour, *First Years,* 334. The local papers made no mention of the Walker incident. The Cuban Giants are found in Jerry Malloy, comp., *Sol White's History of Colored Baseball, with Other Documents on the Early Black Game, 1886–1936* (Lincoln: University of Nebraska Press, 1995), 136.

57. Before July 24 the team averaged 1,345 spectators at home games. After that date, it averaged 670. Total attendance for the year was over 49,000. Figures calculated from attendance reports in the papers. *Sporting Life,* June 3 (first quotation) and August 5, 1885 (second quotation). Carpenter's theft is noted in *Sporting Life,* August 12, 1885. Nash and Johnston's sale is found in *Richmond Daily Dispatch,* August 22, 1885. David K. Walthall to Guy Reeves, August 24, 1885, Reeves Family Papers, Virginia Historical Society, Richmond.

58. *Richmond Daily Dispatch,* September 1 (first quotation) and 20 (second quotation), 1885; *Richmond Daily Whig,* September 18, 1885; *Sporting Life,* September 23, 1885.

59. Notice of the Nationals' demise is in Nemec, *Beer and Whiskey League,* 5. For the 1885 Eastern League, see Albert G. Spalding, ed. *Base Ball Guide for 1886* (Chicago: A. G. Spalding and Brothers, 1886), 67. *Richmond Daily Dispatch,* August 22, 1885 (first quotation); *Sporting Life,* September 30, 1885 (second quotation). The treatment of the players is in *Richmond Daily Dispatch,* September 24 and 25, 1885. Simmons denied the charge and pledged to fight in court, but I found no evidence of the case's final disposition. He stayed in baseball, managing the Syracuse Stars in 1891, a team whose catcher was Moses Fleetwood Walker. Zang, *Fleet Walker's Divided Heart,* 76. Richmond had several amateur teams in the late nineteenth century before a professional team joined the Virginia State League in 1894. Calisch, "Birth of Baseball in Richmond," 2–3.

3. "Dear Sisters" and "Hated Rivals": Athletics and Gender at Two New South Women's Colleges, 1893–1920

PAMELA DEAN

"BASKETBALL IS the most popular game women play," Senda Berenson declared in 1901, when Spaulding first published her rules for a female version of the game.[1] Within months of its invention in 1891, women had begun adopting and adapting basketball to their (then widely accepted) special needs and capacities. College women especially took to the new game and poured onto improvised courts on campuses across the country.[2] Despite the popular reputation of southern women's schools as breeding grounds for languid belles, the region's women were as quick to embrace team sports as their northern sisters.

Although Senda Berenson, athletic director at Smith College, is usually credited with the creation of women's basketball, in fact Clara G. Baer, of Sophie Newcomb College in New Orleans, published a somewhat different version nearly six years before Berenson's came out. However, her modifications of the game were so "radical," she admitted, that when she approached basketball's inventor James Naismith for permission to publish them, he suggested she use some other name.[3] Thus, the rules Baer published in 1895 were for "basquette."

Baer and her feminine/diminutive version of basketball represent one point in a range of possibilities for young southern women in a time of complex change, an example of one view of women and of sports in the New South. At another point, not the polar opposite, certainly, but nonetheless distinct, we might find North Carolina's Normal and Industrial College. In Baer's rules and in the development of athletics at the Normal, as it was affectionately known, we can see some of the strategies New Women in the New South adopted and some of the tensions and anxieties they faced as they negotiated the contested ground of gender redefinition at the turn of the century.

Neither school was what one might call a typical southern women's college. If such an institution existed, it was more apt to have been a seriously underfunded church-affiliated school that functioned, at best, on a secondary level, or one that more nearly fitted the stereotype of a finishing school. In contrast, Newcomb, a privately endowed coordinate college of Tulane University, would be one of the first southern women's colleges to be accredited and thus deemed to offer a liberal arts curriculum comparable to that available to men. Moreover, it was located in and drew many of its students from one of the predominantly rural South's few established cities, a cosmopolitan city shaped in part by its Spanish, French, and Catholic heritage in contrast to the strong Anglo-Saxon and evangelical Protestant culture of much of the rest of the region.[4] The Normal College, by virtue of being a state school explicitly designed to prepare women for gainful employment in classrooms and offices, also stood out among the plethora of institutions claiming to provide higher education for women in the region.

Although both schools might thus be considered anomalies, they were nonetheless in the vanguard of the movement to create a New South. Higher education served as midwife to the New Woman and the New South. It fostered new roles for women and nurtured a generation of reformers that would lead the South into the modern industrial world. Advocates of the New South sought to put the rancor of war and reconstruction behind them and to adopt what they saw as the best of northern values, habits, and institutions. Only by doing so, they argued, could the region grow and prosper. While boosters eagerly touted the benefits of railroads, mills, cities and other accoutrements of a commercial capitalist economy, others feared that progress and prosperity would come at too high a price if the South abandoned its own cherished values. Greed for the almighty dollar and the impersonal workings of the market would replace southern gentility, honor, and the face-to-face relationships that were the base of the region's small-town and rural society.[5]

By its very nature the Normal College was in the center of this debate. Its founder, Charles McIver, was a leading advocate of the New South and worked closely with northern businessmen and philanthropists through the Southern Education Board. Education, he preached, was the key to ending the weakness, ignorance, and poverty that beset the region. He was determined that his college would produce thoroughly competent teachers for public schools, professionals who would also be public advocates for better schools. The school's very existence was challenged repeatedly in the state legislature. Among the critics were the heads of the denominational colleges who had already begun to attack public subsidies for the state universities as an immediate threat to their own struggling institutions, as well as to the concept of higher education as moral training for society's leaders and thus the proper responsibility of the churches. With the advent of the Normal College, they also became concerned about what a secular education might do to susceptible young women, on whom the moral health of the family and the community rested. They might, one predicted, "come back from there a pack of infidels and the whole world will go to the dogs."[6]

Other opponents saw the professionalization of teaching that McIver and his allies advocated as an assault on local control of essential community institutions.[7] There is more than a bit of irony in the fact that many who held this position were Populists, a group closely identified with small farmers who were hardest hit by the transition from a subsistence-based agricultural system to a commercial economy. The irony lies in the fact that a plurality of the college's students were the daughters of yeoman farmers, women who had to "make their own way in the world," as one applicant's mother wrote McIver.[8] Like him, these young women saw the Normal College as the answer to their problem, not a manifestation of the alienation of power from the individual to distant—usually northern—institutions. It promised a way for them as individuals to take control of their own lives and to provide for themselves what their fathers could no longer promise, economic security.

McIver was as passionately committed to expanding opportunities for women as he was to improving the state's schools. "How galling dependence must be to a sensible woman," he acknowledged to his wife, Lula Martin McIver. Lula, who had wanted to follow in her father's footsteps as a doctor, had continued to work as a teacher and lady principal at a women's college even after her marriage to Charles McIver and the birth of their children. Although McIver conceded in the early years of their marriage that he regretted not being able to provide her with a home—the minimal responsibility of husband to wife—he frankly admitted that "the fact is when we do get a home and a competency you will have done at least as much to earn it as I have. It will not be mine to give, but ours to share."[9] Remarkably, McIver found no threat to his manhood in this situation.

McIver passed on to his students his zeal for both improving schools and empowering women, telling them that it would be up to them to aggressively propagate the values and skills that southerners needed if they were to move from the region's impoverished agrarian past to the urban, industrial future of the coming century.[10] They, he told them, must be the vanguard in the battle to create a New South.

As a well-endowed private school, Newcomb never faced the kind of criticism McIver and the Normal endured. President Brandt Dixon recalled that in the early years his greatest challenge was to convince parents of prospective students for what he envisioned as a first-class college on the northeastern model that seventeen was the minimum age for admission to college, not the age at which they should expect their daughters to be "finished." Although the liberal arts curriculum Dixon instituted at Newcomb was perhaps more rigorous than some parents anticipated, it was also more broadly focused than that of the Normal College. Drawing on the port city's growing middle class, it also sought to prepare its students for careers and leadership in their New South communities, but it placed greater emphasis on a somewhat less assertive version of ideal womanhood than the one McIver articulated and perhaps was best known for its design training and the famous art deco Newcomb pottery.[11]

For both schools, the fulfillment of their mission demanded a new female archetype, one that would sanction women's invasion of the public sphere in a way that the image of the more domestic and dependent antebellum lady never could. By the late nineteenth and early twentieth centuries there was a critical mass of urban residents in the South who espoused values of thrift, sobriety, self-control, industry, and civic duty and thus began to form a self-conscious urban middle class. New patterns of work, new standards for judging worth, and new mechanisms for maintaining order were required in the fluid, anonymous, urban world.[12] If the timing meant that the South could borrow from the North, it would do so with a southern twist. College women and their teachers would be vital participants in the process of defining values and styles of self-presentation appropriate to this new class and the New South.[13] But like all cultural change, this process was complex and fraught with ambivalence and anxiety as well as heady delight in new powers and possibilities. And it was played out in all its complexity in the gymnasia and on the basketball courts, between teams of young women who were "dear sisters" as well as "hated rivals."

Games and other forms of recreation have been explored by anthropologists and cultural historians as rituals that can reveal a society's most deeply rooted values and assumptions. By the turn of the century, sports and physical fitness had become national passions and central motifs in a heated debate on gender roles and "the woman question." Robust exercise and especially team sports came to be seen as quintessentially male activities, as definitions of gender began to shift from those based on character—for men, fulfilling duty to God, family and community; for women, purity and piety—to an emphasis on male physical prowess and female "Gibson Girl" grace and vitality.[14]

Earlier in the century, arbitrators of female norms such as Sara Josepha Hale, the influential editor of *Godey's Lady's Book,* and Catharine Beecher, author and education reformer, had advocated mild physical activity for young women.[15] Beecher thought housework the best form of exercise for women, although walking could be substituted for those with domestic help. By the turn of the century, eugenicists, fearing for the vigor and cultural dominance of the Anglo-Saxon race, argued that frail, nervous, sickly women would produce increasingly defective children and predicted that the "better" classes would soon be overtaken by the more robust and fecund immigrants from eastern and southern Europe.

Linked to these concerns was the fear that the brightest daughters of the middle and upper classes were sacrificing their health and endangering their reproductive capacities in the pursuit of higher education. These apprehensions were based on the assumption that the body contained a finite store of energy. Energy drawn to the brain for intellectual activity was energy denied to the reproductive organs—a dangerous proposition, especially during the delicate and formative years of puberty.[16] Too much exercise, however, could be just as detrimental as too little. Excessively enthusiastic indulgence in what was, after all, a quintessentially male activity might make a woman hard, even masculine, with "muscles . . . so developed [that they would appear] in lumpy protuberances."[17]

Women educators had answers for these fevered fantasies. Rather than concluding that women should eschew either education or athletics, they argued that moderate physical activity, carefully supervised to avoid excess, would strengthen young bodies and relieve the strain of studying. Programs based on such principles soon became part of the curriculum at all women's colleges.[18] While the program at Newcomb College was under the direction of Clara Baer, a graduate of a training program for physical education teachers, at the Normal it was the school's physician—first Dr. Miriam Bitting and then her successor Dr. Anna Gove—who served as director of physical culture.

Lula McIver is credited with insisting that the faculty include a female doctor. Charles McIver solicited recommendations from the leading medical schools that admitted women, and from their responses it appears that he may have specified a preference for a southerner.[19] In any event, Marian Bitting, a native Virginian, daughter of a prominent Baptist clergyman, and graduate of the Woman's Medical College of Philadelphia, was hired. She held this position for the first year, teaching physiology, hygiene, and physical culture in addition to treating student ailments. When she left, Anna M. Gove, one of the original applicants, replaced her. A New Hampshire native who was trained at the Woman's Medical College of New York Infirmary, Gove was the only member of the faculty in the early years without a southern background. Her professional credentials made her a welcome addition to the college's intellectual community, but it was her friendship with her fellow MIT alumna, science teacher Dixie Lee Bryant, in addition to her graciousness and "infallible . . . taste in conduct" that assured this Yankee's acceptance in the social community, which, enlightened as it may have been, was nonetheless profoundly southern.[20]

Bitting and Gove not only tended to fevers, female complaints, and minor injuries, they practiced preventive medicine as well. Fresh air, daily walks, individually designed exercise programs, personal hygiene, and the elimination of tight corsets constituted the prescription. Thus, each afternoon at the Normal, every girl opened the windows and door of her dorm room to give it a good airing and went out for an hour's brisk turn around campus. The walking period, as it was known, was as much a social occasion as an exercise period, providing an opportunity for the girls to make dates with their "best girl (no boys allowed)." As one student described it, "Every afternoon at 4:15 'that Normal bell' rings, dormitories open and girls pour forth. . . . We make a regular engagement with our chum . . . clasp arms, saunter, and listen laddies! We talk love."[21] A staple of antebellum female academy life, the walking period helped defuse anxieties about the impact of academics on women's health without substantially altering assumptions about women's physical capacities or the primacy of marriage as the career of choice.[22]

More structured programs of physical culture or therapeutic gymnastics were designed not only to balance the stresses of intellectual pursuits but also to correct defects the girls brought with them. Along with such common problems as poor posture and bad feet, these might include, according to Baer, "psychic nervous conditions," "defects of the respiratory organs," "disturbances of the pelvic organs with functional irregularities," "derangements of the digestic organs," and "skin troubles." Baer suggested that the latter two were often due "to the general want of understanding of the efficient use of water as a therapeutic agent and of fundamental principles of personal hygiene."[23] Baer alludes to the growing concern with cleanliness that cultural historians have noted was a defining feature of the middle class in the nineteenth century. This suggests that, even in the city of New Orleans, many incoming college students had not yet fully assimilated those standards.[24]

Concern for the health of the students was closely linked to concern for their appearance. The stated aim of the physical culture program at the Normal College was "to correct careless physical habits, develop the body symmetrically, and give to the student that erect, strong, reliant, dignified, and graceful carriage and deportment that always characterize the cultured woman."[25] The shining hair and clear complexion that proper diet and hygiene ensured and the "erect" posture and "graceful carriage" of a "symmetrically" developed body were the external indicators of both health and the new standards of femininity. These standards were best realized through calisthenics or gymnastics rather than more vigorous sports, many in the field argued, because they emphasized "the aesthetic element; girls in general desire to appear delicate and graceful." Physical education should not sacrifice "tender femininity" for the sake of "Spartan toughness."[26]

Baer and Bitting and their colleagues walked a fine line when they advocated exercise for southern women. Brandt Dixon, the founder of Newcomb College, recalled parental objections to the "supposed tendency" of athletics "to render the young ladies coarse and unfeminine," with one father going so far as to contend that his daughter got enough exercise in the summer and needed none at school.[27] Only so long as they could demonstrate that grace and femininity went hand in hand with exercise could advocates of women's physical culture succeed.

At the Normal College, the popularity of the Indian club, fan, and scarf drills and similar "physical culture entertainments" as part of annual commencement programs illustrates the balance sought. Dressed in gym bloomers and midi blouses with clubs, fans, or scarves in hand, the girls went through carefully choreographed routines that emphasized grace as well as fitness. The inclusion of these performances among the graduation rituals suggests that students and college administrators alike considered them as significant as the sermons and commencement speeches.[28] Their popularity with parents was apparent from the standing-room-only crowd (ladies only) that a two-hour exhibition drew in 1894.[29]

Certainly the Normal College's president had no hesitancy in praising the results of Bitting's program of calisthenics and walking. In the first annual catalog of the college, he reported that during the past year "many chests increased in girth, shoulders straightened, arms became stronger, and the general bearing much improved."[30] McIver, seeking to inculcate in his students a sense of mission and assertive self-confidence in their roles as teachers and advocates for the New South, was prepared to go beyond "delicate," "graceful," "tender femininity" to achieve a certain robustness that would be appropriate, even necessary, in their new roles. So, even under Bitting's carefully moderated system, the Normal girls would embody a fresh image of southern women, "strong" and "reliant" as well as "graceful."[31]

Speaking at the college's first commencement, Dr. T. H. Pritchard, the former president of Wake Forest College, seemed to affirm McIver's observations, but one must wonder just what the young women in his audience heard when he spoke. There were three ways to recognize a Normal girl, he reported. "She doesn't flirt with the boys, she walks erect and throws her shoulders back well, and she has a large waist." Not being a flirt was a good thing, they may well have agreed. They were, after all, going out to be professional teachers and leaders in their communities, goals quite incompatible with idle flirtation. Good posture was also a desirable characteristic. But a large waist . . . that might have given any girl pause. Pritchard's comment, no doubt, was a tribute to Bitting's lessons on the detrimental effects of tight lacing, which had led two-thirds of the students to discard their corsets.[32] But it also reflected the ambivalence that a young woman of serious mien and determined stride might encounter in the turn-of-the-century South.

Dress reform, like issues of health and appearance, was closely linked to the changing forms of women's sports. Those defects of the respiratory and digestive organs Baer cited were likely results of those same corsets Bitting railed against, as, in part, was the female frailty that worried eugenicists. Unlike North Carolina farmers' daughters, New Orleans ladies were so attached to their tiny waists that Baer met more initial resistance than Bitting. Until 1894, tightly laced corsets, covered with voluminous petticoats, skirts, and shirtwaists, were de rigueur in the gymnasium as well as the classroom. When Baer introduced the less restrictive bloomers and midi blouses, she found the girls reluctant to don so immodest an outfit. To suggest they abandon their stays at the same time, Baer feared, would be too much. Thus she simply let them pant through a few gymnastic workouts in both their tight corsets and voluminous bloomers, until they "sweat[ed] the corsets off."[33]

Bloomers had been the much-ridiculed symbol of the mid-nineteenth-century women's movement. The pioneer suffragists Elizabeth Cady Stanton and Amelia Bloomer, for whom the garment was named, were among the few who recognized the liberative potential of sports for women. Writing in Bloomer's newspaper, *The Lily,* Stanton asserted, "We cannot say what the woman might be physically, if the girl were allowed all the freedom of the boy, in romping, swimming, climbing and playing ball."[34]

Fodie Buie, Normal College class of 1896, recalled the all-enveloping black stockings and blue serge bloomer-and-midi-blouse outfits that the girls ran up on the domestic science department's sewing machines. "We were not allowed even to so much as to walk out in the halls with a gym suit on, cumbersome and all-concealing though it was," she recalled. "No papas and not even any grand papas were allowed to be present."[35] No men at the physical culture exhibition, none in the gymnasium. Bloomers, with their resemblance to trousers, conjured up visions of gender reversal. Even Stanton gave up bloomers for street wear, acknowledging that the controversy they generated distracted from more significant issues in the feminist agenda; however, they did become the accepted costume for the gymnasium and the playing field.

For more public and potentially heterosexual activities such as tennis, golf, or bicycling, modifications in dress were less extreme and the subversion of gender conventions more subtle. Skirts and white midi blouses were the preferred attire on the tennis court. Bicycling, which became widely popular among women, necessitated slightly shortened skirts, a seemingly minor alteration. But Fodie Buie and her mother understood the implications when she bought a bicycle to help her get to and from her work as a court reporter, one of the many jobs she took to help pay for her sister's as well as her own education. "To be able to ride at all, my skirts had to stop at my shoe tops," she recalled. "And if one's skirts did not touch the ground, one was looked upon with suspicion, if not downright disapproval, and somewhat ostracized by the 'best ladies' in the community. But I wore my disgracefully abbreviated skirts, and managed to live down the disapproval of the natives."

The bicycle, Buie continued, "was a great help when I was on reporting trips." The railroads did not charge to carry a passenger's bicycle, and "the Powers-that-Be didn't have to send for me and send me home; and that was bad too, for ladies did not go places alone. Mother was sensible. She told me to go ahead and always behave myself, and all would be well."[36] The minor modification of fashion Fodie Buie adopted with her mother's approval was more than just a symbolic challenge to the standards of the "best ladies." It meant that Buie and women like her could venture alone into heretofore forbidden public territory, from railroad stations to courthouses. But in the process they needed to find modes of dress and behavior that would allow them the freedom of movement necessary to take on new roles and do new jobs in the evolving economy without fatally scandalizing the "best ladies" of the old South. As school teachers and as the future wives of bankers, engineers, and manufacturers, college women might be poised to take over the role of social reformers in their communities, but they would not succeed if their dress or demeanor branded them as outside the circle of respectable society.

Basketball posed a more difficult challenge to the delicate balance sought by southern advocates of women's athletics than any of the previously discussed activities. Team sports were fundamentally different from walking, calisthenics, or even tennis or bicycle riding. To begin with, they were games invented for men. Moreover, even when played by men, they smacked of the modern sensibilities traditionalists in the region condemned. Their codified rules, which inherently promoted not only teamwork but also competition, were in tune with an urban industrial society. Southern churchmen charged that team sports tended to glorify the body over the spirit and were another deplorable example of southerners aping Yankee ways.[37]

Clara Baer was sensitive to these concerns and would address them with her revision of basketball. Baer, a native of Algiers, just across the Mississippi from New Orleans, had been trained in "expression" and oratory in Boston, where she also attended the Posse Normal School of Physical Education.[38] She returned to New Orleans in 1891 to start a physical education program at the recently established Sophie Newcomb College and introduced basketball to her students in 1893. It was, however, a "crude and rough" game, she recalled, and its introduction was "not entirely satisfactory."[39] While Baer offers no other details, accounts of early Smith College matches describe "a mad game" with wild play and riotous cheering, in which players tended to "grow bitter in feeling and lose self-control," which "makes the girls rough, loud-voiced and bold."[40] Distressed at such wildness and lack of control, Baer felt compelled to abandon the game. Nonetheless, basketball offered many benefits, Baer realized, and the following year she reintroduced it in a much-refined version.

Like Senda Berenson at Smith, Baer sought to create a game that her students would enjoy, that would promote healthy exercise and teamwork, but that at the same time was one in which physical contact, exertion, and disorderly commotion would be minimized. In common with the modifications Berenson would later promote, Baer divided the court into zones with players assigned to each to reduce the unseemly rushing about that boys' full-court rules encouraged. But Baer called for seven zones to Berenson's three, and on the subject of dribbling and guarding she went far beyond Berenson, eliminating these features entirely.[41]

Baer argued that her division of the court and team into center (spanning the width of the court), right and left forward guards, right and left backward guards, and a twelve-by-twelve-foot goal zone surrounding the basket allowed players of differing abilities to participate. It also insured that excessive exertion would be eliminated and that players would be protected from "personal contact and shock." In addition, she built frequent rest periods into the game, requiring that all other movement stop whenever a girl attempted a basket. There was to be no guarding of any sort, nor "any interference whatever . . . allowed when a player pauses to aim for a basket." No "striking" or "snatching" or "rolling" or "tapping" the ball, or running with it, or talking during the game, or "needlessly rough play," or even falling. All counted as fouls.

Baer's directions did not stop with her extensive list of fouls. She went on to specify, "In throwing for basket . . . the throw is with one hand. This secures a more upright and graceful position of the body; it places the ball in the line of vision and it secures freer respiration. . . . In tossing the ball with both hands, there is a constant inclination of the shoulders forward, with consequent flattening of the chest." The result would be, Baer concluded, "a most ungraceful position for girls."[42]

This concern with the compression of the chest was based on the philosophy of Baer's teacher, Baron Nils Posse. Posture and correct breathing were central to his teachings on physiology. Baer had attended Posse's school in Boston, and his emphasis on breathing capacity reinforced her earlier training in elocution and oratory. Baer was not the only physical culture teacher at a southern women's college who had been trained in elocution. Mary Settle Sharp who, under Gove's direction, taught physical education at the Normal, had a similar background and would later be responsible for campus debates and staging elaborate May fetes. Posture, graceful gestures, and lung capac-

The jump for basket—illustrating perfect poise. (Reprinted from Clara G. Baer's *Basket Ball Rules for Women and Girls,* Special Collections, Tulane University Library)

ity were equally important to college theatrics, debates, and declamations as to gymnastic routines and to Baer's game of basquette. Properly played, the game "cultivates grace, as well as skill, of movement," Baer insisted.[43] Making a basket was not the point; form, poise, and grace while doing so were. This was indeed a different game than the one Naismith had invented or even the one many women already were playing elsewhere.

It was not until several years later, in 1898, that the Normal College students in North Carolina took up the game, when the junior class invited the other classes to join them in basketball and cricket matches. By 1902 150 girls, about a quarter of the student body, were involved in the Athletic Association, which sponsored interclass tournaments.[44] If basketball would foster many qualities that would be valuable for these new women, at the Normal the first, perhaps, was ingenuity. Learning the game was something of a case of the blind leading the blind. "We had no coach or director," recalled Berta Albright. "Each class had a student coach or referee who studied the rules & told the others what she thought about it. Never having seen a game—or heard of one before in some instances—it must have been very 'individualistic!'"[45] Numerous photographs from college annuals suggest that it was not Baer's rules the "coach" was so creatively interpreting, since two-handed shots and close guarding abound.

Newcomb College girls in long dresses playing basketball according to Clara Baer's rules. (Special Collections, Tulane University Library)

In 1900, the Normal College's board of directors put their seal of approval on the idea of games for women by authorizing the creation of an outdoor playing field. However, they added a proviso that made it clear that their endorsement was not unqualified. An evergreen hedge or other screen would enclose the field, protecting the young athletes from public gaze.[46]

This "hedging" was but one more of the many aspects of female athletics that sought to deny the implicit challenges of which Fodie Buie on her bicycle was so aware. Men's sports were played before stands full of spectators, women's behind hedges. While men emphasized the competitive aspects of sports, women downplayed competition. Neither the Normal College nor Newcomb, as Baer emphasized, "ever entered into contest with other colleges in athletics. While competition may be necessary to life, extremes in competition have never been encouraged at Newcomb College. The South has always been considered conservative but it is a conservatism," she contended, "that has often saved us from making mistakes. Certainly we know that undue excitement is not to the well-being of the girls."[47] "Play-day" rather than play-offs marked the end of basketball season for girls, with games between mixed teams that included players from each of the schools. Undue excitement from spectators was discouraged as well. "Wouldn't it be lovely to be able to cheer like the boys," a coed sighed wistfully in a student's short story. Each class did have a cheer: "Hoopala! Hoopala! Red and Blue. We are the girls of 1902. Hoopala! Hoopala! Ri! Ra! Ru! Hoopala!"[48] But the female partisans, student and faculty, massed on the sidelines were much more apt to sing songs such as this, to the tune of "Polly Wally Doodle":

> Oh! the Junior team may be a good team,
> But the Sophomore team is too,
> And the Junior team may play a good game
> But so does the White and Blue
> Persevere! Persevere!
> Our slogan through the fray
> Oh! the Sophomore team will win the game
> For Blue and White today.[49]

Why the concern with concealing fences, confining hemlines, and modified rules? Like male sports, these games were cultural performances, rituals that played out some of a society's most deeply held assumptions. On the football field, for example, men manifested belief in the rewards of hard work and self discipline, equality, luck, loyalty, teamwork, and aggressive competition. Promoters of basketball for women, including Senda Berenson, considered the game particularly useful in teaching women similar qualities. If women were to succeed in previously male fields, contemporary advocates of physical education contended, they would need physical stamina and the type of teamwork and loyalty that, it was assumed, came naturally to men but not women.[50] And that, of course, was just the problem. For women who potentially might be competing with men in the workplace, it was doubly necessary that they not appear to be challenging men athletically. Thus, on their playing fields they manifested ambivalence as clearly as other more empowering attributes. The fields were carefully screened, and "no papas or even grand papas" ever saw those bloomers. They played different games—football for boys, field hockey for girls—and when they did play the same games, such as basketball, there were different rules and conventions, differences that both denied and concealed the reality that games might teach both sexes similar lessons.[51]

Young women might feel every bit as strongly about the victory of their class colors as men did. Berta Albright certainly did when she recalled the sophomore class's attempt to beat their "hated rivals," the juniors. "The Duke-Carolina games can hardly stir up as much feeling," she asserted.[52] But the quotation marks around "hated rivals" are hers, for such sentiments could be expressed only in jest. She and her schoolmates moderated their competitiveness with an overlay of sorority, as another song illustrates.

> Seniors, dear, we want to tell you,
> Though the Blue may fight the red,
> Oh, Sophomores love the Seniors,
> What'er is done or said
> Who'er may win the victory,
> What's the difference in the end?
> Don't you see dear sisters,
> 'Tis in the family just the same.[53]

Regardless of who won or lost, it was all in the family, a loving family of sisters. No matter how enthusiastic the cheers, no matter how hard fought the game—Albright maintained that her class lost the tournament to those "hated rivals" only when their two best players were sidelined with a turned ankle and an injured collarbone—at heart, the song suggests, they were ladies, graceful and gracious. Whether this was truly the heart of the matter or a thin veneer, they probably could not have said.

Nonetheless, the game was hard fought at the Normal in marked contrast to the restricted scope of movement Baer's version allowed. The progression from walking to calisthenics to team sports reflected an expanding vision of what was possible and acceptable for southern women. McIver's praise for straight shoulders and strong arms contrasts with Baer's assertion that "un-

The Normal College girls in a hard-fought game. (Special Collections, Jackson Library, University of North Carolina at Greensboro)

due excitement" and "extremes in competition" were "not to the well-being of the girls" and suggests that the new images of the New Woman were accepted in varying degrees at different places.

The Normal girls' songs, however, reveal that this process was never without some anxiety and ambivalence. The concealing screens of fences, modest bloomers, and sisterly song helped moderate these anxieties and allowed the women and their society to deny the emerging reality that southern college women might in fact be learning to be strong, self-reliant, and competitive as well as graceful, loyal, and cooperative. On and off the courts their demeanor and dress would change as college women both shaped and were shaped by the new standards for new women in the new middle-class urban South. The anxiety and ambivalence may have remained, but in the end educated women did begin to challenge men in the shops and offices of the New South, in the school rooms and on the school boards, and in the court rooms as well as on the basketball courts.

Notes

An earlier version of this chapter appeared in *Journal of Sport History* 24 (Fall 1997): 341–57.

1. Senda Berenson, "Editorial," *Basket Ball for Women: Spaulding's Athletic Library,* October 1901, quoted in Roberta J. Park, "Sport, Gender, and Society in a Transatlantic Victorian Perspective," in *From "Fair Sex" to Feminism: Sport and Socialization of Women in the Industrial and Post-Industrial Eras,* ed. J. A. Mangan and Roberta J. Park (London: Frank Cass and Co., 1987), 58–93 (quote on 86). Park provides an excellent overview of the relevant issues for middle-class women at the turn of the century. However, she emphasizes the commonalities across British and American culture, denying not only national but also regional differences.

2. On the early history of women's basketball, see Janice Ann Beran, "The Story of Six-player Girls' Basketball in Iowa," in Reet Howell, ed. *Her Story in Sport: A Historical Anthology of Women in Sports* (West Point, N.Y.: Leisure Press, 1982), 552–61; Lynne Emery, "The First Intercollegiate Contest of Women: Basketball, April 4, 1896," in Howell, ed., *Her Story in Sport,* 417–23; and Paula Welch, "Interscholastic Basketball: Bane of Collegiate Physical Educators," in Howell, ed., *Her Story in Sport,* 424–31.

3. Clara G. Baer, *Basket Ball Rules for Women and Girls* (New Orleans: Tulane University, n.d.), 5.

4. On the variety and quality of institutions of higher education available to southern women in this period, see Elizabeth Avery Colton, "Southern Colleges for Women," *Proceedings of the Seventh Annual Meeting of the Association of Colleges and Preparatory Schools of the Southern States* (Nashville: ACPSSS, 1911): 484–68. Colton, a professor at Meredith College in Raleigh, N.C., surveyed women's schools in the South in 1910 and found more than 140 that either called themselves colleges or gave degrees of some sort. Only four were accredited—Agnes Scott in Georgia, Goucher in Maryland, Randolph-Macon in Virginia, and Sophie Newcomb. On the Normal College, see Pamela Dean, "Covert Curriculum: Class and Gender at a New South Women's College" (Ph.D. dissertation, University of North Carolina at Chapel Hill, 1995). On Newcomb, see Brandt V. D. Dixon, *A Brief History of H. Sophie Newcomb Memorial College, 1887–1919: A Personal Reminiscence* (New Orleans: Hauger Printing Co., 1926).

5. Paul Gaston, *The New South Creed: A Study in Southern Mythmaking* (Baton Rouge: Louisiana State University Press, 1976).

6. Fodie Buie Kenyon, "Little Pictures of Old Times, Part II," (North Carolina Women's College) *Alumni News* 30:3 (February 1942): 6.

7. For an excellent discussion of the ideology and tactics of the college's opponents, see James Leloudis, *Schooling the New South: Pedagogy, Self, and Society in North Carolina, 1880–1920* (Chapel Hill: University of North Carolina Press, 1996), chap. 4.

8. Mary D. Moulton to Charles D. McIver, June 30, 1892, McIver Papers, Jackson Library, University of North Carolina at Greensboro.

9. Charles McIver to Lula McIver, March 3, 1890, McIver Papers, Jackson Library, University of North Carolina at Greensboro.

10. Charles McIver, "Educational Statesmanship," *State Normal Magazine* 5 (February 1902): 187–98. For a broader discussion of McIver and his students, see Dean, "Covert

Curriculum." On McIver and school reform in North Carolina, see Leloudis, *Schooling the New South.*

11. Dixon, *Brief History of H. Sophie Newcomb Memorial College,* 25.

12. On the development of the middle class, see Stuart Blumin, *The Emergence of the Middle Class: Social Experience in the American City, 1760–1990* (Cambridge: Cambridge University Press, 1989); Leonore Davidoff and Catherine Hall, *Family Fortunes: Men and Women of the English Middle Class* (Chicago: University of Chicago Press, 1987); and Mary Ryan, *Cradle of the Middle Class: The Family in Oneida County, New York, 1790–1865* (Cambridge: Cambridge University Press, 1984). Burton Bledstein, in *The Culture of Professionalism: The Middle Class and the Development of Higher Education in America* (New York: W. W. Norton and Co., 1976), explores the links between higher education and the middle class. John F. Kasson, in *Rudeness and Civility: Manners in Nineteenth-Century America* (New York: Hill and Wang, 1990), stresses the importance of manners and styles of self-presentation in defining the middle class and defending its preeminence. On the development of southern cities and a southern middle class, see Don H. Doyle, *New Men, New Cities, New South: Atlanta, Nashville, Charleston, Mobile, 1860–1910* (Chapel Hill: University of North Carolina Press, 1990). See also William Link, *The Paradox of Southern Progressivism, 1880–1930* (Chapel Hill: University of North Carolina Press, 1992); and Edward Ayers, *The Promise of the New South: Life after Reconstruction* (New York: Oxford University Press, 1992), for other perspectives on the New South.

13. For a brief discussion of this process, see Pamela Dean, "Learning to Be New Women: Campus Culture at the North Carolina Normal and Industrial College," *North Carolina Historical Review* 68:3 (July 1991): 286–306.

14. For example, see Clifford Geertz, "Deep Play: Notes on the Balinese Cockfight," in *Myth, Symbol, and Culture,* ed. Clifford Geertz (New York: W. W. Norton, 1971), 1–37; and Ted Ownby, *Subduing Satan: Religion, Recreation, and Manhood in the Rural South, 1865–1920* (Chapel Hill: University of North Carolina Press, 1990). On changing definitions of masculinity, see E. Anthony Rotundo, "Body and Soul: Changing Ideals of American Middle Class Manhood, 1770–1920," *Journal of Social History* 16 (Summer 1983): 28–37; Michael S. Kimmel, "The Contemporary 'Crisis' of Masculinity in Historical Perspective," in *The Making of Masculinities,* ed. Harry Brod (Boston: Allen and Unwin, 1986); and Ownby, *Subduing Satan.*

15. Sara Josepha Hale, *Godey's Lady's Book* 23 (July 1841): 41–42, and Catharine E. Beecher, *Physiology and Calisthenics for Schools and Families,* both cited in Park, "Sport, Gender, and Society," 64–65.

16. The physician Edward Clarke's *Sex in Education; or, A Fair Chance for the Girls,* published in 1873, was one of the best-known explications of this position. Dio Lewis, a leading proponent of physical training in schools and colleges, noted other dangers in his 1866 prospectus for his Family School for Young Ladies. "American girls, especially of the higher classes, are too often pale, nervous and fragile, with stooping shoulders, weak spines and narrow chests. In studying under the ordinary systems of education, such girls imperil their chances of health, compromise their enjoyment of life, and often break down in the midst of their labours." Quoted in Thomas Woody, *A History of Women's Education in the United States* (New York: Octagon, 1926), 115.

17. Paul Atkinson, "The Feminist Physique: Physical Education and the Medicalization

of Women's Education," in *From "Fair Sex" to Feminism: Sport and Socialization of Women in the Industrial and Post-Industrial Eras,* ed. J. A. Mangan and Roberta J. Park (London: Frank Cass and Co., 1987), 38–57. See also Carroll Smith-Rosenberg and Charles Rosenberg, "The Female Animal: Medical and Biological Views of Women and Their Role in Nineteenth-Century America," *Journal of American History* 60 (September 1973): 332–56. The quote is from Winnifred Ayers, quoted in Karen Kenney, "The Realm of Sports and the Athletic Woman 1850–1900," in Reet Howell, ed., *Her Story in Sport: A Historical Anthology of Women in Sports* (West Point, N.Y.: Leisure Press), 109.

18. Allen Guttmann, *Women's Sports: A History* (New York: Columbia University Press, 1991).

19. Elizabeth Bowles, *Good Beginning* (Chapel Hill: University of North Carolina Press, 1964), 39–40; W. D. Booker to Charles McIver, May 12, 1892, McIver Papers, Jackson Library, University of North Carolina at Greensboro. Booker recommended two candidates, noting that they had "no appearance of being in the advanced women's movement." McIver might well have supported women's suffrage, as his wife and students would, had he not died in 1906. However, in the early embattled years of the college's existence, he was adamant about keeping the school out of what he saw as peripheral issues, such as racial equality and women's suffrage.

20. *Some Pioneer Women Teachers* (Raleigh, N.C.: Delta Kappa Gamma Society, 1955), 90–93; Bowles, *Good Beginning,* 39–40; Anna M. Gove to Charles McIver, May 13, 1892, McIver Papers, Jackson Library, University of North Carolina at Greensboro. Gove's letters of recommendation included one from Dr. Emily Blackwell, the niece of Elizabeth Blackwell, the first American woman physician.

21. Berta Albright Moon to J. I. Foust, March 1935, Foust Papers, Jackson Library, University of North Carolina at Greensboro; quote from *State Normal Magazine* (February 1898), cited in Richard Bardolph, "Physical Culture," *University of North Carolina at Greensboro Alumni News* 80:1 (Spring 1992): 18.

22. For examples of walking periods at antebellum schools, see Mary Lynch Johnson, *History of Meredith College* (Raleigh, N.C.: Meredith College, 1956), 67; Frances Griffin, *Less Time for Meddling: A History of Salem Academy and College, 1772–1866* (Winston-Salem, N.C.: John F. Blair, 1979), 85; Helen Lefkowitz Horowitz, *Alma Mater: Design and Experience in the Women's Colleges from Their Nineteenth-Century Beginnings to the 1930s* (Boston: Beacon Press, 1986): 25; and Christie Anne Farnham, *The Education of the Southern Belle: Higher Education and Student Socialization in the Antebellum South* (New York: New York University Press, 1994), 124, 126.

23. Clara G. Baer, "Therapeutic Gymnastics as an Aid in College Work, with Some Observations of Specific Cases," *American Physical Education Review* 10 (December 1916): 1–7.

24. Richard L. Bushman and Claudia L. Bushman, "The Early History of Cleanliness in America," *Journal of American History* 74:4 (March 1988): 1213–38.

25. *First Annual Catalogue of the Normal and Industrial School* (Greensboro: Normal and Industrial School, 1893), 33.

26. Moritz Kloss, a leading proponent of the German system of gymnastics, quoted in Guttman, *Women's Sports,* 94.

27. Dixon, *Brief History of H. Sophie Newcomb Memorial College,* 75–76.

28. *State Normal Magazine* 1:6 (June 1898): 308; Richard Bardolph, "Potted Palms, 'The

Forgotten Man,' and Glistening Pomposities: Commencement Exercises of 1897 and 1898," *Alumni News* 70:4 (Summer 1982): 10–13.

29. Bowles, *Good Beginning,* 114.

30. *First Annual Catalogue of the Normal and Industrial School,* 30.

31. For a discussion of the efficacy of stretching sanctioned words and images to include unsanctioned actions, see Anne Firor Scott, "The Ever Widening Circle: The Diffusion of Feminist Values from the Troy Female Seminary, 1822–1872," *History of Education Quarterly* 19 (Spring 1979): 3–25. She argues that by attaching traditional language to potentially revolutionary actions, Emma Willard was able to achieve far more than a head-on assault on Victorian gender norms would have accomplished.

32. *New Bern (N.C.) Journal,* June 22, 1893.

33. "Newcomb Athletics," clipping, ca. 1922, in the Sophie Newcomb Scrapbook II, Tulane University Archives, quoted in Joan Paul, "Clara Gregory Baer: An Early Role Model for Southern Women in Physical Education," paper presented at the National Association of Sports and Physical Education History Academy, Minneapolis, 1983.

34. Elizabeth Cady Stanton, "Improper Education of Women," *The Lily* 7 (April 1, 1855): 5, quoted in Park, "Sport, Gender, and Society," 66.

35. Kenyon, "Little Pictures of Old Times," 5.

36. Ibid., 6–7.

37. See Patrick B. Miller, "The Manly, the Moral, and the Proficient: College Sport in the New South," in this volume.

38. Paul, "Clara Gregory Baer."

39. Clara G. Baer, "The History of the Development of Physical Education at Newcomb College," *National Education Association* 3 (1914): 701–4.

40. Cited in Susan K. Cahn, *Coming on Strong: Gender and Sexuality in Twentieth-Century Women's Sport* (New York: Free Press, 1994), 85.

41. Berenson divided the floor into front-, center-, and backcourt, with players designated as forwards, centers, or guards and confined to their section of the court. One dribble (later three) was allowed, and no physical contact or effort to hinder the shooter was allowed. Cahn, *Coming on Strong,* 86. Baer's emphasis on inclusiveness presaged national themes in women's athletics.

42. Baer, *Basket Ball Rules for Women and Girls,* 11; Clara G. Baer, *Newcomb College Basketball* (New Orleans: Tulane University, 1911). Paul also notes that Baer's use of the one-handed shot preceded the introduction of this now common technique in men's basketball. Paul, "Clara Gregory Baer," 7.

43. Baer, *Newcomb College Basket Ball for Women: Collegiate Rules* (New Orleans: Tulane University, 1914), 37.

44. Bowles, *Good Beginning,* 141; *State Normal Magazine* 4:3 (October 1902): 70.

45. Berta Albright Moon to J. I. Foust, March 1935, Foust Papers, Jackson Library, University of North Carolina at Greensboro.

46. Bowles, *Good Beginning,* 73.

47. Baer, "History of the Development of Physical Education at Newcomb College," 704.

48. (Normal College) *Decennial* (Greensboro, N.C.: Normal and Industrial College, 1903), 27, 32.

49. Normal College Songbook, 1915–19 (pamphlet in the University of North Carolina at Greensboro archives), p. 4.

50. Park, "Sport, Gender, and Society," 86.

51. Jennifer A. Hargreaves, "'Playing Like Gentlemen While Behaving Like Ladies': Contradictory Features of the Formative Years of Women's Sport," *British Journal of Sports History* 2 (May 1985): 50, quoted in Park, "Sport, Gender, and Society," 87.

52. Berta Albright Moon to J. I. Foust, March 1935, Foust Papers, Jackson Library, University of North Carolina at Greensboro. Moon was of course referring to the two universities' male teams.

53. Normal College Songbook, 1915–19, p. 6.

4. Turning the Tide: College Football and Southern Progressivism

ANDREW DOYLE

THE SOUTHERN poet and critic Donald Davidson asserted that the South of the 1920s "disproved the axiom that two bodies cannot occupy the same space."[1] An emerging urban society built upon the secular gospel of progress and innovation coexisted uneasily with an agrarian society wedded to a more traditional value system. The fondest dreams of an earlier generation of New South boosters reached at least partial fruition during that decade. Rapid economic growth over the previous half-century had extended industrial capitalism, mass culture, and the ethos of consumerism into a region still largely rooted in the mores of a rural folk culture and conservative evangelical Protestantism. While the southern commitment to sectional reconciliation on northern terms was irrevocable, the terms of this phase of the long surrender were hard for all but the most ardent of southern modernizers to swallow. The South of the 1920s was moving inexorably closer to the American cultural and economic mainstream, but the rise of religious fundamentalism, the revival of the Ku Klux Klan, and the increasing intensity of sectional hostility revealed the profound misgivings with which most white southerners beheld the emerging order.

Southern college football presents a complex and richly nuanced cultural text that offers insights into the searing internal conflicts that beset the South during this period. The University of Alabama's stunning upset victory over the University of Washington in the 1926 Rose Bowl is arguably the most significant game in southern football history, but it did more than establish the legitimacy of southern football. This game possessed a multifaceted symbolic importance that illustrates the profoundly mixed emotions with which white southerners beheld their fitful and incomplete movement into the American cultural and economic mainstream.[2]

Like the New South movement itself, early southern college football was an amalgamation of innovation and tradition. In the early 1890s, progressive-minded southerners eager to build a rationalized industrial society adopted the fashionable sport of the northeastern bourgeoisie as a cultural component of their modernization program. Many tradition-minded southerners, especially the leaders of southern evangelical denominations, were aghast that students at venerable southern universities had taken up this brutal new Yankee pastime. Yet southern football proponents muted this opposition by imbuing the sport with the trappings of sectional pride. They grandly proclaimed that the personal combat of the gridiron recalled the glories of the southern martial tradition and compared southern football heroes to Lee, Jackson, or Stuart. The faithful sang "Dixie" at games at a fast tempo to rouse the fighting spirit of their heroes and at a slow tempo as an anthem, and observers likened southern college cheers to the rebel yell.

Southern football achieved overnight popularity during the 1890s despite the embarrassing weakness of southern teams. In 1890, Princeton defeated the University of Virginia, then the strongest team in the South, by the embarrassing score of 116-0. This first major intersectional game portended thirty years of repeated humiliation at the hands of Yankee teams. Crippled by woefully inadequate budgets, tiny enrollments, and the two-decade head start enjoyed by their northern counterparts, southerners were nonetheless eager to test themselves against northern competition. Northern universities took advantage of this southern desire for intersectional competition and scheduled southern teams as designated victims in early season warm-up games, offered southerners highly unfavorable splits of gate receipts, and rarely deigned to play southern teams on their home fields. This was in keeping with the ordained order of things, for as the sports historian Michael Oriard observes, "commoners come to kings, not kings to commoners." From the 1890s through the early 1920s, southern teams embarked on trips invariably described as "northern invasions," invariably lost the games, and returned home to congratulations for having defended the honor and traditions of the South. A sportswriter for the *Nashville American* was so thrilled that Vanderbilt managed to lose to Michigan by the respectable score of 18-0 in 1905 that he proclaimed the game to be Vanderbilt's "greatest triumph since the team was organized."[3]

Southern football improved dramatically during the 1920s. Thanks to the region's burgeoning high school football programs, southern coaches no longer had to teach the fundamentals of the game to incoming freshmen. (Prior to World War I, many southern college football players first laid eyes on a football at their initial collegiate practice session.) Urban middle-class southerners with rising levels of discretionary income and a yen for commercialized entertainment flocked to football games in record numbers, and the increased revenues that poured into athletic departments paid for the recruitment and training of quality teams. Intersectional success, however, remained elusive. Occasional upsets of northern teams by Georgia Tech, Centre College, or Alabama were cause for much rejoicing among southern fans, but such victories were the exception rather than the rule. The sports editor of the *Atlanta Journal* lamented that southern colleges had lost fifteen of the sixteen intersectional games that he had covered in the early 1920s.[4] Southern teams seemed to carry the historical stigma of regional inferiority with them into intersectional games, and they suffered defeat after heartbreaking defeat despite having achieved a rough parity of athletic talent and coaching skill. Following a pattern that held true in many other aspects of southern life, southerners defiantly asserted that their boys played first-rate football while they remained perplexed by the Sisyphean futility of their efforts.

A First for the South: Alabama Goes to the Rose Bowl

The 1925 Alabama team won all nine regular-season games against southern teams, but their record failed to impress the northern sportswriters and coaches who constituted the cognoscenti of the national football establishment. No southern team had ever played in the prestigious and financially lucrative Rose Bowl, and under ordinary circumstances Alabama would never have been considered. In November 1925, however, the University of Illinois halfback Red Grange sparked a renewal of the long-standing controversy over the excessive commercialism of college football when he dropped out of college to play professional football just days after playing his last collegiate game. Educators and editorialists immediately embarked on one of the periodic episodes of soul-searching and self-flagellation over the inherent contradiction between the big-money entertainment spectacle of college football and the educational mission of the university. The perplexingly illogical notion that postseason games were somehow a more craven surrender to commercialism than regular-season games led Dartmouth, Michigan, Colgate, and Princeton to decline invitations to meet the University of Washington Huskies in the 1926 Rose Bowl. As the fourth-ranked team in the leading college football poll, Alabama was the next obvious choice. However, the Rose Bowl committee's agent charged with securing an opponent for Washington initially refused even to consider the Tide. "'I've never heard of Alabama as a football team,'" he sniffed, "'and I can't take a chance on mixing a lemon with a rose.'" The increasingly desperate Rose Bowl sponsors overcame their aversion to southern teams and reluctantly extended an invitation to Alabama a mere four weeks before the game.[5]

The University of Alabama's president, George Denny, and head coach, Wallace Wade, were incensed by this public display of disrespect, but the allure of the Rose Bowl was too powerful to refuse. Denny did force the Rose Bowl sponsors to cool their heels for several days before accepting the bid, disingenuously explaining that he had to seek the approval of both the Southern Conference and the Alabama faculty athletic committee. The *Birmingham News* claimed that the entire episode was one more example of the Yankee propensity to denigrate any southern achievement, grumbling, "were she an eastern eleven, [Alabama] would have been the first invited."[6]

Virtually none of the "experts" believed that Alabama stood much of a chance. West Coast gamblers made the Huskies a two-to-one favorite. Lawrence Perry, a leading New York sportswriter, declared that "a crushing defeat of Alabama is indicated." S. V. Sanford, the president of the University of Georgia and head of the Southern Conference, observed that West Coast football fans believed that Alabama "would offer no more opposition than could be furnished by any California high school team." Even Ed Danforth, who as sports editor of the *Atlanta Georgian* had long been a staunch defender of southern football, worried that "Alabama would travel all the way out there, get spanked, and come home with a good record dented."[7]

Washington apparently subscribed to the conventional wisdom, for their pregame preparation was rumored to be lackadaisical. Wallace Wade, however, was a stern disciplinarian who kept his team focused on the task at hand. The team left Alabama thirteen days prior to the game, and Wade conducted twice-daily briefings on his game plan and repeatedly discussed scouting reports during the four-day train journey. Players got off the train to run at every stop and conducted a scrimmage on a dusty high school field in Arizona. Leaving nothing to chance, Wade even brought along drums of drinking water from Alabama to eliminate the possibility of water-borne disease. The Tide arrived in Pasadena on Christmas Eve, and Wade put his team through a hard-hitting practice on Christmas Day. He reluctantly allowed his players to engage in sightseeing for a couple of days, but soon called a halt to all distractions. "In order to get in the right mental attitude, no more entertainment will be indulged in," he declared.[8]

Given the dismal intersectional track record of southern teams, most southerners were only cautiously optimistic about Alabama's prospects. Still, most could not help but make an enormous emotional investment in this game. A Rose Bowl victory by Alabama would diminish the stigma of southern football inferiority, but it would also be a sublime tonic for a people buffeted by a historical legacy of military defeat, poverty, and alienation from the American political and cultural mainstream. Denny approvingly noted the "overwhelming interest and enthusiasm that our trip has evoked, not only in Alabama, but the entire South." He promised that Alabama would "strive to represent worthily our great commonwealth and our great section." The *Atlanta Georgian* declared that Alabama had "the reputation of an entire section to uphold." Wade acknowledged that the ardor of southern fans placed added pressure on his team. "'Every southerner in California is trying to do something for us,'" Wade said. "'We must make a good showing.'"[9]

On New Year's Day 1926, nervously hopeful crowds of Alabamians assembled in theaters, auditoriums, and in windswept city streets to follow the play-by-play account of the game as it flashed in over a special Associated Press wire. A free football matinee sponsored by the *Montgomery Advertiser* filled that city's Grand Theater to standing-room capacity, while hundreds more clamored at the doors for admission. *Advertiser* officials hastily arranged a second free presentation from the balcony of the newspaper office two blocks away, and police roped off a block of Dexter Avenue, Montgomery's main downtown street, for those willing to stand outside for two hours in cold winter weather. Even students at Auburn University packed their campus auditorium to follow the wire reports and cheer the Tide. Auburn students found, perhaps to their dismay, that sectional pride superseded an intrastate rivalry so intense that all athletic relations between the two schools had been severed after the 1907 season.[10]

Alabamians sweated out the final minutes before the kickoff balanced on a razor's edge between anxiety and enthusiasm. The tension was unbearably high, the psychological stakes enormous. Several Alabama radio stations were broadcasting a studio re-creation of the same wire transmission, and these Alabamians might have listened to the same game details at home. They chose instead to gather together in an act of communal solidarity to listen to the game, much as their parents and grandparents had gathered around telegraph offices to await news of Lee's fate at Gettysburg.

The first game details that flashed over the telegraph lines shattered the anxious optimism of the Alabama faithful. George Wilson, Washington's All-American halfback, intercepted a pass on Alabama's first possession, and the Huskies then marched eighty-five yards through a porous Alabama defense for a touchdown. Early in the second quarter, Wilson threw a twenty-yard touchdown pass to put the Huskies ahead 12-0. The vaunted Alabama defense, which had surrendered only one touchdown in nine regular-season games against southern opponents, floundered helplessly in the face of the Washington attack. The worst fears of southern partisans appeared to have been realized. Alabama, the pride of the Deep South and champion of the South-ern Conference for two consecutive years, faced total humiliation.[11]

During the halftime intermission, the forlorn and joyless crowd on Dex-ter Avenue in Montgomery milled about quietly as the short winter afternoon waned into evening. Some fans stopped for a wistful glance at the front win-dow of the Rosemont Gardens florist shop, which proudly displayed an Al-abama team photograph inside a huge, horseshoe-shaped arrangement of red roses. In Court Square, several blocks away at the western end of Dexter Avenue, local civic organizations had stockpiled dozens of torches and a cache of fireworks for a postgame parade. This was the same Court Square in which Montgomery citizens staged a wild celebration sixty-five years earlier, when the news of the fall of Fort Sumter came over the telegraph. That memory still lived on in the hearts of Alabamians, and the city fathers planned a sim-ilar celebration if Alabama could successfully defend the honor of the region on the football field. While the parade was scheduled to be held regardless of the outcome of the game, it threatened to become more of dirge than a party if the game continued along its present course. The crowd on Dexter Avenue and their counterparts throughout the state faced the painful real-ization that the Yankee sportswriters who had long dismissed southern foot-ball as hopelessly inferior and smugly questioned the wisdom of inviting Alabama to the Rose Bowl might have been right after all.[12]

The Tide Turns: Alabama Takes the Championship

In the third quarter, the Crimson Tide mounted a dazzling comeback that confounded the critics and brought joy to the believers. Alabama recovered a Washington fumble and drove for a touchdown that cut the Washington lead to 12-7. Alabama's rugged quarterback, Pooley Hubert, carried the ball five consecutive times on a forty-two-yard touchdown drive, scoring on a one-yard plunge. Pandemonium reigned on Dexter Avenue when the Alabama halfback Johnny Mack Brown put the Tide ahead 14-12 with a sixty-three-yard touch-down reception. Brown, a speedster described by a sportswriter as "slicker than an eel in a sea of stewed okra," then made a spectacular over-the-shoulder catch of a Hubert pass, eluded one tackler, stiff-armed another, and crossed the goal line with Alabama's third touchdown of the quarter.[13]

Alabama scored three touchdowns in seven minutes in an era when sound defensive teams rarely permitted such explosive offensive performances. The stunned Washington team regrouped and scored a fourth-quarter touch-down, but Alabama killed a final Huskie drive with an interception and held on for a 20-19 upset victory. Coach Enoch Bagshaw of Washington, humiliated

Quarterback Pooley Hubert scored Alabama's first touchdown in the third quarter on a one-yard plunge through the center of the Washington line. Hubert demonstrated his undisputed team leadership by calling his own number on all five plays of a forty-two-yard scoring drive. (Paul W. Bryant Museum, University of Alabama)

End Johnny Mack Brown and quarterback Pooley Hubert were the two leading stars of Alabama's 1926 Rose Bowl team, and their exploits are still celebrated by Alabama football fans born decades after the game. Brown went on to become a movie star, appearing in more than 150 films between 1927 and 1966. (Paul W. Bryant Museum, University of Alabama)

by this upset loss to mere southerners, stormed off the field after the game without offering as much as an insincere handshake to Wallace Wade. Stanford coach Pop Warner, who had predicted a Washington victory, reflected the surprise of the national sporting establishment when he called the Alabama victory "a shock to everybody."[14]

The crowds that packed the streets, theaters, auditoriums, and fraternal lodges across the state of Alabama exploded into a joyous frenzy when the words "Alabama wins" flashed over the wire. Alabama's performance instantly transcended the realm of sports and became a symbolic vindication of southern honor. Whites throughout the Deep South reveled in the victory. "Alabama was our representative in fighting for us against the world," declared Vanderbilt coach Dan McGugin. "I fought, bled, died and was resurrected with the Crimson Tide." The *Birmingham News* exclaimed that mere words on newsprint could never do justice to the "miracle at the Rose Bowl"; instead, it should be announced to the world on "a ten league canvas with brushes of comet's hair." The *Pensacola Journal* proclaimed "South Wins West Coast Grid Classic" in a front-page, banner headline. The *Atlanta Georgian* proudly announced that the line score of the game should actually read, "The South 20, the West 19." Beneath the headline "Dixie Acclaims Her Heroes," the *Atlanta Journal* asserted, "All southern hearts are happy today over the outcome." In a similar spirit of pan-southern ecumenism, the *Birmingham Age-Herald* declared in a front-page editorial that the game was "an impressive victory for the entire South."[15]

New Orleans residents lavished an ecstatic reception on the Tide as they passed through that city on their homeward journey, but an even more frenzied welcome awaited the team back home in Tuscaloosa. People from all over the state thronged the railroad station to greet the team train, and a few adventurous students perched precariously on the station's red-tile roof to get a closer look at their heroes. Merchants, professionals, laborers, and farmers on muleback joined Governor William Brandon and other state political leaders in paying homage to the Tide. In a scene that resembled the return of a Roman legion from a war of conquest, the team rode in a procession of decorated wagons pulled through the crowded streets by university freshmen. Euphoric citizens packed the streets so tightly that the caravan took an hour to inch along the three-quarter-mile route from the train station to downtown. A local attorney and civic leader told the jubilant crowd, "'When the band plays "Dixie" over the team, it can whip eleven Red Granges.'" He also chortled that the members of the Washington team and several generations of their descendants would henceforth "'speak with a soft southern accent.'"[16]

The Crimson Tide followed this triumph with another undefeated season in 1926, and Alabama was invited back to defend its Rose Bowl title on New Year's Day 1927. The pundits who had been embarrassed the previous year confidently predicted that Pop Warner's powerful Stanford team would give these southern upstarts their comeuppance. Stanford dominated the game statistically, gaining 350 yards to Alabama's 117, but could manage only a single touchdown against a tenacious Tide defense. Alabama repeated its miracle comeback of the previous year when it converted a blocked punt into a game-tying touchdown in the final minutes of the game and came away with a 7-7 tie. Southern editorialists, politicians, and business leaders led a reprise of the hallelujah chorus that followed the victory over Washington. They crowed over how foolish the self-proclaimed experts who had dismissed the 1926 victory as a fluke now appeared, and they celebrated the tie game as a "moral victory" for "our boys" and the "Solid South" that had faithfully backed them. At the homecoming celebration in Tuscaloosa, Governor-elect Bibb Graves, himself a former Alabama football player, declared, "'The hearts of all of Dixie are beating with exultant pride.'" The Tide, Graves said, "'upheld the honor of the Southland and came back to us undefeated.'"[17]

Judge James Mayfield of Tuscaloosa was part of the Solid South that had stood behind the Tide. Mayfield, a noted jurist and politician, suffered a fatal heart attack as he listened to the Alabama-Stanford game on the radio. (This was the first Rose Bowl to be broadcast live to a nationwide radio audience.) The *Montgomery Advertiser* declared that Mayfield "died as he had lived, loyal to Alabama and her traditions and loyal to the men who were upholding Alabama in a far away state." The *Advertiser* mourned that cruel fate had decreed Mayfield should die "before he knew of the glorious feat of Alabama in tying Stanford . . . before the spirit of Alabama which he loved so well and which he gloriously emphasized had been really asserted." His last words were, "'Why don't they resort to the pass?'"[18]

Fashioning a New South Ideal from the Old South Myth

At the simplest level, the deluge of sectionalist passion that greeted Alabama's triumphant Rose Bowl performances reflected the perennial desire of southerners to exact vengeance for the many humiliations they had suffered at the hands of the Yankees. This long-smoldering sectional hostility had intensified during the 1920s. The sectional rapprochement that began fitfully during the Gilded Age and flowered during Woodrow Wilson's first term ended abruptly after World War I. The image of the "Benighted South" became firmly fixed in the national consciousness during the 1920s, a period that Donald Davidson has dubbed the "cold Civil War."[19] H. L. Mencken and a coterie of his disciples and imitators delighted in lampooning the South in the pages of literary and opinion journals. They labeled the region a cultural desert and a bastion of repressive Puritanism amid the gaiety and glamour of Jazz Age America. Lurid exposés of southern backwardness and barbarity filled the pages of mass-circulation magazines. A reader could hardly pick up a copy of *Harper's, McClure's, Collier's,* or *Scribner's* without reading about such evils as political demagoguery, the Ku Klux Klan, convict leasing, lynchings, share-cropping, or debt peonage. The national image of the South had not been so negative since the end of Reconstruction. Southerners regarded this glorious victory over the outlanders as an emotionally satisfying response to this torrent of outside criticism.[20]

One criticism was especially galling to southerners steeped in the traditions of an honor culture: while antebellum northern polemicists saw their southern counterparts as a threat to be feared and despised, contemporary critics dismissed southerners of the 1920s as backward hayseeds worthy only of contempt and scorn. Southerners well knew that their storied forefathers had defended their honor on the field of battle rather than submit to such abuse, while they had now become supplicants who meekly sought favorable legislation from Congress and outside capital from Wall Street. Alabama's display of masculine strength and virility in Pasadena was interpreted as proof that the martial prowess and chivalric dash of their mythologized ancestors were still alive in the modern world. Southerners had long held that one Confederate soldier was worth five Yankees on the battlefield, and Alabama's proficiency in a sport with strong martial overtones reinforced this belief.

The florid praise that southerners showered on the Crimson Tide was liberally sprinkled with allusions to this idealized past. The *Atlanta Georgian* called the 1926 Rose Bowl "the greatest victory for the South since the first battle of Bull Run." Alabama's performances were a godsend to southerners who, even six decades after Appomattox, still nursed the grievances they felt over military defeat and the humiliation of "bayonet rule" during Reconstruction. The civil religion of the Lost Cause was, in the words of the southern Presbyterian theologian Robert Dabney, "the holy of holies." It reflected the core values of the dominant culture in the postbellum South. Monuments to the fallen heroes of the Civil War dominated the courthouse squares of most southern cities and towns, and Confederate Memorial Day and Robert E. Lee's birthday were state holidays observed with special church services. Tens of thousands of southerners purchased commemorative coins during the mid-1920s to finance the project that sculpted the equestrian images of Lee, Jefferson Davis, and Stonewall Jackson onto the granite face of Stone Mountain near Atlanta. The *Atlanta Journal* compared the Crimson Tide to this monument to the Lost Cause, declaring, "The Crimson Tide no longer belongs exclusively to Tuscaloosa and the state of Alabama. It belongs to the whole South just like the Stone Mountain Memorial."[21]

Southerners explicitly attributed Alabama's Rose Bowl success to the living legacy of the Old South. Governor Brandon evoked the crusading spirit of the Confederacy in a message wired to the Alabama team the day of the Stanford game. "Alabama's glory is in your hands," he declared. "May each member of your team turn his face to the sun-kissed hills of Alabama and fight like hell as did your sires in bygone days." Brandon linked their victory to the premodern virtues of the Old South that southerners sought to preserve. "Chivalry never found truer representatives than in that team which waded across the glory field in Pasadena," he proclaimed. Similarly, S. V. Sanford declared that Alabama "upheld the traditions and fighting spirit of the Old South." The *Birmingham News* disdainfully noted Washington coach Enoch Bagshaw's churlish postgame behavior and contrasted it with Alabama's adherence to "the honored tradition of the Old South—gentlemanly sportsmanship."[22]

Southerners also imbued football with rituals that recreated the ambience of the antebellum southern aristocracy. George Trevor, a New York sportswriter, contrasted the "romantic glamour" and "medieval pageantry" of southern football with the "blasé indifference of the young moderns" of the Ivy League. Much of this "medieval pageantry" centered on the ceremonial role of female team sponsors. In a ritual worthy of a Walter Scott novel, beautiful young society women acting as sponsors played the role of the medieval damsel at a tournament joust, bestowing a pregame benediction on the young warriors poised to do battle in their honor. Although the increasing commercialism of the game had diminished the importance of the sponsorship ritual since the earliest days of southern football, it was still very much alive in the 1920s. A young Tuscaloosa woman sponsored the Tide at the 1927 Rose Bowl, leading the team onto the field in a colorfully decorated horse-drawn carriage while a band played "Dixie." This chivalric vision of young aristocrats vying on the field of honor for the affection of young ladies linked the relatively new tradition of southern football with the hallowed and timeless values of the antebellum planter aristocracy and the cavalier tradition they supposedly embodied.[23]

Southerners also saw football as an effective means of retaining the essence of premodern masculinity as the South belatedly adopted bourgeois conceptions of gender that had long been prevalent in the Northeast. The cultural "feminization" associated with the rise of bourgeois capitalism was especially threatening to the growing southern middle class. Unlike the urban working class and farmers of the region, young middle-class males were now coming of age in a physically undemanding world of material comfort. The late nineteenth-century northeastern elite found football so alluring in part because it reaffirmed the value of male strength, which was becoming economically irrelevant to the professional and managerial class. Modern sports were developed as part of what Donald Mrozek calls a "strategy of regeneration" designed to counteract the social and moral decline that many social observers feared was inherent in modernity. The lag in southern economic development meant that southerners as a whole were confronted with the challenge of redefining middle- and upper-class masculinity in the 1920s, a generation or more after their northeastern counterparts. Also, the legacy of the code of rough masculinity integral to the antebellum southern honor culture made southerners even more eager to embrace the aggressively masculine sport of football. Sanford declared that football helped "to foster and keep alive . . . the aggressive manliness" so prized in the Old South. He proclaimed, "Football meets that unforgotten need of the race which in the days of chivalry had to be satisfied by the tournament and the joust."[24]

Conservatives had begun to see football as an especially valuable counterweight to the liberal ideas and intellectual fads of the 1920s that threatened to undermine adherence to the cult of the strenuous life. The South could, paradoxically, reaffirm the vision of aggressive masculinity that had initially been popularized among the northeastern elite by such reformers as Thomas Wentworth Higginson and Theodore Roosevelt. Sanford maintained that football's popularity in the South was evidence that "modern youth is not jaded, or in a state of pseudo-sophistication, but that youth is still strong, virile, and manly."[25] A short story published in *Sport Story Magazine,* a national sports pulp fiction magazine, reflects the common perception that southern football remained a bastion of the manly attributes that decadent northeasterners had already lost. The hero of this story, which was published only a few months after the 1927 Rose Bowl, is an upper-class northeastern youngster who spends so much on intellectual pursuits that he risks squandering his considerable athletic gifts. His father, concerned that the boy reads books on philosophy and psychoanalysis "written by birds who change their minds twice a day and their shirts twice a month," arranges for his son to attend the University of Alabama. The son had attended a Long Island prep school "where they play football for healthful exercise and serve tea and cookies for the players between halves." At Alabama, however, he learns "hard, bruising football" under the tutelage of a southern coach who possesses the masculine virtues of toughness, discipline, and a strong work ethic. After a suitably difficult rite of passage, the son leads Alabama to victory in the 1926 Rose Bowl.[26]

Southern college football in general and the Alabama Rose Bowl champions in particular thus served as a link to an idealized conception of the Old South. Yet the post-Reconstruction South was hardly an idyllic plantation society populated by dashing cavaliers eager to refight the War for Southern Independence. The southern politicians and editorialists who lauded the Crimson Tide for its chivalric virtues did not reject modernity. Instead, their paeans to the Old South helped facilitate an orderly transition to modern industrial capitalism. The devotion that postbellum southerners lavished upon the ideals of the Old South were in reality part of what C. Vann Woodward calls the "Great Recantation"—the abrupt and unseemly abandonment of the social order that the Confederates had sacrificed so much to preserve. The Lost Cause and the myth of the Old South were popularized in the same post-Reconstruction period in which southern leaders irrevocably committed the region to urbanization and industrialization. The rising southern bourgeoisie adopted the progressive worldview of the North with the zeal of converts, but they could not overtly repudiate the ideals of the Old South. Paying lip service to a mythologized vision of the old order eased this transition by obscuring the deep southern commitment to the modern society that would inevitably destroy the social foundation of that order.[27]

Southern college football clearly illustrates how southerners expressed fervent devotion to the ideals of the past while simultaneously transforming those ideals in the service of a radically new socioeconomic regime. The numerous allusions to the Old South and the bellicose declarations of sectional pride that followed Alabama's Rose Bowl triumphs had always been an integral part of southern football rituals. Yet they obscured the emergence of southern football as a powerful symbol of progress, modernity, and sectional reconciliation.

Since the 1890s, southerners had followed the lead of the northeasterners who created football by celebrating it as a metaphor for the machine age. The game's hierarchical command structure, highly specialized division of labor, complex teamwork, and precise execution of elaborately choreographed plays reflected the "time and motion" industrial management theories of Frederick W. Taylor rather than the work rhythms of the farm or the plantation.[28] The lexicon of southern football contained far more allusions to the modern industrial order than to the cavalier myth. Like their northern counterparts, southern journalists and fans commonly referred to football teams as "machines," and they lauded successful teams for possessing "efficiency," a "scientific" style of play, and a "perfectly synchronized attack." The *Birmingham News* called the Alabama team a "modern juggernaut" and hailed the Alabama coach Wallace Wade as "the disciple of precision." The *Montgom-*

ery Advertiser warned its readers prior to the 1926 Rose Bowl that the Washington team was a "deadly man-killing machine, every cog in it being of the same temper and metal as every other cog." The victory of the Alabama "machine" over Washington implied that the South had risen to the challenge of the industrial era. The Crimson Tide embodied the technical complexity and innovative spirit that had transformed Birmingham from a sparsely populated rural backwater in 1870 into a booming industrial center only thirty years later.[29]

Like the industrial order itself, football was adopted by progressive southerners eager to emulate Yankee innovations. Students and professors who had learned football while attending northern schools brought it to southern campuses in the 1890s. That generation of southern collegians had grown up in the progressive-minded world of the New South, and they ardently proclaimed their desire to imitate the sporting preferences of the northeastern elite. Southern daily newspapers published reams of wire service copy about northeastern and midwestern football during the first quarter of the twentieth century, often according them more prominence than accounts of southern games. Until the 1930s, virtually every southern college employed northern coaches to teach their superior skills and techniques to southerners. (Wallace Wade was a Tennessee native, but he played his collegiate football at Brown University.) Robert Dabney, the Presbyterian minister and leading theologian of the Lost Cause, warned southerners of the 1880s not to succumb to the blandishments of the sinful Babylon to the north. Dabney admonished postbellum southerners to avoid the temptation to "'become like the conquerors . . . and to share, for a few deceitful days, the victor's gains of oppression.'"[30] Most southern evangelical leaders vehemently denounced early southern college football, in part because of its violence and its association with drinking and gambling, but also because it was such a shameless emulation of Yankee culture. Southerners paid a minimal degree of homage to the warnings of Dabney and the evangelical opponents of football by flavoring this Yankee game with an atmosphere of militant sectionalism and surrounding it with the trappings of the Old South.

The southern fervor for a machine-age game that was strongly associated with the northeastern bourgeoisie was a tacit acceptance of sectional reconciliation on northern terms. The alumni and academics who controlled southern college football were members of the nascent upper middle class of the region, and they were anxious to use the game as a means of attaining respectability in the eyes of the national sport establishment. Sanford worked diligently during 1925 and 1926 to raise twenty-five thousand dollars from southern colleges and universities as part of a national effort to build a memorial on the Yale campus honoring the recently deceased Walter Camp. Camp was revered in national sporting circles as the "Father of American Football," but southerners resented his indifference to and ignorance of southern football, which was symbolized by his refusal to name more than a token southern player or two to his annual All-American teams.[31] Raising money for a memorial that few southerners would ever see and that honored a self-consciously elitist Ivy Leaguer who pointedly ignored southern football was a difficult undertaking for a southern college president. Sanford acknowledged these difficulties but believed that his efforts would bring the South recognition within the elite sporting fraternity. He undertook the awkward and thankless task of dunning perennially impoverished southern colleges because he wanted the Southern Conference "to be something more than a local body . . . I did not wish it to be said that this conference fell down on the first national work it was asked to have a leading part in."[32]

The Rose Bowls of 1926 and 1927 reveal how southerners simultaneously and apparently without contradiction saw intersectional football both as a recapitulation of the Civil War and as a meeting of equals on the fields of friendly competition. Alabama's performances served both as symbolic vengeance over historic enemies and as a plea for respect from those same enemies. The *Memphis Commercial-Appeal* declared that the Alabama victory over Washington was "another reminder that the South in its manhood, as in other things, is a great section of this great country of ours." The *Birmingham News* compared Alabama's Rose Bowl performances to the battles won by Allied troops in World War I as well as to those won by Confederate troops in the Civil War. Tuscaloosa civic organizations decorated the lampposts of that city with American, Confederate, and Alabama flags for the 1926 victory celebration. Southerners appreciatively noted that the Pasadena Elks Club band played "Dixie" at the Rose Bowl to honor the Tide, but in a victory celebration three days after the game, the New Orleans Police Department Band serenaded the team train with a rendition of "The Star Spangled Banner."[33]

Alabamians' obsession with the reception of their team in Pasadena reflects the long-standing desire of the postbellum southern middle and upper classes for acceptance by the rest of the nation.[34] The Alabamians who attended the 1926 and 1927 Rose Bowls were pleasantly surprised by and made numerous references to the friendly welcome extended them by their California hosts. Denny was moved by the "spontaneous and overwhelming ovation" that Rose Bowl spectators gave Alabama, and he expressed "profound appreciation for the wonderful support given us by the people of Lower California." The team was feted at Hollywood movie studios and heard a sermon entitled "The Crimson Tide" at a Pasadena church service. Members of the Ala-

bama party played golf at local country clubs, and the team's business manager had a lengthy chat with the reigning Miss America at a party and ex-
tracted a promise from her to visit Alabama. Southern sportswriters were
ecstatic over the Rose Bowl crowds' cheers for the Alabama team and the
Pasadena Elks Club Band's rendition of "Dixie." The sports editor of the
Atlanta Journal observed, likely with some surprise, "The people of Pasadena are crazy about the Crimson Tide," and added, "the Los Angeles and Pasadena papers gave the Tide a square deal in the write-ups." The *Tuscaloosa
News* approvingly noted that sportswriters in southern California had made
the underdog Tide a sentimental favorite and quoted a *Los Angeles Times*
headline that declared, "Sportsmanship and Courtesy Make Tide Popular."
The sectionalist rhetoric that followed the Alabama victories might imply that
the Alabama party in Pasadena and their counterparts among the elite back
home were a group of dedicated warriors suffused with a spirit of romantic
alienation from the dominant national culture and eager to avenge ancient
injustices. Yet they were also aspiring members of a charmed circle who were
happy to be accepted as equals rather than treated as redneck interlopers.[35]

The media frenzy that surrounded the 1925 prosecution of John Scopes for
teaching evolution in a Tennessee high school aroused high levels of defensiveness among many middle- and upper-middle-class southerners. They
were eager that the world not confuse them with the stereotyped image of
the uneducated, malnourished, ill-clothed rural and working-class southerners who swelled the ranks of the Ku Klux Klan and the religious fundamen-
talist movement. Grover Hall, the editor of the *Montgomery Advertiser,* published an apologia in *Scribner's* in 1928 in which he attempted to portray
urban middle-class southerners as prosperous, progressive, fun-loving people who were fast forgetting the Civil War and who had little "genuine religious passion." In a lighthearted tone that masked a palpable defensiveness,
Hall asserted that the image of the South as a bastion of backwardness was
exaggerated and misleading. Like Hall, the southern journalists who covered
the 1927 Rose Bowl were eager to dispel that image. They published sly allusions to an excursion by members of the Alabama traveling party to bars and
casinos in Ciudad Juarez, Mexico, during a stop in El Paso and to the sizable
sums of money Alabama partisans won by betting at favorable odds on the
underdog Crimson Tide. Conspicuous participation in the fashionable vices
of the Jazz Age smart set and then noting this with a wink and a nod in the
newspapers was a perfect way for these mostly urban, upper-middle-class
southerners to refute the stereotype that all southerners were puritanical
religious zealots. Their pursuit of good pleasure offered testimony that, contrary to Mencken's assertion, not all southerners were offended by the idea
that someone, somewhere, might be having a good time.[36]

The Business Progressive leadership reacted with horror to the torrent of unfavorable publicity generated by the Scopes trial. Advertising and public relations had become indispensable tools in the "Age of Ballyhoo," and southern politicians and businessmen invariably considered themselves expert in the sophisticated new techniques of manipulating mass opinion. Alabama's victory over Washington was a serendipitous public relations windfall that fell into the laps of southern boosters only six months after the nightmarish Scopes trial. Two themes repeatedly reverberate in the southern reaction to the 1926 and 1927 Rose Bowls: satisfaction over proving something to those smug Yankees and enthusiastic pronouncements that the victory would provide a public relations bonanza. The South had made extraordinary economic progress in the previous twenty-five years. The southern economy had grown at an annual rate of 2.65 percent between 1900 and 1920, expanding more than twenty percent faster than the American economy as a whole. While Progressive Era reform efforts often lagged behind similar efforts in non-southern states, they had laid the foundation for a modern, rationalized, bureaucratized society in the region. By the 1920s, prosperous industrial cities with skyscrapers and streetcar suburbs dotted the landscape, and southern boosters were eager to use the Crimson Tide to advertise these changes to the world. Southerners may have extolled the Tide as a defiant symbol of a bygone era, but in virtually the same breath, they touted the team as proof that the region was every bit as modern and progressive as the rest of the nation. These Rose Bowls became part of the noisy and incessant booster campaign that had been a central feature of southern modernization efforts since the New South creed had become the region's secular gospel in the 1880s.[37]

Newspapers across the South gleefully proclaimed that the Crimson Tide could become the centerpiece of a campaign of economic boosterism. Editorialists, politicians, and business leaders practically counted the investment dollars they confidently expected to come pouring in as a direct result of Alabama's Rose Bowl performances. The *Anniston Star* paid editorial homage to the Tide for upholding the proud martial tradition of the southern past in the 1927 Rose Bowl, but it followed this with as assertion that the game "gave this state advertising that is of incalculable value." A speaker introduced Wallace Wade to the 1927 homecoming reception as "a man who had advertised Alabama more in the past three years than any other man in the past fifty years." The *Gadsden Star* euphorically claimed, "There is no calculating the material benefit that is sure to result" from the win over Washington. The *Atlanta Journal* compared the game to that notorious triumph of salesmanship over good sense, the Florida land boom, proclaiming them to be the "two great outstanding events of the past three years." (This comparison was made only a few months before the speculative bubble ingloriously burst.) The Crimson Tide returned to the Rose Bowl for a third time in 1931, and Governor Bibb Graves made that team a selling point in the neverending crusade to attract outside capital to Alabama. "We have been hampered industrially by an unfair picture the world seems to have of Alabama as a state of undersized, weak people living in swamp lands full of malaria and tuberculosis," Graves asserted. "None who have seen Wade's Tide in action . . . will continue to embrace the idea." Southern college football thus became an all-purpose symbol that combined the chivalric valor of Robert E. Lee with the business acumen and public relations genius of the Madison Avenue advertising executive Bruce Barton.[38]

The splendid athleticism of the Alabama players was a godsend to the southern boosters eager to refute the popular image of the "Lazy South." The prevalence of hookworm infestation was a particularly touchy subject in the 1920s. Hookworm victims exhibited a chronic torpor easily interpreted as simple laziness, and many of them compulsively engaged in the practice of "dirt eating." Many southerners believed that the northern press accentuated hookworm disease because it reinforced negative stereotypes about southerners and helped to perpetuate the region's quasi-colonial status within the national economy. Some southern states even declined to accept money for hookworm eradication from northern philanthropic organizations because doing so would be a tacit admission that hookworm was indeed a serious problem.[39] The *Montgomery Advertiser* optimistically announced that Alabama's victory over Washington "should go far to dissipate certain popular illusions concerning hookworm and malaria in the South."[40] Governor Brandon eradicated the hookworm by rhetorical fiat when he proclaimed, "This team has proven that there is no hookworm in Alabama."[41] In a letter to George Denny, a New Orleans resident said that southerners should "stop doubting, hesitating, explaining. Southern health, young manhood, vigor, power is no longer to be explained away. Victories like these . . . are worth ten thousand essays, speeches, advertisements. . . . Maybe we will have to do less explaining hereafter about swamps, mosquitoes, hookworm, dirt eating, runts and so forth."[42]

Southerners of the 1920s thus saw college football as a public relations vehicle that could present an image of progress and middle-class respectability to the rest of the nation. Yet image-conscious urban boosters were embarrassed by the dearth of modern stadiums in which to stage their football spectacles. Most southern games were played in the low-rent confines of minor league baseball parks or, worse, on chalked-off sections of college campuses or city parks. Southern fans watched games from cheap wooden bleachers, milled about the sidelines, and all too often spilled across barbed-wire barriers onto the field. After World War I, civic leaders across the South led campaigns to finance the construction of modern concrete and steel stadiums that local boosters invariably proclaimed to be nearly as impressive as the Yale Bowl. Staging mass-market sporting events in modern stadiums was a highly visible way to showcase the progressive urban society of the twentieth-century South. It fairly shouted that the South had acquired "big league" status. Southern boosters equated stadium building with the self-confident spirit of the American Century. The *Gadsden Times-Journal* proclaimed, "A town that can give the right kind of support to athletics can do anything."[43]

Birmingham business leaders combined civic boosterism, devotion to the Crimson Tide, and the middle-class distaste for mixing too closely with the lower orders when they sold bonds to finance the construction of Legion Field in 1927. Everyone who paid one hundred dollars for what a later generation would call a "personal seat license" acquired the right to purchase two reserved seats for any football game played there. The "all seats reserved" policy of the new facility appealed to a middle class concerned about the "rough neck element" that had a nasty habit of "invading" the reserved-seat section of football games held at the local baseball park. The Birmingham Junior Chamber of Commerce sold the bonds in a heavily promoted sales campaign that coincided with Alabama's appearance in the 1927 Rose Bowl. After Alabama's "moral victory," citizens were urged to purchase the few remaining bonds as a show of gratitude toward their heroes then returning from Pasadena. "Stadium Fund Goal in Sight as Tide Nears," announced an *Age-Herald* headline. A Birmingham salesman jumped aboard this booster bandwagon despite his frank admission that he had never seen a football game and had absolutely no interest in the sport. He purchased a stadium bond because he was "interested in anything that will uplift humanity and be of benefit to our city." Dozens of southern cities used bond subscription campaigns to finance the construction of cotton mills in the 1880s and 1890s. Birmingham and other southern cities tapped that same brimming reservoir of New South boosterism in the 1920s to build football stadiums. The growing power of the mass-market entertainment industry enabled the football stadium at least partially to supplant the factory as the most visible symbol of civic progress, even at the apogee of the machine age. The iconic significance of the stadium reflected the larger national transition from a culture of production to a culture of consumption.

Football, like southern progressivism itself, represented an attempt to synthesize the best of the old and the best of the new. The essence of southern progressivism was a tenuous and often contradictory marriage of bourgeois liberalism with the antimodernist elements of the southern tradition. The southern elite eagerly sought the benefits of material progress and modernization, but they also clung with desperate intensity to the proud traditions of the old order. This desire to reconcile contradictory tendencies, although rooted partially in sentiment, served the practical end of helping to perpetuate the hegemony of the progressive southern elite. Widespread popular allegiance to an idealized vision of the southern past provided the social cohesion and cultural continuity that blurred class divisions and mitigated the psychic dislocation caused by the ascendancy of the culture of mass production and mass consumption.[44]

The Lost Cause and the myth of the Old South promoted this white cultural unity and served as what Eric Hobsbawm calls "invented traditions." These rituals were "responses to novel situations which take the form of reference to old situations, or which establish their own past by quasi-obligatory repetition." They inculcated the timeless values of the past and created a shared culture that minimized the societal instability that was an inherent aspect of industrialization. These invented traditions solidified the hegemony of the Big Mule–Black Belt alliance from the end of Reconstruction until the mid-twentieth century by fostering the white social and cultural unity so crucial to the Herrenvolk ideology that formed the foundation of the racial caste system.[45] They also promoted allegiance to the new social order by draping it with a mantle of historical legitimacy.[46]

The bellicose assertions of sectional pride and the ceaseless allusions to the glories of the southern past that were an integral part of the dramaturgy of southern college football dovetailed nicely with the Lost Cause and made the sport an invented tradition in its own right. Yet the Lost Cause and the myth of the Old South were the progeny of southern defeat. They exuded a fatalism and obsession with the past that were ill-suited to the needs of the prosperous middle-class South of the 1920s. They perpetuated a crippling sense of self-doubt and alienation from the American mainstream that hindered postbellum southern economic development. The invented tradition of southern college football was more flexible. It perpetuated the mythology of the southern past while embodying a progressive vision of the future. The Business Progressives of the 1920s sought to maintain regional traditions while they integrated the South into the national economy, and they believed that college football could serve both of those ends. They embraced football as a means of inculcating the competitive self-confidence so vital to capitalism while simultaneously upholding the traditions that bolstered the southern social order. Southerners could continue to revere the beau geste rendered in a noble but doomed crusade, but they now could admire and emulate the

hard work and systematic preparation that had produced Alabama's spectacular Rose Bowl triumphs. John Temple Graves, a Birmingham newspaper editor and leading Business Progressive spokesman, believed that the
Alabama Rose Bowl teams played a key role in grafting this new ethos of victory onto the southern character. Writing in 1941, Graves declared: "For all
the last stands, all the lost causes and sacrificings in vain, the South had a
heart. And a tradition. But the South had a new tradition for something else.
It was for survival, and for victory. It had come from the football fields. It
had come from those mighty afternoons in the Rose Bowl at Pasadena, when
Alabama's Crimson Tide had rolled to glory. . . . The South had come by way
of football to think at last in terms of causes won, not lost."[47]

The stabilizing force of tradition and a resolute faith in progress comprised
two elements of the tripartite social foundation of the early twentieth-century South. College football offered assurances that these antithetical forces
could harmoniously coexist. The racial caste system and the attendant ideology of white supremacy formed the third component, and the all-white
teams fielded by segregated southern universities embodied this social ideal
as well. The urban middle-class progressives who formed the core constitu-
ency of southern college football were usually willing to extend a minimal
level of government services to blacks in the interest of social and economic
efficiency. They also generally looked with disdain upon the virulent hate
mongering and racially motivated violence associated with lower-class whites.
Yet virtually all progressive white southerners possessed, in the words of
Ulrich Bonnell Phillips, the preeminent southern historian of the era, "a
common resolve, indomitably maintained—that [the South] shall be and
remain a white man's country." Most white southerners also subscribed to
the racialist theories and nativist sentiments prevalent during the 1920s and
thus took pride in the Anglo-Saxon heritage of the majority of the southern
white population. Denny echoed these sentiments at the homecoming celebration after the 1927 game with Stanford. "'I come back,'" Denny said,
"'with my head a little higher and my soul a little more inspired to win the
battle for this splendid Anglo-Saxon race of the South.'" Denny possessed
impeccable progressive credentials, and his willingness to interpret Alabama's
1927 Rose Bowl performance as a vindication of white supremacy accurate-
ly reflected the racial views of virtually all southern progressives.[48]

Southern progressives espoused a program that united disparate and
sometimes mutually contradictory elements. They envisioned an economically vibrant society buttressed by rigid lines of caste and class. This social
rigidity enabled the southern elite to maintain control in the face of the social, cultural, and economic disruptions caused by rapid industrialization and

urbanization. The southern progressive elite molded the symbolism of college football to fit this social vision. Football was flexible enough to sustain southern orthodoxies while it simultaneously enhanced the New South vision of sectional reconciliation and dynamic industrial growth within a modern, rationally ordered society. White southerners saw the Alabama Rose Bowl teams of 1926 and 1927 as the embodiment of the efficiency and complexity of the machine age, yet the players possessed the martial spirit of the hopelessly outgunned student cadets who had bravely but unsuccessfully defended the university against a federal cavalry assault in 1865. The Crimson Tide was a glorious instrument of vengeance loosed upon old enemies, yet it also served as an entrée into national circles of middle-class respectability. The cultural text of southern college football possessed a symbolic plasticity that allowed southerners to mold its interpretation to serve their disparate and often conflicting needs.

Notes

This chapter is reprinted, with minor editorial changes, from *Southern Cultures* 3:3 (Fall 1997): 28–51. © 1997 by the University of North Carolina Center for the Study of the American South. Used by permission of the publisher.

1. Donald Davidson, *The Attack on Leviathan: Regionalism and Nationalism in the United States* (Chapel Hill: University of North Carolina Press, 1938), 141.

2. All further references to "southerners" or "Alabamians" should be understood to refer to whites. For a discussion of the cultural conflict in the South during the 1920s, see George B. Tindall, *The Emergence of the New South* (Baton Rouge: Louisiana State University Press, 1967), 184–253; and Dewey Grantham, *Southern Progressivism: The Reconciliation of Progress and Tradition* (Knoxville: University of Tennessee Press, 1983), 410–22.

3. Michael Oriard, "Local Heroes: Football and the Popular Press, 1920–1960," address delivered at the 1995 conference of the North American Society for Sport History, Long Beach, California; Fuzzy Woodruff, *A History of Southern Football, 1890–1928*, 3 vols. (Atlanta: Walter W. Brown Publishing, 1928), 2:116, 2:141–153, 3:85; Edward L. Ayers, *The Promise of the New South* (New York: Oxford University Press, 1992), 313–16; *Atlanta Journal*, October 16, 1905, 14.

4. *Atlanta Journal*, October 2, 1926, B-2.

5. *Birmingham News*, November 17, 1925, 15; *Montgomery Advertiser*, December 8, 1927, 1; John D. McCollum, *PAC-10 Football: The Rose Bowl Conference* (Seattle: The Writing Works, 1982), 42; William Warren Rogers et al., *Alabama: The History of a Deep South State* (Tuscaloosa: University of Alabama Press, 1994), 457–58.

6. *Montgomery Advertiser*, December 8, 1925, 1, 2; Clyde Bolton, *The Crimson Tide: A Story of Alabama Football* (Huntsville, Ala.: Strode Publishers, 1973), 86–87.

7. *Atlanta Journal*, January 1, 1926, 15; 1926 Report to the Southern Conference, S. V. Sanford Papers, box 15, "Speeches by Sanford, Athletics" file, University of Georgia Ar-

chives, Athens; *Birmingham News,* January 3, 1926, B-4; column from *Atlanta Georgian,* reprinted in *Birmingham News,* January 3, 1926, B-4.

8. Bolton, *Crimson Tide,* 88–92; *Birmingham News,* December 20, 1925, D-2, December 23, 1925, 18.

9. *Birmingham News,* December 20, 1925, D-2; column from *Atlanta Georgian,* reprinted in *Birmingham News,* January 3, 1926, B-4; *Montgomery Advertiser,* December 27, 1925, 6.

10. *Montgomery Advertiser,* January 1, 1926, 1, 2, 5; January 2, 1926, 1, 2; *Birmingham News,* January 4, 1926, 10.

11. Bolton, *Crimson Tide,* 92; *New York Times,* January 2, 1926, 16; *Birmingham Age-Herald,* January 2, 1926, 1, 8, 10.

12. *Montgomery Advertiser,* January 1, 1926, 1, 4, 5; January 2, 1926, 1, 2.

13. Bolton, *Crimson Tide,* 93–94; *Birmingham Age-Herald,* January 2, 1926, 1, 8, 10, 15; *New York Times,* January 2, 1926, 16; *Birmingham News,* November 5, 1925, 18.

14. *Birmingham Age-Herald,* January 2, 1926, 10; *Birmingham News,* January 2, 1926, 6.

15. *Atlanta Journal,* January 4, 1926, 12; *Birmingham News,* January 2, 1926, 6; *Pensacola Journal,* January 2, 1926, 1; column from *Atlanta Georgian,* reprinted in *Birmingham News,* January 3, 1926, B-4; *Atlanta Journal,* January 2, 1926, 2; *Birmingham Age-Herald,* January 2, 1926, 1.

16. *Birmingham News,* January 4, 1926, 10, January 5, 1926, 1.

17. For an account of the game, see *Montgomery Advertiser,* January 2, 1927, 12; for declarations of a "moral victory," see *Montgomery Advertiser,* January 2, 1927, 4; *Anniston Star,* January 3, 1927, 4. Graves quoted in *Tuscaloosa News,* January 5, 1927, 1.

18. *Montgomery Advertiser,* January 2, 1927, 1, 2.

19. Donald Davidson, *Southern Writers in the Modern World* (Athens: University of Georgia Press, 1958), 34.

20. For a discussion of the deteriorating national image of the South during the 1920s, see George B. Tindall, "The Benighted South: Origins of a Modern Image," *The Virginia Quarterly Review* 40 (Spring 1964): 281–94; see also Fred Hobson, *Serpent in Eden: H. L. Mencken and the South* (Chapel Hill: University of North Carolina Press, 1974).

21. Editorial from *Atlanta Georgian,* quoted in *Birmingham News,* January 3, 1926, B-4; *Montgomery Advertiser,* December 7, 1925, 4, December 7, 1926, 4; *Atlanta Journal,* January 2, 1926, 2.

22. *Birmingham Age-Herald,* January 1, 1927, 11; *Birmingham News,* January 2, 1926, 8, January 5, 1926, 1.

23. George Trevor, "Southern Football's Challenge," *Outlook and Independent* 156 (November 12, 1930): 425, 436; *Atlanta Journal,* January 2, 1927, C-2; *Tuscaloosa News,* January 6, 1926, 1.

24. S. V. Sanford Papers, box 15, "Speeches by Sanford, Athletics" file, University of Georgia Archives, Athens. For a discussion of sport and elite regeneration, see Donald Mrozek, *Sport and American Mentality, 1880–1910* (Knoxville: University of Tennessee Press, 1983); and T. J. Jackson Lears, *No Place of Grace: Anti-Modernism and the Transformation of American Culture* (New York: Pantheon Books, 1981).

25. S. V. Sanford Papers, box 15, "Speeches by Sanford, Athletics" file, University of Georgia Archives, Athens.

26. Arthur Grahame, "Alabama: A Story of the 'Crimson Tide,'" *Sport Story Magazine* 17 (October 8, 1927): 12.

27. C. Vann Woodward, *Origins of the New South, 1877–1913* (Baton Rouge: Louisiana State University Press, 1951), 142–74, esp. 154–55. See also Richard M. Weaver, *The Southern Tradition at Bay: A History of Postbellum Thought* (Washington, D.C.: Regnery Gateway, 1989); and Charles Reagan Wilson, *Baptized in Blood: The Religion of the Lost Cause, 1865–1920* (Athens: University of Georgia Press, 1980), 79–87.

28. Michael Oriard, *Reading Football: How the Popular Press Created an American Spectacle* (Chapel Hill: University of North Carolina Press, 1993). See also Michael Oriard, *Sporting with the Gods: The Rhetoric of Play and Games in American Culture* (New York: Cambridge University Press, 1991), 12–13.

29. Woodruff, *History of Southern Football,* 2:54, 3:110, 3:132, 3:249; *Birmingham News,* October 30, 1925, 18, December 6, 1925, C-5, November 28, 1924, 34; *Montgomery Advertiser,* December 8, 1925, 4.

30. Dabney quoted in Wilson, *Baptized in Blood,* 86.

31. Zipp Newman, *The Impact of Southern Football* (Montgomery, Ala.: Morros-Bell, 1969), 5.

32. S. V. Sanford Papers, box 13, "Writings by Sanford, Athletics" file, University of Georgia Archives, Athens.

33. Editorial in *Memphis Commercial-Appeal,* reprinted in *Montgomery Adviser,* January 5, 1926, 4; *Birmingham News,* January 2, 1926, 8; *Tuscaloosa News,* January 5, 1926, 1.

34. Woodward, *Origins of the New South,* 150.

35. *Birmingham News,* January 2, 1926, 8; *Atlanta Journal,* January 4, 1927, 15; *Birmingham Age-Herald,* December 29, 1926, 11; *Birmingham News,* January 3, 1926, B-3; *Atlanta Journal,* January 3, 1927, 10; *Tuscaloosa News,* January 3, 1926, 6.

36. Grover Hall, "We Southerners," *Scribners* 83 (January 1928): 82–88; *Birmingham Age-Herald,* December 24, 1926, 11, December 31, 1926, 10; *Atlanta Journal,* January 2, 1927, C-1.

37. Richard A. Easterlin, "Regional Income Trends, 1840–1950," in *American Economic History,* ed. Seymour Harris (New York: McGraw-Hill, 1961), 525–47; Paul M. Gaston, *The New South Creed: A Study in Southern Mythmaking* (Baton Rouge: Louisiana State University Press, 1976).

38. *Anniston Star,* January 3, 1927, 4; *Montgomery Advertiser,* January 6, 1927, 6; *Gadsden Star* editorial reprinted in *Tuscaloosa News,* January 4, 1926, 4; *Atlanta Journal,* January 4, 1926, 12; Wayne Hester, ed., *Century of Champions: The Centennial History of Alabama Football* (Birmingham, Ala.: Seacoast Publishers/Birmingham News, 1991), 12.

39. Tindall, *Emergence of the New South,* 276–82.

40. *Montgomery Advertiser,* January 9, 1926, 1.

41. *Birmingham Age-Herald,* January 5, 1926, 1.

42. *Birmingham News,* January 5, 1926, 14.

43. Editorial in *Gadsden Times-Journal,* reprinted in *Tuscaloosa News,* January 4, 1926, 4.

44. *Birmingham Age-Herald,* December 29, 1926, 1, December 31, 1926, 1, 8, January 9, 1927, B-6; *Birmingham News,* October 30, 1924, 16.

45. Eric Hobsbawm, "Introduction: Inventing Traditions," in *The Invention of Tradition,* ed. Eric Hobsbawm and Terence Ranger (Cambridge: Cambridge University Press, 1983), 1.

46. George M. Fredrickson, *The Black Image in the White Mind: The Debate on Afro-American Character and Destiny, 1817–1914* (New York: Oxford University Press, 1971), 256–82.

47. John Temple Graves, *The Fighting South* (New York: George Putnam's Sons, 1943), 90–91.

48. Ulrich Bonnell Phillips, "The Central Theme of Southern History," *American Historical Review* 34 (October 1928): 30–43; *Montgomery Advertiser,* January 6, 1927.

PART 2

Race Relations and Southern Sport: Athletics "Behind the Veil" and the Process of Desegregation

5. To "Bring the Race Along Rapidly": Sport, Student Culture, and Educational Mission at Historically Black Colleges during the Interwar Years

PATRICK B. MILLER

"ATHLETICS IS the universal language," an editorialist asserted in the Howard University campus newspaper in the spring of 1924. "By and through it we hope to foster a better and more fraternal spirit between the races in America and so to destroy prejudices; to learn and to be taught; to facilitate a universal brotherhood."[1] Such sentiments had been enunciated since the turn of the century, but it was during the interwar years that the athletic ideal resonated most intensely for various commentators on the prospects for racial reform. Capturing the belief shared by numerous African American leaders that the football gridiron and baseball diamond, the track oval, and even the boxing ring offered significant platforms for proving equality, the Howard student writer carefully articulated the widespread desire that black athletes might engage white society in a broad-based dialogue about democratic principles and practices. Ideally, the success of African Americans in sport would provide powerful lessons in "interracial education."[2]

Acting on these hopes, many spokesmen for uplift and assimilation strenuously promoted the organization of sports in the schools and colleges of the South. Working behind the veil of segregation in an environment overwhelmingly hostile to any claims of black self-worth, a new generation of African American educators and students remained extremely conscious of their isolation, as well as their need for circumspection. They believed, nevertheless, that the cultivation of playing fields possessed enormous significance: athletic accomplishment could strengthen the sense of racial pride among black southerners and at the same time encourage them to identify with "national" pastimes. At the very least, games and races might relieve for a short time the burdens of labor, the daily ordeal of enforced deference. Edwin Bancroft Henderson, perhaps the most prominent commentator on African American sport during the first half of the twentieth century, stated his appraisal clearly, if condescendingly: "The glare and glamour [of athletics] attracted to scholastic halls many a backwoods boy and girl who would have been plowing and mating in the countryside untrained and in humdrum living, but who now are being turned into high class more useful products of society." Conceived in terms such as self-respect and social engagement, sport served many purposes. For many "New Negroes," its potential role in forging racial solidarity as well as channeling the energy and aspirations of southern blacks seemed immense.[3]

From an early date, the ideal of muscular assimilationism was elaborated in educational practice. In 1906 the African American educator Samuel Archer extolled sport for the qualities of self-reliance and self-control that it was said to inculcate. The conditions under which games were then being played in the black colleges, he argued, were "very favorable for the development of the strong and aggressive in union with the gentle and the just."[4] Abiding by the athletic creed, many of those who sought to raise up the next generation similarly enumerated the values ascribed to disciplined training for competition on the playing fields. After the turn of the century, for instance, the catalog of Wiley College proudly announced that "'athletic sports are not only allowed, but encouraged.'" At that small college in Marshall, Texas, institutional policy stressed the notion "'that the best education is that which develops a strong, robust body as well as other parts of the human makeup.'"[5]

Subscribing to the principles addressed by Samuel Archer and the Wiley catalog, though observing the racial landscape from a different perspective, an array of journalists and reformers vigorously applauded the efforts of stellar black athletes who won places on the teams of the predominately white colleges of the North. Those athletes especially, Edwin Henderson declared, did "much to soften racial prejudices" and to advance "the cause of blacks everywhere."[6] In both substantive and symbolic terms, college sport offered a model for African American activists: the fulfillment of the gospel of athletic success would be manifest not only in headline performances, world records, and Olympic medals, but also in an increasing number of victories over Jim Crow and breaches of the color line. From the publicity won by such stars as Fritz Pollard, Paul Robeson, and Jesse Owens, to the occasions in the late thirties when the football squads of the University of North Carolina and Duke agreed to travel north and face a black competitor on a rival team, race leaders could take pride in the present and gather strength for future struggles.[7]

To many spokesmen for the "talented tenth," such as the editors of *Crisis* and *Opportunity* or the publishers of the *Pittsburgh Courier* and the *Chicago Defender*, the goal of integrating sport—in order "to facilitate a universal brotherhood"—was no less compelling than their concern about uplift. Within the boundaries of far-flung playing fields, prevailing biases could be contested and defeated, black reformers suggested. Similarly, what for a growing number of African Americans was a newfound boldness could be forcefully communicated: athletic distinctions underscored the enormous potential of black Americans for achievement in all walks of life. In a telling commentary written in praise of two track-and-field champions from the 1932 Olympic Games, Arthur Howe, the president of Hampton Institute, asserted that the gold and silver medals won by Eddie Tolan and Ralph Metcalfe, respectively, should not be considered as merely a "source of pride and inspiration" for African Americans. The performances they registered, Howe maintained, also bespoke "many less advertised victories . . . in more significant realms." Ultimately concerned about the ways to move black Americans from the margins to the mainstream of the political, economic, and social life of the nation, racial reformers hoped that such triumphs would challenge the dominant culture "to give the Negro his due in justice and opportunity."[8] Thus the leaders of the NAACP and the National Urban League enlisted muscular assimilationism in the civil rights crusade.

At the same time that sports gained respect as a source of pride and a "vehicle" for social change, however, some African American observers recognized the enormous qualifications and conditions that shadowed the contributions hard work at play might make to the advancement of the race. During the 1920s and 1930s, numerous traditionally black institutions of higher education became embroiled in controversies over athletics similar to the scandals that plagued predominantly white colleges, where the violations of rules had become as well documented as they were flagrant and widespread. This was a cause of consternation among racial reformers like W. E. B. Du Bois, who feared that such episodes would draw public attention away from the hard-won scholastic achievements of black Americans. As a consequence, the proper organization and regulation of the strenuous life in the southern schools—among the larger obligations of educational authorities to racial uplift—remained a constant concern for African American leaders through the first half of the twentieth century.

A more general apprehension, though one that would become sharper and ever more significant over the years, concerned the misrepresentation of black achievement in sport. Even before the tenets of "scientific" racism were projected onto the playing field, some African Americans anticipated that claims for equality of opportunity made through the bodies of black athletic heroes would provoke substantial resistance from the dominant culture. As early as 1905, William Pickens, a professor at Talladega College, averred that "whites would accept from a Negro physical and athletic superiority but . . . stand aloof when one approaches with moral or intellectual superiority."[9]

Such presentiments would be confirmed several decades later, when black activists came to witness the betrayal of their trust in the notion that triumph in athletics readily translated into social progress. The notions of "manly character" and "courage" had long connected physical prowess with other cultural ideals, such as the attributes of great generals and presidents. Yet in response to African American ascendancy in sport, the mainstream press replaced those images with allusions to survival in some distant jungle or to a distinctive anatomy and physiology, references not to the cultivation of character and the hallmarks of modern civilization but to the natural and the primitive. Herein lay the paradox of muscular assimilationism as a strategy for racial reform: the standards and values by which African Americans strove to be judged have always been susceptible to manipulation by white America. Still, open competition remained an ideal central to civil rights activism. And numerous black physical educators and cultural commentators fervently embraced the athletic creed. Through achievement in sport they ultimately hoped to demonstrate "the same traits of courage" said to characterize the dominant race.[10]

The substantial hopes held by many black Americans thus engaged the subtle fears of a few concerning the influence of athletics in revising social arrangements in the United States. Since so much was at stake, college students and their teachers as well as journalists and reformers of many stripes contributed to the discussion about the proper means and ends of sporting competition, the role of athletics in black higher education, and the relative effectiveness of sport in subverting prevailing stereotypes. In addition to the wide-ranging conversation black athletes ideally would initiate with white America, "internal debates" among blacks addressed the problematics as well as the promise of sport as a platform for social change. The discussions took place in many forums. Yet perhaps nowhere else were they conducted more extensively or energetically than on the campuses of traditionally African American colleges during the interwar era.

* * *

In the years following the death of Booker T. Washington, a "New Negro" was said to have appeared on campus, provoking dramatic controversies over both the mission and methods of black higher education in the South. Significantly, many students and alumni, as well as a growing number of instructors and several college presidents, drew inspiration from the cultural renaissance associated with Harlem. Concerning liberal learning, they spoke the language of Du Bois and endeavored to use their talents in the full range of professional opportunities and intellectual pursuits. Many of them advanced the notion, moreover, of a thoroughgoing black "manhood," which in the context of their essays and speeches bespoke self-confidence and the assertion of civil rights. Manly independence meant a resistance to the stifling conformity that for the new cohort characterized the atmosphere of many historically black institutions. It also encouraged an increasing militancy in the face of discriminatory public policies in the nation at large. One obvious correlative of such a mentality lay in the sanctioned aggressiveness, the images of heroism, and the display of strength and energy that infused competitive sports.

Against these voices for change, traditionalists mounted a resolute defense. Maintaining the visions of the founders of industrial training institutions and missionary schools, many educational authorities, both black and white, also subscribed to the conservative principles set forth by such funding agencies as the General Education Board and the Phelps-Stokes endowment. Thus throughout the first decades of the twentieth century, numerous principals and presidents of the old school, supported by their boards of trustees or by lily-white state legislatures (or both), continued to impose a strict discipline on many student activities and to enforce what might be called a policy of "distance or deference" concerning race relations in the South.

Such considerations about the boundaries of the curriculum were closely related in the thoughts of many traditionally minded educators to the control of undergraduate conduct. The regulation of nearly every hour and virtually every facet of campus life at some institutions suggested a fear that students were incapable of self-governance, that they were somehow disposed to range out of control. Likewise, the academically modest, often outright regressive vocational programs at numerous schools—legacies of the Washingtonian creed—represented formidable restraints upon both the preparation and aspirations of black students, regarding not only their immediate educational concerns but also their entire working lives.[11]

Across the generations, the most crucial issue remained the claims of liberal learning over and against vocational training. Beyond that controversy, though, at many schools the relative influence accorded the extracurriculum, especially sports, provoked some of the most striking confrontations. While intercollegiate athletic competition was in many ways related to other campus activities, its symbolic significance often loomed larger than that of student government and campus journalism. And though the bonding within fraternities and sororities, like the rituals of dating and mating, occurred day to day, it was the drama of the big game that for many students converted the semester into a season.[12]

Sport stimulated campus spirit, its advocates declared. A game like football offered memorable examples of competence and vitality just as it represented one of the principal measures of institutional prestige, both within the African American community and beyond. As one undergraduate journalist declared in 1893, black collegians were justified in their anxiousness to play against other institutions, for "to excel in athletics as well as other things" would be to "raise the honor" of the school. Yet intercollegiate rivalries also raised numerous questions for students and educators concerning the ways of gaining victory, the relationship between athletics and academics at financially challenged but ambitious institutions of learning, and ultimately about the proper purposes of "play" for black collegians.[13]

The first facts regarding black college athletics customarily pinpoint the date and location of the initial forays by college teams into extramural competition, whether it was the ball games played between the students of Hampton Institute and clubs from several towns in southeastern Virginia or the contests between Howard and visiting squads from northern colleges. The 1892 football competition in North Carolina, matching Biddle (now Johnson C. Smith) and Livingstone, was the first black intercollegiate game on record for that sport. Within two years Howard and Lincoln as well as Tuskegee Institute and Atlanta University had commenced their rivalries, and by the turn of the century, Morgan College, Atlanta Baptist, and Virginia Union had also entered the intercollegiate athletic fray. With notable pride, Wiley College boasted in 1901 of the introduction of "football, as it is played at Yale and other Eastern colleges." Variations on the theme of precedence abounded. Though the inauguration of off-campus athletics was often in reality quite a modest affair, through memory and nostalgia it became a prominent part of the early histories of schools from Wilberforce in Ohio to Talladega in Alabama.[14]

The date and outcome of an athletic contest became a matter of record. Beyond such information, the first generation of black college athletes offered more vivid characterizations of the origins and development of black college sport, including the invention of traditions and reminiscences of triumph and travail. In adopting familiar team colors and nicknames, African American students in the New South hoped to give their schools a prominent place on the collegiate map. Thus, from the menagerie of ferocious mascots available to them, black collegians at Atlanta Baptist chose to become Tigers, while at Livingstone they adopted the nickname Bears. Other schools distinguished themselves as the Lincoln Lions, Wiley Wildcats, and Howard

Bisons, though the Tornadoes of Talladega and the Trojans of Virginia State departed from the dominant zoological theme. The early teams from Fisk were named after the school's president, Erastus Milo Cravath, and played as the Sons of Milo. Happily, in later years they renamed themselves the Bulldogs. And inevitably, perhaps, numerous Agricultural and Industrial schools would be called Aggies on and off the field. To join a national intercollegiate culture, African American students created small distinctions between their institutions and selected rivals, but they also conformed to patterns of self-representation already well established.[15]

Significantly, too, black athletes took enormous pride in their efforts to start up and maintain their teams, innovation in the face of scarcity looming large in their recollections of spring and autumn sporting rituals. While the photographs of many of the early varsities portray neat uniforms and a noteworthy formality, they do not explain the many sacrifices athletes and institutions made during a season of competition. The members of the first Livingstone squad chipped in to buy a single regulation football outfit from the Spalding Sporting Goods Company. From this model, the young women in the Sewing Department made patterns for the other uniforms. At Langston during the early years, athletes bought their own uniforms from the Sears and Roebuck catalog. Some players nailed small squares of old leather to their shoes, presumably for better traction on a dusty football field, though perhaps to repair damage after a rough season. And while a few relatively well-heeled students might have purchased shin protectors, nose guards, and mouthpieces, during the 1920s most athletes could not afford shoulder pads. Head gear was "thin, light, or nonexistent," several former players remembered. For many schools the provision of equipment remained largely makeshift or make-do; even so, the teams generated considerable pride and excitement.[16]

Concerning the exhilaration and pageantry surrounding black college sport, it would be difficult at a distance to measure the jubilation on campus following an invitation to the Penn Relays, a vast—and racially mixed—track-and-field carnival, widely known during the 1920s as the "Negro Olympics." From current affairs, perhaps, one might get a sense of the college spirit (and spirits) that once animated the bonfire rally on the eve of a dramatic contest between arch rivals Lincoln and Howard or Tuskegee and Atlanta. The rituals black colleges shared with their predominately white counterparts were significant in cultural terms; their differences were more important still. At least one rite attending football at historically African American institutions contrasted sharply with the autumn spectacles enacted on the campuses of northern and western colleges. This was the "Rabbles." A halftime pageant at several schools, the "rabbles" occurred when the grandstands emptied and students, clad in their finest, some carrying their own musical instruments, danced around the field, perhaps in conscious contrast to the precision marching bands that were the pride of many predominately white universities. "The ending of the first half was the cue for 'rabble' exhibitions," reported the *Howard University Record* about the game against Lincoln in 1921: "The rabbles of both schools pounced upon the field in spite of its mud-soaked condition and the continuous rain. The 'Blue and White' rabble, headed by its band, executed a wild snake dance while the Lincoln horde did its serpentine dance. The weather forbade society exhibitions . . . and kept the ladies in their seats, prohibiting the fur coat parade of last year."[17]

As another periodical, the *Howard Alumni Sentinel,* observed, athletic rituals not only attested to the exuberance that infused the black athletic experience, they also offered a way to "keep alive" the "spirit of tradition" on the college scene. By other accounts as well, sport stood at the center of campus culture. According to the president of Florida A&M University, "'No school in this day can expect to attract promising men or women that does not give organized athletics a foremost place. Where there are no athletics, it is very likely true that only deadheads are attracted. Young men and women of promise desire to be connected with an institution that has spirit and force.'" Such ebullience would also characterize the response of some faculty members to the sporting spectacle. In 1920, for instance, Professor Clara Standish of Talladega College wrote proudly to her friends that "'our football team has won every game so far and is considered one of the finest in the South.'" Describing a crucial contest against Tuskegee not merely as the triumph of skill over superior weight but also with a strong sense of academic status, Standish boasted that it was a "'decided victory for higher as compared with industrial education.'"[18]

Ultimately, as a response to prevailing notions of African American inferiority, organized athletics was a telling assertion of pride and accomplishment. Set against the backdrop of contrasting educational ideals, the phenomenon suggested not only the vitality of student culture on black campuses but also the gradual loosening of institutional restraints on undergraduate activity. For many contemporary commentators, athletics seemed to offer at least a limited means through which historically African American schools could become assimilated, on their own terms, to a national collegiate culture.

By the 1920s nearly every black college sponsored teams in football and baseball, as well as in basketball and track and field. Significantly, women students also participated in intramural athletic activities and traveled to intercollegiate basketball and track contests. During the Depression, several runners, such as Alice Coachman and Christine Petty, gained national prominence, while a few southern schools assembled formidable teams, Tuskegee winning eleven out of twelve Amateur Athletic Union track championships between 1937 and 1948. The African American sporting community not only offered women more opportunities to compete but also accorded more prestige to their accomplishments than did predominately white colleges. Yet alumni periodicals and the African American press abided by the prevailing gender ideology; it was principally the combined energy and expertise of male athletes that they extolled as representing institutional honor and carrying the cause of the race. Whether it was in the person of such stars as Francis Alfred "Jazz" Byrd and Harry "Wu Fang" Ward or the collective achievement of black Olympians, the male image held a central place in the African American athletic ideal.[19]

In more strictly organizational terms, the black colleges sought to emulate the most successful white intercollegiate programs at institutions such as the University of Virginia or distant Yale. Most schools hired coaches and trainers at least on a part-time basis. An increasing number of colleges joined the athletic conferences devised to organize sporting affairs. And they acknowledged—in one form or another—the existence of rules and standards governing amateur competition. Established in 1911, the Colored Intercollegiate Athletic Association (CIAA) enlisted the majority of traditionally black institutions in the upper South. During the next two decades, the Southern Intercollegiate Athletic Association, the South-Atlantic Intercollegiate Athletic Association, and the Southwestern Athletic Conference were formed to regulate black sport, though often they were much more loosely organized than the CIAA. These conferences disseminated materials that had originated with the Amateur Athletic Union and the National Collegiate Athletic Association (NCAA), although many individual cases fell outside the broad principles defining "pure and simple" amateurism, a class-based Victorian construct if ever there was one. Meetings were held and rules passed, but the foremost agencies of regulation often seemed ineffective. This only served to sharpen the debate over sports, educational mission, and the progress of the race.[20]

Belying the assumptions about sportsmanship that lay at the foundation of the athletic creed and revealing the weakness of the early governing organizations, problems concerning perceived corruption and inadequate control began to occur more frequently in the 1920s. What had long been keen competition on the field escalated during the interwar years into conduct that, for some commentators, threatened to tarnish the collegiate image they had endeavored so strenuously to create. And it was owing to the belief that intercollegiate sporting competition had suddenly lurched out of control that the subject of athletics began to play into larger controversies concerning student autonomy, presidential authority, and the aims of black education.

Throughout the 1920s and 1930s the athletic programs of numerous black colleges came under criticism for their unfair recruiting practices and indifference to academic standards of eligibility, as well as for the subsidization of their best passers, pitchers, and runners. Accusations about violations of rules filled the mails traveling from one campus to another. Such allegations also flowed from the pages of *Crisis*, where W. E. B. Du Bois and his protégé, George Streator, periodically railed against a long litany of abuses in sports, breaches of the spirit if not always the letter of the "laws" then defining amateurism. Claflin College admitted athletes without reviewing their transcripts, Streator reported in one lengthy article, while South Carolina State College fielded several athletes who had seen considerable action around Orangeburg during the preceding eight years and several more who had played collegiate ball elsewhere. The indictment ran to several fact-filled pages, and Streator even ranked black colleges according to the extensiveness of their athletic excesses.[21]

One school enrolled a man in a music class for an hour each week so he could compete on the football team, Streator asserted. Other colleges used players from the preparatory department or the theological seminary to fill out their squads. Fisk's most prominent football player, "Jumping" Joe Wiggins, had one year's experience at Virginia State and then two years' more at Atlanta University before lending his talents to the Nashville institution for three years of competition. During the mid-twenties Archie Lewis distinguished himself on the gridiron for John Carroll University, a Jesuit school in Cleveland, Ohio, then contributed his services for four years more to Lincoln University in Pennsylvania. The success of Wilberforce on the gridiron, Streator concluded, was "less a tribute to the skill of the coaches than to the experience of the players." The list of infractions seemed endless, highlighted by editorial charges that athletic officials at many schools had abandoned their broader responsibilities and succumbed to the demand for victory at any cost.[22]

For the most part, critics and reformers ignored the exploitation of athletic labor, concentrating mainly on the issue of unfair competition. In 1929 Frank A. Young of the *Chicago Defender* refused to pick an All-America team because he considered it unfair to compare the playing ability of performers who had competed for seven or eight years with those who had participated for only two or three. Tuskegee had not lost a game in years, Du Bois noted in 1930. "I ask, why should she?" he wondered. "Has she not kept the same team practically intact for six or seven years? The name [Benjamin Franklin] Stevenson has appeared in Tuskegee's lineup for no less than six

years. Unless there is a radical change of policy, it will appear next year."
Numerous practices of this sort not only called into question the sportsmanship of some schools, Du Bois contended; such conduct also suggested the
need for substantial reform. A vital student culture was laudable, but athletic scandals indicated too great an emphasis on matters not related to the
academic purposes of higher education. For many African American leaders, "self-government" had long been an issue of great concern, and they
strove to dispel prevailing images regarding poorly formed habits and values among black youth. Simply stated, the reputation of centers of learning
needed to be protected.[23]

Significantly, both the long list of schools violating athletic rules and the
stated concern about academic status were not unique to black higher education. In fact, Streator's indictment of such institutions as Lincoln, Wilberforce, and South Carolina State paralleled reports in the mainstream press
about the recruiting practices of the University of Pittsburgh, for instance,
or the ways athletes at the University of Southern California were maintained
by local alumni and civic boosters. Throughout the twenties, while a number
of sportswriters documented instances of illegal "proselytism" and subsidization at predominately white colleges and universities, educational authorities and cultural commentators inveighed against the increasing commer-
cialization and professionalization of college sport. What was occurring on
the black college scene, then, was part of a much larger pattern, and the
specific recommendations advanced by African American reformers of sport
would have been familiar to their counterparts in the white collegiate establishment.[24]

The policies advocated by Du Bois and Streator, for instance, included one
rule limiting athletic eligibility to three years and another that required an
athlete to sit out one year of competition after changing schools. According
to this plan of action, all black colleges should be bound by common standards governing the recruitment of high school athletes and the use of students not regularly enrolled in the collegiate program. Athletes would not be
allowed to participate on professional teams during the off-season; likewise,
it would be illegal for schools to remunerate players for their services. Beyond these stipulations, Streator argued for increased faculty control of
sports, periodic meetings among deans and registrars to address athletic
problems, and a more forceful national body to coordinate, and ultimately
to supervise, the activities of the respective regional conferences.[25]

Cast largely within the framework of progressive reform—emphasizing
high morals and effective administration—both the indictments and the
remedies that emanated from *Crisis* journalism between 1930 and 1932 closely

resembled the charges and programs set forth in the famous Carnegie Report of 1929, the most detailed critique of (white) college sport ever assembled. Within this context, the motives of many reformers seemed clear: New Negroes were supposed to play the same games in the same manner as the athletes at the most upright institutions found in the Northeast or Midwest. As Du Bois asserted: "Now that Negro colleges are being admitted to the associations of standard colleges, and even now are debating with these colleges and universities, it is even possible that some Negro college will play games with the members of the 'Big Ten' or some other Carnegie-investigated groups. I wonder if we will have the nerve to say that 'Chicago exhibited great racial prejudice in refusing to play unless Fisk benched Brown, her mainstay in the backfield for the last ten years?'"[26]

The promulgation of numerous rules and regulations constituted one dimension of the larger discussion concerning the prominence—some would have said the overexposure—of sports at black colleges. There remained other voices in the dialogue as well, maintaining a deep and widespread pride in the accomplishments of African American athletes and continuing to assert that sporting competition admirably projected the image of black manhood. Ostensibly, the debate conformed to the classic outlines of generational conflict, pitting student demands for more expansive means of self-expression and autonomy within the extracurriculum—in alliance with those who advocated a new model of liberal learning—against the claims of an old guard, insistent on the tight control of the entire educational enterprise and identified with a circumscribed curriculum.

Yet as the concerns of Du Bois suggest, the controversy over the boundaries of student culture actually cut across rival notions of academic mission. At several institutions, for instance, educational innovators were intent on transforming their schools into universities of the first rank; at the same time, they were notable for their extreme hostility to sports as distractions from greater goals. It was the library and laboratory, not the playing field, that should feature the highest demonstrations of African American potential, some college presidents asserted through both word and deed. Many "new" students and alumni, however, showed less support for curricular innovation and educational excellence than they did for the development of sports as a measure of institutional pride. In protesting the edicts that would weaken or eliminate the football team, they sought to challenge the traditional structure of authority because it had become so demoralizing. But they also showed considerable tolerance of the athletic scandals that threatened the academic reputation of their schools.

Ultimately, some notably progressive black commentators sided with heavy-handed college leaders on behalf of strong academic programs as the basis for racial uplift, while many students and their supporters saw in the expansion of sport one of the best means of cultivating their own sense of race pride. In light of such crossings of lines, the familiar dichotomy setting apart Washingtonians and the New Negro needs to be revised in order to explain how the curriculum and extracurriculum often stood as rivals within the broad campaign for improving race relations. In significant ways, the controversies at two of the most prominent institutions of black education illustrate the dynamics of these debates as well as the complexity of the relationship between muscular impulses and racial progress.

The situation at Fisk University during the first part of the 1920s suggests that strong personalities as well as competing ideals played a large part in the debate over the extracurriculum. Fayette Avery McKenzie, who had been the president of the school since 1915, stood among several other educators of the era who seemed to combine Washingtonian means as to institutional authority with the ideals of Du Bois concerning the full development of the academic realm. McKenzie's motto was "Let us dare to be a university." Accordingly, he endeavored to improve academic standards as well as to expand the curriculum, raising substantial sums from the General Education Board and Carnegie Corporation to carry out his plans. Yet at the same time, his rule on campus was said to be "tyrannical," a program "of petty authority in aggravated form" that set off a campus revolt. McKenzie elaborated a strict code of discipline, regulating dress and conversation as well as curtailing those undergraduate activities that were not already prohibited, such as student government and campus journalism. Additionally, he discontinued intercollegiate baseball and track, and as students complained, he presided over the decline of football "to the point where Fisk had recently fallen to Tuskegee by a score of sixty-seven to zero."[27]

Responding to what he perceived to be athletic "overemphasis," the bogey haunting many educators, McKenzie created problems of morale so extensive that they overwhelmed his academic ambitions and his program of reform for Fisk. In several dramatic presentations, Du Bois entered the fray on behalf of the students, the controversy went public, extending far beyond the Nashville community, and McKenzie was eventually persuaded to resign. What many envisioned as an ideal balance between the offerings found in the course catalog and the extracurriculum had not been struck at Fisk. Nor would it be in subsequent years, when athletic preeminence was followed by revelations of impropriety, and the rancorous contest between athletics and academics was rejoined.[28]

The troubled atmosphere at Fisk had a counterpart in the sour relations between two forceful presidents of Howard University and many of their students. Resembling the case involving McKenzie, the hostilities on the hilltop in the District of Columbia initially centered on a white college president with an authoritarian disposition and the growing militancy of a black academic community widely regarded as "the capstone of Negro education." During the early 1920s, J. Stanley Durkee drove Howard toward Class-A accreditation for an increasing number of the college divisions as well as the professional schools, a formal status allowing the school to compare itself to the most prominent institutions in the "Middle States" region, including segregated Georgetown, George Washington, and American Universities in the District of Columbia as well as the Maryland Agricultural College—significantly, not until 1920 renamed the University of Maryland—a few miles away. In the process, however, Durkee alienated many African American educators at the university and ran afoul of the alumni as well as many undergraduates. There were many dimensions to the confrontation at Howard. The racial composition of the board of trustees and the relative power of the president were crucial issues. So too was Durkee's condescending attitude toward the faculty, as strong-willed as it was in many ways eminent.[29]

But debates concerning the role of athletics also contributed to the discord on campus. A controversy over the eligibility of a football player named Robert Miller, who had transferred from Lincoln University, occurred during the 1924 season and extended into the first months of 1925, late on Durkee's watch. It involved strained relations with other institutions and with the governing athletic association, but mainly it focused attention on the rivalry between athletics and academics at Howard. The immediate outcome was the withdrawal of Howard from the CIAA. But what the Miller imbroglio actually foreshadowed was a reevaluation of the mission of the most prominent black university in the nation. Combined with numerous other actions that outraged the black community, the controversy over sports helped forge an alliance that challenged the entire educational administration. Durkee did not weather the storm; he was forced to resign in 1926. To a significant extent, it would be his successor who would reap the athletic whirlwind.[30]

In numerous respects, Mordecai Wyatt Johnson, the first black president of Howard, took over where his predecessor left off, striving to achieve educational excellence with missionary zeal, imposing his program on students and teachers who had a strong sense of their own contributions to Howard's reputation. Not simply a legacy of the Durkee years but also a matter of policy early in Johnson's own administration, sport became a core issue. Soon after his inauguration, the crisis over athletics polarized the campus and provoked an enormous outpouring of resentment toward those who would scuttle successful football teams in order to consolidate academic reputation. In the first instance, Johnson pursued a broad-based program of exercise and physical activity. John H. Burr had been appointed Dean of Physical Education for Men during the Durkee years, but he won Johnson's support as well. Owing to his experience in the YMCA movement and his belief in "Athletics for All," he endeavored to reorient Howard sporting programs toward the gymnasium and the intramural playing fields. Johnson, also attached to the YMCA ideal, subscribed to this conception of physical training and competition, and though once a varsity athlete himself, he sought to diminish the influence of intercollegiate sports on college life.[31]

Arguing that both expense and equity—an athletic budget deficit of twenty-one thousand dollars and the need to help students struggling economically—required the reduction of sports programs, in 1927 Johnson abolished athletic scholarships, the training table, and compensation for room and board. The immediate consequence was a strike—though a short-lived one—on the part of the football squad. To the consternation of fans, on campus and beyond, Johnson's plans meant a diminished athletic program. In ensuing years, Howard teams won "moral victories" on gridiron and diamond, according to one editorialist, but few real ones. And after another brief period of expansion and another round of cuts, in 1936 Howard athletes went on strike again, with the overwhelming support of the student body but without much success against the entrenched academic authorities.[32]

As Howard's athletic fortunes fell, several African American leaders emerged to defend Johnson's ideals and program. One of them was Du Bois, who in this case defended an imperious administrator, lauding Johnson's "attempt to purge the lists at Howard of those students who were not maintaining scholastic efficiency." Along the same lines, Du Bois castigated the "rabid sports lovers of the country" for subverting the proper purposes of the academy. Within a wide-ranging indictment of campus culture run amok, which he delivered at the Howard commencement of 1930, Du Bois emphasized the ill effects of athletic excess: "The average Negro undergraduate has swallowed hook, line and sinker the dead bait of the white undergraduate, who, born in an industrial machine, does not have to think and does not think. Our college man today, is, on the average, a man untouched by real culture. He deliberately surrenders to selfish and even silly ideals, swarming into semiprofessional athletics and Greek-letter societies, and affecting to despise scholarship and the hard grind of study and research."[33]

The debate had two sides, of course, both keen to the ways in which American society worked and played. For the defenders of sport, it was desirable if not imperative that Howard excel in a variety of fields to demonstrate that it was a fully-fledged educational institution. Yet this purportedly more expansive notion of the collegiate enterprise turned out to be just as disparaging of strict academics as the followers of Johnson and Du Bois could be about the overemphasis of athletics. According to one of the administration's critics, it seemed that the great aim of the university was to make "literary geniuses, philosophers, and Phi Beta Kappa men out of football players." Athletics was being destroyed at Howard, many students complained, because no one was encouraging players "in a material way" comparable to the manner in which other colleges subsidized sports, or as some might have stated, comparable to the means used to improve the Howard law school or biology department.[34]

Beyond the campus setting, black commentators assessed the relationship between the curriculum and the most notable aspect of student culture. The *Amsterdam News* in New York editorialized in 1929 that the "public expects the best in everything from Howard; the best scholarship, the best sportsmanship, and the best athletic competitions." But as a writer for the same newspaper suggested eleven years later, for many African Americans it was sports that mattered most. After Lincoln trounced Howard by a score of 63-0, the journalist lamented that "mediocrity in football or any other form of intercollegiate competition doesn't help the school's prestige." Howard officials would be well advised, he continued, "either to get a football team or do like the University of Chicago, 'throw in the sponge.'" The circumstances notwithstanding, such a comparison of academic institutions doubtless would have been praised by Du Bois, just as it might have pleased Johnson, who lasted as president of Howard until 1960, held in awe by many in the community but still largely unliked.[35]

The controversy over the value of sport in enhancing the prestige of an institution or in improving race relations would continue long past the end of Johnson's tenure at Howard or the departure of W. E. B. Du Bois from the offices of *Crisis*. Arguments on behalf of athletics as an emblem of pride and an avenue of opportunity have largely prevailed. Such endorsements appear on the halftime television commercials sponsored by the NCAA; they inform the stories of success and surpassing that fill the daily sports pages; they often inspire the rhetoric of prominent political figures. Yet against such claims, many commentators have voiced their misgivings about the utility of sport in shaping social change or about the concentration on athletics to the neglect of other demonstrations of prowess and pride.

Those who addressed the issue during the interwar period were as eloquent as any who came after. But of all the critical observations on sport, perhaps

the most acute expression of doubt about athletic ideals and practices occurred in a verse published in *Crisis* in 1928 by a young African American
scholar, whose lines, both earnest and sardonic, were addressed to "The Second Generation" at historically black colleges:

> Juggling basketballs
> And women
> You won't work,
> You won't study,
> You won't marry.
>
> But you have four "letters"
> And a fraternity pin.
>
> College education
> Of a hundred like you every year
> Will bring the race along rapidly.[36]

In response to the various pronouncements about sport, "the universal language," the poem by Allison Davis—who in 1942 became the first African
American professor hired by a predominately white university—highlights
the problems of a student culture not directed outward to larger social concerns. It implies, from an academic's point of view, what higher ideals black
collegians ought to strive for. And it suggests a more profound apprehension
than what African Americans have succeeded in doing with their bodies has
not communicated, for the dominant culture, the entire range of black aspiration and capability.

* * *

Cast within the context of the development of African American higher education and in terms of black manhood, the ideal of "muscular assimilationism" has become a part of a broad-based cultural conversation about equality and opportunity in America. For many black leaders sports have afforded
a source of self-expression and fostered self-esteem. Athletics have called
attention to youth and energy, consequently directing thought and imagination toward the future, presumably a better future. Even before the turn
of the century, a hopeful writer for the *Fisk University Herald* had declared,
"We do not agree with Pindar, who said, 'No man is great who is not great
with his hands and feet'; but we do believe that not only the brain but also
hands and feet ought to be cultivated. For well has it been said that only strong
arms can make men and nations free."[37]

But for those white Americans who have wished to limit its significance,
athletics could also be interpreted as yet another form of physical labor, sim-

ply a matter of sweat and muscle. In many ways, the dominant culture has historically conceded black strength and endurance; from the perspective not only of the cultural critic but also of the athlete on the field, the equation of playing fields and cotton fields is not difficult to discern. What amounted to the inversion of the athletic creed, which long had linked the strong body to idealized notions of character and courage, proceeded in racialist terms from the metaphor of servitude. Mere brawn could be abstracted from the traits of discipline, self-sacrifice, and other long-lauded values, many sportswriters and athletic officials contended. Critically, it was precisely at the time when black athletes had begun to register more victories in interracial competition—winning boxing championships and Olympic gold medals—that such formulations achieved a wider currency among white commentators.

Thus by the 1920s and 1930s prevailing generalizations about black athletic achievement, whether predicated on custom or the claims of pseudoscience, departed from the notion of the acculturating dimension of the playing fields and emphasized "instinct," "natural ability," and the legacies of a "primitive" existence in Africa. Such thinking became even more expansive in its assertions that superior physicality indicated a lack of intelligence and creativity or somehow compensated for their absence. Fifty years after the Fisk undergraduate declared his belief in the value of sports "to make men and nations free," and less than two decades following the statement of faith by the Howard University student that athletics constituted "a universal language," a white track coach could explain African American success in sports with references that thoroughly undermined the ideal of "muscular assimilationism." "It was not long ago," Dean Cromwell casually averred in 1941, "that his [the black athlete's] ability to sprint and jump was a life-and-death matter to him in the jungle. His muscles are pliable, and his easygoing disposition is a valuable aid to the mental and physical relaxation that a runner and jumper must have."[38]

During the interwar years some African Americans challenged the hypocrisy involved in altering the dialogue concerning athletics achievement, the cultivation of character, and racial progress.[39] The paradox would be seized upon in later years by black activists, Harry Edwards foremost among them, as well as by cultural historians who have studied the relationship of the body to power in modern society. Their considerations delineate the contours of social control and the subtleties of hegemony; they also emphasize the linkages among the categories of "race," gender, and class, especially as they have been deployed in elaborate systems of subordination.[40]

Ultimately, the best means of achieving "racial reconciliation" or overcoming structures of oppression continues to be debated. But statements made by prominent white sports figures in the late 1980s that black athletic achievement does not translate into the "necessities" of leadership suggest how deeply embedded some stereotypes remain in the popular consciousness. Likewise, a recent journalistic venture, which portrays African Americans' success in sport not in terms of cultural values and social practices but as an issue once again requiring "scientific" investigation, offers further cause for concern. It is significant to point out that the vast majority of geneticists and physical anthropologists strongly dispute the biodeterminism that dotes on connections between "race" and athletic accomplishment. It is equally important to note that many historians and sociologists hear, in such assertions, echoes of the racist ideology that attempted to justify slavery and segregation throughout much of the nineteenth and early twentieth centuries. What remains, beyond grim irony, is substantial reason to doubt the efficacy of sport in playing through the formidable prejudices that continue to clutter the social landscape.[41]

Notes

An earlier version of this chapter appeared in *History of Education Quarterly* 35 (Summer 1995): 111–33.

1. *(Howard University) Hilltop,* April 29, 1924.

2. On the African American experience in sports generally, see Edwin B. Henderson, *The Negro in Sports* (Washington, D.C.: Associated Publishers, 1939); Edwin B. Henderson, *The Black Athlete: Emergence and Arrival* (New York: Publishers Co., 1968); Ocania Chalk, *Pioneers of Black Sport: The Early Days of the Black Professional Athlete in Baseball, Basketball, Boxing, and Football* (New York: Dodd, Mead, 1975); Ocania Chalk, *Black College Sport* (New York: Dodd, Mead, 1976); and Arthur Ashe Jr., *A Hard Road to Glory: A History of the African-American Athlete* 3 vols. (New York: Warner Books, 1988). The qualification for boxing is noteworthy. While newspapers extolled the achievements of black boxers, periodicals like the *Crisis,* edited from 1910 to 1933 by W. E. B. Du Bois, opposed prizefighting as an emblem of racial pride and aspiration. On blacks and boxing, see Randy Roberts, *Papa Jack: Jack Johnson and the Era of the Great White Hopes* (New York: Free Press, 1983); and Jeffrey Sammons, *Beyond the Ring: The Role of Boxing in American Society* (Urbana: University of Illinois Press, 1988), 34–53.

3. Concerning black education in the South, the principal works are James Anderson, *The Education of Blacks in the South, 1860–1935* (Chapel Hill: University of North Carolina Press, 1988); and Raymond Wolters, *The New Negro on Campus: Black College Rebellions of the 1920s* (Princeton, N.J.: Princeton University Press, 1975). See also August Meier, *Negro Thought in America, 1880–1915: Racial Ideologies in the Age of Booker T. Washington* (Ann Arbor: University of Michigan Press, 1966). Quote in Edwin B. Henderson, "Sports," *The Messenger* 8 (February 1926): 51. See also David K. Wiggins, *Glory Bound: Black Athletes in a White America* (Syracuse, N.Y.: Syracuse University Press, 1997), 221–40.

4. Samuel H. Archer, "Football in Our Colleges," *Voice of the Negro* 3 (March 1906): 199–205.

5. Wiley College Catalog, 1901, quoted in Michael Heintze, *Private Black Colleges in Texas, 1865–1964* (College Station: Texas A&M University Press, 1985), 171.

6. Edwin B. Henderson, "Few Headliners in Northern Colleges," *The Messenger* 9 (February 1927): 52. On the value of sport, see Edwin B. Henderson, "The Colored College Athlete," *Crisis* 2 (July 1911): 115–19; Ira F. Lewis, "Our Colleges and Athletics," *The Competitor* 2 (December 1920): 290–92; and Robert Vann, "Football as Vehicle," *Pittsburgh Courier*, December 1, 1923.

7. Several of these themes are explored more broadly in Patrick B. Miller, *The Playing Fields of American Culture: Athletics and Higher Education, 1850–1945* (New York: Oxford University Press, forthcoming), chaps. 7 and 8. For a sense of the breakthroughs as well as the setbacks in the desegregation of college sport during these years, see Donald Spivey, "'End Jim Crow in Sports': The Protest at New York University, 1940–1941," *Journal of Sport History* 15 (Winter 1988): 282–303; and Patrick B. Miller, "Harvard and the Color Line: The Case of Lucien Alexis," in *Sports in Massachusetts: Historical Essays*, ed. Ronald Story (Westfield, Mass.: Institute for Massachusetts Studies, 1991), 137–58. For newspaper files on black sports heroes, see Scrapbook Collection, Sports, Schomburg Center for Research in Black Culture, New York, N.Y., and the Tuskegee Institute News Clipping Files, Division of Behavioral Research, Carva Research Foundation, Tuskegee Institute, Ala. See also Jules Tygiel, *Baseball's Great Experiment: Jackie Robinson and His Legacy* (New York: Vintage Books, 1983); William Baker, *Jesse Owens: An American Life* (New York: Oxford University Press, 1986); Martin Duberman, *Paul Robeson* (New York: Alfred A. Knopf, 1988), 19–24; and John M. Carroll, *Fritz Pollard: Pioneer in Racial Advancement* (Urbana: University of Illinois Press, 1992).

8. Arthur Howe, "Two Racers and What They Symbolize," *Southern Workman* 62 (October 1932): 387. See also W. E. B. Du Bois, "Athletics in Negro Colleges" and "Postscript," *Crisis* 37 (June 1930): 209–10; George Streator, "Negro Football Standards," *Crisis* 38 (March 1931): 85–86; George Streator, "Football in Negro Colleges," *Crisis* 39 (April 1932): 129–30, 139–41; and Edwin B. Henderson, "The Negro Athlete and Race Prejudice," *Opportunity* 14 (March 1936): 77–78. For an appraisal of this endeavor, see David K. Wiggins, "Wendell Smith, the *Pittsburgh Courier-Journal*, and the Campaign to Include Blacks in Organized Baseball, 1933–1945," *Journal of Sport History* 10 (Summer 1983): 5–29.

9. William Pickens, letter to the editor, *Voice of the Negro* 2 (August 1905): 560. Pickens went on to become a high-ranking official in the NAACP. See William Pickens, *Bursting Bonds* (formerly *The Heir of Slaves: The Autobiography of a "New Negro"*), ed. William L. Andrews (Bloomington: Indiana University Press, 1991). See also Sheldon Avery, *Up from Washington: William Pickens and the Negro Struggle for Equality, 1900–1954* (Newark: University of Delaware Press, 1989).

10. See Ismael P. Flory, "Walter Arthur Gordon: A Biographical Sketch," *Opportunity* 10 (September 1932): 283–84, 292; Elmer Carter, "The Negro in College Athletics," *Opportunity* 11 (July 1933): 208.

11. Wolters, *New Negro on Campus*, offers the most detailed assessment of academic culture in the 1920s.

12. See Monroe H. Little, "The Extra-Curricular Activities of Black College Students,

1868–1940, *Journal of Negro History* 65 (Spring 1980): 135–48; Randolph Edmonds, "Some Whys and Wherefores of College Dramatics," *Crisis* 37 (March 1930): 92, 105.

13. It was Charles W. Snyder Jr. who wanted "to raise the honor" of his school, in the *Fisk Herald,* January 1893, 5. I am indebted to Beth Howse, Director of Special Collections at Fisk University, for making this and other materials available to me. Little, "Extra-Curricular Activities of Black College Students." For sporting developments, see Henderson, "Colored College Athlete"; and Chalk, *Black College Sport;* as well as institutional histories such as Joe M. Richardson, *A History of Fisk University, 1865–1946* (Tuscaloosa: University of Alabama Press, 1980); Clarence A. Bacote, *The Story of Atlanta University: A Century of Service, 1865–1965* (Atlanta: Atlanta University, 1969); Zella J. Black Patterson, *Langston University: A History* (Norman: University of Oklahoma Press, 1979); and F. A. McGinnis, *A History and an Interpretation of Wilberforce University* (Wilberforce, Ohio: Brown Publishing Co., 1941).

14. See Henderson, *Negro in Sports,* 100; Chalk, *Black College Sport,* 199–200; Heintze, *Private Black Colleges in Texas,* 171; Michael Hurd, *Black College Football, 1892–1992: One Hundred Years of History, Education, and Pride* (Virginia Beach, Va.: Donning Co., 1993), 28; and Ashe, *Hard Road to Glory,* 2:100.

15. See Hurd, *Black College Football,* 153–62; Richardson, *History of Fisk,* 157.

16. Patterson, *Langston University,* 172–75.

17. *Howard University Record* 16 (December 1921): 126. Concerning distinctive halftime activities in more recent years, see Michael Hurd and Stan C. Spence, "Halftime: The Band Be Kickin'!" in Hurd, *Black College Football,* 123–29.

18. *Howard Alumni Sentinel* 6 (February 1923): 13–14. J. R. E. Lee quoted in Leedel W. Neyland, *The History of Florida A&M University* (Gainesville: University of Florida Press, 1963), 127; Standish quoted in Miriam Jones and Joe Richardson, *Talladega College: The First Century* (Tuscaloosa: University of Alabama Press, 1990), 95.

19. On the relation of gender and sport in the black community, see Linda Williams, "An Analysis of American Sportswomen in Two Negro Newspapers: The *Pittsburgh Courier,* 1924–1948, and the *Chicago Defender,* 1932–1948" (Ph.D. dissertation, Ohio State University, 1987); and Susan Cahn, *Coming on Strong: Gender and Sexuality in Twentieth-Century Women's Sport* (New York: Free Press, 1994), 110–39. See also Rita Liberti, "'We Were Ladies, We Just Played Like Boys': African American Women and Competitive Basketball at Bennett College, 1928–42," in this volume; and Pamela Grundy, *Learning to Win: Sports, Education, and Social Change in Twentieth-Century North Carolina* (Chapel Hill: University of North Carolina Press, 2001), chaps. 5 and 8.

20. See *The Competitor* 3 (May 1921): 40; Charles H. Williams, "Twenty Years Work of the C.I.A.A.," *Southern Workman* 61 (February 1932): 65–76; *Norfolk Journal and Guide,* April 16, 1932; Henderson, *Negro in Sports,* 288–301; Chalk, *Black College Sport.*

21. George Streator, "Football in Negro Colleges," 129, 141. The list of the worst offenders included Lincoln (Pa.), Wilberforce, South Carolina State, Allen University, Claflin, and Morris Brown. "Medium, in need of further reform," were Fisk, West Virginia State, Knoxville, and Kentucky State. Streator ranked Hampton, Howard, Morehouse, Wiley, and Tuskegee as good.

22. Ibid.

23. Richardson, *History of Fisk,* 158; Streator, "Negro Football Standards," 85–86; Du

Bois, "Athletics in Negro Colleges," 209. Stevenson, perhaps the greatest black college football player of his era, played for eight seasons in all. See Ashe, *Hard Road to Glory,* 2:101.

24. See, for instance, Upton Sinclair, *The Goose-Step: A Study of American Education* (Pasadena, Calif.: n.p., 1923); and more importantly Bulletin Number Twenty-three of the Carnegie Foundation for the Advancement of Teaching: Howard J. Savage, with Harold W. Bentley, John T. McGovern, and Dean F. Smiley, M.D., *American College Athletics* (New York: Carnegie Foundation for the Advancement of Teaching, 1929). This was an exhaustive, thoroughly documented survey of the athletic practices of more than one hundred (white) institutions of higher education. See also John R. Tunis, *Sports: Heroics and Hysterics* (New York: The John Day Company, 1928); and Reed Harris, *King Football: The Vulgarization of the American College* (New York: Vanguard Press, 1932). Recent appraisals of the issue include Murray Sperber, *College Sports Inc.: The Athletic Department vs. the University* (New York: Henry Holt, 1990); and John R. Thelin, *Games Colleges Play: Scandal and Reform in Intercollegiate Athletics* (Baltimore: Johns Hopkins University Press, 1994), esp. 13–37.

25. Streator, "Negro Football Standards," 85–86, and "Football in Negro Colleges," 129–30.

26. Du Bois, "Athletics in Negro Colleges," 210. Howard had already played football against Cooper Union of New York City and baseball against Columbia University. Louis L. Wilson, "A New Athletic Policy at Howard University," *Howard Alumnus* 3 (January 15, 1925): 60–61.

27. Wolters, *New Negro on Campus,* 29–69; Abigail Jackson to Du Bois, January 20, 1925, cited in Wolters, *New Negro on Campus,* 45; Richardson, *History of Fisk University,* 157–58; Anderson, *Education of Blacks in the South,* 265–70.

28. See *Washington American,* April 25, 1925; and *Chicago Whip,* February 27, 1926. Concerning the next round of debates, see Du Bois, "Athletics in Negro Colleges," 209–10.

29. For Howard under Durkee, see *The Competitor* 1 (January 1920): 10–11; *Crisis* 23 (February 1922): 157, 162; *Howard University Record* 18 (October 1923): 29; and Wolters, *New Negro on Campus,* 70–136. See also Walter Dyson, *Howard University: The Capstone of Negro Education—A History, 1867–1940* (Washington, D.C.: The Graduate School, Howard University, 1941), 396–98; and Rayford Logan, *Howard University: The First One Hundred Years, 1867–1967* (New York: New York University Press, 1969), 187–246. I am indebted to the late Hylan Garland Lewis, a former professor of sociology at Howard, for pointing out (with a certain flourish) the date of the transformation of the University of Maryland.

30. For the Miller case, see Edward P. Davis, "Howard and the C.I.A.A.," *Howard Alumnus* 3 (January 15, 1925): 48–49, 52, 59; *Howard Alumnus* 4 (May 15, 1925): 139–40; and Chalk, *Black College Sport,* 236–37.

31. On Howard in the Johnson years, see Dyson, *Howard University,* 66, 398–401, 433–38; and Logan, *Howard University,* 247–406. Interesting perspectives can be found in Genna Rae McNeil, *Groundwork: Charles Hamilton Houston and the Struggle for Civil Rights* (Philadelphia: University of Pennsylvania Press, 1983); Kenneth R. Manning, *Black Apollo of Science: The Life of Ernest Everett Just* (New York: Oxford University Press, 1983), esp. 208–10; and Kenneth R. Janken, *Rayford W. Logan and the Dilemma of the African-American Intellectual* (Amherst: University of Massachusetts Press, 1993), 202–14. Robert Cohen

nicely captures the many dimensions of Johnson in *When the Old Left Was Young: Student Radicals and America's First Mass Student Movement, 1929–1941* (New York: Oxford University Press, 1993), 219, 395 n.104.

32. On athletic matters, see Wilson, "New Athletic Policy at Howard University," 60–61. On the strikes, see *(Howard University) Hilltop,* October 18, 1927; Chalk, *Black College Sport,* 245–48.

33. Du Bois, "Education and Work," in *The Seventh Son: The Thought and Writings of W. E. B. Du Bois,* ed. Julius Lester. 2 vols. (New York: Random House, 1971), 1:563. See also Edward P. Davis, "The Function of a Board of Athletic Control," *Howard Alumnus* 5 (February 1927): 115.

34. *(Howard University) Hilltop,* November 7 and 14, 1927. See also the clippings, reports, and other materials in Ralph Bunche Papers, box 25, Manuscripts Collection, Schomburg Center for Research in Black Culture, New York, N.Y.

35. *(New York) Amsterdam News* quoted in Chalk, *Black College Sport,* 275–76. See also Edwin B. Henderson, "Sports," *The Messenger* 8 (May 1926): 149, and 8 (August 1926): 247; Henderson, *Negro in Sports,* 356–59.

36. Allison Davis, "The Second Generation: College Athlete," *Crisis* 35 (March 1928): 87.

37. L. W. G. Moore, "College Athletics," *Fisk University Herald,* November 1894.

38. Dean B. Cromwell and Al Wesson, *Championship Techniques in Track and Field* (New York: McGraw-Hill, 1941), 6. See also John McCallum and Robert H. Pearson, *College Football USA, 1869–1973* (Greenwich, Conn.: Hall of Fame Publishers, 1973), 231; and Martin Kane, "An Assessment of Black Is Best," *Sports Illustrated* 18 (January 18, 1971): 72–83. On scientific racism generally, see Stephen Jay Gould, *The Mismeasure of Man* (New York: W. W. Norton, 1981); Kenneth Ludmerer, "American Geneticists and the Eugenic Movement, 1905–1935," *Journal of the History of Biology* 2 (Fall 1969): 337–62; Manning, *Black Apollo of Science,* 49–50; and Elazar Barkan, *The Retreat of Scientific Racism: Changing Concepts of Race in Britain and the United States between the World Wars* (New York: Cambridge University Press, 1992).

39. For criticism of the various explanations among whites that emphasized distinctive anatomical and physiological advantages, see the *Peoria Transcript,* July 9, 1933; Henderson, "Negro Athlete and Race Prejudice," 79; and W. Montague Cobb, "Race and Runners," *Journal of Health and Physical Education* 7 (1936): 3–6. The best historical assessment of the issue is David K. Wiggins, "'Great Speed but Little Stamina': The Historical Debate over Black Athletic Superiority," *Journal of Sport History* 16 (Summer 1989): 158–85. See also Gary Sailes, "The Myth of Black Sports Supremacy," *Journal of Black Studies* 21 (June 1991): 480–87; and Patrick B. Miller, "The Anatomy of Scientific Racism: Racialist Responses to Black Athletic Achievement," *Journal of Sport History* 25 (Spring 1998): 119–51.

40. Harry Edwards, *The Revolt of the Black Athlete* (New York: Free Press, 1969); Harry Edwards, *The Sociology of Sport* (Homewood, Ill.: Dorsey Press, 1973). See also Henry Louis Gates Jr., ed. *"Race," Writing, and Difference* (Chicago: University of Chicago Press, 1986), esp. 185–261; John Hoberman, *Darwin's Athletes: How Sport Has Damaged Black America and Preserved the Myth of Race* (Boston: Houghton Mifflin, 1998); and Miller, "Anatomy of Scientific Racism."

41. Philip Hoose, *Necessities: Racial Barriers in American Sports* (New York: Random House, 1989). In April 1989, NBC News aired a documentary entitled "Black Athletes—Fact and Fiction." For impressive assessments of this program, see Laurel R. Davis, "The Articulation of Difference: White Preoccupation with the Question of Racially Linked Genetic Differences among Athletes," *Sociology of Sport Journal* 7 (1990): 179–87; Hoberman, *Darwin's Athletes,* 204–5. Notwithstanding the criticism of the program, one of the people involved in its production pursued the subject, first on email lists, then in a book. See Jon Entine, *Taboo: Why Black Athletes Dominate Sports and Why We're Afraid to Talk about It* (New York: Public Affairs, 2000). For the relationship of pseudoscience, the racial lore concerning sport, and public affairs, see Miller, "Anatomy of Scientific Racism."

6. "We Were Ladies, We Just Played Like Boys": African American Women and Competitive Basketball at Bennett College, 1928–42

RITA LIBERTI

THROUGH THE efforts of a handful of sport history scholars, in recent years our knowledge and understanding of the collegiate athletic experiences of African American women has grown significantly. Although in its infancy, this scholarship has moved beyond the analytic categories of race and gender to engage the complexities of class, helping to bring about an end to the mythical notion of a monolithic black female sport history. The conclusions drawn in these studies suggest that among elite black colleges and universities the tendency throughout the 1920s and 1930s was to abandon an earlier commitment to women's intercollegiate basketball.[1] School leaders at Howard, Fisk, Morgan, and Hampton believed that women's participation in competitive intercollegiate basketball ran counter to a middle-class feminine ideal grounded in refinement and respectability. Thus, support once given to intercollegiate basketball was channeled to less competitive structures, such as intramurals and play-days, with emphasis placed on activities that were deemed more suitable for female involvement, including badminton, archery, and table tennis.[2]

While some African American schools actively sought to dismantle their female basketball programs through the late 1920s and early 1930s, others were just beginning to invest institutional resources. Reflecting on this rise in involvement, in 1927 the *Chicago Defender* concluded that "women [*sic*] athletics are booming among dixie institutions."[3] To varying degrees, many public and private black colleges and universities across the South participated in women's basketball competition.[4] In Arkansas, for example, the Philander Smith College women's team, after having defeated all of the competition, declared themselves state champions in 1918.[5] Beginning in 1926, the

Georgia–South Carolina Athletic Association, which represented seven schools in the two states, announced that the conference title and trophy was to be awarded to the women's team that played at least seven games with at least four different teams in the schedule.[6] In North Carolina several private black institutions initiated women's intercollegiate basketball teams in the 1920s, including Shaw University, Livingstone College, Barber-Scotia College, Immanuel Lutheran College, and Bennett College in Greensboro.[7] The wide range of institutional support of women's basketball by black colleges and universities reflects a spectrum of responses and attitudes concerning female participation in sport from the 1920s through the 1940s.

The purpose of this essay is to examine more closely the athletic experiences of African American women within a middle-class collegiate setting, specifically Bennett College. Bennett is a fascinating exception to the pattern of elite black colleges discontinuing basketball for women during the 1930s and, as a result, provides a unique location to examine African American women's sport history. My intent is to explore the tension between a middle-class ideology that in part supported traditional conceptualizations of gender relations and the support Bennett gave competitive female athletic participation in basketball. Although there was debate within the black community concerning the appropriateness of female involvement in competitive basketball, Bennett College enthusiastically supported a team, becoming one of the most successful basketball programs in the nation by the mid-1930s.[8] However, by the early years of the 1940s Bennett discontinued intercollegiate basketball and instead focused energy and resources on intramural and play-day events. I argue that this transition not only reflects a middle-class ideology that precluded women's participation in rigorous athletic activity but also illustrates the multiple and often contradictory and shifting roles of black middle-class women during this period.

Black women who enrolled as students and athletes in colleges and universities during this period both challenged and yielded to the boundaries of class, race, and gender arrangements in their community. This ongoing process of negotiation exposes a history shaped by multiple and intersecting identities. The juxtaposition of black women's collegiate athletic experiences with those of black men and white women, for example, provide further evidence of the varied historical experiences that emerge among particular groups in our culture. Patrick B. Miller and Pamela Dean, in their essays on college sport among black men and white women, respectively, help to expose this notion of the myriad of histories that are constructed and shaped by specific historical and cultural contexts. As Miller notes, black male collegiate athletic achievement during the interwar years was promoted as another avenue for blacks to demonstrate their worthiness of inclusion into the dominant culture.[9] Although women's collegiate athletic experiences were generally viewed as acceptable by the black community, their activities in sport were not put forth with the same intensity and enthusiasm. Occasional ambivalent reactions to female athleticism by members of the black community reflected adherence by some to more restrictive notions of gender and the unease surrounding women's involvement in rigorous sport. However, opposition to female participation in athletics was not universal in the black community in part because the lived experiences of women necessitated and exposed a wider range of attitudes.

The view of female physicality in the black community, which did not necessarily preclude being a woman and a participant in competitive sport, translated into different participation patterns for black and white women enrolled in colleges in the South. Although dissimilar with regard to the level of involvement in competitive intercollegiate athletic activities that their respective communities deemed suitable, white and black women who enrolled as students in colleges shared a common bond in their efforts to, at times, challenge existing gender ideologies. Pamela Dean's study of the athletic activities of white women at Sophie Newcomb College and North Carolina Normal and Industrial College illustrates the diversity of women's experiences generated from competing ideals of womanhood. As Dean argues, whether at Newcomb College or at the Normal College, white women constructed athletic activities within the confines and parameters of wider cultural misgivings concerning female participation in physical games.[10] The basketball history at Bennett College reflects a similar negotiation of prescriptive class and gender ideologies.[11]

The Methodist Episcopal church founded Bennett College in 1873 as a coeducational institution for African Americans. The college's initial mission was to train men for the ministry and women as teachers to help meet the enormous need to educate newly freed blacks. In 1926 the Woman's Home Missionary Society of the Methodist Episcopal church decided to refocus the direction of the school from a coeducational to a women's college, with the emphasis on teacher training remaining in the forefront.[12] Writing in 1928, Carol Cotter provides an early account of the philosophy of Bennett College: "If Americans of African descent are ever to step upon their rightful platform in the destiny of nations it must be at least partially through the efforts of the sisters to our men."[13] From its inception, Bennett College served as an important avenue for black women to be active participants in the struggle for racial equality and justice.

Under the leadership of the college president, Dr. David Jones, the enrollment of the newly reorganized Bennett quickly rose from ten women in 1926 to 138 by 1930.[14] The growth of basketball at Bennett seemed to parallel the general development of the college, with intercollegiate athletic contests beginning during the 1928–29 academic year.[15] In addition to giving early support to intercollegiate basketball, Bennett also appeared committed to the general health and physical well-being of all of its students, requiring them to take two years of physical education. The 1929–30 college catalog reassured those interested that "there is ample space for skating, tennis, basketball, hockey and all the games that delight a robust, growing girlhood."[16] By 1930, the position of physical education and intercollegiate basketball seemed fairly well established and aligned with the overall educational direction of the college.

The support that college officials at Bennett provided to its basketball program and other extracurricular activities reflected the broader aims of the college, which were to "provide its students with opportunities for the development of self-expression, leadership, and skill along individual lines of interest."[17] Bennett students from the 1930s recall the encouragement that Jones and other college faculty gave to the basketball program. Ruth Glover, a star Bennett forward from 1934 to 1937, remembers that Jones was in attendance at all home games and "was right there on the sidelines rooting!"

The Bennett College team circa 1933. (Greensboro Historical Museum)

The Bennett College team in 1934. (Greensboro Historical Museum)

The Bennett women are standing on a diagonal in a row from shortest to tallest player.
(Mrs. Ruth Glover Mullen)

Her teammate, Amaleta Moore, adds that for away contests Jones offered his vehicle and driver to transport the basketball squad. When describing attitudes toward basketball across the entire Bennett College community during the mid-1930s, Glover says that "the spirit was on the campus."[18] Frances Jones, a Bennett student and the daughter of President Jones, explains that basketball served as the centerpiece for campus activity, in part because African Americans had such limited access to other forms of recreation and leisure activities in the segregated South. In addition, Frances Jones fondly recalls that "we all loved our basketball" and that the popularity of the game at Bennett was due, in part, to the fact that "we beat everybody," making attendance that much more enjoyable.[19]

As Bennett president, David Jones was well aware of the obstacles that black women encountered, and he worked to create an environment at the college that would prepare students to enter the world and be full participants in it. According to Jones, the "role of Negro women in the past has been a heroic one as mother, teacher, and civic leader. The responsibilities of the educated Negro woman of the future will be no less burdensome or challenging."[20] Understanding the significance of sexism and its implications within higher education for women, Jones stated that "the struggle of women to achieve status in the American economy has been a long and sometimes discouraging and baffling effort. The idea that the woman's place is in the home is so deep-rooted, and the resistance of men to female competition so keen that the achievements of women in politics, in economics, in science have been won oft-times only because of superior qualifications and because of compensatory effort on the part of the so-called weaker sex."[21]

Under Jones's leadership the educational mission of Bennett was to train women on a number of different levels and in a wide range of settings to bring about the most effective positive change for the entire race. The 1929–30 college catalog makes clear Bennett's broad educational goals by stating that "attention should be given to matters relating to the refinements of family and community life . . . also that the most vigorous standards of scholarship should be maintained in all subjects of the curriculum."[22] Emphasis on academic rigor, civic responsibility, and homemaking best characterized the elements of a Bennett College education during this period. The components of this strategy were not meant as competing ideals but were viewed in totality as the best means to effect social change.

Bennett sought to uphold middle-class standards of refinement and respectability among its students in part to counter lingering stereotypes of African Americans as immoral and uncivilized. Although efforts to "uplift" the entire race rested upon middle- and upper-class African Americans, as "keepers of social standards . . . and guardians of spiritual values" black college women in particular were considered conveyers of character and culture.[23] The historian Stephanie Shaw notes that many educated blacks believed that upstanding behavior by black college women reflected positively not only on the individual woman but also on the entire black community. College personnel carefully molded and monitored students' behavior, deeming actions seen as unbecoming for a "lady" inappropriate and discouraging them.[24] For students at Bennett, including Ruth Glover, being a lady meant, for one thing, dressing the part, with a clear understanding that the dress code had much more serious implications than fashion. Glover explains: "Oh, you didn't go shoppin' or uptown . . . without your hat and gloves. You had to be dressed like you were goin' to a formal affair . . . *we could get respect you see.*"[25]

Moreover, white assaults on the black community were often centered on the notion that African American women contributed to moral degradation with unkempt and uncivilized homes. As a result, emphasis on homemaking became a core element in the educational process at many black colleges and universities, including Bennett College. Beginning in 1927 the "Homemaking Institute" became an annual meeting at Bennett College, with conference presentations and discussions focused on improving the home and family relations.[26] In addition, Bennett required each student to satisfactorily complete a course entitled "The Art of Right Living," which aimed, among other things, to "help students find and solve their own problems in relation to personal hygiene, food and nutrition, clothing, family and community relationships."[27] Former Bennett students with whom I have spoken recognize the practical importance of their exposure to homemaking skills and responsibilities. However, they also were clearly provided with the tools to move beyond the home and pursue leadership and professional roles in the community after graduation. Amaleta Moore notes that throughout the 1930s the basic premise of a college education for black women was "that you were training for a given profession, to go and contribute to the community where you lived."[28]

Not only did their academic preparation equip Bennett women with the skills to enhance the lives of others in the black community, basketball presented another way in which these women could give something back to those around them. After graduating from Bennett, all of the basketball players of the 1930s that I interviewed assumed careers as teachers and basketball coaches on the elementary and high school level.[29] Graduating with a degree in French from Bennett in 1934, star center Lucille Townsend recalls that the principal at the black elementary school in Pinehurst, North Carolina, asked if she would consider teaching the fourth grade primarily because the district needed a girls' basketball coach.[30]

With an educational philosophy similar to that of many black colleges and universities throughout the late nineteenth and early twentieth centuries, Bennett College consistently underscored the notion of the relationship between college-educated blacks and the community. Writing in 1937, James T. Morton Jr., who served on the faculty at Bennett, argued that "whether we are inclined to agree with W. E. B. Du Bois in all of his details concerning the solving value of the TALENTED TENTH, we must admit that among our group, leadership should come from the trained and aggressive."[31] Bennett administrators and faculty strove to ensure that the school was "far from being an ivory tower, or the traditional combination of finishing school and blue-stocking factory," and they supported student initiative to take academic learning beyond the classroom to assist in the development of racial pride and justice.[32] The historian Glenda Gilmore argues that black women who were graduates of North Carolina colleges in the early twentieth century took with them "more than just a finite body of knowledge or set of skills"; rather they were "armed with a full quiver of intellectual weapons to aim at . . . discrimination."[33]

The 1937–38 protest and boycott of the downtown movie theaters in Greensboro, led by the Bennett first-year student Frances Jones, reflected an educational structure and philosophy that instilled civic duty and responsibility. When students learned that white theater owners in North and South Carolina refused to show films in which "Negro and white actors appear[ed] on an equal social basis," as opposed to stereotyped depictions of blacks, they organized a campaign by members of the black community to boycott the movie establishments. After months of picketing, their efforts were successful, leading the *Carolina Times* to conclude that "the step taken by the students in the two Negro schools in Greensboro shows more courage on the part of Negro youth than we have any record of anywhere else in the south." Within the context of the Jim Crow South, the paper added that the bold actions by the college students would lead America into a "new day."[34] Frances Jones recalls that the success of the boycott was significant because it symbolized the fact that segregation was no longer considered an impenetrable "solid wall" incapable of being eradicated. Although Jones was fully aware of the potential harm that could have been perpetrated against her, she notes that there was "no room for fear." Several years after the boycott Jones learned that her father, the president of Bennett College, had been "visited by the Federal Bureau of Investigation and other government agencies" who "tried to force him to get us to stop."[35] Frances Jones remembers that her father's continued support of the students throughout the protest was an example of the fact that he demanded excellence in all of his students and encouraged their participation in various activities that fostered pride and self-respect.

Interestingly, while Bennett officials created an environment that supported acts of civil disobedience in protest of racial injustice, they continually demanded that students exhibit behaviors that maintained a level of dignity. In an effort to instill ideals such as good manners, proper conduct, and self-control, college officials at Bennett and other black schools enforced strict rules and rigid codes of behavior for all students, especially women. Bennett freshmen were given the Greensboro bus and train schedules their first day on campus and told by president Jones that they would be leaving the same day via one of those routes if they broke the rules. Bennett women were rarely given the opportunity to leave campus unless on officially sanctioned business, in which case a chaperone accompanied them.[36] Participation in basketball provided student athletes with a degree of autonomy not typical of many of their peers. Travel to away basketball contests presented such a rare and special occasion to leave campus that it led some of the Bennett players to resist and ultimately bend the rules. Amaleta Moore recalls that she and her teammates risked punishment by "sneaking the team mascot out of the dormitory" so that she too could travel with the team. Practice sessions were also considered an opportunity to escape the regulations the general student body had to follow. Basketball practice for Bennett began after study hour each evening and lasted from 9:00 P.M. to 11:00 P.M. As the other students returned to the dormitory from the library, athletes made their way to the gym. Moore acknowledges that practice sessions "were a privilege because we could get out of the dormitory that time of night."[37]

Bennett faculty and administrative staff may have extended the higher level of personal freedom to basketball players because they were committed to the notion that physical development on the basketball court or in a physical education class reinforced their efforts to impart conduct becoming a "lady." This is suggested in college literature that promoted the physical education program by asserting that the activities "involve total body control as they take place under conditions requiring physical exertion, intellectual accuracy and emotional control simultaneously."[38] Having the chance to travel across the roads of North Carolina was sometimes used by players as a way to mock a segregated South, turning racism on its head, if only for a brief moment. Moore remembers that "we would be riding along the highway and you'd meet some white fellas thumbing . . . and we'd hang our heads out the window and say, 'Jim Crow car!'"[39]

The moral standards Bennett women were trained to practice and possess off the basketball court occasionally contrasted with opponents' ideas concerning respectable actions and appropriate behavior. Such was the case when Bennett, after a very successful 1934 season, competed in a three-game series against the *Philadelphia Tribune* team. The contests even attracted the white press, which ordinarily gave little attention to events in the black community.[40] Press reports indicate that over one thousand spectators attended the initial game of the series, reflecting the enormous interest in women's basketball in the community.[41] The *Greensboro Daily News* prefaced the upcoming series: "After having met and defeated in rapid succession all of the college teams that would accept to play, the undefeated Bennett College team, seeking larger worlds to conquer, will risk its reputation against Otto Briggs' Tribune female team. . . . The Tribune girls, led by the indomitable, internally famed and stellar performer, Ora Washington, national women's singles champ in tennis, comes with an enviable reputation."[42]

The *Tribune* team was housed on the Bennett College campus during the series, and Lucille Townsend remembers their arrival, particularly her first impression of Ora Washington. "She [Washington] looked like the worst ruffian you ever wanted to see. She looked like she'd been out pickin' cotton all day, shavin' hogs, and everything else."[43] Washington's rugged appearance stood in opposition to the feminine ideals that Townsend and other black college educated women were trained to regard as "earmarks of a lady," which included "always being well-groomed, appropriately dressed, scrupulously clean in body and attire with hair carefully arranged."[44]

Townsend recalls that the first game of the series was played in downtown Greensboro at the sports arena, and "ordinarily colored didn't play there . . . it was the largest place we had ever played and I was scared."[45] She remembers that the game was replete with thrills on and off the court. In many ways the game did not resemble the type the Bennett players were accustomed to participating in and was thus both exciting and unsettling. Townsend explains: "They [the *Tribune* team] changed uniforms, they had red and white uniforms one half, and gold and purple the next half, and socks to match!" The game itself was also a departure from the Bennett team's encounters with high school and college opponents. Although Townsend had played in a number of games throughout her career that she considered physical contests, none compared to the match-up against Ora Washington and the *Tribune* team. She recalls, "I told the referee she's [Ora's] hittin' me in the stomach every time I jump . . . he caught her when she hit me one time . . . I doubled over and went down."[46]

Off-court actions by some members of the *Tribune* team provide important evidence of the diverse notions of womanhood and respectable behavior within the black community during this period. Townsend recalls the events that took place while sharing the locker room with the opposing team during halftime. "We went to the locker room, and that's when them girls pulled out little half pint jars, they had corn liquor in it." She continues, "now all of them didn't have it . . . two or three of them didn't. But the rest of them would take two or three big swigs and set it down somewhere over there and go right on out and play!"[47]

The series between Bennett College and the *Philadelphia Tribune* team not only illustrates the popularity of women's basketball but also highlights the tensions, ambiguities, and divisions within the black community along class and gender lines during this period. Like other black college women, Bennett students were taught to always present themselves in a refined and dignified manner. Reflecting on the actions by Ora Washington and the *Tribune* team, both on and off the basketball court, Lucille Townsend draws a clear line of distinction between herself and the members of the Philadelphia squad. In assessing the series and the *Tribune* team, she concludes that "they were a different class of people."[48]

Although Bennett lost the three games against the *Philadelphia Tribune* team, the 1934 and 1935 seasons were extremely successful for the Bennett cagers, with twenty-four victories and no defeats versus college, high school, and community teams.[49] Ruth Glover explains Bennett College's basketball dominance through the mid 1930s: "We used to practice against a group of high school boys . . . Dudley High School . . . they scrimmaged us. They would come down and teach us the tricks of the trade . . . you know, how to take that ball in like that [demonstrates a one-handed shot]. That's where we learned . . . a lot of that type of getting over that floor."[50]

Beyond the basketball court, interaction between the sexes was viewed by some within the black community as unladylike and was thus discouraged. In this instance, however, whatever conflict, if any, was present in the minds of Bennett personnel was surpassed by the desire to elevate the level of play of the women's basketball program by practicing against local high school boys.

By the 1934 *Tribune* series, basketball was an extremely popular activity at Bennett, despite the continuing and growing ambivalence within the black community over the suitability of the competitive game for girls and women. The National Association of College Women (NACW) was one group that spoke out strongly against intercollegiate competition for black women. Founded in 1910 by Mary Church Terrell as the College Alumnae Club, the NACW expanded to a national organization in 1923, and over the next three decades it did more than any other association to advance the position of black women as students and professionals within higher education.[51] Under the auspices of the NACW, a conference composed of deans and advisors to women in black colleges and universities was held at Howard University in 1929. The conference participants met to consider major problems in connection with the education of black women. The position of intercollegiate athletics for women was the central focus of one of four issues that it tackled at the 1929 meeting. The *NACW Journal* summarized the position of the women in attendance: "Inter-collegiate athletics should not be encouraged with all their undesirable physiological and sociological features. Inter-class and intra-class games serve every good purpose of the inter-collegiate games, and avoid all the harmful effects."[52]

In October 1940, the NACW restated their position with regard to women's sport in the following recommendation: "That the Association go forward with a proposal made in 1938 to the effect that we use our efforts as an organization to eliminate from our schools intercollegiate athletics for women, urging the substitution of intramural contests and intercollegiate non-competitive play activities."[53] Similarly, Maryrose Reeves Allen, the director of the physical education program for women at Howard University during this period, deemed activities such as dance, light games, archery, and badminton appropriate physical activities in which women should be encouraged to engage. While basketball is not mentioned explicitly, Allen makes a distinction by disapproving of certain activities. In 1938 she wrote that "the heavier sports . . . have no place in a woman's life: they rob her of her feminine charms and often of her good health."[54]

The tension between femininity and athleticism is no more clearly illustrated than in the writings of Ivora (Ike) King, the sports columnist for the *Baltimore Afro-American,* who argued that "the girl who is too athletic is on the wrong track to becoming a wife. Men want feminine women, not creatures who are half like themselves and the other half resembling something else. It is only natural and logical because we loathe men who act effeminate and desire a man, all man. Men want women all women . . . being too athletic and consequently too mannish, prevents her from being [so]."[55] Heterosexual appeal rested firmly on a woman's ability to remain within the confines of particular gender arrangements. For King, denying femininity to the athletic woman threatened to corrupt her gendered and sexual identities and in doing so forfeited her existence as a real woman.

To Bennett women, however, a feminine ideal of black womanhood and participation in competitive athletics remained negotiable. The Bennett teammates Amaleta Moore and Ruth Glover clearly felt this way. Moore recollected that Bennett never competed against women from neighboring white schools during the mid-1930s, noting that "they were little southern ladies, that was too rough for them." But as Glover's words show, this did not mean that the Bennett women felt they compromised their respectability or womanliness by playing basketball: "We were ladies too, we just played basketball like boys."[56] Her classmate Almira Henry underscores and clarifies the notion that being athletic and female was not a contradiction for Bennett women. "Being a lady does not mean being prissy, it's just an inward culture . . . always being polite and not saying things to hurt people's feelings. You could be tough as I don't know what on that basketball court, but you still have those same principles."[57] For these women and the institution that supported their involvement in intercollegiate basketball in the 1930s, the notion that being female and athletic was dichotomous remained a falsehood. As I have briefly illustrated here, there was a wide range of responses among members of the black community to women's participation in athletics, and this reflects the multiple roles and expectations of African American women, especially those who were in the middle class or who aspired to middle-class status.

Thus, while some within the black community opposed all basketball competition for girls and women, others encouraged the sport but sought to place limitations on the style of play, preferring girls' rules or six-player basketball versus five-member teams.[58] Throughout the 1920s and 1930s the debate among members of the black community over the suitability of five- or six-player basketball competition for girls and women was played out on several occasions in the black press. Proponents of games played under girls' rules argued that five-player basketball was too rough for women and that "girls always look inadequate and butter-fingered under boy's [*sic*] rules."[59] J. H. N. Waring Jr., the principal and girls' basketball coach at Downington Industrial and Agricultural School in Pennsylvania, strongly opposed female participation in five-player basketball. Like other critics, Waring argued that the five-player game was too strenuous and did not bring out "the finer qualities in girls."[60] Furthermore, according to Waring, female basketball contests played under five-player rules did not draw spectators because the limited physical capabilities of girls and women resulted in slow and unexciting play. He also insisted that games were "disgusting to athletic fans who do not enjoy seeing young school girls pulling and tugging and roughing each other like so many alley cats."[61] Waring opposed female involvement in five-player basketball because he feared for the physical well-being of the athletes who competed, but also because such participation disturbed his own sensibilities concerning appropriate behavior for girls and women.

Others directly opposed Waring's vision of womanhood and the resulting restrictive impact on female physicality, illustrating the wide spectrum

of attitudes concerning girls' and women's participation in five-player basketball. A former basketball player and current coach argued in a letter to the
Baltimore Afro-American in 1930 that "Girls of today are red-blooded, virile
young creatures, and are no longer content to conform to the masculine ideal
of feminine inferiority and frailty. The clinging vine has given way to the
freely moving, sensibly clad young Amazon of today. Such fineness of physique cannot be maintained or secured through the inadequacies of girls'
rules in basketball."[62] The correspondent's conceptualization of femininity
and womanhood was in contrast to that presented by Waring, indicating that
there was a divergent and wide range of opinions among members of the
black community concerning the compatibility of being female and engag-
ing in a rigorous athletic activity, such as five-player basketball. These oppo-
sitional views of the five-player basketball issue reflect the tensions and negotiations of the boundaries of black womanhood that were ongoing during
the 1920s and 1930s.

Despite the wide range of opinions concerning the appropriateness of five-
player basketball, girls' rules began to influence college play in North Carolina, including Bennett and other colleges in the state. By 1936 North Carolina colleges and universities reconsidered their earlier devotion to five-player
basketball and began to compete using six-player rules. The move away from
five-player basketball "hampered the style of quite a number of the old varsity members" on Bennett's team, but they still claimed a share of the state
title with Shaw University, making it their fourth championship of the decade.[63] Following an undefeated 1937 season, one of the nation's most popular black newspapers, the *Chicago Defender,* dubbed Bennett "the nation's
best female cage team"; but this would be the last state championship that
Bennett would win.[64]

Not only were basketball rules in a state of transition at Bennett College
by the latter half of the 1930s, direction and control of the sport was also in
flux. Throughout the 1920s and 1930s black physical educators and others
interested in female participation in sport debated the issue of men coaching women's athletics, and some supported the notion that women should
organize and direct female involvement in sport and physical activity.[65] Although female physical educators were on staff from the inception of Bennett as a women's college in 1926, male coaches directed the basketball team
for many of the years between 1928 and 1938.[66] Similarly, as at other black
colleges in North Carolina, female chaperones accompanied the women's
basketball teams, but in most instances male faculty members assumed the
coaching duties.[67] By the late 1930s this pattern of male coaching dominance
began to change somewhat. In 1938 the female physical education instruc-

tor Mildred Burris became only the second female coach at Bennett in ten years of basketball competition.[68]

Though Bennett continued to support intercollegiate basketball through the 1941 season, by the late 1930s its athletic interests appeared to be headed in another direction. In 1939 the college became the first of four black North Carolina schools to join the Women's Sports Day Association (WSDA). The WSDA was founded in 1938 by female physical education leaders at Virginia State and Hampton and Maryrose Reeves Allen at Howard University. The goals of the association clearly promoted the personal philosophy of Allen, endorsing a structure that was noncompetitive and activities that "develop in women the qualities of beauty of movement, poise, femininity by affording each individual who participates an opportunity to play in an atmosphere of dignity, courtesy, and refinement."[69] The WSDA promoted a class-bound ideal of womanhood grounded in female frailty, and its influence was reflected in the activities pursued on the Bennett campus. In November 1940 Bennett served as "hostess" to the handful of other colleges in the association, including Howard University, Virginia State University, Hampton University, and North Carolina Agricultural and Technical (A&T) College, at the first of two Sports Days. Each school sent twenty-five women who were then divided among the other participants into teams so that "group sportsmanship among the colleges [was] emphasized."[70] This was a significant shift for Bennett from intercollegiate basketball, which emphasized competition, travel, and winning, to the intramurals and play-days of the WSDA. By 1942 the shift was complete, and Bennett withdrew its support of women's intercollegiate basketball.[71]

I found no evidence to suggest who initiated the changes from intercollegiate basketball to play-day events at Bennett. However, given the promotion of play-days by the WSDA and the continued anticompetition rhetoric put forth by the NACW, it is highly likely that intercollegiate basketball for women at black colleges in North Carolina, including Bennett, came under increasingly heavy scrutiny. By 1937, for example, under the auspices of the NACW, seven colleges in North Carolina, including Bennett, sent representatives to the eighth annual conference of the Deans and Advisors to Girls and Women in Colored Schools, more than in any previous year.[72]

On the state level, Bennett was not alone in its increased focus on play-days versus intercollegiate basketball competition for women.[73] The director of physical education for women at North Carolina College during the first half of the 1940s, Vivian Merrick, recalls a successful intramural and play-day structure at the college. When asked to speculate on possible reasons for the demise of women's intercollegiate basketball during the 1940s, Merrick suggests that the war crisis combined with the belief among some in the black community that "our [women's] physical make-up" was not suited for the rigors of basketball competition.[74] Interestingly, while World War II did have enormous impact on college athletic programs, North Carolina officials worked to sustain men's basketball teams. In fact, men's basketball at several colleges in North Carolina not only continued but flourished, with teams playing extensive schedules and traveling to compete against out-of-state opponents.[75] The same pattern cannot be seen for women enrolled as students at North Carolina black colleges and universities, as they found increasingly limited opportunities to compete in basketball through the 1940s.

The historian Cindy Himes-Gissendanner notes that nearly a decade before Bennett's reorganization away from intercollegiate play several black colleges in the early 1930s dismantled competitive women's basketball on their campuses and promoted activities that placed less emphasis on athletics. Himes-Gissendanner argues that this movement away from competitive sport reflects ambivalence among some college officials, especially those at elite black schools, concerning the suitability of women's continued involvement in rigorous athletic activity. While I contend that Himes-Gissendanner's conclusions have merit, the Bennett basketball history through the 1930s problematizes her thesis somewhat and forces scholars to recognize the complexities of an ongoing negotiation of boundaries surrounding female physicality in the African American community.[76]

This transition to less competitive activities during the early 1940s on the campus of Bennett College signaled the end to a brief yet illuminating period in the history of African American women's sport. The tensions surrounding female athleticism on the Bennett campus and in the larger black community reflect diverse responses to and attitudes concerning women's involvement in sports such as competitive basketball and provide scholars with insights into the ways in which class informs race and gender identity. From the late 1920s through the 1930s Bennett's administration, faculty, and student athletes balanced and negotiated various understandings of class, race, and gender arrangements as they supported competitive women's basketball.

In a more general sense, Bennett personnel articulated a position that illustrated the societal tensions that informed their efforts to forge their identity as a black women's college. In a presentation to the NACW in 1937, the Bennett faculty member Merze Tate argued that "The presidents of women's colleges are not endeavoring to turn out an army of masculine counterparts. Neither in the light of rapid historical progress and a sense of humor is there any longer a need to turn out an army of feminists."[77] Tate's interest in sculpting the public perception of Bennett as an institution for women that did not "masculinize" them may have been in response to fears among some in the wider African American community that college-educated black women disrupted gender norms and might make unsuitable marriage companions to men.[78] Aware of societal gender restrictions, Bennett College officials balanced those tensions while challenging assumptions in educating black women, as Tate's further comments make clear: "In the light of present-day thought and experiments, does the challenge of responsibility for the home involve women alone. Between the ultra-feminism of women's rights forever, and the ultra-feminists in the idea of women always to serve the men, to produce the race, and to keep the home, is the stimulating vision of women making their fullest contribution to life, whether in the home, in other service, or in both fields of activity."[79] The particular conceptualization of womanhood constructed by some middle-class blacks, including those at Bennett, simultaneously endorsed and rejected aspects of middle-class femininity. The complexity of that continual process of cultural construction is symbolized in women's basketball, the history of which evolved and changed over the course of a decade and a half, much like the fluid notion of what it meant to be black, female, and middle-class during this period. These multiple identities at times merged and blended and in other instances were contradictory forces, exposing a history that cannot be categorized as static or fixed but is rather dynamic and shifting. Bennett College basketball from the late 1920s to the early 1940s illustrates the tensions between individual agents creating their own histories and societal expectations and constraints.

Notes

An earlier version of this chapter appeared in *Journal of Sport History* 26 (Fall 1999): 567–84.

1. Martha H. Verbrugge, "The Institutional Politics of Women's Sports in American Colleges, 1920–1940," paper presented at the North American Society for Sport History, Auburn, Ala., May 1996; Cindy Himes-Gissendanner, "African-American Women and Competitive Sport, 1920–1960," in *Women, Sport, and Culture*, ed. Susan Birrell and Cheryl Cole (Champaign, Ill.: Human Kinetics, 1994), 81–92. Susan Cahn's discussion of ideals surrounding black womanhood concludes with the assertion that "it is not clear whether wealthier African Americans approved of women's involvement in sports like basketball." Susan Cahn, *Coming on Strong: Gender and Sexuality in Twentieth-Century Women's Sport* (New York: Free Press, 1994), 312.

2. Verbrugge, "Institutional Politics of Women's Sports in American Colleges," and Himes-Gissendanner, "African-American Women and Competitive Sport," suggest this transition to less competitive athletic structures. For the athletic philosophy at Hampton Institute, see Elizabeth Dunham, "Physical Education of Women at Hampton Institute," *Southern Workman* 53 (April 1924): 161–68. At Morgan College in Baltimore women's

basketball seemed popular, frequently filling the sports pages of the *Baltimore Afro-American* from 1921 to the early 1930s. Apparently, by 1933 intercollegiate basketball for women at Morgan had ceased. See Olga H. Bowers, "Just between Sportswomen," *Baltimore Afro-American,* February 18, 1933, 16. At Howard University competitive basketball was frowned upon, due at least in part to the philosophy of the chairperson of the physical education department, Maryrose Reeves Allen. See Maryrose Reeves Allen, "The Development of Beauty in College Women through Health and Physical Education" (Master's thesis, Boston University, 1938). Significantly, female students at Howard were permitted to compete in an exhibition badminton tournament with women from Swarthmore College, a white school located within a day's distance. The suitability of the game of badminton—a noncontact sport—as opposed to basketball is apparently the reason for this interaction. See "H.U. Badminton Team to Meet Swarthmore," *Baltimore Afro-American,* March 18, 1939, 23; and "H.U. Badminton Team Leaders Selected," *Baltimore Afro-American,* March 25, 1939, 21.

3. "Dixie Doings," *Chicago Defender,* February 12, 1927, 8.

4. This conclusion is based on an examination of the *Baltimore Afro-American, Chicago Defender, Atlanta Daily World, Pittsburgh Courier,* and *Carolina Times.*

5. "Philander Smith Wins Championship," *Chicago Defender,* April 9, 1921, 11.

6. "Pinson Re-Elected Head of Ga.-Carolina Athletic Assn.," *Chicago Defender,* February 13, 1926, 11.

7. Rita Liberti, "'We Were Ladies, We Just Played Basketball Like Boys': A Study of Women's Basketball at Historically Black Colleges and Universities in North Carolina, 1925–1945" (Ph.D. dissertation, University of Iowa, 1998).

8. Newspaper accounts of women's basketball competition in the black press suggest that Bennett had one of the most successful basketball programs in the mid-1930s. See, for example, "Shaw University Girls Hand Bennett Sextette First Defeat in Three Years," *Norfolk Journal and Guide,* March 28, 1936, 14; and "Nobody Has Licked Them for Two Years," *Baltimore Afro-American,* April 13, 1935, 21. Tillotson College for Women in Austin, Texas, also had a very successful team during the mid-1930s. See "Tillotson Wins Texas Tournament," *Chicago Defender,* March 24, 1934, 16; and "Tillotson Five Tops May Allen," *Chicago Defender,* March 16, 1935, 16.

9. Patrick B. Miller, "'To Bring the Race Along Rapidly': Sport, Student Culture, and Educational Mission at Historically Black Colleges during the Interwar Years," in this volume.

10. Pamela Dean, "'Dear Sisters' and 'Hated Rivals': Athletics and Gender at Two New South Women's Colleges, 1893–1920," in this volume.

11. I include the work of Miller and Dean because each serves as an example of the range of histories that emerge given race, class, and gender considerations during the early to middle decades of the twentieth century. However, a detailed discussion of the collegiate athletic experiences of African American men and white women during the first few decades of the twentieth century is beyond the scope of this essay. Moreover, I contend that a compare/contrast model serves to marginalize the experiences of African American women by perpetuating normative standards as male and white. See Elsa Barkley Brown, "'What Has Happened Here': The Politics of Difference in Women's History and Feminist Politics," in *"We Specialize in the Wholly Impossible": A Reader in Black Women's His-*

tory, ed. Darlene Clark Hine, Wilma King, and Linda Reed (Brooklyn, N.Y.: Carlson, 1995), 39–54; and Patricia Hill Collins, *Black Feminist Thought: Knowledge, Consciousness, and the Politics of Empowerment* (New York: Routledge, 1990), xii–xiii.

12. Beverly Guy-Sheftall, "Black Women and Higher Education: Spelman and Bennett Colleges Revisited," *Journal of Negro Education* 51 (1982): 278–87; Barbara Solomon, *In the Company of Educated Women* (New Haven, Conn.: Yale University Press, 1985), 152–53, 168, 179; Hugh Victor Brown, *A History of the Education of Negroes in North Carolina* (Raleigh, N.C.: Irving Swain Press, 1961), 73–76; Willa Player, "Improving College Education for Women at Bennett College: A Report of a Type A Project" (Ed.D dissertation, Columbia Teachers College, 1948). For an early account of Bennett College before it became a women's college in 1926, see Jay S. Stowell, *Methodist Adventures in Negro Education* (New York: Methodist Book Concern, 1922).

13. Carol Cotter, "Bennett College: An Opportunity for Negro Womanhood," *Opportunity* 6 (May 1928): 145.

14. Bennnet College for Women, catalog, 1929–30, p. 12, in Miscellaneous Box, Bennett College Archives, Greensboro, N.C. Bennett players testified to the enormous support that Jones gave to them as student athletes and to the basketball program. Author's interviews: Edythe Robinson Tweedy (Rocky Mount, N.C.), August 10, 1995; Lucille Townsend (Richmond, Va.), August 6, 1995; Clarice Gamble Herbert (Philadelphia, Pa.), July 31, 1995; Amaleta Moore and Ruth Glover Mullen (West Cape May, N.J.), July 30, 1995.

15. *Baltimore Afro-American,* February 23, 1929, 10, January 18, 1930, 14, and February 15, 1930, 14. By the early 1930s several other colleges and universities in North Carolina began playing basketball, including North Carolina Agricultural and Technical College, Shaw University, Livingstone College, Fayetteville State Normal, North Carolina College, and Lutheran College. On the development of high school basketball among North Carolina black schools, see Charles H. Thompson, "The History of the National Basketball Tournaments for Black High Schools" (Ph.D. dissertation, Louisiana State University, 1980).

16. Bennett College for Women, catalog, 1929–30, p. 17, in Miscellaneous Box, Bennett College Archives, Greensboro, N.C.

17. Velma B. Hamilton, "An Adventure in Women's Education," *Journal of the National Association of College Women* 13 (1935): 32.

18. Moore and Mullen interviews.

19. Author's interview with Frances Jones Bonner (Newton Centre, Mass.), February 1, 1998.

20. David D. Jones, "The War and the Higher Education of Negro Women," *Journal of Negro Education* 11 (July 1942): 337.

21. Ibid., 329.

22. Bennett College for Women, catalog, 1929–30, p. 12, in Miscellaneous Box, Bennett College Archives, Greensboro, N.C.

23. Florence M. Read, "The Place of the Women's College in the Pattern of Negro Education," *Opportunity* 15 (September 1937): 268. For further discussion of the dissemination of middle-class values among college students of this period, see James D. Anderson, *The Education of Blacks in the South, 1860–1935* (Chapel Hill: University of North Carolina Press, 1988); Raymond Wolters, *The New Negro on Campus: Black College Rebellions of the 1920s* (Princeton, N.J.: Princeton University Press, 1975); Kevin K. Gaines,

Uplifting the Race: Black Leadership, Politics, and Culture in the Twentieth Century (Chapel Hill: University of North Carolina Press, 1996); Linda M. Perkins, "The Impact of the 'Cult of True Womanhood' on the Education of Black Women," *Journal of Social Issues* 39 (1983): 17–28; and Evelyn Brooks Higginbotham, *Righteous Discontent: The Women's Movement in the Black Baptist Church, 1880–1920* (Cambridge, Mass.: Harvard University Press, 1993).

24. Higginbotham, *Righteous Discontent*, 19–46; Stephanie Shaw, *What a Woman Ought to Be and to Do: Black Professional Women Workers during the Jim Crow Era* (Chicago: University of Chicago Press, 1996), 80–90.

25. Mullen interview.

26. Flemmie P. Kittrell, "Home Economics at Bennett College for Women," *Southern Workman* 60 (1931): 381–84; "Homemaking Institute at Bennett College, March 17–25," *Carolina Times*, March 15, 1941, 3.

27. Constance H. Marteena, "A College for Girls," *Opportunity* 16 (October 1938): 307.

28. Moore interview.

29. Moore, Mullen, Townsend, Herbert, and Tweedy interviews.

30. Townsend interview.

31. James T. Morton Jr., "The Relationship of the College and Its Community," *Bennett College Bulletin* 12 (December 1937): 1, in Miscellaneous Box, Bennett College Archives, Greensboro, N.C.

32. Lois Taylor, "Social Action at Bennett College," *Opportunity* 20 (January 1942): 8.

33. Glenda E. Gilmore, *Gender and Jim Crow: Women and the Politics of White Supremacy in North Carolina, 1896–1920* (Chapel Hill: University of North Carolina Press, 1996), 31.

34. "The Voice of Youth," *Carolina Times*, January 15, 1938, 4. For additional information on the boycott, see William H. Chafe, *Civilities and Civil Rights: Greensboro, North Carolina, and the Black Struggle for Freedom* (New York: Oxford University Press, 1980), 26–27; and "What About It Students?" *Carolina Times*, February 12, 1938, 4.

35. Bonner interview.

36. Moore and Mullen interviews.

37. Moore interview.

38. "The Basketball Team," *Bennett College Bulletin* 9 (May 1934): 12, in Miscellaneous Box, Bennett College Archives, Greensboro, N.C.

39. Moore interview.

40. "Bennett Cage Team Facing Two Games," *Greensboro Daily News*, March 9, 1934, 12; "Tribunes Triumph over Bennett Team," *Greensboro Daily News*, March 13, 1934, 10; "Bennett Meets Eastern Squad," *Greensboro Record*, March 9, 1934, 10.

41. "Tribunes Dazzle Down Home Fans in Victorious Tour," *Richmond Planet*, March 24, 1934, 6; "Tribune Girls Defend Record on Cage Tour through South," *Norfolk Journal and Guide*, March 31, 1934, 12. In the third game of the series, held at the Bennett College gym, the black press reported that fans traveled from distances of over one hundred miles to see the game. "Tribgirls Dazzle Down Home Fans in Victorious Tour," *Philadelphia Tribune*, March 22, 1934, 10.

42. "Bennett Cage Team Facing Two Games," *Greensboro Daily News*, March 9, 1934, 12.

43. Townsend interview.

44. Charlotte Hawkins Brown, *The Correct Thing to Do—to Say—to Wear* (Durham, N.C.: Seeman Printery, 1940), 49–50.

45. Townsend interview. The sports arena was located on Commerce Plaza in downtown Greensboro. According to J. Stephen Catlett of the Greensboro Historical Museum, it was a multipurpose building used for athletic events and social gatherings (personal communication, March 15, 1996).

46. Townsend interview.

47. Ibid.

48. Ibid.

49. "Bennett Girls Win 14 Games, Claim Title," *Baltimore Afro-American*, March 31, 1934, 19; "They Stand Out as Real Champions," *Chicago Defender*, April 13, 1935, 16.

50. Mullen interview.

51. On the NACW, see Hilda Davis and Patricia Bell-Scott, "The Association of Deans of Women and Advisors to Girls in Negro Schools, 1929–1954: A Brief Oral History," *Sage: A Scholarly Journal on Black Women* 6 (Summer 1989): 40–44; Linda Perkins, "The National Association of College Women: Vanguard of Black Women's Leadership and Education, 1923–1954," *Journal of Education* 172 (1990): 65–75; and Mary Carter, "The Educational Activities of the National Association of College Women, 1923–1960" (M.Ed. thesis, Howard University, 1962).

52. "Summary of the Conference of Deans and Advisors to Women in Colored Schools," *Journal of the National Association of College Women* 6 (1929): 38.

53. E. Estelle Thomas, "The Personnel Point of View," *Quarterly Review of Higher Education among Negroes* 8 (October 1940): 231.

54. Maryrose Reeves Allen, "The Development of Beauty in College Women through Health and Physical Education," in Maryrose Reeves Allen Papers, box 160-4 (folder 4), Moorland-Spingarn Research Center, Howard University, Washington, D.C.

55. Ivora (Ike) King, "Feminine yet Athletic," *Baltimore Afro-American*, September 19, 1931, 13.

56. Moore and Mullen interviews.

57. Author's interview with Almira Henry Wilson (Iowa City, Iowa), October 22, 1996.

58. The debate within the black community concerning the type and style of basketball to be played by girls and women was evident throughout the 1920s, 1930s, and 1940s. "Woman Makes Season's Record," *Baltimore Afro-American*, March 5, 1927, 14; J. H. N. Waring, "Selects All Star Court Team from Schoolgirls," *Philadelphia Tribune*, April 16, 1931, 11; Ivora (Ike) King, "Women in Sports," *Baltimore Afro-American*, January 23, 1932, 15; C. T. Edwards, "What to Do with Athletics," *North Carolina Teachers Record* 4 (January 1933): 18; "Clark's Undefeated Girls' Team," *Atlanta Daily World*, February 26, 1937, 5; Sarah L. Humphries, "Women's Sports," *Atlanta Daily World*, March 10, 1940, 8.

59. "Clark Co-eds Boast a Splendid Quintet," *Atlanta Daily World*, February 18, 1937, 11.

60. J. H. N. Waring, "Hear Me Talkin' to Ya," *Baltimore Afro-American*, March 22, 1930, 15.

61. J. H. N. Waring, "Waring Picks an All-Star Girls' Team," *Baltimore Afro-American*, April 7, 1934, 19.

62. J. H. N. Waring, "Hear Me Talkin' to Ya," *Baltimore Afro-American*, April 5, 1930, 14.

63. "Bennett Girls Face 6 More Games at Home," *Norfolk Journal and Guide*, February 8, 1936, 14.

64. "Meet the Nation's Best Female Cage Team," *Chicago Defender*, March 27, 1937, 14.

65. Amelia C. Roberts, "Women in Athletics," *Chicago Defender*, March 12, 1927, 9; Ivora

(Ike) King, "Women in Sports," *Baltimore Afro-American*, March 19, 1932, 15; "Athletic Leaders Confer at Howard," *Baltimore Afro-American*, May 24, 1930, 14.

66. According to the interviews I conducted with Bennett athletes, the male coaches included Dean Staley in the early 1930s, Coach Streator from 1932 to 1934, Coach Wormley in 1935, and Coach Trent Jr. in 1936 and 1937. Evidence suggests that the physical education teacher Dorothy A. Barker coached the team in the late 1920s. See "Bennett Lassies Win," *Baltimore Afro-American*, February 15, 1930, 14. Barker was a graduate of the Sargent School of Physical Education and joined the Bennett faculty in 1927. See Bennett College for Women, catalog, 1929–30, p. 11, in Miscellaneous Box, Bennett College Archives, Greensboro, N.C.

67. Exceptions to a male coaching staff included Barber-Scotia College and Winston-Salem Teachers' College.

68. Burris joined the Bennett faculty in 1936. She completed her undergraduate degree at Temple University and graduate study at Harvard and Columbia. See "Athletics," *Bennett College Bulletin, 1939–1940*, 85, in Miscellaneous Box, Bennett College Archives, Greensboro, N.C.

69. *Handbook of the Women's Sports Day Association*, 32. (I located this handbook among miscellaneous files in the Livingstone College Archives, Salisbury, N.C. The document is undated, but since Livingstone entered the WSDA in 1957, the handbook must have been written after that date.) Bennett joined the WSDA in 1939, and they were followed by North Carolina A&T in 1940, North Carolina College (Central) in 1943, and finally Livingstone in 1957. For primary source accounts of the activities of the WSDA, see "College Coeds Vie for Honors at Howard Pool," *Baltimore Afro-American*, March 1, 1941, 21; "Sports Day at Bennett College," *Baltimore Afro-American*, November 16, 1940, 21; and "Beauties in Sports at Bennett College," *Carolina Times*, November 30, 1940, 7.

70. "Sports Day to Be Held Nov. 16," *Bennett Banner*, November 1940, 2.

71. "Bennett Has Intramural Basketball," *Future Outlook*, March 21, 1942 (found in scrapbook, newspaper clippings file, Bennett College Archives, Greensboro, N.C).

72. Papers of the National Association of College Women, box 90-8 (folder 4), Moorland-Spingarn Research Center, Howard University, Washington, D.C.

73. "Women Form Athletic Association," *A&T Register*, October 1937, 5; "Intercollegiate Athletics for Women Banned," *A&T Register*, March 1938, 6; "Immanuel Lutheran's Purposes Are Stated," *Norfolk Journal and Guide*, May 22, 1937, 15.

74. Author's interview with Vivian Merrick Sansom (Durham, N.C.), August 10, 1996.

75. "CIAA Reaffirms Carry-on Stand for War Duration," *Baltimore Afro-American*, May 22, 1943, 22; Lem Graves Jr., "Sports Are Important to Us," *Norfolk Journal and Guide*, February 20, 1943, 13; "A&T Aggies Set for Exhibition Game," *Atlanta Daily World*, March 11, 1943, 5; "N.C. State Championship Claimants," *Norfolk Journal and Guide*, March 11, 1944, 10.

76. Himes-Gissendanner, "African-American Women and Competitive Sport."

77. Merze Tate, "The Justification of a Women's College," *Bennett College Bulletin* 12 (1937): 15, in Miscellaneous Box, Bennett College Archives, Greensboro, N.C.

78. Gaines, *Uplifting the Race*, 139–40.

79. Tate, "Justification of a Women's College," 15.

7. Integrating New Year's Day: The Racial Politics of College Bowl Games in the American South

CHARLES H. MARTIN

EARLY IN THE evening of November 23, 1948, a rapidly growing crowd of agitated students gathered around a huge bonfire on the central quadrangle of Lafayette College in Easton, Pennsylvania. Virtually the entire student body soon assembled there, leaving nearby dormitories almost totally deserted. The emotional issue that mobilized so many undergraduates on a cool November evening was a controversial faculty decision earlier that day concerning the school's football program. In an unexpected move that shocked the campus, the college faculty had voted to reject an invitation for Lafayette's highly successful football team to participate in the Sun Bowl football classic on New Year's Day. Since the Leopards had not played in a bowl game for twenty-six years, students at the all-male school had responded enthusiastically to news of the anticipated trip to El Paso, Texas, and were bitterly disappointed by the sudden change in plans. After much debate, nearly fifteen hundred concerned young men marched to the nearby home of the school's president, Dr. Ralph C. Hutchison, to demand an explanation. His dinner interrupted, Hutchison hastily defended the unpopular faculty action by attempting to shift the blame to narrow-minded Sun Bowl officials. The main reason that the faculty rejected the bowl invitation, the beleaguered president explained, was because southern racial customs would have barred senior halfback Dave Showell, an African American, from the contest. "'It is fundamentally wrong,'" Hutchison declared, "'for any team to go and play a game and leave any player behind because of his race, color, or religion.'"[1]

Caught off guard by this revelation, the students urged Hutchison to inform Sun Bowl officials that the college still wished to participate in the January 1 game, provided that Showell could play. Impressed with the students'

The presence of halfback David Showell on the 1948 Lafayette College football team set off a racial controversy concerning the Sun Bowl that exposed the continuing discrimination against black athletes in the South. (Lafayette College Special Collections)

passion, and perhaps intimidated by their numbers, Hutchison agreed to reverse the faculty decision. The president then quickly placed a telephone call to the chairman of the selection committee, who curtly replied that Showell could not participate and that a replacement team had already been contacted. Disappointed by this negative response, the students subsequently marched to downtown Easton, where they held an orderly protest rally and sent off a telegram to President Harry S. Truman denouncing the Sun Bowl's action. The following day, nearly a thousand Lafayette students staged "a civil rights demonstration" in the school's auditorium, at which they adopted resolutions condemning intolerance in American society and endorsing the principle that "all Americans have equal rights under the law."[2]

The national publicity surrounding the Sun Bowl controversy of November 1948 deeply embarrassed Lafayette College administrators, bowl officials, and El Paso residents. More importantly, however, the incident is historically significant because it widely exposed the exclusion of African American football players from most college bowl games and dramatically highlighted the Deep South's fanatical insistence on maintaining segregation in all local sporting events. The controversy also demonstrated that northern students were increasingly willing to challenge the continuing presence of a color line in big-time college sports. By the fall of 1948 New Year's Day had become the single most important date in the college football season, with most of the top-ranked squads battling each other in a half-dozen or more bowl games. Since four of the five best-known postseason contests were held in the Deep South, southern racial policies controlled these events. This strategic grip on January 1 thus enabled whites in Dixie to impose their racial values on non-southern teams, in effect "Southernizing" the national sport.

An examination of the rise and fall of racial exclusion in college bowl games held in the American South between 1935 and 1965 reveals much about the shifting trends in national race relations. During the 1930s and early 1940s, conservative white southerners demanded total conformity to Jim Crow and used the leverage of bowl games' profits and prestige to force opportunistic northern universities to abandon their black players. After World War II, northern colleges increasingly defended democracy on the gridiron, forcing southern bowl committees to modify segregation in order to recruit the top national teams. After 1954, however, militant segregationists, worried about the mounting threat to the foundations of the Jim Crow system, attacked this racial moderation in sports and attempted to reestablish a rigid color line. The eventual defeat of their conservative crusade finally permitted southern bowl games to implement a permanent policy of racial egalitarianism. This study will trace these events by focusing on the racial histories of the Cotton, Sugar, and Orange Bowls, the most prestigious southern classics of that era, and the Sun Bowl, the oldest and best known of the so-called second tier bowl games.

During the 1920s college football captured the fancy of the American sporting public and became the nation's second most popular team sport, surpassed only by major league baseball. According to historian Benjamin G. Rader, "Between 1921 and 1930, attendance at all college games doubled and gate receipts tripled." This rapid surge in new spectators enticed many universities to launch a wave of stadium construction and expansion. The growing frequency of intersectional matches featuring North-South or East-West battles contributed substantially to this exploding fan enthusiasm. Despite several efforts to establish special postseason games, however, the famous Rose Bowl match remained the only continuous New Year's Day classic in operation. In the 1930s and 1940s, however, additional civic groups and individual promoters experimented with several new postseason contests. Festivals like the Dixie Bowl, Salad Bowl, Pineapple Bowl, Harbor Bowl, and Oil Bowl failed to attract enough fans to sustain themselves, as did the short-lived Bacardi Bowl in Havana, Cuba, and the Spaghetti Bowl in Florence, Italy.[3]

From this wreckage of failed dreams, four new postseason classics emerged as survivors: the Sugar Bowl in New Orleans, the Orange Bowl in Miami, the Sun Bowl in El Paso, and the Cotton Bowl in Dallas. Because all four host cities were located in the ex-Confederate South, they naturally adhered to the region's prevailing ideology of white supremacy, which prohibited all "mixed" athletic competition between blacks and whites. This custom dictated that if any northern team invited to a southern bowl game included African Americans on its roster, it would agree in advance to withhold them from the contest. Moreover, southern white college teams during the 1920s and 1930s went even further and demanded that non-southern teams bench black players for those intersectional games played *north* of the Mason-Dixon line. Until the late 1930s, most northern universities automatically acquiesced to such demands, demonstrating that southern schools had succeeded in imposing their racial code on intersectional competition. This capitulation by northern coaches and administrators also reflected their tolerance for racial discrimination, the small number of black players on their squads, the marginal status of African American students on campus, and the growing lure of generous payouts and national prestige that bowl games provided.[4]

The Rose Bowl served as the model for these new regional ventures. However, on racial policy the California classic took a more egalitarian position than did its southern imitators. Inspired by a one-time football match held in Pasadena in 1902, the modern Rose Bowl contest began in 1916 and was staged by the Tournament of Roses Committee, which already sponsored a wide variety of festivities to call attention to southern California's mild winter weather. After a few lean years, the renewed game became a smashing success, attracting huge crowds and providing generous payments to participating teams. Although race relations in southern California were far from ideal, the Rose Bowl accepted African American players from the start. In 1916 festival organizers invited Brown University to represent the East against the host school, Washington State College, fully aware that Brown's star player was black halfback Fritz Pollard, a future All-American. Although Pollard encountered some discrimination in public accommodations while visiting California, the game's sponsors apparently made no efforts to prevent his appearance. This precedent of including black players was reinforced in 1922 when single-wing quarterback Charles West of Washington and Jefferson College played the entire game for the Presidents against the University of California.[5]

During the mid-1930s, promoters successfully launched four new bowl games in Deep South cities. These New Year's Day events were organized by businessmen and civic boosters who, seeking the Holy Grail of national press coverage, hoped to exploit the publicity generated by matches between top football powers to expand tourism and foster local economic growth. In Miami civic leaders staged the Palm Festival in 1933 and 1934, with the local University of Miami squad hosting a visiting team from the North both years. In the later half of 1934, these boosters and additional football fans formed the Orange Bowl Committee, which held its first contest on January 1, 1935. In New Orleans a lengthy campaign by several journalists finally resulted in the creation of the Mid-Winter Sports Association, which organized its first Sugar Bowl game also on January 1, 1935. The Sun Bowl in El Paso began operations on that same date, although its first contest matched two high school teams. In 1936 the West Texas festival hosted its first game between college teams. On New Year's Day in 1937, Texas oilman J. Curtis Sanford, inspired by Southern Methodist University's participation in the 1936 Rose Bowl, organized the first Cotton Bowl match in Dallas. Because of local skepticism about the venture's viability, Sanford personally financed the first few games before eventually turning the event's management over to the Cotton Bowl Association.[6]

All four of these new bowl games suffered problems with attendance and profits during their first few years. After Sanford reportedly lost six thousand dollars on the 1937 Cotton Bowl and twenty thousand dollars on the 1940 contest, critics jokingly referred to the event as "Sanford's folly." In Miami the first Orange Bowl match drew a sparse crowd of only 5,135 fans, some of whom were curious neighborhood pedestrians admitted for free. Nonetheless, the creation of four new bowl games greatly expanded postseason opportunities for college football teams. At the same time, however, the fact that all four of the new events were located in the Lower South created possible conflicts for those northern schools whose rosters included one or more black athletes.[7]

The 1940 Cotton Bowl and the 1941 Sugar Bowl revealed the fierce determination of white southerners to maintain the color line in college football and the willingness of ambitious northern universities to abandon their black players in pursuit of athletic success and financial rewards. Unlike intersectional games during the regular season, when northern teams possessed some leverage, bowl games in Dixie were controlled by white southerners who defined the "rules of engagement" to exclude blacks. Since the Cotton Bowl did not yet have an automatic contract with the Southwest Conference champion in 1940, the classic that year featured Clemson against Boston College.

An emerging powerhouse in the Northeast, Boston College aggressively pursued its first-ever bowl bid, even though the team's starting lineup included black halfback Lou Montgomery. In preliminary discussions, Cotton Bowl officials made it clear that southern custom precluded Montgomery's participation. Although Coach Frank Leahy publicly grumbled about the exclusion, BC nonetheless quickly accepted the invitation. In reality, benching Montgomery presented no great moral dilemma for the Jesuit-run institution, since the school had already done so twice during the 1939 regular season, for *home* games against Auburn and the University of Florida. The following year Boston College enjoyed even greater gridiron success, going undefeated and earning a bid to the 1941 Sugar Bowl. But once again school administrators ignored criticism from a few sportswriters and students and cravenly agreed to withhold Montgomery from postseason play. As a small concession, New Orleans officials did permit him to accompany the team and watch the game from the press box.[8]

Although Boston College displayed no inhibitions about abandoning Lou Montgomery in 1940 and 1941, a few radical and liberal northern students did challenge racial exclusion in college sports during the immediate prewar years. Their numbers and clout grew enormously after 1945. As a result of the wartime campaign against Nazi doctrines of Aryan supremacy, liberal attitudes favoring equal opportunity in sports became commonplace on northern campuses. Consequently, northern teams stopped the custom of benching African American players for intersectional games at home, and some of these colleges also began to challenge this policy of racial exclusion for games played in Dixie. This new toughness by Yankee schools forced the cancellation of several games and the termination of a few intersectional rivalries in the late 1940s. The trend also forced southern bowl committees to reevaluate their commitment to racial purity on the gridiron, since it now threatened to interfere with their desire to offer the public the most exciting possible matchup and to maximize their own revenues.

The first important defection from the traditional southern policy of racial exclusion came with the January 1, 1948, Cotton Bowl clash between Southern Methodist University and Penn State University. The game's tremendous success established a precedent for other southern bowl games and gave the Cotton Bowl a temporary recruiting advantage over them. Taking place only two and one-half months after the University of Virginia had shattered southern tradition by hosting an integrated Harvard team in Charlottesville, the SMU–Penn State showdown was reportedly the second integrated major college football contest ever held in the ex-Confederate South and the first in Texas. In mid-November 1947, when the Cotton Bowl selection committee compiled the names of possible visiting teams, it placed Penn State at the head of the list. Winners of the Lambert Trophy, symbolic of football supremacy in the East, the Nittany Lions finished the 1947 season undefeated and ranked fourth in the Associated Press poll. However, the presence of two African Americans, fullback Wallace Triplett and end Dennis Hoggard, on the team's roster complicated the selection process.[9]

The Penn State administration and athletic department strongly supported the policy of racial egalitarianism in college sports. Located in an isolated spot in central Pennsylvania, the university was not the type of school normally associated with intellectual or political liberalism. Hence Penn State's firm stand demonstrated the growing insistence on democratic ideals in sports that spread across most northern campuses after the war. The university had first confronted southern racism in 1940, when the U.S. Naval Academy refused to let sprint champion Barney Ewell run in a track meet at Annapolis. Refusing to compete without their African American sprinter, Penn State forced the academy to move the meet to State College. In the fall of 1946, a similar confrontation developed between the college and the University of Miami after officials at the Florida school discovered that the Nittany Lion squad included Triplett and Hoggard. Miami authorities insisted that the two black players could not participate in their scheduled November matchup in the Orange Bowl Stadium because such a contest might result in "unfortunate incidents."[10]

Reflecting the new liberal attitude on northern campuses, Penn State students strongly criticized the Miami demand. One senior summed up this philosophy when he told the student newspaper that PSU should play sports "the democratic way" or not all, since "the ideals of Democracy are more important than any football game." After several weeks of negotiations, the two colleges finally called off the game. Afterwards, Penn State issued a formal statement that declared, "It is the policy of the college to compete only under circumstances which will permit the playing of any or all members of its athletic teams." In July 1947 the school reaffirmed this policy when the Athletic Advisory Board declined an invitation to send the school's boxing team to the 1947 Sugar Bowl boxing tournament, from which African American boxers were excluded. The action was based entirely on principle, since there were no black boxers on the current team. Penn State's position was well known nationally and understood by most Cotton Bowl officials from the start.[11]

Cotton Bowl officials were delighted when local favorite SMU, led by All-American halfback Doak Walker, captured the Southwest Conference title with an 8-0-1 record. As a result, the bowl could now showcase the third- and fourth-ranked teams in the AP poll, creating "the top attraction in the nation on New Year's Day" and the most exciting matchup in the classic's brief history. (Number one–ranked Notre Dame did not participate in postseason play at that time.) After the SMU coach, Matty Bell, and the Mustang players enthusiastically endorsed playing the Nittany Lions, the Cotton Bowl extended a formal invitation to the university.[12]

Although they quickly accepted the bid, Penn State administrators remained concerned about the rigid pattern of segregation and discrimination that characterized most aspects of Dallas life. Bowl officials worked carefully behind the scenes to ease their fears and avoid any unexpected confrontations with Jim Crow, especially in off-field social activities. The Penn State coach, Bob Higgins, insisted that all of his players, including Triplett and Hoggard, stay together, but the major downtown hotels were segregated. Cotton Bowl planners cleverly resolved this issue by arranging for the visiting squad to reside in the bachelor officer quarters of the Dallas Naval Air Station near suburban Grand Prairie, fourteen miles from downtown. Bowl officials also scaled down some of the traditional social activities for the two teams, but all of the players, including Triplett and Hoggard, attended the postgame awards banquet at a downtown hotel, violating local segregation customs.[13]

The major Dallas newspapers openly reported the racial complications surrounding the possible selection of Penn State for the 1948 game. Once the Nittany Lions accepted the Cotton Bowl invitation, however, the white press temporarily refrained from making any references to Triplett and Hoggard or the larger significance of the racial milestone that was approaching. Since these newspapers did not report any local criticism of the decision to drop the color line, it seems likely that influential local whites preferred to downplay the impending racial change as much as possible to avoid stirring up extreme segregationists. The *Dallas Morning News* did note one Pennsylvania sportswriter's description of the Nittany Lions as "a melting pot football team" composed of players from Polish, Irish, Italian, Ukrainian, and Negro lineage. Finally, on the day of the eagerly awaited showdown, the *Morning News* rediscovered Wallace Triplett, belatedly identifying him as Penn State's "star Negro fullback . . . who is both a fast and elusive runner, and a superb defensive player." Unlike their mainstream counterparts, the black press paid close attention to the racial issue and interpreted the contest as an important step forward in race relations. The *Pittsburgh Courier* noted the game's larger significance and proudly reported that Triplett and Hoggard were always treated courteously by whites during their stay. The local black newspaper, the *Dallas Express,* praised SMU for its willingness to break with southern tradition and Coach Bell for his "courage and character." Other newspapers around the nation, especially those with a liberal, assimilationist philosophy, also celebrated this racial breakthrough. Perhaps influenced by Jackie Robinson's integration of major league baseball earlier in the year, the *Christian Science Monitor* even argued that the integrated football game carried "more significance than does a Supreme Court decision against Jim Crowism or would a Federal Fair Employment Practices Act."[14]

The pairing of the eastern champion against the local favorite SMU, as well as the substantial box office appeal of the Mustangs' All-American halfback Doak Walker, produced a record-setting demand for tickets. The Cotton Bowl ticket office received over a hundred thousand ticket applications in the first four days of mail sales, and one newspaper estimated that 150,000 tickets could have been sold if additional seats had been available. Penn State officials received twenty thousand requests for its allotment of three thousand tickets. An overflow crowd of nearly forty-seven thousand packed the stadium on January 1 for what one sports writer described as "a hell of a game." Paced by Doak Walker, SMU took an early lead, but Penn State rallied to tie the score at 13-13 on a third-quarter touchdown by Wallace Triplett. The game ended in a deadlock when a deflected last-second pass dramatically slipped off Dennis Hoggard's fingertips in the SMU end zone. The tremendous enthusiasm generated by the contest aided the Cotton Bowl in another area. Bowl officials had already planned to float a bond issue in order to expand the stadium's seating capacity, and the 1948 game's success made sale of the securities an easy task. By the time of the 1949 classic, the newly enlarged stadium now held just over sixty-seven thousand seats.[15]

Delighted with the game's tremendous success, the Cotton Bowl attempted to repeat this "milestone achievement" the following year when it invited another integrated team, the University of Oregon Ducks, to participate in the 1949 contest. The popular SMU Mustangs, ranked ninth in the nation, returned as the Southwest Conference champion, guaranteeing a large crowd. Moreover, the selection of SMU halfback Doak Walker for the Heisman Trophy, awarded annually to the top college player, fueled even greater interest in the match. The first team from the Pacific Coast Conference to visit the Cotton Bowl, Oregon had finished the season with a 9-1 record, a share of the league championship, and the number-ten national ranking. However, the Ducks had been unexpectedly passed over in favor of the University of California for the conference's Rose Bowl slot. Paced by flashy quarterback Norm Van Brocklin, the Oregon squad contained three African American players, including starting halfback Woodley Lewis. Declining accommodations at the Naval Air Station, the visitors from the Pacific Northwest instead selected a downtown hotel. The three black players were housed separately at the private homes of prominent black Dallas residents but joined their

teammates at the hotel for most of their meals. The bowl's reception committee included several African Americans, an interracial step bold for its day.
The game itself provided exciting, hard-hitting play and was free of racial
incidents. An overflow crowd of seventy thousand applauded the action as
the Mustangs posted a thrilling 21-13 victory. Clearly the Cotton Bowl and
SMU had followed a policy of racial moderation at a time and in a city where
such flexibility was uncommon, and local politicians had not attempted to
interfere. The gamble paid off handsomely, as the Cotton Bowl profited enormously from the two consecutive outstanding pairings. Although race relations in Dallas were conservative and paternalistic, bowl officials and city
fathers understood the financial and public relations benefits that their city
could gain from flexibility in athletic scheduling. The Cotton Bowl's willingness to breech the color line for one day each year also gave it a competitive
advantage over the Sugar Bowl and Orange Bowl in recruiting top-ranked
non-southern teams, since these two competitors retained their policies of
racial exclusion.[16]

   In El Paso, the Sun Bowl also directly confronted the problem of segregation in the late 1940s, but with less success than the Cotton Bowl. The Southwestern Sun Carnival Association, which had been formed in 1934 by members of several local service clubs, sponsored the New Year's Day event. During
the 1940s, the contest pitted the champion of the Border Conference against
a strong challenger, usually from another western conference. Although the
Sun Bowl was located in the border city of El Paso in far West Texas, it historically followed the prevailing southern and Texas custom of excluding
black players. The game was held each year at Kidd Field, located on the campus of the Texas College of Mines and Metallurgy (later known as Texas
Western College and now as the University of Texas at El Paso). Since the
college was a branch of the University of Texas at Austin, the bowl association adhered to the UT board of regents' policy against interracial athletic
games within the state. In the late 1930s, the College of Mines had upheld this
southern tradition by requiring visiting football teams from Arizona State
College and Northern Arizona College to bench their black players for games
at Kidd Field. Faced with a similar demand in 1938, however, Santa Barbara
State College unexpectedly rejected these Jim Crow demands and canceled
an October 29 contest in El Paso rather than leave the team's two African
American members behind in California.[17]

   In December 1946 the Sun Bowl association encountered the first of several postwar confrontations over this exclusion policy. The search for two
teams to play in the January 1, 1947, classic proved unusually difficult, as several schools, including Border Conference champion Texas Tech, unexpect-

edly declined invitations. After Virginia Polytechnic Institute (VPI) eventually agreed to fill one slot by serving as the home team, the Sun Bowl selection committee turned in desperation to the University of Cincinnati football squad, whose impressive 8-2 season record featured victories over Indiana and Michigan State. Cincinnati players and fans responded enthusiastically to the news of the first bowl invitation ever in the school's history. However, local opinion soon became divided after the athletic director, Charles Mileham, revealed that Sun Bowl officials would not permit senior Willard Stargel to participate in the contest because of his race. Such a demand was not new to Stargel or the university. Earlier in the 1946 season Cincinnati had withheld the outstanding right end from a home game against the University of Kentucky and a road game at the University of Tulsa, both of which the Bearcat squad lost.[18]

Unlike other northern college teams faced with a similar dilemma after World War II, the Cincinnati squad and athletic department officials were apparently not troubled at all by the issue of racial exclusion. With Stargel absent, the Bearcat players voted unanimously to accept the invitation, a decision that the athletic committee promptly endorsed. But once news of the Sun Bowl's color line spread across the campus and the city, considerable local opposition to the trip began to appear. The university's board of directors exercised the final authority on such matters, and on Monday, December 9, the board met to consider the invitation. Troubled by the racial issue, President Raymond C. Walters recommended to the group that the bid be rejected and urged the board to base its decision "solely on ethical and patriotic principles." Charles Mileham supported the trip, arguing that the players and coaches all wanted to go and that Stargel had not fully recovered from injuries suffered during the season. Various communications from students and alumni groups split on the matter. A pro–Sun Bowl student petition decried racial prejudice but warned that "futile attempts to eliminate racial discrimination" could seriously "cripple" the university's athletic program. Stressing the trip's potential benefits, one enthusiastic board member argued that participation in the El Paso classic would bring "prestige" and "national publicity" to Cincinnati, while also attracting more "football-minded youths" to the school. Opponents of accepting the invitation filed a petition with a thousand student signatures on it, stressing their objections to racial discrimination against Stargel.[19]

On the first vote, the board found itself divided and recessed for lunch. At an afternoon session, with one additional member now present, the board narrowly voted 4-3 to accept the invitation and Stargel's exclusion. Despite this action and the ensuing burst of public excitement over the bowl game

against VPI, critics continued to condemn the decision. One sports columnist pointedly suggested that "the board's conscience gave in for the sake of
what's called the honor and glory of Cincinnati." Furthermore, the local city
council unanimously adopted a resolution commending President Walters
for his stand against the trip. Stargel, who was married over the Thanksgiving weekend, declined to talk to reporters about the incident and dropped
off the basketball team, reportedly because there were "quite a few southern
teams on the schedule." At the New Year's Day game in El Paso, the Bearcats
overpowered the VPI eleven by a score of 18-6 before ten thousand fans.
However, the excitement over this victory back in Cincinnati did not fully
silence Stargel's supporters, some of whom urged the university never again
to schedule southern schools unless they agreed not to discriminate.[20]

Two additional incidents involving the exclusion of African American players from football games at Kidd Field embarrassed the Sun Bowl and focused
further national attention on the color line in southern college sports. In the
fall of 1947, College of Mines officials barred halfback Morrison "Dit" Warren of Arizona State University from a Border Conference match at the stadium. Not only did Arizona State officials complain about this discrimination, but many El Paso fans joined them in criticizing the University of Texas
system's policy. The Miner coach, Jack Curtice, publicly commented that
Warren's participation was acceptable to him and pointed out that no one
had "objected when we played against several Negroes in Tempe last year."
Just over one year later, the selection process for the January 1, 1949, Sun Bowl
produced yet another embarrassing racial incident. After Border Conference
champion Texas Tech declined an invitation to serve as home team, the selection committee offered the host spot to the College of Mines, the conference runner-up. The committee then extended a formal offer on November
20 to Lafayette College, which had just completed a successful 7-2 season.
Because the Pennsylvania university had not participated in a bowl game
since 1923, its students responded with wild enthusiasm to the news.[21]

An unexpected racial problem soon threatened to disrupt the Sun Bowl's
plans. After receiving the official invitation, Lafayette's president, Ralph C.
Hutchison, informed College of Mines administrators about the presence of
halfback Dave Showell, an African American, on the squad. Although apol-
ogetic about the exclusion rule, the El Pasoans nonetheless emphasized that
Showell could not play and that there was nothing local people could do
about the regents' exclusion policy. When Lafayette officials told Showell
about the ban, the popular World War II veteran graciously urged his teammates to carry on and make the trip without him. This burden lifted from
their consciences, both the team and the athletic council voted to accept the

Sun Bowl invitation. But the proposal still needed formal approval by the college faculty.[22]

On Tuesday afternoon, November 23, the Lafayette faculty met and debated the issue. Opponents of the El Paso trip stressed the school's tradition against postseason play, missed class time by athletes and students returning from the game, low grades by many football players, and the racial ban. After much discussion, the assembled professors voted overwhelmingly to reject the bid. Hutchison promptly informed Sun Bowl officials of the faculty's decision. He later claimed that he did not specifically cite the racial issue in his explanation to the El Pasoans because he did not want to appear ungrateful for the invitation.[23]

Hutchison's announcement immediately sent the Sun Bowl selection committee into a frantic search for a replacement team and touched off the series of demonstrations by Lafayette students discussed at the start of this essay. In interviews after the student protests, Hutchison carefully avoided mentioning any faculty concerns other than the racial issue. For their part, Sun Bowl officials desperately attempted to divert attention away from the UT Regents' policy against interracial games and back to Lafayette's alleged indecisiveness.[24] The resulting national publicity about the incident created a public relations fiasco for the Sun Bowl. At the College of Mines, the student newspaper reported that most of the school's football players and students opposed the racial ban and were embarrassed by the affair. Many influential El Pasoans were also upset over the negative publicity that their city had received and resented the fact that the ultimate decision about who could play at Kidd Field remained in the hands of UT regents, not local people. On November 24, West Virginia University agreed to play in the Sun Bowl as Lafayette's replacement, and eventually the controversy subsided.[25]

Two years later, however, another embarrassing incident over racial policies at Kidd Field further alarmed Sun Bowl officials and El Paso residents. After the 1950 fall season had begun, Loyola University of Los Angeles suddenly canceled its scheduled September 30 game against the Texas Western College Miners because local officials had barred African American halfback Bill English from the match. Although TWC administrators blamed Loyola for reneging on an alleged "gentlemen's agreement" not to bring English, most El Pasoans instead directed their criticism at the racial ban. The directors of the Sun Carnival Association, the city council, and several civic organizations adopted resolutions urging the UT board of regents to repeal the rule, warning that the current policy endangered the future of the Sun Bowl and Texas Western athletics. One month later, at their regular October meeting, the regents voted 6-3 to repeal the exclusion policy specifically for Kidd

Field, but they retained the general rule for all other state university facilities. This modification greatly relieved the Sun Bowl's sponsors, since it now freed them to select teams from a much larger national pool. Just over a year later, the bowl invited its first integrated team, the College of the Pacific from Stockton, California. On January 1, 1952, Pacific halfback Eddie Macon became the first African American to play in the Sun Bowl when he took the field against host Texas Tech.[26]

The Orange Bowl classic in Miami experienced similar problems during the late 1940s and early 1950s. Since the Orange Bowl Stadium was owned by the city of Miami, the Orange Bowl Committee lacked the power to unilaterally set its own racial policies. Traditionally, all athletic competition in Florida had been segregated. Moreover, in the late 1940s the State Board of Control adopted a formal policy specifically prohibiting all public colleges from hosting integrated home games. Despite a thriving tourist industry aimed at northern visitors, both Miami and its sister city Miami Beach, located to the east across the bay, were very much southern cities with extensive segregation. The Orange Bowl Stadium, unlike most southern facilities, even lacked a segregated all-black spectator section until 1950, when it added one behind the east end zone. Florida's athletic color line first gained national exposure in the fall of 1946, when Penn State and the University of Miami canceled their scheduled intersectional football match at the Orange Bowl Stadium because of the racial ban. Embarrassed by the ensuing negative publicity, many Miami students criticized city officials and school administrators over the policy. Praising the student outcry, the sports editor of the college newspaper wrote that it had been most "heartening to note that a violation of one of the basic principles for which this last war was fought and for which over 250,000 Americans gave their lives, has caused a positive sentiment to sweep the campus." In January 1947 the local racial ban received additional national publicity when Duquesne University canceled an outdoor basketball game in the stadium against Miami. Duquesne decided not to make the trip south when it received confirmation that Charles Cooper, the college's black star, would not be allowed to play. Several other intersectional football and basketball games were canceled across the state in the late 1940s and early 1950s for similar reasons.[27] In a pivotal 1950 decision, however, the Miami *city* government reversed its position and permitted the *private* University of Miami to host the University of Iowa football team at the stadium. The Iowa traveling squad included five African American players, all of whom saw action in the Hawkeyes' loss to the Hurricanes.[28]

The Orange Bowl Committee successfully ducked the racial issue for several years by selecting all-white teams. Whether this invitational pattern represented a deliberate policy of avoiding integrated squads or merely reflected random chance (since several prominent northern teams lacked black players) is unclear. Nonetheless, ambitious bowl officials eventually adopted a color-blind policy when a major opportunity to enhance the bowl's national stature appeared. In November 1953 the festival pulled off a major coup when it signed an agreement with the Big Seven (later the Big Eight) Conference and the Atlantic Coast Conference to match their champions annually in Miami. Since all of the Big Seven schools except for Oklahoma and Missouri had recently begun to recruit African Americans for their football teams, the new contract guaranteed that most future Orange Bowl games would be integrated. This new lineup also brought the festival its first national television contract, another important milestone. Clearly, the Orange Bowl Committee and the city government had jettisoned Jim Crow in order to elevate the bowl's national status and increase its financial strength. The city's expanding tourist industry and growing northern-born population may have aided this pragmatic decision. But Miami civic leaders acted without statewide support, as the rest of Florida firmly retained the traditional policy of exclusion.[29]

The Orange Bowl's first integrated game took place on January 1, 1955. In the second match of the new ACC–Big Seven series, the Nebraska Cornhuskers used two black players during their 34-7 loss to Duke. The local press did not take any special note of this racial milestone, perhaps to avoid stirring up segregationists around the state. Integrated games subsequently became the norm for the Orange Bowl in its city-owned stadium, while the University of Florida, Florida State University, other state colleges, and Florida high schools continued to prohibit mixed competition at their state-regulated facilities well into the 1960s. This loyalty to Jim Crow made scheduling additional intersectional games increasingly difficult. For example, in November 1958 the University of Buffalo rejected an invitation to play in the Tangerine Bowl in Orlando because of racial restrictions. Even though bowl officials were willing to host an integrated football match, the local school district, which owned the city's major stadium, refused to waive its ban against African American players.[30]

The Sugar Bowl in New Orleans experienced far more political interference from segregationist politicians than did all three of its major southern competitors combined. Local custom dictated that seating and other facilities at Tulane University Stadium, the game's annual site, be strictly segregated. By the late 1940s, Sugar Bowl tickets even stated that "this ticket is issued for a person of the Caucasian race" and warned that any other person using it could be ejected from the stadium. In the early 1950s, northern journalists began to criticize this seating policy. Even though not all northern colleges had African Americans on their team rosters, black students usually participated in marching bands and in fan delegations traveling to the games, thus creating a new source of potential conflict. In response to these complications, the Mid-Winter Sports Association quietly modified its guidelines for the January 1955 match, allowing unrestricted seating in the visitors section while maintaining the traditional Jim Crow area for black fans in one end zone. This compromise allowed the U.S. Naval Academy, a recent convert to racial egalitarianism, and its integrated midshipman corps to participate in the 1955 New Year's Day classic against Ole Miss.[31]

The U.S. Supreme Court's *Brown v. Board of Education* decision declaring segregated public schools to be unconstitutional, announced in May 1954 and reaffirmed one year later, ignited an explosion of southern white resistance. This political crusade greatly complicated the Sugar Bowl's operations. For embattled segregationists, maintaining racial purity in athletics now became a crucial battle in the larger war to defend the entire Jim Crow system. Judge Hugh Locke of Alabama, who in 1954 led a successful campaign to restore a Birmingham municipal ordinance barring interracial football and baseball games, voiced the extreme segregationist position when he warned ominously that "allowing a few Negroes to play baseball here will wind up with Negroes and whites marrying." Across the Deep South and also in Virginia, state legislators and political leaders eventually embarked on a sweeping campaign of "massive resistance" to federally mandated desegregation. According to one historian of the modern South, "Legislatures in the former Confederate states enacted some 450 segregationist laws and resolutions" during the ten years following the *Brown* ruling. This southern white backlash against racial change ran directly counter to the increasingly flexible athletic policies being implemented by southern bowl games and a few white southern universities.[32]

Sugar Bowl directors unintentionally crashed headlong into this tidal wave of massive resistance in late 1955 when they took the daring step of inviting an integrated University of Pittsburgh team to play Georgia Tech in the January 1, 1956, match. With the regular season champions of the ACC, the Big Seven, and the Southwest Conference all bound contractually to rival New Year's Day contests, the Sugar Bowl found it increasingly difficult to secure an attractive matchup for its game. Its task became even more difficult if it excluded integrated northern teams. Even though the Pitt squad included only one African American, fullback Bobby Grier, his solitary presence was sufficient to alarm rabid segregationists in both Georgia and Louisiana. Before Georgia Tech administrators accepted the bid, they prudently verified that key university boosters and Governor Marvin Griffin had no objections. But on Friday, December 2, 1955, after receiving complaints from influential segregationists, Griffin unexpectedly reversed course and urged the board of regents of the University System to prohibit Tech's trip. In apocalyptic language the governor warned, "The South stands at Armageddon. The battle is joined. We cannot make the slightest concession to the enemy in this dark and lamentable hour of struggle. There is no more difference in compromising the integrity of race on the playing field than in doing so in the classroom. One break in the dike and the relentless seas will rush in and destroy us."[33]

Griffin's dramatic shift outraged Georgia Tech students. That evening hundreds of young men gathered on the Tech campus, eventually burning Griffin in effigy. As more students and sympathetic residents joined their ranks, the crowd decided to march downtown to the state capitol. Eventual-

On January 2, 1956, Pittsburgh fullback Bobby Grier became the first African American to break the color line in the Sugar Bowl. (Sports Information, University of Pittsburgh)

ly a mob of about two thousand people assembled at the capitol building, where they hanged another effigy of the governor and damaged a few doors and trash cans. Still not satisfied, part of the group then marched to the governor's mansion, where two dozen law enforcement vehicles and a phalanx of policemen greeted them. After voicing their complaints to reporters, the protesters peacefully dispersed and headed home in the early morning hours. The following Monday, the state board of regents met and debated Georgia Tech's Sugar Bowl invitation. Despite considerable pressure from the governor and militant segregationists, the regents approved the trip. However, the board did adopt formal guidelines requiring state colleges to honor Georgia's customs and traditions in all future home games.[34]

The so-called Tech riot and the larger political controversy over the Yellow Jackets' trip focused unusually heavy attention on the Sugar Bowl. In order to avoid patronizing segregated hotels in downtown New Orleans, Pitt established its team headquarters uptown at Tulane University, where it also held practices. Bowl officials again modified seating policies in the stadium for the visitors section, and increased attendance by black fans helped make the game a sell-out. In a somewhat dull contest, Georgia Tech won a narrow 7-0 victory, with its lone touchdown being set up by a questionable pass interference call against Bobby Grier. That evening, Grier broke another racial barrier by attending the awards banquet at a downtown hotel, mingling easily with several Georgia Tech players. However, he skipped the formal dance afterwards and instead attended a special party at historically black Dillard University.[35]

Militant segregationists in the Georgia state assembly and the Louisiana legislature refused to accept this abandonment of racial exclusion. Members of both political bodies viewed integrated athletic competition as an opening wedge for further desegregation, and both were determined to do everything possible to protect the now endangered Jim Crow system. The Georgia assembly responded with a flood of new laws reinforcing segregation, especially in the public schools. In early 1956 and again in early 1957 state legislators debated but narrowly failed to approve a bill that would have outlawed all athletic competition between blacks and whites. Louisiana segregationists were more successful than their Cracker cousins. In July 1956, as part of a wave of regressive legislation designed to forestall desegregation in the state, the legislature adopted bills that prohibited interracial sporting contests and required segregated seating at all public events. Despite pleas from Sugar Bowl officials that these measures would no doubt "seriously damage our sports program," Governor Earl Long reluctantly signed the bills into law. A few weeks later, though, a Long supporter privately offered financial assistance to the New Orleans NAACP if it would initiate a legal challenge to the sports ban, but the civil rights group responded that the governor should stand up for his convictions and file his own suit.[36]

The new Louisiana laws resegregated the Sugar Bowl and made it virtually impossible to attract non-southern teams to the New Year's Day game or any of the associated athletic events. Immediately after the legislature's action, three northern basketball squads pulled out of the December 1956 Sugar Bowl basketball tournament. Both the football game and the basketball tournament subsequently became regional events exclusively between all-white southern teams, thereby reducing their national visibility. Northern schools also canceled nearly a dozen scheduled football and basketball games with Louisiana colleges over the next two years. In 1958 a federal district court invalidated the sports segregation law, an action that the U.S. Supreme Court upheld in May 1959. This decision did not greatly aid the Sugar Bowl, however, since the segregated seating law remained intact and northern universities maintained their boycott. Finally, in January 1964 the Supreme Court struck down this law as well. With this racial burden now lifted from its back, the Sugar Bowl resumed a nondiscriminatory invitational policy and convinced Syracuse University, whose squad included eight African Americans, to play LSU in the 1965 match. The Syracuse invitation produced no public outcry, except for one complaint to LSU by the Southern Louisiana Citizens Council. After expressing its "sincere concern" over the school's decision to meet an integrated team, the Citizens Council warned that "LSU owes its greatness, academically and athletically, to its Anglo-Saxon heritage." The ensuing January 1, 1965, Sugar Bowl contest between Syracuse and LSU marked the end of "southern exceptionalism" concerning racial policy for bowl games and offered further proof that the high tide of racial resistance in the Deep South had now ebbed. Nonetheless, it still took the New Orleans classic several years to fully erase its previous stigma and reestablish strong television ratings.[37]

Racial controversy concerning the Sugar Bowl reappeared unexpectedly in the 1970s. These new incidents expanded the issue of racial exclusion far beyond the physical boundaries of the playing field. Just before the 1972 contest, African American players from the University of Oklahoma complained that only one black woman had been invited to any of the major social events held for the squad. In the fall of 1973 a New Orleans civil rights coalition threatened to picket the upcoming contest unless the Mid-Winter Sports Association appointed several African Americans as associate members of the group. In December, after extended negotiations, the organization named six prominent black civic leaders, including future mayor Ernest N. Morial, as its first nonwhite associate members, finally extending the principle of racial inclusion to its own ranks. Despite this concession, civil rights activists continued throughout the decade to press the Sports Association for greater black representation in its membership.[38]

During their early years, southern bowl games clearly reflected prevailing white racial values in the Deep South. To grant equality on the playing field, even if only for three hours, represented an unacceptable symbolic action because it suggested the possibility of equality in other areas of southern life. After 1945, however, as part of the crucial shift in racial values unleashed by World War II, northern universities gradually adopted an athletic policy of democratic egalitarianism. Confronted with a new firmness by these colleges, southern bowls began to waver in their loyalty to Jim Crow, fearing that they might lose the status and profits of attractive intersectional matchups if they did not modify their policies. Since the principal sponsors of these bowl games were urban businessmen and civic leaders interested in attracting favorable national publicity and increased tourism to their communities, they tended to be pragmatic moderates on racial policy rather than rigid ideologues. Eventually they came to view the abandonment of traditional racial exclusion as a necessary concession to new national standards. The resulting integrated games began to acclimate some white southerners to black and white cooperation in one important aspect of social life. Thus integrated bowl contests provided an important precedent for additional desegregation and reflected a modest liberalization in southern race relations.

The southern white response to the 1954 *Brown v. Board of Education* ruling brought this emerging trend to a sudden halt. During the ensuing period of "massive resistance," militant segregationists attacked all deviations from ideological purity in an effort to shore up the collapsing Jim Crow order. Postulating a racial "domino theory," they feared that integrated athletic events would serve as an opening wedge for more sweeping changes in southern race relations. This conservative counterattack interfered with intersectional competition at Deep South universities from Louisiana to South Carolina for up to a decade or longer. Yet because their host cities were located literally and culturally on the margins of the South, the Sun Bowl and the Orange Bowl remained unaffected by the segregationist counterattack. In Dallas interracial athletic competition had become so deeply ingrained that the substantial local resistance to public school integration did not interfere with the Cotton Bowl's activities. But because it was located in Louisiana, one of the most recalcitrant Deep South states, the Sugar Bowl was seriously harmed by this white resistance well into the 1960s.

By 1964, however, even the Sugar Bowl had finally joined the other major southern bowls in adopting inclusive racial policies based on national as opposed to regional values. This successful transition from segregated to integrated competition represented a form of sectional reconciliation in athletics indicating that the high tide of southern white resistance to racial change had ebbed. Yet it should be noted that despite the widespread acceptance of integrated bowl games by the mid-1950s outside of Louisiana, most southern white universities did not rush to host integrated football matches on campus at that time or to recruit African American athletes for their own squads. In fact, many colleges still refused to accept black undergraduates, thereby revealing the limitations of this racial liberalization. Nonetheless, the triumph of pragmatism and self-interest that integrated bowl games embodied reflected a strong desire by most white southerners to participate fully in the national sporting culture, rather than maintain an extreme regional identity and risk further marginalization and isolation. Thus each year on the sacred day of January 1, if not necessarily on the other 364 days, Dixie had become "Americanized."

Notes

An earlier version of this chapter appeared in *Journal of Sport History* 24 (Fall 1997): 358–77.

1. *New York Times,* November 24, 1948, 27. The team had earlier voted to accept the invitation after Showell told them he would not object to sitting out the game.

2. *New York Times,* November 24, 1948, 27; *Lafayette* (Lafayette College), December 3, 1948; *El Paso Times,* November 23, 24, and 26, 1948; *El Paso Herald-Post,* November 23–24, 1948; *New York Times,* November 24, 1948, 27. The student telegram to the White House read: "Denied Sun Bowl game because we have a Negro on our team. Is this democracy?"

3. Historically black colleges also staged special postseason matches, the best known of which was the Orange Blossom Classic. Begun in 1933, the game was held at various Florida cities over the years and matched Florida A&M against a top-ranked black college team. Benjamin G. Rader, *American Sports,* 2d ed. (Englewood Cliffs, N.J.: Prentice Hall, 1990), 182–88; Anthony C. DiMarco, *The Big Bowl Football Guide,* rev. ed. (New York: Putnam, 1976), 6–7.

4. For an overview of racial policies in southern college sports, see Charles H. Martin, "Racial Exclusion and Intersectional Rivalries: The Rise and Fall of the Gentlemen's Agreement in Big-Time College Football," paper delivered at the Annual Meeting of the Southern Historical Association, New Orleans, La., November 1995.

5. One California sportswriter joked about the relatively unknown Pennsylvania squad, "All I know about Washington and Jefferson is that they are both dead." DiMarco, *Big Bowl Football Guide,* 1–3; Joe Hendrickson, *Tournament of Roses: The First 100 Years* (Los Angeles: Knapp Press, 1989), 1–42; John M. Carroll, *Fritz Pollard: Pioneer in Racial Advancement* (Urbana: University of Illinois Press, 1992), 79–90.

6. DiMarco, *Big Bowl Football Guide,* 3–4; Carlton Stowers, *The Cotton Bowl Classic: The*

First Fifty Years (Dallas: Host Communications, 1986), 7–16; Loran Smith, *Fifty Years on the Fifty: The Orange Bowl Story* (Charlotte, N.C.: East Woods Press, 1983), 3–10.

7. Stowers, *Cotton Bowl Classic,* 10–11; Smith, *Fifty Years on the Fifty,* 5.

8. Despite Montgomery's absence, there still were sectional overtones to the 1940 match. At the pregame coin flip, one Boston College captain joked, "Let's not have any North-South bitterness. Remember, when your grandfathers were fighting Yankees, our grandfathers were in Poland and Czechoslovakia." *Pittsburgh Courier,* December 23 and 30, 1939; Glen Stout, "Jim Crow, Halfback," *Boston Magazine,* December, 1987, 124–31; Wright Bryan, *Clemson: An Informal History of the University, 1889–1979* (Macon, Ga.: Mercer University Press, 1988), 207.

9. *New York Times,* November 27, 1947, 51; *Daily Collegian* (Pennsylvania State University), November 25, 1947; *Pittsburgh Courier,* October 18 and December 13, 1947; *Dallas Morning News,* November 24, 26–27, 1947.

10. *Centre (Pa.) Daily Times,* November 6, 1946; *New York Times,* November 6, 1946, 33.

11. The university did permit a popular distance runner on the track team to compete as an *individual* in the Sugar Bowl track meet, prompting complaints on campus that the school was being inconsistent on its racial policy. *New York Times,* November 6, 1946, 33; *Daily Collegian* (Pennsylvania State University), November 1 and 6, 1946, July 29, September 26, November 25, December 10, 16, and 19, 1947, January 9, 1948; *Pittsburgh Courier,* December 13, 1947.

12. *Dallas Times Herald,* November 25 and 27, December 9, 1947; *Dallas Morning News,* November 27, December 21, 1947.

13. Several of the Penn State players, mostly ex-servicemen, later complained about being housed on a military post, but their irritation was aimed more at the lack of evening entertainment, Higgins's rigorous training schedule, and military food than at their black teammates for causing the housing problem. *New York Times,* November 27, 1947, 51; *Dallas Morning News,* December 21 and 24, 1947, January 6, 1948; author's telephone interview with Felix R. McKnight, April 23, 1996; *Daily Collegian* (Pennsylvania State University), January 6–7, 1948; Rich Donnell, *The Hig: Penn State's Gridiron Legacy* (Montgomery, Ala.: Owl Bay Press, 1994), 186–87, 201–2.

14. *Dallas Morning News,* December 1–31, 1947, January 1, 1948; *Dallas Times Herald,* December 1–31, 1947; *Dallas Express,* January 10, 1948; *Pittsburgh Courier,* December 13, 1947, January 3 and 10, 1948; McKnight interview; *Christian Science Monitor* quoted in *Centre (Pa.) Daily Times,* n.d., 1948.

15. The individual team payout was $66,453. *Dallas Morning News,* January 2 and 6, 1948; *Dallas Express,* January 10, 1948; *Pittsburgh Courier,* January 3 and 10, 1948; Lee Cruse, *The Cotton Bowl* (Dallas: Debka Publishers, 1963), 36–39; Stowers, *Cotton Bowl Classic,* 77–78; McKnight interview; Ridge Riley, *Road to Number One: A Personal Chronicle of Penn State Football* (New York: Doubleday, 1977), 305.

16. *Pittsburgh Courier,* December 4 and 11, 1948; *Dallas Express,* December 11 and 25, 1948, January 8, 1949; Cruse, *Cotton Bowl,* 39–41.

17. *El Paso Times,* October 13–15, 1938; *El Paso Herald-Post,* October 13–14, 1938; miscellaneous clippings in University Archives, University of California, Santa Barbara; *State Press* (Arizona State University), April 14, 1977; *Phoenix Arizona Republic,* August 4, 1980.

18. *El Paso Times,* November 22–December 6, 1946; *El Paso Herald-Post,* December 2–

6, 1946; Kevin Grace, "The Stargel Story: One Measure of Progress," *UC Currents*, October 23, 1992, 2; *Cincinnati Times-Star*, December 6, 1946; and miscellaneous clippings, all in Archives Department, University of Cincinnati.

19. The El Paso newspapers hardly mentioned the controversy over Stargel's participation, apparently because they assumed that Cincinnati would automatically withhold the outstanding senior without any debate. *El Paso Herald-Post*, December 6 and 7, 1946; *El Paso Times*, December 7 and 14, 1946; Minutes, Board of Directors, University of Cincinnati, December 9, 1946; *Cincinnati Enquirer*, December 7, 1946; and miscellaneous clippings, all in Archives Department, University of Cincinnati; Grace, "Stargel Story."

20. Diary of Raymond C. Walters, December 9, 1946; Minutes, Board of Directors, December 9, 1946, both in Archives Department, University of Cincinnati; *Cincinnati Post*, December 9, 12, and 13, 1946; *Cincinnati Enquirer*, January 17, 1947.

21. *Prospector* (College of Mines), November 1 and 8, 1947, November 20, 1948; *El Paso Times*, November 4, 1947, November 16, 19, 1948.

22. The *Pittsburgh Courier* reported a rumor that state officials in Austin were worried that permitting an integrated football game in El Paso might undermine the university's defense against a pending law suit brought by the NAACP and Heman Sweatt, which sought to integrate the UT School of Law. *El Paso Times*, November 22, 1948; *El Paso Herald-Post*, November 22, 23, 1948; *Pittsburgh Courier*, January 1, 1949.

23. Faculty Minutes, November 23, 1948, Statement by the President, November 24, 1948, in College Archives, Skillman Library, Lafayette College, Easton, Pa.; *El Paso Times*, November 24, 1948; *El Paso Herald-Post*, November 24, 1948.

24. *New York Times*, November 24, 1948, 27; *Lafayette* (Lafayette College), December 3, 1948; Albert W. Gendebien, *The Biography of a College* (Easton, Pa.: Lafayette College, 1986), 234–35.

25. C. D. Belding of the selection committee accused Lafayette officials of attempting "to saddle me with the blame by trumping up this racial discrimination story" and claimed that Lafayette's original decision had been based primarily on nonracial factors. *El Paso Herald-Post*, November 24, 1948; *Prospector* (College of Mines), December 4, 1948.

26. The writer Larry L. King later recalled Texas Tech partisans yelling "kill that black ape" and other racial slurs at Macon early in the game but later applauding his excellent play. *Prospector* (Texas Western College), September 30 and October 28, 1950; *El Paso Herald-Post*, September 29, October 11, 12, and 28, 1950, December 26, 1951, January 2, 1952; *Oklahoma City Black Dispatch*, November 11, 1950; *El Paso Times*, September 30 and October 28, 1950; Larry L. King, *Confessions of a White Racist* (New York: Viking, 1971), 68.

27. Two University of Miami government professors, both World War II veterans, also publicly criticized the Penn State cancellation, asserting that the action was "contrary to the American tradition of democracy in education, and a perversion of the spirit of sport." *Hurricane* (University of Miami), November 8, 15, and 22, 1946, January 9, 1947, December 8, 1950; *New York Times*, November 6, 1946, 33, January 10, 1947, 26, November 25, 1947, 41; Charlton W. Tebeau, *The University of Miami: A Golden Anniversary History, 1926–1976* (Coral Gables, Fla.: University of Miami Press, 1976), 176–78, 236; author's telephone interviews with Howard Kleinberg, August 18 and 23, 1997; Howard Kleinberg to the author, August 27, 1997.

28. An editorial in the Miami student newspaper reported that the black players' par-

ticipation took place "with a minimum of fanfare," adding that the contest "was a big, big step in the right direction." *New York Times,* October 18, 1951, 39; *Pittsburgh Courier,* November 25, 1950, January 20 and October 20, 1951; *Daily Iowan* (University of Iowa), November 25, 1950; *Hurricane* (University of Miami), December 1, 1950. The five black Hawkeyes later reported that they did not experience any racial problems with Miami players or residents, but they were required to stay at a separate hotel.

29. Smith, *Fifty Years on the Fifty,* 83, 231; Bruce A. Corrie, *The Atlantic Coast Conference* (Durham, N.C.: Carolina Academic Press, 1978), 49–50; Howard Kleinberg to the author, August 27, 1997.

30. The Gator Bowl, founded in 1946 in Jacksonville, did not host an integrated game until 1961. Florida State University's first integrated home game finally took place in 1964 against New Mexico State. A. S. "Doc" Young, *Negro Firsts in Sports* (Chicago: Johnson Publishing, 1963), 254; *El Paso Times,* January 2, 1955; *New York Times,* November 29, 1958, 22; Vaughn Mancha to the author, January 31, 1995; Smith, *Fifty Years on the Fifty,* 91, 178–79.

31. By the mid-1950s, the service academies had finally become sensitive to racial discrimination against any of their cadets, whether as competitors or spectators. *New Orleans Times-Picayune,* January 1, 1948; *Atlanta Daily World,* January 8, 1955; *Pittsburgh Courier,* January 15, 1949; *Miami Herald,* December 24, 1954.

32. William Warren Rogers, Robert David Ward, Leah Rawls Atkins, and Wayne Flynt, *Alabama: The History of a Deep South State* (Tuscaloosa: University of Alabama Press, 1994), 539; Numan V. Bartley, *The New South, 1945–1980* (Baton Rouge: Louisiana State University Press, 1995), 187–260.

33. *Atlanta Constitution,* December 1 and 3, 1955; "Tempest O'er the Sugar Bowl," *Tech Alumnus,* December 1955, 8; *Atlanta Daily World,* December 1, 1955.

34. *Atlanta Journal,* December 3, 5–6, 1955; *Atlanta Daily World,* December 7, 1955; *Atlanta Constitution,* December 3–6, 1955; Robert C. McMath Jr. et al., *Engineering the New South: Georgia Tech, 1885–1995* (Athens: University of Georgia Press, 1985), 283.

35. *Atlanta Constitution,* January 5, 1956; *Atlanta Daily World,* January 3, 1956; *Pittsburgh Courier,* December 10, 1955; *New York Times,* January 3, 1956, 33; author's telephone interview with Bobby Grier, June 23, 1994.

36. *Atlanta Constitution,* February 15–23, 1957; Charles H. Martin, "Racial Change and Big-Time College Football in Georgia: The Age of Segregation, 1892–1957," *Georgia Historical Quarterly* 80 (Fall 1996): 532–62; *New York Times,* July 17, 1956, 13, October 16, 1956, 14; *New Orleans Times-Picayune,* January 1, 1984; Adam Fairclough, *Race and Democracy: The Civil Rights Struggle in Louisiana, 1915–1972* (Athens: University of Georgia Press, 1995), 205–6, 232–33.

37. The *New York Times* strongly endorsed the 1959 Supreme Court ruling and suggested that expanded interracial contact through athletics would bring increased racial tolerance. The newspaper contended that "there has been no one channel of understanding that has been better than that of sport." *New York Times,* October 16, 1956, 14, November 29, 1958, 22, May 26, 1959, 1, and January 7, 1964, 20; DiMarco, *Big Bowl Football Guide,* 60–63; *New Orleans Times-Picayune,* January 1, 1984; *Red and Black* (University of Georgia), November 15, 1956; Fairclough, *Race and Democracy,* 219, 335–36; 1985 Sugar Bowl Media Guide; Ken Rapport, *The Syracuse Football Story* (Huntsville, Ala.: Strode Publishers, 1975), 254–56.

38. The Orange Bowl Committee eventually broadened its membership after receiving public complaints that it was not representative of the area's diverse population. *New Orleans Times-Picayune,* January 1, 1984; Fairclough, *Race and Democracy,* 219, 335–36; *Los Angeles Times,* December 23, 1973; *New Orleans States-Item,* December 26, 31, 1973, in Amistad Collection, Tulane University, New Orleans, La.; Howard Kleinberg to the author, August 27, 1997.

8. Baseball's Reluctant Challenge: Desegregating Major League Spring Training Sites, 1961–64

JACK E. DAVIS

THE ENTIRE affair made little sense to Bill White, the first baseman for the St. Louis Cardinals. "'I think about this every minute of the day,'" he told a reporter in March of 1961.[1] As a professional baseball player, he had visited cities throughout the country, participated in many different social functions, and never once had he caused trouble. He was articulate, educated, personable, and middle-class. "'I think I'm a gentleman and can conduct myself properly,'" he insisted. Yet White and his black teammates on the Cardinals had been excluded from the invitation list to the St. Petersburg, Florida, "Salute to Baseball" breakfast, sponsored annually by the local chamber of commerce. City and team officials maintained that they had not intended the breakfast to be a white-only engagement and that the team invitations were meant to include all players. But White and the others had not found the invitations so explicit, and they understood by precedent and custom that the protocol of race applied to such affairs. No longer willing to accept excuses for discrimination, White used the incident to publicly condemn the discriminatory racial policies at spring training locations in Florida. "'This thing keeps gnawing at my heart,'" he stated grimly. "'When will we be made to feel like humans?'"[2]

Whether an oversight or intentional, the exclusion of black players from the 1961 breakfast was consistent with past and existing practices in spring training. More than a decade after the major leagues desegregated, racial policies in the spring season continued to reflect southern social patterns. In 1961, thirteen of the eighteen major league teams trained in eleven Florida cities. All of the clubs—with the exception of the Dodgers—routinely housed their black players in segregated accommodations, usually private homes or boardinghouses in the black districts.[3] By sanction of law and custom, Jim Crow established the standard when dining, lodging, socializing, and traveling. Florida ballparks also adhered to that standard by seating their fans in segregated sections.[4]

Throughout the 1950s, team and league management refrained from challenging these practices and from disrupting the southern social order. "The segregation of the hotels was the hardest thing to break down," Henry Aaron reflected thirty years after integration. "There wasn't a white man in Florida or in baseball, for that matter—who was going to change things just out of his sense of decency."[5] But even black players, who during this period quietly tolerated unequal treatment, had inadvertently contributed to the retention of discrimination. When Bill White took his grievances before the public in 1961, his forthrightness followed a break from the black players' tradition of reticence. Many had recently come forward to protest the inequities of spring training and demand that baseball management contest the South's unsavory form of hospitality. The impetus of that new assertiveness, however, had not originated within the ranks of baseball. Bill White and the others were actually following the lead of Florida black citizens who were engaged in their own struggle for equality.[6]

Segregated seating at Al Lang Field in St. Petersburg, Florida. (*St. Petersburg Times* and Pinellas County Historical Museum)

In some ways that argument diverges from traditional interpretations. Many scholars and ballplayers writing about sport have been inclined to emphasize that professional baseball served as a precursor of positive change in American race relations. Four years after Jackie Robinson became the first black man to play in the major leagues, Walter White, the executive director of the National Association for the Advancement of Colored People (NAACP), observed that the "'most visible sign of change to most Americans is the cracking of the color line in professional sports, particularly professional baseball.'"[7] The Hall of Fame member Monte Irvin maintained at the height of civil rights activity in 1964 that "'Baseball has done more to move America in the right direction than all the professional patriots with their billions of cheap words.'"[8] Speaking from a more objective standpoint than Irvin, but probably no less congratulatory of baseball's experiment with integration, the historian Jules Tygiel concludes that "the events unleashed by the historic alliance between [Jackie] Robinson and [Branch] Rickey significantly altered American society."[9]

As the nation's pastime, baseball was indeed woven into the fabric of American society and culture. From the time of its conception in the nineteenth century, baseball as a recreational sport quickly evolved into a mass culture, one that transcended class, race, ethnic, and gender lines. In its institutional and professional form, the minor and major leagues, baseball did not begin to promote a similar widespread sense of cultural and social unity until its integration in the 1950s. Yet even by then its impact was limited. In the South, the white power structure chose not to follow the American pastime's example of racial integration, and until the 1960s disunity more often than unity characterized the spring seasons.

The South's first encounter with integrated professional baseball in the twentieth century came in 1946, when the Brooklyn Dodgers' farm club, the Montreal Royals, traveled to Florida for spring training. With them they brought the minor leagues' first black recruits, John Wright and Jackie Robinson. The Royals' experience in Florida that spring revealed that not everyone favored baseball's changing complexion. Many communities were opposed to blacks and whites playing together on the same ball field. In Jacksonville, the recreation commissioner locked the Royals out of the ballpark to prevent interracial participation. Two days later, Deland city officials achieved the same results with the excuse of a faulty lighting system. When the Royals tested the reception in Sanford, the chief of police ordered the removal of Robinson and Wright from the ballpark.[10]

Although reactionary forces in some Florida communities tried to obstruct baseball's new direction in race relations, municipalities across Florida and the South were not unified in their response to integrated play. A number of Florida cities launched ambitious recruitment campaigns for the chance to host the Dodgers in 1947, even in anticipation of Robinson's rise to the major leagues. Professional sports teams provided a lucrative draw for communities that depended heavily on the winter tourist trade. Opposition to interracial baseball generally came less from the fans and business leaders than from extremist elements and a few intransigent authority figures. When spring training tours introduced integrated major league baseball to other parts of the South in the late 1940s, the response was equally mixed as in Florida. Minor league teams with new black recruits as well encountered both opposition and acceptance. While many southern communities in the early 1950s chose to give up their minor league franchises rather than a Jim Crow custom, other communities were eager for the opportunity to provide a new home to a previously spurned team.[11]

Baseball management generally dealt with lingering pockets of resistance by avoiding such places. Still, hostility to black players occasionally surfaced unexpectedly as late as 1954. In March of that year, the police chief of the rural citrus town of Winter Garden informed Zinn Beck, the general manager of the Chattanooga Lookouts, that talk in town opposed the presence of the Lookouts' seven black Cuban players. "'[W]e don't allow our [Negro] boys to play out there,'" the police chief warned. Fearing for the safety of his black players, Beck removed them to the Orlando training camp of the Washington Senators, the parent team of the Lookouts.[12]

The hometown connection of the Senators drew the attention of some important people. In a speech before the annual conference of the National Civil Liberties Clearing House, Attorney General Herbert Brownell Jr. pointed to the Winter Garden incident as a glaring example of the nation's race relations problems. Commenting on the incident from the White House, President Eisenhower wrapped his message on race relations in cold war rhetoric when he told Americans, "'we must constantly remember that the struggle against foreign tyranny can scarcely be won by any people who lightly regard their own people.'" Sounding a similar patriotic note, but finding a target for blame, the Washington NAACP director Clarence Mitchell insisted that it "'almost seems the Winter Garden police chief and commissioners are trying to give some free service to the Communist propaganda mill.'" Mitchell proposed a boycott of Winter Garden citrus and called for the Justice Department to take immediate action against the police chief and local officials.[13]

The overall response in Washington and Florida went little beyond public denunciations. The Winter Garden city council extended a formal apology to the Lookouts and assured the future safety of their Cuban players. The

FBI looked into the matter but apparently determined that it did not warrant a full investigation.[14] The affair in Winter Garden represented the first and last time the federal government directed its attention to the racial problems of organized baseball in the South. It also revealed the southern white racial ambivalence to black players. By the time of the Winter Garden incident, numerous black players had asserted a formidable presence in the major leagues, and open opposition to integrated competition became the rare exception. Professional baseball had managed to topple a landmark of segregation and, while doing so, illuminate the conflict between time-honored traditions and the benefits of social progress. Yet a victory for professional sports and black athletes did not necessarily translate into defeat for the white South. Southern whites could enjoy a better game of baseball and reap the economic and social benefits from it. Change had been confined to the baseball diamond. Local officials conceded no more than what they deemed necessary to keep professional baseball alive in their communities, and they had done so while keeping the traditional racial order intact. For many observers, that idea had been mostly lost in the general enthusiasm for baseball's impressive accomplishments in race relations. The media were wont to portray the major leagues as the nation's most racially progressive institution. In a 1954 editorial that fostered such an image, the *New York Times* noted that professional baseball was responsible for "some of the most intelligent and effective work against racial discrimination." Black players "have done more than could have been accomplished by volumes of polemics to demonstrate the stupid folly of prejudice."[15] But what baseball players had accomplished by their skills on the playing field was not enough to break down the segregation barriers in spring training accommodations. The separation of players by race in lodging, dining, and ballpark bleachers continued to go largely unchanged and unchallenged through the 1950s.

Yet beneath the seeming lethargy of black players floated a latent desire for change. Black players had traditionally stood their ground in personal confrontations with gross injustice, but collectively they had retreated from publicly condemning the problems in the spring season. Despite their personal accomplishments and their positive contributions to baseball, many felt open protest would jeopardize the progress blacks had made in the major leagues. Spring training lasted only a few weeks of an eight-month season, and players concentrated on winning a spot on the team, not with ending Jim Crow. Still, they were not content with the existing conditions. Some players had expressed their concerns to the Florida NAACP in informal and subtle ways. When in 1960 two members of the NAACP chapter in St. Petersburg, Ralph Wimbish and Robert Swain, suggested coming out publicly against racial policies in spring training, black players pledged their support.[16]

Both Wimbish and Swain were prominent members of the black community in St. Petersburg, and they played important roles in the struggle to end social segregation there. A young physician, Wimbish was president of the local chapter of the NAACP. Swain, a dentist with a budding practice, was a behind-the-scenes money man in the desegregation movement. Both owned rental properties, and for years they had enjoyed the financial windfall that came with housing black players in St. Petersburg for the New York Yankees and the St. Louis Cardinals. But in the torrid climate of the times, they came to terms with the paradox of that practice. If they continued to lodge black players, the two men reasoned, they would be contributing to the condition of forced segregation and betraying the very principles for which they were fighting.[17]

The two black leaders did not single out spring training for any specific reason. Its segregated conditions reflected the broader social problem, and the attack against it was consistent with NAACP policy to challenge segregation wherever it existed. For that reason, NAACP state headquarters gave its full endorsement to the Wimbish and Swain plan, and did so without consideration of anticipated publicity. The NAACP did expect an infusion of national attention and support, nonetheless, and intended to welcome it as an added benefit to the ongoing struggle in Florida and St. Petersburg.[18]

As the recognized "capital of spring training," St. Petersburg made a fitting locale for the forthcoming protest. Tourism had been the foundation of growth for the Gulf Coast city of 181,000. Northerners had been making winter retreats to St. Petersburg since before its incorporation in 1892. Retirees especially found its reputed medicinal climate enticing, and city boosters actively promoted the retirement community image. Sometimes to the chagrin of local boosters, St. Petersburg's demographic distinctiveness often became the substance of drollery for journalists. In one example of mirthful prose, Carl Biemiller of *Holiday* magazine wrote, "There are no old people in St. Petersburg, just young folks seventy-five years of age or better, most of whom spend their time playing shuffleboard, pitching horseshoes fantastically well, guzzling oceans of orange juice while seated on park benches, or playing foot[s]ie somewhere along the twenty-two miles of silver beaches which border the westward boundaries of the city."[19]

But the resort city's outwardly serene appearance veiled what many white observers often overlooked: the Deep South characteristics. St. Petersburg was 13 percent black in the 1950s and was thoroughly segregated, from its schools to its public facilities. The majority of St. Petersburg's "silver" beaches was restricted to white use only, and its acclaimed world's largest drugstore, Webb City, maintained Jim Crow lunch counters. Known worldwide as the City of Green Benches, an appellation that suggested friendly hospitality, St. Petersburg denied blacks the privilege of sitting on these landmarks. Blacks were even prohibited from driving their automobiles on the famed Million Dollar Pier. "'It bothered all of us,'" recalled Earnest Ponder, a black school teacher during St. Petersburg's segregated days.[20]

The organized challenge to those conditions had no specific beginning. "You just wake up one morning and all of a sudden these things are happening," Robert Swain remembered.[21] Following the 1954 *Brown v. Board of Education* decision, which determined the unconstitutionality of segregated public schools, blacks across the South began testing the legality of segregation in places outside of public education. In Florida the NAACP encouraged blacks to accommodate themselves to the tourist state's segregated beaches, and in the summer of 1955 swimming facilities in St. Petersburg became the targets of swim-ins. The next year, local blacks won a federal lawsuit ordering the desegregation of the municipal beaches and swimming pool. The legal victory was temporarily spoiled, however, when St. Petersburg officials closed the swimming facilities. Their actions initially received widespread public support. But opposition mounted as it became increasingly evident that St. Petersburg residents and tourists would be denied a major recreation for a long period. Under pressure from downtown businesses and the *St. Petersburg Times,* coupled with that from the black community, officials finally reopened the beaches and pool in 1959.[22]

The next major victory for local blacks came two years later. St. Petersburg was one of the sixty-nine southern cities caught in the wave of lunch counter sit-ins that had begun in 1960 with four black students in Greensboro, North Carolina.[23] In November of that year, beginning with a McDonald's restaurant located near the black junior college, St. Petersburg black students in cooperation with the NAACP launched a boycott and picketing movement against segregated lunch counters. The NAACP provided the monetary backing and organizational experience. The students provided the manpower and youthful energy. Lasting less than a month, the protests were relatively peaceful, and few arrests were made. In January 1961, seventeen establishments, including Webb City, ended their discriminatory policies.[24]

Riding on the momentum of their success, black leaders in St. Petersburg directed their attention to the segregated lodging of baseball's spring trainees. On the last day of January Ralph Wimbish called a press conference. The St. Petersburg physician told reporters that he would no longer act as the Yankees' unofficial housing representative. For years he had located accommodations for the team's black players and had himself provided housing for Elston Howard. To demonstrate his commitment to the cause, Wimbish announced that he would not offer the Yankee catcher accommodations that

Students demonstrating against segregated lunch counters in St. Petersburg, Florida, in December 1960. (*St. Petersburg Times* and Pinellas County Historical Museum)

season, and he urged other black landlords to follow his lead. He then concluded by calling on Yankee and Cardinal officials to push for an end to segregated practices at their respective headquarters, the Vinoy Park and Soreno hotels. "'It's time the management of the clubs takes a hand,'" he insisted.[25] The NAACP state president A. Leon Lowry seconded Wimbish's statement by sending letters to all of the clubs training in Florida urging them to seek a resolution to the problem of "racial bias."[26]

In response to Wimbish's demands, the Yankee president and co-owner Dan Topping called his own press conference. He insisted that the Yankees' four black players "'mean as much to our ball club as any other players and we would like very much to have the whole team under one roof.'" Topping then requested his general manager, Roy Harney, to work with Soreno management and St. Petersburg Chamber of Commerce officials to find a solution. Yet, according to the *Fort Lauderdale News,* Topping's actions may have been less than sincere. An anonymous source close to the Yankee organization claimed that Wimbish's demands had "'backed [Topping] against a wall.'" New York state's antidiscrimination laws made it "illegal to condone segregation." Whether or not the law applied in this case, alleged the source, Topping requested integrated quarters to avoid any possible entanglements with New York authorities.[27]

Whatever the motivation of Topping's request, the Yankees' efforts to end segregation met strong resistance. The chamber of commerce offered a spurious excuse that others would later use to defend conventional practices. "'The city is full of tourists and guests,'" the chamber of commerce statement read. "'Neither the hotel management nor city officials care to risk jeopardizing the existing social structure at a time when the tourist business is at the highest of the season.'" Florida's chairman of the Governor's Baseball Committee, Elon "Robie" Robison, later concurred with the chamber of commerce's position. "'The baseball clubs are caught in the middle,'" he fumed, while revealing his frustration with Wimbish's demands. "'We can't upset the traditions of generations in a single day or a single year.'"[28]

The spring training controversy quickly captured the national spotlight. The New York Times assiduously kept its readers abreast of the story with investigative reports, as did the major black newspapers. In cooperation with the NAACP, the Pittsburgh Courier launched a media campaign to end racial discrimination at Florida's training camps.[29] Branch Rickey, the former Dodger president and the man who signed Jackie Robinson to the major leagues, supported the campaign and called the segregation policies an "outrage," adding: "'There is no earthly reason why Negro players shouldn't stay in the same hotels and eat in the same restaurants as the other players.'"[30] Elston Howard, one of the Yankee players at the center of the controversy, expressed the grievances that black players had generally kept to themselves. "'It is my feeling that all players should be accorded the same treatment,'" the normally taciturn Howard contended. "'We get it on the field but not off.'"[31]

The accusations of Howard and the others were not excessive caviling, especially in light of the disparities between black and white accommodations. For white players, the four-to-six-week hiatus in Florida resembled that of any tourist vacationing in the Sunshine State. Ball clubs generally housed their white players in top-rated hotels offering amenities such as room and maid service, dining facilities, wall-to-wall carpeting, private baths, and a swimming pool. The "lavish" Vinoy Park Hotel in St. Petersburg, where the Cardinals headquartered, boasted not only a waterfront location but "Moorish arches and tile-lined cupolas, elegant Georgian-style ballrooms with leaded glass windows and carved beam ceilings, scores of crystal chandeliers and ornamental urns, and 367 lavishly appointed rooms."[32] After a day at the ballpark, players could spend time at the beach or on the golf course, dine in fine restaurants, or enjoy a movie, amenities restricted to whites only. For many white players—particularly established veterans—spring training served the dual purpose of a family vacation. Players who brought their wives and children lodged away from the team hotel in locations of their choosing and owned their own houses. Like any white tourist, they had access to Florida's beaches, restaurants, and amusement parks.

The black players' accommodations contrasted sharply with the fine appointments found in hotels such as the Vinoy Park. Many facilities were located in the poorest section of the black district. Players often bunked two or more to a room, shared a common bathroom, and ate prearranged meals.[33] At the team hotels, white players "'ordered dinner from a full menu card,'" recalled Monte Irvin, the ace batter for the New York Giants. "'We ate whatever was shoved before us.'"[34] The boardinghouse in Tampa where the Cincinnati Reds third baseman Frank Robinson lodged provided only a bathtub and no shower for three players.[35] Overnight travels created additional problems. Henry Aaron remembered the scene when sharing the Bradenton boardinghouse leased by the Milwaukee black players of visiting teams: "'Sometimes the place is so crowded that they have two guys sleeping in the hall.'"[36]

Black players also lacked access to many local public facilities. The ubiquitous "Black Only" and "White Only" signs were a disturbing feature both to local and visiting blacks. Jim Crow in Florida restricted nonwhites to certain parts of town, and black and white players found socializing together difficult. In some places, blacks could not even ride in buses with their white teammates; nor could they be transported in taxis with white drivers. In restaurants, theaters, nightclubs, and other establishments that did accommodate blacks and whites, segregation policies were observed, in some cases with the sanction of the law. The Florida state sanitary code required restaurants that served or employed both races to provide separate toilet and lavatory facilities.[37] In Tampa, Jim Crow policies were enforced at the jai alai fronton, where blacks were barred, and the dog track, where, according to Frank Robinson, the black section was so far away that the dogs looked like rabbits and the rabbits like fleas. An admitted addict of the big screen, Robinson sometimes watched two or three movies in a single day. But in Florida he spent much of his time confined to his room because local theaters restricted black seating to the balconies, where he refused to sit. "No movies, no bowling, nothing. It was watch our step every time we went on the street."[38] Most golf courses, theme parks, recreational complexes, and beaches were off limits to blacks. Some places provided Jim Crow beaches, but these were typically located on the most unattractive and least accessible sections of the waterfront. Like Frank Robinson, many black players chose to limit their social activities and spare themselves from humiliating encounters with Jim Crow.

For the few blacks who took their families to Florida, the inhospitable conditions often frustrated their visits. Elston Howard described the difficulties of having his family join him in St. Petersburg: "'I can't make plans until I get down there and see what kind of house I can rent. The other players can rent from an agent in advance, but I can't. It's not pleasant.'"[39] After two weeks in Fort Lauderdale, Hector Lopez sent his wife back to Panama. She was afraid to go out "on account of this thing in the South," Lopez later recalled.[40] Billy Bruton's wife, who accompanied the Braves player south for five seasons, never saw her husband play in Florida. She refused to attend the games because segregation policies at ballparks prohibited her from sitting with the wives of the white players.[41] Most black players kept their families isolated from these problems by simply leaving them at home in the North or Latin America.

The forced segregation, inadequate facilities, and constant abuse that came off the field contradicted treatment on the field, where black players could become the heroes of whites. Despite their national popularity and middle-class distinction, black players became part of an undifferentiated whole of racial subordinates in southern society. The indignity of the white-imposed social order was illuminated whenever the team bus dropped off the non-white players at the edge of the black district and their white teammates rode on to enjoy the privileges of their race. Joining in the chorus of public denunciations, Wendell Smith of the *Pittsburgh Courier* incisively described the paradox of the black players' experience in Florida: "despite all your achievements and fame, the vicious system of racial discrimination in Florida's hick towns condemns you to a life of humiliation and ostracism."[42] It was this sort of double standard black players and locals alike sought to eradicate. "'It's a matter of pride,'" one black spokesperson in Florida pointed out. "'They don't want to be second-class citizens.'"[43]

Once the injustices prevalent in spring training were exposed in St. Petersburg, Florida's other spring training sites were compelled to qualify their stand on the housing question. St. Petersburg blacks had directed their grievances toward the Yankees and Cardinals and did not expect such a windfall of response from the other communities. But it soon became evident that team and local officials throughout the state had misinterpreted the black players' feelings toward segregation. Club management equated the black players' years of silence with contentment and asserted that their players were happy with the present conditions. City and team officials typically addressed the problem by denying that one existed. To them, the real problem was the possibility of black agitation jeopardizing business relations in Florida.

In Bradenton, team and city officials tended to overlook the concerns of black players in such a manner. Responding to Wimbish's public statement, the executive vice president of the Braves, George "Birdie" Tebbetts, assured the press that segregation had never presented a problem and that Milwaukee's black players were satisfied with their housing arrangements. One Bradenton city council member, C. B. Tipton, agreed: "We have never had any trouble and we don't expect any this year."[44]

But trouble of the sort to which Tipton referred soon followed. The Braves players Henry Aaron, Wes Covington, and Billy Bruton flatly denied the accuracy of Tebbetts's statement and criticized him for making it. Their accommodations in a local boardinghouse were adequate, the three acknowledged, but it lacked the comforts of the team hotel, which should be open to blacks as well. Aaron told Tebbetts, "'It's about time you all realized that we're a team and we need to stay together.'"[45] Bruton held management responsible for finding a solution. "'I realize the ball clubs are small compared to states, but they take a lot into the cities and they're important enough to be listened to. After all, take the Braves out of Bradenton and what have you got?'"[46]

Nonplussed by these accusations, Bradenton and Braves officials turned defensive. "We have never had any complaints before from any of our Negro players," insisted a surprised Duffy Lewis, the Braves' traveling secretary. With similar conviction Bradenton's mayor, A. Sterling Hall, claimed, "The Negro players have always told me they were well satisfied." The mayor then suggested that the problem could be solved by the ball clubs leasing complete housing facilities or by building their own training complex, as the Dodgers had done in Vero Beach. Birdie Tebbetts was certain that the teams and local communities would eventually find a solution, but not "by pressure methods, and not overnight." The teams, he maintained, had no business trying to change local customs. The black players "want us to tell a hotel in Florida to take all our men, or none, when there is a state law which says owners of a private hotel can refuse to admit anyone he pleases. Where do we stay then?"[47]

This sort of temporizing reverberated around the state that February. In Ft. Myers, where locals extended a cheerful welcome to the world champion Pittsburgh Pirates, city officials claimed confidently that the black players had "'excellent accommodations in private homes.'" Across the state in Pompano Beach, spring home of the Washington Senators, the chairman of the local Citizen's Baseball Committee assured: "'We have no problems.'" He added that the black players were happy in their private two-story home, and "'actually [were] more comfortable than their teammates.'"[48] From his spring headquarters in West Palm Beach, general manager Frank Lane declared that the Kansas City Athletics were "'not spearheading any political movements.'"[49]

The call for change did not rest well with hotel owners and managers, either. A *New York Times* reporter investigating the housing question found hotel managers "generally jumpy and gun-shy." The strongest resistance to integration was expected to come from the Tampa Bay region (which included St. Petersburg), a popular winter resort area and spring home to seven major league clubs. Explained one anonymous hotel manager, "'our hotels are almost like private clubs this time of year. If we opened our dining rooms and other facilities to just any one, you can see what would happen.'" Some managers privately admitted that they were not personally opposed to integration and they were willing to go along with a uniform change in policy. But they were not willing to take the initiative and risk losing business to their competitors who continued to maintain white-only accommodation. A few acknowledged they were waiting to follow the direction of the Soreno Hotel in St. Petersburg.[50]

That wait was a short one. Within a day of the Yankees' request for desegregated facilities, Soreno management announced its decision. Assistant manager Norville H. Smith declared that the hotel would continue to house the Yankees only on "'the same basis as we've always had them by making arrangements for some of the players outside.'" From Tulsa, Oklahoma, C. H. Alberding, the owner of both the Soreno and Vinoy Park, supported his assistant manager's statement, and firmly added that if the Yankees and Cardinals insist on housing blacks with whites, they "'should look for other hotels.'"[51]

Alberding's pronouncement marked the end of Yankee efforts that winter to end segregated housing. Club officials had proceeded along a cautious line, asking rather than pressing for change and quickly backing down in the face of opposition. Publicity director Bob Fishel affirmed a fleeting commitment to immediate integration when he acknowledged that the Yankees had contracted to lodge at the Soreno that spring. He then recommended reaching a resolution through additional private talks "'at a more leisurely pace.'" On a seemingly positive note, Fishel announced that the Yankees tentatively planned to move to Fort Lauderdale next spring, suggesting that the move might resolve the housing problem.[52]

Dan Topping later confirmed the anticipated change. "'But moving has nothing to do with the problem of segregation,'" the Yankee president clarified. Intimates had known Topping to refer to St. Petersburg as a "dead city" that was "depressing" to players and fans. For the past few years, the team had been negotiating with Fort Lauderdale officials, who promised lucrative gate receipts and the construction of a new sports complex, larger than the St. Petersburg facilities. Integrated accommodations in Fort Lauderdale would be a "'definite plus,'" Topping pointed out, but they were not a requisite—nor were they assured. Topping further conceded that he had no desire to contest the social order of the South. "'We do not run the State of Florida,'" he declared pointedly.[53]

Other team and league officials took the same noncommittal position. From the beginning of the controversy, St. Louis Cardinals management kept a relatively low profile, though general manager Bing Devine did admit that the policies in St. Petersburg presented a problem. "'But we don't make the rules and regulations for the various locations,'" he explained in a public statement that had anticipated Topping's last announcement.[54] Taking a safe but equivocal position, the American League president, Joe Cronin, gave full support to the Yankee response, while the National League president, Warren Giles, declined to "'comment on a problem I do not know exists.'"[55] Official league policy came from the baseball commissioner's office, where Ford C. Frick advocated caution and stuck by the prevailing view of team management to "not become involved in any sort of controversial racial or religious question."[56]

Florida state officials were equally cool in their response. Governor Farris Bryant's sole statement on the housing situation reflected the state's low-keyed position. Bryant pledged his commitment to keeping major league baseball in Florida and asserted his belief in the "freedom of association." Yet the governor who had run for office on a platform of social segregation also declared that integrated accommodations in spring training baseball would "go against custom."[57] Throughout the affair the state government avoided a potentially explosive issue. The recent rush of civil rights activity had placed other southern states and communities under national scrutiny, often resulting in increased intervention and condemnation from the North, protracted confrontations with the federal government, and restructured social policies. In Florida, negative publicity could jeopardize the tourist trade. But since baseball officials had taken a nonassertive position, the state government was able to minimize its role in the controversy and safeguard its principal industry, as well as the traditions of Jim Crow.

Probably most disappointing to the advocates of change was the lack of support from landlords, white and black. Some landlords were openly appalled by accusations that their facilities were somehow substandard. The elderly landlady for the Braves' black players felt personally slighted when Aaron and the others, who she had always treated "'like my own sons,'" went public with their demands to be accommodated in the team hotel.[58] At the same time, desegregation threatened an added source of income. Renting to the major league teams was a lucrative business that brought up to three or four times the standard rental rates. Most landlords at Florida spring training sites declined to join Wimbish and Swain in their stand against segregated housing. In the St. Petersburg area, at least one black landlord and more than one white landlord provided lodging for the players Wimbish and Swain had turned aside.[59]

Despite the pervasiveness of resistance, the actions of many intractable Floridians masked a growing belief that change was imminent. Local civil rights activity had triggered what many regarded as unavoidable. "'You can't fight it—it's got to come,'" one hotel manager admitted. Even Robie Robison, the state baseball committee chairman, grudgingly conceded that baseball teams "'will someday be forced to yield to the pressure. When they do we will have to make arrangements to meet their demands.'" At the same time, he blamed local blacks for unleashing the forces behind that inevitable process.[60]

While some officials speculated on future probabilities, others took steps to move away from past policies and practices. Responding to Wimbish's press conference, Chicago White Sox president Bill Veeck made the first official gesture toward desegregation. In March 1961, Veeck canceled reservations at the McAllister Hotel in Miami after its management refused to lodge his black players during an upcoming exhibition game with the Baltimore Orioles. He then asked the nearby Biscayne Terrace Hotel to take both white and black players. "'I mulled it over in my mind for three or four weeks,'" the hotel manager, Randy Kippel, said of his decision to house the White Sox. Veeck was pleased. "'This is a real sign of progress.'"[61]

Others followed Veeck's initiative. In March, the Braves ended Jim Crow policies at their ballpark in Bradenton by abolishing segregated seating requirements and removing discriminatory signs at washrooms, ticket windows, and gates. Other ballparks made similar changes in policy.[62] Desegregated accommodations for most of the players came the next spring season. The Yankees moved to the new training facilities in Fort Lauderdale, while local and team officials in St. Petersburg worked behind the scenes to arrange for integrated accommodations, at hotels other than the Soreno and Vinoy Park, for the Cardinals and the newly arriving New York Mets.[63] Many other teams moved their headquarters to hotels where players could be housed together. Major league and local officials resolved the housing issue quietly and outside of the media spotlight and managed to avoid a repeat of the potentially explosive events of 1961. The only exceptions to the peaceful transition came at the camps of the Philadelphia Phillies and Minnesota Twins. In both cases, blacks at the community level organized the move for integration. After the Jack Tar Harrison Hotel in Clearwater refused to lift segregation policies for the Phillies in 1962, black citizens in Philadelphia announced their intention to picket Connie Mack Stadium during the regular season.

The Clearwater city manager, James Stewart, sought a stale excuse when asked to comment on these developments: "'as far as we are concerned, no problem exists.'" The Phillies management nevertheless acceded to the pressure back home and moved its players to a hotel twenty miles away across Tampa Bay. Two weeks later, the Jack Tar Harrison changed its policy on racial restrictions and signed a contract with the Phillies for the following spring.[64] The Twins encountered a similar dilemma two years later when members of the Congress of Racial Equality in Minnesota threatened to picket home games. The only remaining team lodging in segregated facilities, the Twins moved to a new integrated hotel in Orlando.[65]

Like the hard-fought battles of civil rights activists, the fruits of desegregated accommodations and ballparks proved an incomplete victory for ballplayers. The move to integrated lodging quite often meant a downgrade in accommodations for the white players, and the black players, according to Henry Aaron, left "behind some first-rate chicken and biscuits."[66] Restaurants in many of the team hotels seated blacks behind partitions, and in most other public facilities the discriminatory policies of the past persisted. In short, change at team headquarters did not spill over into the local communities; desegregation was not tantamount to complete integration. Even after the abolition of legal segregation and the passage of the 1964 Civil Rights Act, some places in the South and Florida remained loyal to the old social conventions. One instance of the persistence in white racial sentiment was recorded in 1966, the year the Boston Red Sox returned to train in Florida. Nearby their new spring headquarters in Winter Haven, two different drinking establishments refused service to the Red Sox pitcher Earl Wilson. "'I think I'd rather be in Mississippi,'" Wilson commented on the episode. "'There you know you're not wanted.'"[67]

Although an exceptional incident by the mid-1960s, Wilson's experience in Winter Haven represents a fitting culmination in the spring training ordeal. Change in the South had been a slow and almost evolutionary process, suggesting that regional determinants in race relations circumscribed baseball's influence as a national institution. The integration of the major leagues in the 1950s had set a salutary precedent in American race relations, but it required more than mere example to effect a fundamental shift in the social patterns of the South. With remarkable success, the white-determined social structure had managed to absorb external pressures that fell short of active opposition. It was not coincidental then that the desegregation of spring training paralleled the emerging civil rights movement. When major league teams did finally integrate spring training facilities in Florida they were still conforming to southern society, which by that time was in the midst of transformation.

Notes

An earlier version of this chapter appeared in *Journal of Sport History* 19 (Summer 1992): 144–62.

1. The reporter was Joe Reichler, a UPI sportswriter. Quoted in Henry Aaron with Lonnie Wheeler, *I Had a Hammer* (New York: HarperCollins, 1991), 154.

2. *Pittsburgh Courier,* March 18, 1961.

3. Though racial discrimination did exist in the West where many teams trained, it was not nearly as prevalent or as harsh as in the South; nor did teams training there face the same housing problems. The Dodgers avoided the problems of segregated housing in Florida by converting an abandoned Naval Air Station at Vero Beach into their own self-sustaining facility.

4. For an excellent examination of the black players' experiences in the Jim Crow South, see Jules Tygiel, *Baseball's Great Experiment: Jackie Robinson and His Legacy* (New York: Vintage Books, 1983), 262–302.

5. Aaron, *I Had a Hammer,* 153.

6. Bill White believes his public condemnation of the St. Petersburg baseball breakfast "started the ball rolling" against segregation in spring training. However, Aaron's autobiography makes no mention of the local civil rights activity that dealt directly with the spring training issue and preceded White's March denunciation. Quoted in Aaron, *I Had a Hammer,* 154–55.

7. Quoted in Frederick W. Cozens and Florence Scovil Stumpf, *Sports in American Life* (Chicago: University of Chicago Press, 1953), 249.

8. Quoted in Jackie Robinson, *Baseball Has Done It* (New York: Lippincott, 1964), 96.

9. Tygiel, *Baseball's Great Experiment,* 343.

10. *Baltimore Afro-American,* April 6 and 20, 1946; Tygiel, *Baseball's Great Experiment,* 108–15.

11. See Tygiel, *Baseball's Great Experiment,* 246–84.

12. *Orlando Sentinel,* March 19 and 20, 1954.

13. *New York Times,* March 19, 1954.

14. *Washington Post,* March 19, 1954; *Orlando Sentinel,* March 20, 1954.

15. *New York Times,* March 20, 1954.

16. Ibid.

17. Author's interview with Robert Swain, March 7, 1990.

18. Robert Saunders, the Florida NAACP field secretary at the time, and A. Leon Lowry, the president of the Florida NAACP at the time, confirmed this strategy. Author's interview with Robert Saunders, August 11, 1990; author's interview with A. Leon Lowry, August 1, 1990.

19. Carl Biemiller, "Florida's Baseball Riviera," *Holiday,* March 1955, 70.

20. *St. Petersburg Times,* February 6, 1989.

21. Swain interview.

22. Darryl Paulson, "Stay Out, the Water's Fine: Desegregating Municipal Swimming Facilities in St. Petersburg, Florida," *Tampa Bay History* 4 (Fall/Winter 1982): 619.

23. For relevant books on the sit-in movement, see William Chafe, *Civilities and Civil Rights: Greensboro, North Carolina, and the Black Struggle for Equality* (New York: Oxford

University Press, 1980); and Martin Oppenheimer, *The Sit-in Movement of 1960* (Brooklyn, N.Y.: Carlson Publishing, 1989).

24. Swain interview; author's interview with Nate Oliver (former St. Petersburg resident and 1959 Dodger draftee), May 5, 1990; *St. Petersburg Times,* March 9, 1961.

25. *New York Times,* February 1, 1961.

26. Lowry interview; *St. Petersburg Times,* February 3, 1961. Available evidence indicates that there were no plans to boycott Al Lang Field in St. Petersburg, where the Yankees and Cardinals played their spring season games. Robert Swain recalls that only a small number of black fans attended the games, and segregated seating at Al Lang was not a primary concern of the St. Petersburg NAACP. Swain interview.

27. *Fort Lauderdale News,* February 2, 1961.

28. *New York Times,* February 3 and 19, 1961. Robert Swain said that within a short time after Wimbish's press conference he received a telephone call from a man who identified himself as Elon Robison. The caller warned, "You are going to regret what you are doing." Swain interview.

29. Robert Saunders explained that the NAACP worked closely with the sportswriter Mal Goode of the *Pittsburgh Courier* on discrimination in spring training. The *Courier* acted as a public voice for the NAACP in their activities in Florida. Saunders interview.

30. *Pittsburgh Courier,* February 4, 1961.

31. *New York Times,* February 3, 1961.

32. Raymond Arsenault, *St. Petersburg and the Florida Dream, 1888–1950* (Norfolk, Va.: Donnelly Co., 1988), 202.

33. Interview with Clifford Williams (son of a former boardinghouse owner) by Denise Frontel, February 10, 1990.

34. Quoted in Robinson, *Baseball Has Done It,* 91.

35. Ibid., 154.

36. *New York Times,* February 19, 1961.

37. *Robinson v. Florida,* 378 U.S. 153 (1963).

38. Frank Robinson with Al Silverman, *My Life Is Baseball* (Garden City, N.Y.: Doubleday and Co., 1968), 84, 117; Robinson, *Baseball Has Done It,* 154–55.

39. *St. Petersburg Times,* February 2, 1961.

40. Quoted in Robinson, *Baseball Has Done It,* 115.

41. Ibid., 175.

42. *Pittsburgh Courier,* April 1, 1961.

43. *New York Times,* February 19, 1961.

44. *St. Petersburg Times,* February 2, 1961,

45. Aaron, *I Had a Hammer,* 154.

46. *Bradenton Herald,* February 5, 1961.

47. *Ft. Meyers News Press,* February 10, 1961; *Florida State Statute* 509 092 authorized restaurant and hotel managers "to refuse accommodations or service to any person who is objectionable or undesirable to said owner or manager."

48. *Fort Lauderdale News,* February 2, 1961.

49. *New York Times,* February 19, 1961.

50. Ibid.

51. *New York Times,* February 2 and 3, 1961.

52. *New York Times,* February 3, 1961.

53. *New York Times,* February 4, 1961; *St. Petersburg Times,* February 4, 1961.

54. *New York Times,* February 2, 1961.

55. *New York Times,* February 3, 1961.

56. Quoted in Robinson, *Baseball Has Done It,* 99.

57. *Fort Lauderdale News,* February 3, 1961.

58. *New York Times,* February 19, 1961 (quotation); Aaron, *I Had a Hammer,* 155.

59. Swain interview; *St. Petersburg Times,* March 9, 1961.

60. *New York Times,* February 19, 1961.

61. *St. Petersburg Times,* February 3, 1961; *Bradenton Herald,* February 2, 1961.

62. On the same day of the Braves' announcement to end segregation at the ballpark, a dozen black high school girls tested racial policies at Bradenton's downtown Woolworth's. Except for drawing scurrilous remarks from a few onlookers, the girls were served without incident. *Bradenton Herald,* March 6, 1961.

63. Interview with Jim Toomey (former Cardinals publicity director) by Melody C. Bailey, October 11, 1988.

64. *St. Petersburg Times,* March 10, 1962; *Clearwater Sun,* March 11, 1962 (quotation).

65. *Orlando Sentinel,* March 14, 1964.

66. Aaron, *I Had a Hammer,* 154.

67. *St. Petersburg Times,* February 28, 1966.

9. "Something More Than the Game Will Be Lost": The 1963 Mississippi State University Basketball Controversy and the Repeal of the Unwritten Law

RUSSELL J. HENDERSON

THE RACIAL integration of athletics, when examined as part of the civil rights movement, reveals black efforts for social change and white resistance. After Jackie Robinson broke professional baseball's color barrier in 1947, African American athletes gradually took hold of the new opportunities in organized sport. The resulting desegregation of professional and amateur athletics—like that of lunch counters and bus stations—created vexing problems for the South, as its segregated sports demonstrated that Jim Crow was incompatible with American democratic principles. White southerners remained as firmly, though not as violently, committed to the region's segregated athletic teams and facilities as they did to its segregated schools and voting booths.[1] Nevertheless, in the midst of nationwide social change, sport—like other aspects of southern life—was fundamentally altered.

White southerners' opposition to the integration of athletics was manifest in the hardening of formal and informal policies barring racially mixed collegiate sporting events. These policies stemmed primarily from fears concerning the social ramifications of competing in desegregated contests and secondarily from worries about losing to integrated squads. As the *Jackson (Miss.) Clarion Ledger* warned: "We play integrated teams abroad—next we play integrated teams at home—next we recruit Negro stars to strengthen our teams—and the fast cycle of integration is complete."[2] Some southern state universities had enrolled a few African American students by the early 1960s, though the region's major athletic conferences, the Atlantic Coast, Southeastern, and Southwest, remained unofficially all-white.[3] Teams within these conferences manipulated their regular-season schedules and negotiated "gen-

tlemen's agreements" with integrated northern squads to avoid desegregated games.[4] Postseason championship tournaments were especially troublesome. If there was the possibility of playing against an integrated team in a
postseason football bowl game, that invitation could be politely declined and
an invitation not involving black players accepted. However, in the case of
postseason basketball and baseball play, southern squads wishing not to play
against blacks had only one course of action: to refuse the National Collegiate Athletic Association (NCAA) tournament berth, which obviated the
possibility of postseason play for that team because no other tournaments
existed. Several public controversies arose concerning whether or not all-
white southern teams should participate in racially mixed games, most notably a dilemma over Georgia Tech's invitation to play in the 1956 Sugar Bowl.[5]
In 1955 and 1956 agencies that oversaw state universities in Mississippi, Louisiana, and Georgia banned interracial athletic competition in an effort to
quell interest in such integrated contests.[6]

Mississippi's "unwritten law" against integrated collegiate athletics was
promulgated in the fall of 1955 after Jones County Junior College accepted a
bid to play in the Junior Rose Bowl against an integrated football team from
Compton, California.[7] In order to force state schools to refuse such invitations in the future, Mississippi legislators—in collusion with compliant college administrators—threatened to withhold appropriations from the of-
fending schools.[8] The negotiations among legislators and college officials that
resulted in Mississippi's "unwritten law" occurred simultaneously with other
attempts by the state legislature to defy desegregation.[9] Unlike Mississippi's
overt, public defiance of federal integration statutes, the unwritten athletic
law "was never mentioned on the floor of either House and what happened
at the meeting did not leak out for a long time."[10] Both black and white institutions of higher learning were subject to the "law"; these political mach-
inations, in essence, placed Jim Crow on the rosters of each Mississippi collegiate athletic team in Mississippi.

Several of Mississippi's public colleges and universities ran afoul of the unwritten law during its eight-year existence.[11] But no athletic team confronted
the law as many times as Mississippi State University's (MSU) basketball
team—in fact, the unwritten law was first implemented after MSU competed
in a racially mixed basketball game in December 1956.[12] Controversy over the
unwritten law embattled the Magnolia State each time the MSU Maroons competed for the Southeastern Conference (SEC) basketball title because the conference championship brought an automatic berth into the integrated NCAA
tournament. If accepted, the NCAA invitation would have compelled the all-
white Mississippi State squad to compete against desegregated teams, thereby

violating the "unwritten, iron-clad policy" against interracial athletics.[13] Mississippi State captured conference championships in 1959, 1961, and 1962; but, because of the threats in the unwritten law, the school's administration turned down each invitation to participate in the NCAA playoffs. The *Jackson Daily News* concluded after MSU's 1962 SEC championship that only a "change of heart by Mississippi's politicians" would permit the team to play in the nationwide basketball tournament.[14] One year later, the 1963 Mississippi State basketball team again won the SEC title, and the resulting controversy forced a "change of heart" by Mississippi's race-baiting politicians—and finally allowed Mississippi collegiate teams to participate in racially mixed games.

By the end of 1962 segregation appeared to most white Mississippians to be on the verge of complete collapse. Though Mississippi remained one of only three southern states (along with South Carolina and Alabama) that retained segregated elementary and secondary schools, its politicians and citizens had not been able to prevent the integration of the University of Mississippi ("Ole Miss") in September 1962.[15] As statewide turmoil over James Meredith's enrollment at Ole Miss continued during the 1962–63 academic year, Mississippi State's basketball team won seventeen games and on Feb-

Mississippi State University, 1962–63 Southeastern Conference Champs. (University Archives Photograph Collection, Special Collections Department, Mitchell Memorial Library, Mississippi State University)

ruary 25 clinched a tie for the championship of the SEC by defeating Tulane University. A few days before MSU's victory, the *Jackson Daily News* acknowledged that "[Mississippi's] racial problems appear to doom the talented Maroons' chances of representing the league in the post-season tournament."[16] After the Tulane game, James H. "Babe" McCarthy, MSU's head basketball coach, appealed on his statewide radio show for Mississippians to support his team's participation in the NCAA tournament. Repeating that it was a "shame" for his squad to again finish its season at home without participating in the playoffs, McCarthy rued: "It makes me heartsick to think that these players, who just clinched no worse than a tie for their third straight Southeastern Conference championship, will have to put away their uniforms and not compete in the NCAA tournament. . . . This is all I can say but I think everyone knows how I feel."[17]

State's students rallied behind their team.[18] Several hundred coeds marched to President Dean W. Colvard's residence immediately after the Tulane game to demonstrate their support for the ball club and its participation in the tournament. Staging a sit-in on the lawn of the president's home, they eagerly inquired about the chances of their team playing in the NCAA tournament. Colvard evasively indicated "that the matter would receive careful consideration."[19] Disappointed with Colvard's answers, several rowdy male students boldly declared their intention to "march on Jackson, to the Capitol on the basketball team's behalf."[20] On February 26 the MSU Student Senate voted unanimously to accept the hoped-for NCAA invitation. Following the vote it prepared a petition, eventually signed by approximately two thousand students, supporting tournament play.[21]

Unlike previous years, in 1963 Mississippi State alumni and fans openly championed NCAA tournament participation. Intimidated by Mississippi's segregationists and enveloped within what the historian James Silver has called the "closed society," MSU faithful had formerly acquiesced to the dictates of the unwritten law.[22] The *Jackson Daily News*, for example, noted in March 1962 that several alumni groups and "highly placed" state officials began "quietly urging" that the basketball team be allowed to compete in postseason action. "But," the paper concluded, "nobody wants to be quoted as favoring the move due to the strong segregationist feeling."[23] The following year, fears of reprisal for challenging the status quo did not seem to concern State followers. Groups of Maroon fans sent President Colvard and the Mississippi Board of Trustees of State Institutions of Higher Learning (College Board) numerous petitions demanding that MSU be granted permission to play in the NCAA tournament.[24] Alumni groups from twenty Mississippi counties as well as clubs in Atlanta, Birmingham, Dallas, Memphis,

New Orleans, and Tuscaloosa also voiced support for the team. The squad received faculty support from the Administrative Council, Faculty Athletic Committee, School of Business, and several individual departments.[25]

On February 27, the SEC commissioner sent a telegram to Wade Walker, Mississippi State's athletic director, mandating March 5 as MSU's "absolute deadline" for accepting or declining the NCAA bid. The commissioner declared March 5 as the deadline because Georgia Tech, the SEC runner-up, had to have enough time to prepare properly for the tournament.[26] Georgia Tech's coach, John Hyder, though pleased at the possibility of representing the SEC, stated, "I have always thought the SEC champion should represent the conference in the NCAA playoffs."[27] Walker did not comment on the deadline, but, in responding to a newspaper reporter's question, he said that he was unaware of any change in state or university policy that would permit the MSU team to play in interracial games. As the *Jackson Daily News* aptly reported: "Joy, tempered by caution, is today's mo[od] at Mississippi State."[28]

For the senior Mississippi State players (Leland Mitchell, Joe Dan Gold, W. D. Stroud, and Bobby Shows), the NCAA postseason tournament again became a source of torment. The quartet had led MSU to three consecutive SEC basketball championships. Mitchell, Gold, and Stroud also captured numerous individual honors and school records, and many Maroon fans, alumni, and students apparently wanted to reward the group's efforts. "'A lot of people who were for us going were still for segregation,'" Mitchell later recalled. "'It was just we'd played four years and we'd won it every time. They wanted to do something for us.'"[29] Yet the players' quest to obtain national laurels had been squelched by Mississippi's racial customs.

Sympathy for the group collided with Mississippi's strident defense of Jim Crow. State government officials remained cautious concerning the basketball issue, fearing that another compromise with integration would forever breech Mississippi's once-impenetrable segregationist barriers. S. R. Evans, the chairman of the College Board's athletic committee, claimed that "'As long as the state policy is like it is, I don't see how they can [play]. If the governor [Ross Barnett] or lieutenant governor [Paul Johnson] or possibly the legislature indicated a desire to let the team play, then I feel that the board would give them their approval.'"[30] Intransigent segregationists implored state officials to prohibit MSU's participation in interracial tournament play. One man asked: "Shall the temporary false glory of a basketball team be our thirty pieces of silver for our honorable heritage and race integrity?"[31] The implications of the latest controversy over the unwritten law, especially in the wake of the Meredith crisis and other events in the South, churned in the minds of concerned white Mississippians.

Mississippi State's basketball coach, Babe McCarthy, clearly understood the dilemma. McCarthy, a Mississippi native and State alum, became State's coach in 1955 even though he never played organized basketball in college.[32] Within four years he guided MSU's basketball program from obscurity to national prominence. His 1958–59 team compiled the nation's best record and became the first State squad to win the SEC's basketball championship. McCarthy led two other Maroon clubs to conference titles (1960–61 and 1961–62), but Mississippi's racial policies barred those teams from the NCAA playoffs. The first time McCarthy confronted the law he claimed to favor participation in the tournament, but he qualified his position. "'As a real true segregationist in Mississippi,'" he said, "'I would not want to jeopardize the segregationist cause in my state.'"[33] After winning additional conference championships, McCarthy cautiously spoke out against the unwritten law, careful not to offend Mississippi's segregationists.[34] By February 1963, he sensed that the aftershocks of the Meredith incident indicated that "'the general sentiment around the state is undergoing a change.'" Declaring that "'these are times when some things need saying,'" he argued that the admission of Meredith into Ole Miss justified a repeal of the unwritten law.[35] More important, McCarthy had formed a special bond with his players, especially the four seniors, who had labored for several seasons without receiving their postseason reward. The reserve guard and team manager Jimmy Wise recalled: "'He committed himself to finding a way to get us into the tournament.'"[36]

Other Mississippians also committed themselves to finding a way for McCarthy and his players to enter the NCAA tournament. People across the state deluged Governor Barnett, members of the College Board, and President Colvard with cards, calls, letters, and telegrams.[37] Ralph Rushing, the spokesman for a group that gathered several petitions, asserted that neither Barnett, the College Board, nor the state legislature should prevent MSU from competing in the playoffs if Mississippi's voters and taxpayers favored the squad's participation: "'We also believe that Coach McCarthy and the players, especially the four seniors on the team who have already won two SEC titles in as many years and then been forced to stay home, have put Mississippi on the map basketballwise and deserve the right to participate for national honors.'"[38] The student resolutions, public petitions, alumni support, and waves of approving cards, calls, letters, and telegrams showed Mississippi's political officials that a substantial number of citizens openly disdained the unwritten athletic law. Hodding Carter, the editor of the *Greenville Delta Democrat-Times,* observed: "what has become increasingly apparent is that there are many, many Mississippians who long ago decided the 'unwritten

law' is for the birds."[39] Apprehensive of another intrusion into public educational affairs in the wake of the Ole Miss fiasco, Mississippi political authorities dumped the responsibility for making the decision onto President
Colvard. The former Dean of Agriculture at North Carolina State University, Colvard had become Mississippi State's twelfth president—the first from
outside the Magnolia State—in 1960. MSU grew extraordinarily during his
tenure, as Colvard also completed the institution's transition from an agricultural and mechanical college to a state university. Colvard calmly steered
Mississippi State through the tumultuous early 1960s, including the peaceful enrollment of its first African American student in 1965.[40]

Controversy over the unwritten law previously occurred twice during
Colvard's term, but, like his executive peers at the other public universities,
he remained uninformed on educational decisions regarding racial issues
made by state officials. He stated in 1962 that he did not "'know who made
the decision last year, and I don't think I will be the one this year. There has
been no change in precedent to my knowledge.'"[41] Mississippi lawmakers and
College Board trustees assumed that collegiate administrators would duti-
fully accept, in the service of segregation, governmental interference in the
operations of the state's public colleges.[42] The College Board president,
Thomas J. Tubb, and other board members assured Colvard "that the board
had no policy on the [basketball] matter and that it had never taken away
from [any Mississippi university] president the authority to act."[43] However, past meddling by politicians in state educational affairs, the unwritten and
unspoken threats of withholding state appropriations, and the Meredith
calamity clearly demonstrated that the board and state government could
capriciously undermine any action deemed detrimental to Mississippi's defense of segregation. Conscious of the internal pressures to sustain segregation and his tenuous position as a non-Mississippian, Colvard chose to construct a rock-solid foundation of support before challenging the unwritten
law.[44] He later reflected: "'I did not feel I was well-enough established to make
a decision. If I made the decision and it was rejected, the "unwritten law"
might have been more firmly established in concrete.'"[45]

Many Mississippians implored Colvard to confront the state's "higher-
ups." "Should a dynamic university be led by a man with the intelligence to
make a decision on the merits of the case and the guts to back it up?" the
Mississippi State student newspaper demanded. "Or, should that university
be led by a man, who out of fear for his job, would listen to and be persuaded by the politicians who are usually trying to create votes?"[46] Moderate
Mississippians, cognizant of the educational and public relations disaster
engendered by the political meddling into James Meredith's enrollment, saw

the basketball issue as a ticket to reenter national affairs. Eager to find "forth-right and realistic" approaches to integration and follow "responsible lead-ership," they pleaded with Colvard to defy the state's political regents.[47] An MSU alumnus challenged him: "Are you . . . under so much of a threat of coercion and intimidation by those for powerful demagogues that you have no choice in the matter?"[48]

Challenged as a leader, confident of alumni, faculty, and student support, emboldened by the public outpouring of sentiment favoring the team's par-ticipation in the tournament, and concerned he "'might not have the oppor-tunity again,'" Colvard took a stand.[49] Presenting the issue as an adminis-trative affair rather than as an educational matter, Colvard notified the College Board president, Thomas J. Tubb, that he would allow the squad to play in the NCAA championships. He recalled in his memoir: "It had begun to look as if our first major racial issue might pertain to basketball rather than to admissions. Although I knew opinion would be divided and feelings would be intense because of the unwritten law . . . I thought I had gained sufficient following that, win or lose, I should take decisive action."[50]

On March 2 Colvard announced MSU's acceptance of the NCAA invita-tion. Fifteen minutes before State's final regular season game against its arch rival Ole Miss in Oxford, he released a statement to the press proclaiming that the Maroons had his permission to compete in the NCAA playoffs. Colvard cautiously declared: "In answer to a manifestation of interest and in light of my best judgment, it is my conclusion that as responsible mem-bers of the academic community and of the Southeastern Conference we have no choice other than to go. Accordingly, as president of Mississippi State University I have decided that unless hindered by competent authority I shall send our basketball team to the NCAA competition."[51]

He claimed that "he made his decision freely and independently" after members of the College Board indicated it had no authority to accept or decline the invitation. Colvard stated that his decision resulted from his sense of duty toward MSU students, fans, and alumni and other Mississippians. He also believed the team worthy, maintained it was entitled to compete against national competition, and insisted that "'the state of Mississippi will have reason to be proud of their representation.'"[52] Colvard's historic dec-laration signified the second major opening in Mississippi's once-impreg-nable barrier against interracial educational activities. The basketball team affirmed Colvard's announcement by defeating Ole Miss, thereby clinching the SEC's automatic NCAA tournament berth.[53]

The ultrasegregationist *Jackson Clarion-Ledger* reported "little immediate adverse reaction to Colvard's decision."[54] Governor Ross Barnett had no official comment, though the columnist Charles M. Hills claimed Barnett privately "deplore[d]" Colvard's act.[55] A member of the College Board asserted that it held the authority to overturn Colvard's decision (contrary to the assurances to Colvard) but lacked a formal policy to prevent acceptance of the NCAA invitation.[56] W. J. Simmons, the leader of the white supremacist Citizens' Council, said that his organization had not considered the matter and declined comment.[57]

Several state legislators, trying to court white voters during an election year, raged that the decision would irreparably harm Mississippi's segregationist cause. State Representative Walter Hester of Natchez charged that Colvard's "'action follows the Meredith incident as an admission that Miss. State has capitulated and is willing for the Negroes to move into that school en masse.'"[58] Russell Fox, the chairman of the House Appropriations Committee, refused to speculate whether MSU's state appropriation would be reduced but added, "'We'll have a brand new legislature next year and I don't know what might be done.'"[59] State Senator Billy Mitts (a former State cheerleader) accused Colvard of striking a "'low blow to the people of Mississippi'" and "'advocate[d] a substantial decrease in the financial appropriation for every university of this great state that encourages integration.'"[60] Mitts also introduced a resolution in the state Senate requesting that the College Board refuse "permission for any institution under its jurisdiction to engage in any athletic contest with integrated teams."[61]

Mississippi's segregationist organs editorialized in the same vein. The editor of the *Jackson Daily News,* James M. Ward, believed that Colvard's decision would subject "young Mississippians to the switch blade knife society that integration inevitably spawns."[62] James B. Skewes, the editor of the *Meridian (Miss.) Star,* cried that Colvard's "'action constitutes a breach of the walls of segregation. Especially in these times we should make no compromise regarding our Southern way of life—we cannot afford to give a single inch.'"[63] The *Jackson Clarion-Ledger* saw a "gross inconsistency" in fighting to keep Jim Crow alive while others struggled to send an athletic team to an integrated event.[64] It also cautioned: "If Miss. State U. plays against a Negro outside the state, what would be greatly different in bringing the integrated teams into the state? And then why not recruit a Negro of special basketball ability to play on the Miss. State team? This is the road we seem to be traveling."[65] Aware of their ability to arouse white resistance, infuriated politicians, editors, and columnists exhorted Mississippians to fight against Colvard's order.

A number of Mississippians responded. The overwhelming majority of those opposed to Colvard's decision appealed, in light of James Meredith's enrollment, to the charge that Colvard was guilty of treason. "Are we willing to sacrifice the principles we professed during the invasion of our state during the Ole Miss crisis?" a Mississippi State student implored and then asked, "Can we sacrifice the principles we profess for a few moments of glory on a basketball court?"[66] A person writing directly to Colvard addressed him as "Quisling," and another correspondent wrote: "Your friend and fellow integrationist Martin Luther King has no doubt expressed his thanks for your effort. Little Brother Bobby Kennedy may award you a medal of honor for the betrayal of State University and the people of Miss[iss]ippi!"[67] Implicit in these harangues was a suspicious hatred of outsiders who sought to change the racial customs of Mississippi and the South.[68] Most of all, the state's hardened segregationists worried that Colvard's decision would tarnish white Mississippi's image of being united against integration. Tom Ethridge, a columnist for the *Jackson Clarion-Ledger,* wondered whether the basketball controversy "was worth the bitterness and bickering generated among Mississippians at a time when unity is sorely needed."[69] Indeed, an anonymous letter writer feared that "something more than the game will be lost" if State violated the unwritten law.[70]

Though the opposition remained steadfast, many Mississippians seemingly endorsed Colvard's decision. Johnny Vaught, the Ole Miss football coach, said: "'Those boys deserved to go and I'm glad they're getting the opportunity.'"[71] The Jackson television station WJTV took a poll of its viewers on the issue and found that 85 percent of the respondents (from twenty-seven Mississippi counties) favored tournament play.[72] Rubel Phillips, the 1963 Republican gubernatorial candidate, and several others insisted that Colvard's decision fully supported states' rights principles.[73] Others reasoned that the desegregation of Ole Miss justified State's participation in the NCAA playoffs.[74] Significantly, Mississippians lauded Colvard's action for bringing a modicum of freedom back to the "closed society." "Your decision," one man wrote to Colvard, "is indicative, I think, of a reduction in the monastic discipline which Mississippi's introverted society has imposed upon itself in utter disregard of reason and reality."[75]

The outpouring of public sentiment supporting the team subdued the usually outspoken Ross Barnett. Fighting federal contempt citations stemming from his interference in the Meredith affair and opposing the admission of another black applicant to Ole Miss, Barnett limited himself in the MSU crisis to one formal statement opposing State's participation in the NCAA tournament.[76] He affirmed: "'The people of Mississippi know that I am a strong believer in and an advocate of segregation in every phase of activity in all our schools. Under Section 213A of the Mississippi State Constitution, the control of our colleges and universities rests with the Board of

Trustees of Institutions of Higher Learning. Personally, I feel that it is not for the best interests of Mississippi State University, the State of Mississippi, or either of the races.'"[77]

A crucial but publicly unstated reason Barnett did not take an active role in the basketball dilemma was the "watch" undertaken by the Southern Association of Colleges and Schools (SACS) upon Mississippi's colleges and universities. In November 1962 SACS placed all of Mississippi's public institutions of higher learning on probation as punishment for Barnett and Lieutenant Governor Paul Johnson's interference in the administration of academic affairs at Ole Miss. SACS also warned the College Board that additional interference, political pressures, or encroachment upon public educational activities by elected officials would result in the forfeiture of accreditation for all of Mississippi's state universities. In order to maintain academic control of university activities, SACS policy required that control of collegiate athletics fall under faculty authority. Some of the Magnolia State's more defiant authorities sought to close all the public colleges rather than integrate or submit to the SACS's demands. Still obsessed with maintaining Jim Crow but stymied by the SACS decree, Barnett passed to his appointed trustees on the College Board the responsibility of defending the Magnolia State's segregationist ramparts.[78]

The authority of the College Board to determine whether MSU could accept the NCAA's invitation remained unclear. The board operated under the guidelines of a 1944 state constitutional amendment designed to eliminate the governor's political influence upon educational activities.[79] The unwritten law, though directly affecting the public universities and thus seemingly falling under the control of the College Board, was actually a policy of the state legislature. Wielding the threat of withholding state funding, the legislature remained the arbiter of the edict. Past College Board presidents interpreted this particular athletic issue—whether or not to participate in postseason play against integrated teams—as an internal administrative matter, similar to formulating schedules or organizing booster clubs, that was to be handled by each public university.[80] The board, therefore, had no formal or informal policy that would prevent institutions under its jurisdiction from interracial contests outside Mississippi.

Prodded by hamstrung political mates and Mississippi's reactionary press, Barnett's five appointed trustees pursued an official policy barring integrated athletic events.[81] At a minimum, they hoped to erect, in the words of Colvard's statement accepting the NCAA invitation, the "hindrance by competent authority" that would halt MSU's quest.[82] M. M. Roberts, a trustee appointed by Barnett, frothed: "we have the greatest challenge to our way of life since reconstruction days, that violence is about to be done to all of Mississippi, that this is the most important subject the board will ever be called on to decide, and that we must be present to accept our responsibility."[83] Unlike the integration of Ole Miss, no federal court order enforced with U.S. marshals and bayonets would interfere with the Barnett administration's attempted solution to the latest segregation crisis.

The College Board met in Jackson on March 9 to discuss Mississippi State's fate. Four white students from nearby Millsaps College picketed in front of the meeting place bearing placards that read: "Don't Confuse NCAA with NAACP," "Go State Go," "Don't Discriminate against Whites, Let State Play." Jackson police dispersed the group after they confronted five local women bearing petitions against the Maroons playing in the tournament.[84] Thomas Tubb called the meeting to order and opened a public forum, the first time citizens had been permitted to attend a board meeting. M. M. Roberts revealed that he "prayed" MSU would not win its last two regular season games because he feared facing "this problem."[85] Other board members "'pointed out that Mississippi teams played in racially mixed events. . . . Before the NAACP got after us.'" "'But,'" the trustee Ray Izard continued, "'I think we should rule out consideration of everything before the 1954 Supreme Court decision.'" Tubb presented information that Mississippi appropriated $120,000 per biennium to send state officials to national integrated meetings, including the U.S. Congress.[86] Several trustees agreed that there was no difference between this type of integration and an interracial basketball game. Tubb added that Colvard "'could not in good conscience'" prevent the team from participating in the tournament, even though Colvard "'knew he might be fired.'"[87] Other members contended that an antiparticipation vote "'would be a slap in the face'" of Colvard and potentially could "'lead to more harm.'"[88]

After the tense deliberations ceased, Roberts moved that Mississippi State not be permitted to participate in the NCAA tournament. The board voted 8-3 in favor of allowing MSU to play. Roberts quickly made a second motion demanding that the board fire Colvard. "'There is no doubt in my mind that he knew he was going against the will of the board,'" Roberts railed. "'I resent that! And I think he should resign! He put us on the spot!'"[89] The motion died when no one seconded it. Tally Riddell then requested that the board "'express its confidence in Dr. Colvard.'" The board approvingly voted 9-2 on Riddell's measure and quickly adjourned.[90] A woman opposing the board's decision confronted Tubb outside the conference room immediately after the meeting. Shaking her finger in his face, she exclaimed, "'You've got blood on your hands!'"[91]

Governor Barnett, recognizing the board's "exclusive legal authority to act in this matter," released a statement acknowledging its decision and adding hopes of a MSU victory.[92] Others were not so gracious. One man wrote to Colvard: "Here's hoping that the niggers . . . beat Mississippi State by a humiliating score."[93] But many Mississippians appreciated the significance of the board's decision. "[T]he State College Board's decision to back the president of Mississippi State University may have been the first meaningful sign that the decent people in Mississippi are sick of letting the professional haters make all the decisions and control the shots," Hodding Carter proclaimed.[94] The College Board's approval of MSU's participation in the NCAA tournament granted, for the first time, official state sanction to an interracial event and signaled Mississippi's return from self-imposed exile.

Ignoring the lessons emanating from the Meredith imbroglio and the SACS "watch," several of Mississippi's politicians mustered to prevent State from playing in the tournament. On March 13 (the day before MSU was scheduled to leave for the tournament) State Senator Billy Mitts and former State Senator B. W. Lawson obtained a temporary injunction in a Hinds County court against the members of the College Board, President Colvard, and Coach McCarthy, barring them from taking the basketball squad out of Mississippi. Mitts and Lawson claimed in the motion that Colvard's decision violated "the announced public policy of the State of Mississippi."[95] They also protested the expenditure of any "State funds, taxes, [or] appropriations . . . to travel from the State of Mississippi to engage in any athletic contest wherein there will be participating mixed races."[96] Mitts and Lawson further stated that the College Board's endorsement of Colvard's action indicated an unlawful "usurpation by administrative government of inalienable public rights" that invaded "areas properly reserved to the individuals."[97] Mississippi State students hung effigies of Mitts and Lawson at a pep rally held for the basketball team later that night.[98]

The team planned to leave Starkville at 8:30 A.M. on Thursday, March 14. After the pep rally a university spokesman declared: "As of 9:30 tonight, we are going to the tournament. We will leave as scheduled tomorrow."[99] Hinds County sheriffs arrived in Starkville around 11:30 P.M. Wednesday to serve the injunction. Mississippi code required law officers from one county wishing to make an arrest or serve an injunction in another county to be accompanied by local officials. The Oktibbeha County sheriff was ill, so the deputy sheriff, Dot Johnson, led the Hinds County police around Starkville looking for Colvard and the others.[100]

Upon learning the Hinds County sheriffs were approaching Starkville, MSU officials hurriedly executed their plan to avoid service of the injunction. Around 8:00 P.M. Colvard and John K. Bettersworth, the university's vice president, drove to Birmingham and checked into a hotel under aliases. Coach McCarthy, the athletic director, Wade Walker, and the assistant athletic director, Ralph Brown, rented a car, drove to Memphis, and flew to Nashville to escape the writ. Colvard later explained: "My feeling was that the officers might arrest the athletic director, the coach or me, but that they would not dare touch the members of the basketball squad."[101] The Hinds County sheriffs returned to Jackson after failing to find those named in the injunction, thereby leaving Deputy Johnson the task of serving the order.

The team devised its own "intriguing plot" to avoid Mitts's injunction.[102] It planned to send a group of freshmen players disguised as the varsity squad to Starkville's airport early Thursday morning, while the first-stringers and key reserves hid in State's athletic dormitory with Jerry Simmons, the assistant varsity coach.[103] Led by the trainer, Werner Luchsinger, this group of "expendables" would serve as decoys in the event Johnson attempted to serve the injunction on them. Luchsinger was to telephone Simmons at the athletic dormitory if Johnson tried to serve the writ. Simmons would then sneak his group to a private plane hidden at the Starkville airport and fly to Nashville to pick up McCarthy, Walker, and Brown. From Nashville they would all take a commercial flight to the game.[104]

Luchsinger's crew anxiously arrived at the airport around 7:30 A.M. There they found no sheriff, no injunction—and no airplane. Thunderstorms in Atlanta delayed the plane, which was scheduled to arrive at 8:00 A.M. Deputy Johnson then arrived at the airport, discovered no plane and no one upon whom to serve the injunction, and returned to the campus. Luchsinger learned at approximately 9:00 A.M. that the tardy plane was near Starkville and called Simmons at the dormitory to hurry the team to the airport. Simmons whisked his players to the airport, and the plane left Starkville around 9:45 A.M.[105] After clearing Mississippi airspace, one player allegedly quipped: "'Now I know how those East Berliners feel when they make it past the wall.'"[106] While no one publicly admitted collusion between MSU officials and Johnson, a team spokesman lightheartedly joked, "'[he] didn't seem to try very hard to find us.'"[107] Later that afternoon, Associate Justice Robert G. Gillespie of the Mississippi Supreme Court issued a stay of the injunction, ruling the writ "was issued without authority of law and improvidently issued without notice."[108]

Loyola University of Chicago defeated the all-white Tennessee Tech basketball team in the opening round of the 1963 Mideast Regional at Michigan State University and earned the tournament position against Mississippi State. (As SEC champion, MSU drew a bye.) Coach McCarthy called Loyola "'the best basketball team we've ever played since I've been at Mississippi

State.'"[109] But of greater moment to State fans and Mississippi citizens, four of Loyola's starters were African Americans. Maroon players "were unanimous" in stating that competition against blacks would be no different than from whites.[110] "'I don't see anything morally wrong with playing against Negroes, Indians, Russians, or any other race or nationality,'" Leland Mitchell explained. "'Most of us boys have already competed against them in high school or hometown sandlot games. In my opinion it's just like playing against anyone else.'"[111]

Though State's players and coaches downplayed the game's interracial angle, some folks back home bemoaned the contest's alleged harm to Mississippi's defense of segregation. A Meridian resident wrote to the *Jackson Clarion-Ledger:* "I know not what the future may hold for the members of the . . . team, but they can always point back and say that I was a member of the team that broke the traditions of my beloved state in order to promote my own selfish interest and that of a few of my friends."[112] Other Mississippians apparently resigned themselves to State's participation and wished the team luck.[113] Percy Greene, the African American owner of the *Jackson (Miss.) Advocate,* editorialized: "When Mississippi State's Maroons go up to that tournament we don't care who they're going to be playing, we are going to be pulling for the Maroons, because our state pride, despite its present handicaps and short-comings, is firmly lodged with the State of Mississippi."[114] After weeks of intrigue and drama, the "most talked about, and awaited, basketball game in the history of the NCAA" finally took place.[115]

During the first few minutes of play the Maroons achieved a quick 7-0 lead. Once Loyola composed themselves, MSU became "plague[d] by publicity and poor shooting."[116] Loyola combined defensive tenacity, streaky scoring, strong rebounding, and overall athletic ability to beat State 61-51.[117] The *Pittsburgh Courier* gleefully noted that Loyola's "four tall and terrific tan shooters" scored all but two of their team's points.[118] Loyola of Chicago eventually won the 1963 NCAA national basketball championship.

The game was fought hard, cleanly played, and without incident; in fact, the game started with a ceremonial handshake between the team captains, Joe Dan Gold of MSU and Jerry Harkness of Loyola.[119] Gold claimed that Loyola's black cagers played like "'perfect gentlemen.'"[120] Coach McCarthy, waving off a racial explanation of the defeat, commented, "'The color didn't make any difference. I don't even want to talk about that because it wasn't important.'"[121] When asked if MSU would play again in the integrated national championship tournament, McCarthy stated: "'There'll either have to be a law forbidding us to come or we'll be back.'"[122] State defeated Bowling Green of Ohio in the consolation game of the Mideast Regional, finishing its season with a record of 22-6 and ranking seventh in the final 1963 basketball poll. Governor Barnett later sent each member of the team an official "Certificate of Appreciation and Commendation" for representing Mississippi at the NCAA tournament.[123]

The legality of the unwritten law and the prospects of future integrated games remained unresolved, though the game had been played. At the College Board's March 21 meeting, the Barnett-appointed trustee Ray Izard proposed a resolution directing Mississippi's university presidents to "come before the Board with recommendations on all controversial matters in connection with athletic events." Mississippi's major newspapers reported that several unnamed college presidents supported Izard's proposal as a measure toward relieving them of the responsibility of making such decisions. The board, nevertheless, rejected Izard's proposal and voted to leave such decisions solely on the shoulders of Mississippi's university officials.[124]

The repeal of Mississippi's unwritten athletic law finally came on April 18, 1963. At that day's board meeting, J. N. Lipscomb, another Barnett appointee, declared:

Today this Board is standing at the fork of the road with respect to decisions pertaining to integration in our schools. . . . Intercollegiate contests, by whatever name known, are the skirmish lines. Whether these advance groups of two opposing philosophies fight or fraternize may determine the outcome of this disturbing conflict. To yield or not to yield, that is the question. . . . I feel that this Board should seriously deliberate the question of choosing between one of three options:

1. No intercollegiate contests with integrated teams.
2. Intercollegiate contests with integrated teams outside our state but not inside our state.
3. Disregard the degree of integration of opposing teams whether these contests are held in Mississippi or beyond our borders.

The board voted 7-5 against considering any of Lipscomb's three options.[125] In its refusal to prohibit future integrated athletic games, the board nullified the unwritten law and acquiesced to the inevitability of integrated collegiate activities.

The confrontation over the unwritten law remains an important, but often overlooked, moment in Mississippi history. It was, chronologically, the next public incident involving race after the integration of the University of Mississippi, and it exposed unexpectedly deep fractures within Mississippi's alleged racial monolith. Moderate Mississippians, mindful of the Ole Miss fiasco, presented MSU's plight as one more example of the representation imposed upon the state by politically powerful segregationists. The MSU basketball player Joe Dan Gold recalled: "'I think people knew it was time to move forward and realized [participation in the tournament] was a positive step. Not only the university, but the state of Mississippi had to do away with the image we projected every time we turned down a bid.'"[126] The overwhelming public support for the MSU basketball team within the state and region demonstrated that many whites grasped the inevitability of racial change and looked for safe areas, such as sport, to ease the transition. These white citizens, unconsciously borrowing tactics of civil rights activists, sought change through vociferous nonviolent protest and defied an unfair law to pursue a just end. As a barrier to progress, the unwritten law rankled many southerners and, according to Hodding Carter, "'undermine[d] the same status quo the men who formulated it strain[ed] at gnats to preserve.'"[127]

The controversy over the unwritten athletic law also exposed the ambivalence that some white Mississippians felt for the "closed society." In certain areas, such as business and sport, white southerners did not seem to approve of segregation when it threatened a value or belief even more cherished than the separation of the races.[128] For example, Susan Gay, a columnist for the MSU student newspaper, wrote in 1963 that "sports is the one area in which negroes are considered equal. If they are not considered so, then it is clearly a case of prejudice, that dirty word."[129] The color line in athletics appeared less rigid, and white sentiment less volatile over its erasure, than in voting, schools, or public accommodations; for instance, some Mississippians were willing to close all the state universities to halt academic integration, yet no one publicly recommended that collegiate athletics be abandoned because of integrated play.[130] Though racist southerners employed athletics as a weapon for the social and political cause of segregation, the values and ideals of sport (especially the enthusiasm for winners, equalitarianism, and reward for achievement) justified white support of MSU's basketball team and allowed previously silenced moderates to espouse disapproval of their "closed society."[131] Athletic tenets later tempered attitudes regarding academic integration throughout the South and eventually mandated racial accommodation.[132] Without assigning too much causal force to one social phenomenon, the integration of sport wielded considerable might in suffocating white devotion to Mississippi's "closed society" and weakened the South's edifice of segregation.

The travails of the Mississippi State basketball team and the repeal of Mississippi's unwritten athletic law, like the larger civil rights movement, involved various forces that pulled the Magnolia State toward more racial integration and countervailing forces that obstructed social change. The consternation over and eventual suspension of the extralegal edict demonstrated that moderate white Mississippians, though not completely ready to

bury Jim Crow, clearly understood the central tenet of the civil rights movement—equality of opportunity—and began to demand it for themselves. In
the winter of 1962–63 the MSU basketball team, Coach McCarthy, President
Colvard, their advocates, and those who desired a different Mississippi and
a different South battled the same foes that black Mississippians fought and
thus conducted their own campaign against the "closed society." "'It was
much more than a basketball game,'" Leland Mitchell later declared, "'We
were making history. We were ambassadors for the South, though none of
us realized it at that time.'"[133] The effort to ensure Mississippi State's participation in the NCAA national basketball championships allowed moderate
whites an opportunity to show that Mississippi had never been completely
closed concerning racial issues, particularly those involving sports.[134] The
repeal of the unwritten law also signified the end to Mississippi's self-imposed
exile and the beginning of its slow reintegration into national affairs. Indeed,
something more than the game was truly lost.

Notes

The chapter is reprinted, with minor editorial changes to endnotes, from *Journal of Southern History* 63 (November 1997): 827–54. Reprinted by permission of the Southern Historical Association.

1. See Jules Tygiel, *Baseball's Great Experiment: Jackie Robinson and His Legacy* (New
York: Vintage Books, 1983); Wilma Dykeman and James Stokley, *Neither Black nor White*
(New York: Rinehart, 1957), chap. 13; Charles H. Martin, "The Integration of Southeast-
ern Conference Athletics," paper delivered to the fifty-sixth annual meeting of the South-
ern Historical Association, November 3, 1990, New Orleans; and Adolf H. Grundman, "The
Image of Intercollegiate Sports and the Civil Rights Movement: An Historian's View,"
Arena Review 3 (October 1979): 17–24.

2. *Jackson (Miss.) Clarion-Ledger,* March 8, 1963, 1, and March 1, 1961, 17. See also *Greenville (Miss.) Delta Democrat Times,* March 1, 1961, 1; and *Jackson (Miss.) Daily News,* March
1, 1961, 10.

3. Martin, "Integration of Southeastern Conference Athletics"; Joan Paul, Richard V.
McGhee, and Helen Fant, "The Arrival and Ascendance of Black Athletes in the Southeastern Conference, 1966–1980," *Phylon* 45 (1984): 284–97; *Jackson Clarion-Ledger,* February 1, 1963, 16; *Pittsburgh Courier,* February 9, 1963, 15; "Texas to Integrate Athletics,
Faubus Opposes," *Jet* 25 (November 28, 1963): 56.

4. Martin, "Integration of Southeastern Conference Athletics," 3; "Desegregating College Sports Creates Scheduling Problems," *Southern School News* 8 (May 1962): 15.

5. Robert W. Dubay, "Politics, Pigmentation, and Pigskin: The Georgia Tech Sugar Bowl
Controversy of 1955," *Atlanta History* 39 (Spring 1995): 21–35; "Time to Grow Up," *Ebony*
11 (February 1956): 88; "Miss. State in Liberty Bowl Brings NAACP Protest," *Jet* 25 (December 26, 1963): 55.

6. *New York Times,* July 29, 1956, 4S; *State Athletic Commission v. Dorsey,* 359 U.S. 533 (1959); Dubay, "Politics, Pigmentation, and Pigskin"; Martin, "Integration of Southeastern Conference Athletics," 5–6; Dykeman and Stokley, *Neither Black nor White,* 248–53; *Jackson Daily News,* February 12, 1963, 11.

7. Robert W. Dubay, "Pigmentation and Pigskin: A Jones County Junior College Dilemma," *Journal of Mississippi History* 46 (February 1984): 43–50; *Los Angeles Times,* October 16, 1994, B-1 and B-3.

8. *Greenville Delta-Democrat Times,* February 22, 1959, 1; *Jackson Clarion-Ledger,* February 22, 1959, 2A; *Jackson State Times,* March 2, 1959, 4B.

9. "14 New Laws Placed on Statute Books," *Southern School News* 7 (July 1960): 7.

10. *Greenville Delta Democrat-Times,* February 22, 1959, 1.

11. *Jackson State Times,* February 10, 1959, 4B; *Greenville Delta Democrat-Times,* February 22, 1959, 1; "State University Turns Down NCAA Bid in Stand against Player Integration," *Southern School News* 5 (March 1959): 2; *Jackson Daily News,* March 1, 1961, 10, and March 2, 1961, 8D; *Jackson Clarion-Ledger,* March 3, 1961, 16, and March 6, 1962, 20; *Jackson Daily News,* March 6, 1963, 12.

12. Martin, "Integration of Southeastern Conference Athletics," 6; Dykeman and Stokely, *Neither Black nor White,* 253; *Jackson Clarion-Ledger,* December 30, 1956, 1; *Jackson Daily News,* December 29, 1956, 1; *New York Times,* December 31, 1956, 13; *Jackson Clarion-Ledger,* February 11, 1959, 15; *Greenville Delta Democrat-Times,* February 22, 1959, 1.

13. *Jackson Clarion-Ledger,* February 11, 1959, 15.

14. *Jackson Daily News,* March 16, 1962, 13.

15. See Russell Barrett, *Integration at Ole Miss* (Chicago: Quadrangle Books, 1965); Walter Lord, *The Past That Would Not Die* (New York: Harper and Row, 1965); James Meredith, *Three Years in Mississippi* (Bloomington: Indiana University Press, 1966); James Silver, *Mississippi: The Closed Society* (New York: Harcourt, Brace, and World, 1966); David G. Sansing, *Making Haste Slowly: The Troubled History of Higher Education in Mississippi* (Jackson: University Press of Mississippi, 1990), 156–95.

16. *Jackson Daily News,* February 12, 1963, 10.

17. *Jackson Clarion-Ledger,* February 26, 1963, 11. See also *Jackson Clarion-Ledger,* February 25, 1963, 9, 10; *The (Mississippi State University) Reflector,* February 28, 1963, 1, 6.

18. *Greenville Delta-Democrat Times,* February 20, 1959, 1, 2; *Jackson Clarion-Ledger,* February 20, 1959, 1; *Jackson State Times,* February 20, 1959, 1A; *Jackson Daily News,* March 1, 1961, 11; *Jackson Daily News,* February 13, 1962, 11–12; *Jackson Clarion-Ledger,* February 14, 1962, 17.

19. Dean W. Colvard, *Mixed Emotions: As Barriers Fell—A University President Remembers* (Danville, Ill.: Interstate Publishers and Printers, 1985), 61–62.

20. *Jackson Clarion-Ledger,* February 28, 1963, 5D; *The (MSU) Reflector,* February 28, 1963, 8.

21. *Jackson Clarion-Ledger,* March 3, 1963, 4C; *The (MSU) Reflector,* February 28, 1963, 8.

22. Silver, *Mississippi.*

23. *Jackson Daily News,* March 1, 1962, 1F; *Jackson State Times,* March 1, 1961, 1; *USA Today,* March 29, 1996, 2A.

24. *Jackson Daily News,* February 28, 1963, 3C; *Jackson Clarion-Ledger,* March 1, 1963, 19. Supportive petitions also originated from several groups of State students and from res-

idents of Hattiesburg, Oxford, and Yazoo City. Box A85-203, vols. 1 and 2, Dean W. Colvard Miscellaneous Collection, Department of Archives, Mitchell Memorial Library, Mississippi State University, Starkville (hereafter cited as Colvard Miscellaneous Collection).

25. Dean W. Colvard Papers, box 2, Department of Archives, Mitchell Memorial Library, Mississippi State University, Starkville (hereafter cited as Colvard Presidential Papers); box A85-203, vols. 1 and 2, Colvard Miscellaneous Collection. See also *Jackson Daily News*, March 6, 1963, 14.

26. *Jackson Clarion-Ledger*, March 1, 1963, 19.

27. *Jackson Daily News*, March 4, 1963, 9 (quotation); *Jackson State Times*, February 14, 1961, 4B.

28. *Jackson Daily News*, March 4, 1963, 9.

29. *Jackson Clarion-Ledger*, March 13, 1988, 12A. Several sources confirm Mitchell's memory. See *Jackson Clarion-Ledger*, March 13, 1963, 6; Buddy Graves to Dean W. Colvard (hereafter DWC), February 26, 1963; Sam A. Coggin to DWC, March 4, 1963; Edwin C. Brown to DWC, March 7, 1963; and R. B. Smith to the Mississippi Board of Trustees for Institutions of Higher Learning, March 7, 1963, all in box A85-203, vol. 1, Colvard Miscellaneous Collection.

30. *Jackson Daily News*, February 27, 1963, 11; *Jackson Clarion-Ledger*, February 27, 1963, 13. See also *Jackson Daily News*, February 26, 1963, 9.

31. Earl F. Guyton to DWC, March 4, 1963, box A85-203, vol. 2, Colvard Miscellaneous Collection.

32. James Harrison McCarthy Vertical File, Department of Archives, Mitchell Memorial Library, Mississippi State University, Starkville; "Mississippi State 1962–63 Basketball Dope Book for Press, Radio, and Television," no. 296, Subject Group 5, Record Group 39, Mississippi Department of Archives and History, Jackson; *Jackson Clarion-Ledger*, February 11, 1959, 16; *Jackson Daily News*, February 9, 1961, 9; *Jackson Clarion-Ledger*, February 10, 1961, 21; *Jackson State Times*, February 16, 1961, 1C; *Jackson Daily News*, March 6, 1962, 10.

33. *Jackson Clarion-Ledger*, February 26, 1959, 1B.

34. *Jackson Daily News*, March 4, 1962, 1.

35. *Jackson Daily News*, March 1, 1963, 7 (quotations), February 14, 1963, 20; *Greenville Delta Democrat-Times*, February 27, 1963, 8; *The (MSU) Reflector*, February 28, 1963, 6.

36. *Jackson Clarion-Ledger*, March 13, 1988, 12A.

37. Box A85-203, vols. 1 and 2, Colvard Miscellaneous Collection.

38. *Jackson Clarion-Ledger*, February 17, 1963, 5D.

39. *Greenville Delta Democrat-Times*, March 4, 1963, 4.

40. Colvard, *Mixed Emotions;* John K. Bettersworth, *People's University: The Centennial History of Mississippi State* (Jackson: University Press of Mississippi, 1980), 341–71.

41. *Jackson Daily News*, March 1, 1962, 1F, February 14, 1963, 2D.

42. Sansing, *Making Haste Slowly,* chaps. 9–11.

43. Colvard, *Mixed Emotions,* 64.

44. *Jackson State Times*, March 1, 1959, 1A, March 2, 1959, 4B; *Jackson Clarion-Ledger*, March 3, 1959, 1.

45. *Jackson Clarion-Ledger*, March 15, 1983, 2C. See also Colvard, *Mixed Emotions,* 19.

46. *The (MSU) Reflector,* March 7, 1963, 1.

47. William Winter to DWC, March 4, 1963, and Franklin P. Howard to DWC, March 8, 1963, Colvard Presidential Papers, box A85-203, vol. 1.

48. J. Andrew Carothers to DWC, undated, Colvard Presidential Papers, box A85-203, vol 1.

49. *Jackson Clarion-Ledger,* March 15, 1983, 2C.

50. Colvard, *Mixed Emotions,* 63–64 and 60 (quotation).

51. "Statement by D. W. Colvard, President of Mississippi State University, Relative to Participation in National Collegiate Athletic Association Championship Competition," box A85-203, vol. 1, Colvard Miscellaneous Collection.

52. *Jackson Clarion-Ledger,* March 3, 1963, 1C; *Jackson Daily News,* March 3, 1963, 1; *Greenville Delta Democrat-Times,* March 4, 1963, 1.

53. Colvard, *Mixed Emotions,* 68–70.

54. *Jackson Clarion-Ledger,* March 4, 1963, 1; *Pittsburgh Courier,* March 16, 1963, 1. See also *Memphis Commercial-Appeal,* March 5, 1963, 16.

55. "Affairs of State," *Jackson Clarion-Ledger,* March 8, 1963, 7A.

56. *Jackson Clarion-Ledger,* March 4, 1963, 1.

57. *Jackson Daily News,* March 4, 1963, 9.

58. *Jackson Clarion-Ledger,* March 5, 1963, 1 (quotation); *Memphis Commercial-Appeal,* March 5, 1963, 15; Secretary's report of telephone call from Walter Hester to DWC, March 4, 1963, box A85-203, vol. 1, Colvard Miscellaneous Collection.

59. *Jackson Clarion-Ledger,* March 4, 1963, 1.

60. *Jackson Daily News,* March 4, 1963, 12; *Memphis Commercial-Appeal,* March 5, 1963, 15; *Jackson Clarion-Ledger,* March 4, 1963, 1.

61. *Jackson Clarion-Ledger,* March 2, 1963, 8. For a full copy of the resolution, see Charles M. Hills's column, "Affairs of State," in the *Jackson Clarion-Ledger,* March 11, 1963, 6. Cecil H. Brown to Billy Mitts, March 5, 1963, box A85-203, vol. 1, Colvard Miscellaneous Collection.

62. *Jackson Daily News,* March 6, 1963, 10.

63. Quoted in *Jackson Clarion-Ledger,* March 9, 1963, 4.

64. *Jackson Clarion-Ledger,* March 8, 1963, 8A.

65. *Jackson Clarion-Ledger,* March 6, 1963, 10.

66. *Jackson Clarion-Ledger,* March 14, 1963, 8A.

67. Anonymous to DWC, undated, box A85-203, vol. 1, Colvard Miscellaneous Collection (first quotation); Lay W. West to DWC, March 6, 1963, box A85-203, vol. 1, Colvard Miscellaneous Collection, William L. Koerber to Thomas Tubb, March 7, 1963, box A85-203, vol. 2, Colvard Miscellaneous Collection.

68. Lay W. West to DWC, March 6, 1963, box A85-203, vol. 1, Colvard Miscellaneous Collection.

69. "Mississippi Notebook," *Jackson Clarion-Ledger,* March 20, 1963, 10A.

70. Anonymous to DWC, March 4, 1963, box A85-203, vol. 1, Colvard Miscellaneous Collection.

71. *Memphis Commercial-Appeal,* March 4, 1963, 16.

72. Owen Alexander to DWC, March 6, 1963, box A85-203, vol. 1, Colvard Miscellaneous Collection.

73. *Greenville Delta Democrat-Times,* February 27, 1963, 2; *Jackson Daily News,* March 8, 1963, 1; C. E. Jones to DWC, March 8, 1963, box A85-203, vol. 1, Colvard Miscellaneous Collection.

74. Patricia W. Shelby to DWC, February 26, 1963, box A85-203, vol. 1, Colvard Miscellaneous Collection; *Pittsburgh Courier,* March 23, 1963, 15.

75. Ben A. Douglas to DWC, March 4, 1963, box A85-203, vol. 2, Colvard Miscellaneous Collection; Howard Dyer Jr. to DWC, March 4, 1963, box A85-203, vol. 1, Colvard Miscellaneous Collection.

76. *Jackson Daily News,* February 1, 1963, 1, 9, February 7, 1963, 1, 12A; *Jackson Clarion-Ledger,* February 2, 1963, 1, 16, February 19, 1963, 1.

77. *Jackson Clarion-Ledger,* March 7, 1963, 1, 12A; *Memphis Commercial-Appeal,* March 7, 1963, 60; E. B. Stribling, Charles S. Whittington, and Hugh Critz to Ross Barnett, March 7, 1963, box A85-203, vol. 1, Colvard Miscellaneous Collection.

78. "SACS Reprimands University but Continues Accreditation," *Southern School News* 9 (December 1962): 14; "Mississippi State May Compete in Biracial Playoffs," *Southern School News* 10 (March 1963): 6; R. B. Smith to College Board, March 7, 1963, box A85-203, vol. 1, Colvard Miscellaneous Collection; *Memphis Commercial-Appeal,* March 9, 1963, 20.

79. "Board of Trustees of the Institutions of Higher Learning," Record Group 39, Mississippi Department of Archives and History, Jackson.

80. *Greenville Delta Democrat-Times,* February 19, 1959, 1; "State University Turns Down NCAA Bid in Stand against Player Integration," *Southern School News* 5 (March 1959): 12.

81. *Jackson Clarion-Ledger,* March 6, 1963, 1, 10, 16, March 8, 1963, 1.

82. *Memphis Commercial-Appeal,* March 8, 1963, 24; *Jackson Clarion-Ledger,* March 6, 1963, 17, 18.

83. *Jackson Daily News,* March 7, 1963, 1, 12A.

84. *Jackson Daily News,* March 11, 1963, 14.

85. *Jackson Daily News,* March 11, 1963, 12; M. M. Roberts to David Sansing, September 23, 1978, 24–25, box 6, Verner Holmes Papers, Department of Archives, John D. Williams Library, University of Mississippi, Oxford.

86. *Jackson Clarion-Ledger,* March 10, 1963, 10A.

87. *Greenville Delta Democrat-Times,* March 10, 1963, 1.

88. *Jackson Clarion-Ledger,* March 10, 1963, 10A.

89. Ibid.

90. Minutes of the Board of Trustees of State Institutions of Higher Learning, March 9, 1963, Department of Archives, Mitchell Memorial Library, Mississippi State University, Starkville.

91. *Jackson Daily News,* March 11, 1963, 12 (quotation); *Memphis Commercial-Appeal,* March 11, 1963, 16.

92. *Jackson Clarion-Ledger,* March 10, 1963, 1A.

93. Lewis Graham to DWC, March 11, 1963, box A85-203, vol. 2, Colvard Miscellaneous Collection.

94. *Greenville Delta Democrat-Times,* March 11, 1963, 4.

95. *Mitts and Lawson v. Board of Trustees of the Institutions of Higher Learning of the State of Mississippi et al.,* Bill of Complaint, Cause No. 62,880, Chancery Court, Mississippi, First Judicial District of Hinds County, 5 (Hinds County Chancery Court Building, Jackson).

96. *Mitts, Mashburn, and Lawson v. the Board of Trustees of the Institutions of Higher Learning of the State of Mississippi, Colvard, McCarthy, and Their Agents, Servants, and Employees,* Writ of Injunction, Cause No. 62,880, Chancery Court, Mississippi, First Judicial District of Hinds County, 1 (Hinds County Chancery Court Building, Jackson).

97. *Mitts and Lawson v. Board of Trustees of the Institutions of Higher Learning of the State of Mississippi et al.,* Bill of Complaint, Cause No. 62,880, Chancery Court, Mississippi, First Judicial District of Hinds County, 6. See also *Jackson Clarion-Ledger,* March 14, 1963, 1, 11; *Memphis Commercial-Appeal,* March 14, 1963, 1; *Greenville Delta Democrat-Times,* March 14, 1963, 1; Colvard, *Mixed Emotions,* 163.

98. Colvard, *Mixed Emotions,* 87–88; *Jackson Daily News,* March 14, 1963, 1E; *Memphis Commercial-Appeal,* March 14, 1963, 62; *The (MSU) Reflector,* March 14, 1963, 1.

99. *Chicago Tribune,* March 14, 1963, sec. 3, p. 1.

100. Colvard, *Mixed Emotions,* 89; "Mississippi State Team in Biracial Game," *Southern School News* 9 (April 1963): 10.

101. Colvard, *Mixed Emotions,* 88. See also Bettersworth, *People's University,* 349–50; *Jackson Clarion-Ledger,* March 14, 1963, 1A.

102. *Jackson Clarion-Ledger,* March 15, 1963, 1.

103. *Jackson Clarion-Ledger,* March 15, 1963, 25, March 15, 1983, 2C.

104. Colvard, *Mixed Emotions,* 88–89; *Chicago Tribune,* March 15, 1963, sec. 3, p. 3.; *Jackson Daily News,* March 14, 1963, 1, 14A, March 15, 1963, 13; *Jackson Clarion-Ledger,* March 14, 1963, 1E, March 15, 1963, 1, 24, 25; *Memphis Commercial-Appeal,* March 15, 1963, 1.

105. *Jackson Clarion-Ledger,* March 15, 1963, 25–26; *Jackson Daily News,* March 14, 1963, 1; *Memphis Commercial-Appeal,* March 15, 1963, 22.

106. *Jackson Clarion-Ledger,* March 15, 1963, 25.

107. *Greenville Delta Democrat-Times,* March 15, 1963, 5; Chancery Summons, Cause No. 62,880, Chancery Court, Mississippi, First Judicial District of Hinds County; *Jackson Clarion-Ledger,* March 15, 1983, 2C.

108. *The Board of Trustees of the Institutions of Higher Learning of the State of Mississippi et al. v. Mitts and Lawson et al.,* Cause No. 62,880, Supreme Court, Mississippi (copy of the original order located in the records of the Chancery Court, First Judicial District of Hinds County, Hinds County Chancery Court Building). See also *Jackson Daily News,* March 15, 1963, 1; *Chicago Tribune,* March 15, 1963, sec. 3, p. 1; Colvard, *Mixed Emotions,* 178–79; and "Mississippi State Team in Biracial Game," 10. The Hinds County Court chancellor, Stokes V. Robertson Jr., officially dissolved the order on March 28. *Mitts and Lawson v. Board of Trustees of the Institutions of Higher Learning of the State of Mississippi et al.,* Order of Dismissal without Prejudice, Cause No. 62,880, Chancery Court, Mississippi, First Judicial District of Hinds County; *Jackson Daily News,* April 2, 1973, 6A.

109. *Jackson Clarion-Ledger,* March 13, 1963, 15; "Desegregating College Sports Creates Scheduling Problems," 15; *Chicago Tribune,* March 14, 1963, sec. 3, p. 1.

110. *Jackson Clarion-Ledger,* March 18, 1963, 3C; *Jackson State Times,* February 23, 1959, 5B.

111. *Jackson Clarion-Ledger,* March 9, 1963, 7 (quotation); *Jackson State Times,* March 1, 1961, 2A.

112. *Jackson Clarion-Ledger,* March 15, 1963, 16.

113. Anonymous family to DWC, March 9, 1963, box A85-203, vol. 1, Colvard Miscella-

neous Collection; and *The (University of Mississippi) Mississippian,* March 5, 1963, 4; *The (MSU) Reflector,* March 14, 1963, 5.

114. *Jackson (Miss.) Advocate,* March 16, 1963, 4; The *Advocate* was a black-owned and -operated newspaper funded partially by Mississippi's Sovereignty Commission, a state agency designed to protect segregation. Julius E. Thompson notes that "the black press in Mississippi had had two voices during the 1960s, one demanding immediate freedom, equality, and justice for blacks, another pressing for gradual changes in black progress." Julius E. Thompson, *The Black Press in Mississippi, 1865–1985* (Gainesville: University Presses of Florida, 1993), 49, 79–80 (quotation).

115. *Chicago Defender,* March 16–23, 1963, 16.

116. *The (University of Mississippi) Mississippian,* March 19, 1963, 8 (quotation); *Jackson Clarion-Ledger,* March 13, 1988, 12A.

117. *Chicago Tribune,* March 16, 1963, sec. 3, p. 1; *Jackson Clarion-Ledger,* March 16, 1963, 9; *Jackson Daily News,* March 16, 1963, 2; *Memphis Commercial-Appeal,* March 16, 1963, 20.

118. *Pittsburgh Courier,* March 23, 1963, 15.

119. *Jet* 23 (April 4, 1963): 53. See also *Chicago Tribune,* March 16, 1963, sec. 3, p. 1; and *Greenville Delta Democrat-Times,* March 17, 1963, 10.

120. *Jackson Clarion-Ledger,* March 16, 1963, 9; *Southern Exposure* 7 (Fall 1979): 77, 80; *Chicago Tribune,* March 31, 1996, sec. 3, p. 6.

121. *Jackson Daily News,* March 16, 1963, 20.

122. *Jackson Daily News,* March 16, 1963, 1.

123. DWC to Ross Barnett, May 25, 1963, box 12, Colvard Presidential Papers.

124. Minutes of the Board of Trustees of State Institutions of Higher Learning, March 21, 1963, Department of Archives, Mitchell Memorial Library, Mississippi State University, Starkville; *Jackson Daily News,* March 21, 1963, 1; *Jackson Clarion-Ledger,* March 22, 1963, 1.

125. Minutes of the Board of Trustees of State Institutions of Higher Learning, April 18, 1963, Department of Archives, Mitchell Memorial Library, Mississippi State University, Starkville.

126. *Jackson Clarion-Ledger,* March 13, 1988, 12A (quotation); Helen Tyson to DWC, March 17, 1963, box A85-203, vol. 1, Colvard Miscellaneous Collection.

127. *Greenville Delta Democrat-Times,* March 2, 1961, 4.

128. James C. Cobb, *The Selling of the South: The Southern Crusade for Industrial Development, 1936–1980* (Baton Rouge: Louisiana State University Press, 1982); Elizabeth Jacoway and David R. Colburn, eds., *Southern Businessmen and Desegregation* (Baton Rouge: Louisiana State University Press, 1982), 1–14; Charles S. Whittington to College Board, March 6, 1963, box A85-203, vol. 1, Colvard Miscellaneous Collection.

129. *The (MSU) Reflector,* February 28, 1962, 4.

130. *Eyes on the Prize: America's Civil Rights Years, 1954–1964,* episode 2: "Fighting Back, 1957–1962," videorecording, prod. and dir. Judith Vecchione (Alexandria, Va.: Blackside, Inc., 1986).

131. Willie Morris, *The Courting of Marcus Dupree* (Garden City, N.Y.: Doubleday, 1983), 100.

132. Bill Finger, "Just Another Ball Game," *Southern Exposure* 12 (Fall 1979): 74–81.

133. *Jackson Clarion-Ledger,* March 13, 1988, 1A.

134. James Silver argues in *Mississippi: The Closed Society* that the quest for complete

racial segregation stifled white dissent. John Dittmer claims that by the fall of 1964 "White Mississippi no longer spoke with a single voice" concerning the maintenance of segregation. John Dittmer, *Local People: The Struggle for Civil Rights in Mississippi* (Urbana: University of Illinois Press, 1994), 314. My contention is that white Mississippians had never spoken with a single voice concerning racial issues, particularly those involving sports, nor had they been completely inhibited from publicly or privately criticizing the effects of segregation upon either themselves or Mississippi's society.

PART 3

Myths, Symbols, and Stereotypes in Southern Sport: The Shaping of a Regional Identity

10. An Atheist in Alabama Is Someone Who Doesn't Believe in Bear Bryant: A Symbol for an Embattled South

ANDREW DOYLE

> As a usual matter, I do not have the time or inclination to answer the slanted news reports concerning this section of the country, but this is too much. The formula is well known—if something is unfavorable about the South, the news is splashed all over the front pages of newspapers across the country, but if the news is favorable to us, then we are either ridiculed in some way or the item is ignored or buried. I submit the article is unfair and unsportsmanlike, and is such an unjust criticism of a great football team (coached by one of the top football coaches of all time) that I feel compelled to reply.
>
> —Letter to the editor, *Los Angeles Times,* December 31, 1964

THE 1961 University of Alabama football team won eleven consecutive games and ended the season ranked number one in both wire service polls. A punishing defense led by the All-American middle linebacker Lee Roy Jordan dominated opponents, giving up only twenty-five points all year. On New Year's Day 1962, it capped its first national championship season in twenty years with a 10-3 Sugar Bowl victory over the University of Arkansas. A national football championship would have been cause for ecstatic celebration in the best of times, but the early 1960s could never have been mistaken for the best of times in Alabama.

The day after the Sugar Bowl victory, U.S. Representative Frank Boykin of Mobile expressed his unbounded joy in a rambling and somewhat incoherent letter to Alabama's head football coach, Paul "Bear" Bryant. He invoked the glorious martial tradition of the Confederacy, declaring, "Your men stood like Stonewall Jackson." He added, "They should now name you not just Bear Bryant, but General Bear Bryant." Boykin effused at length about "the thrill that you and your marvelous, brilliant men" gave to him, his family, and "our colored people that's [*sic*] done such a good job for us over the years."[1]

Yet Boykin believed that the Alabama victory provided him with something more practical than mere thrills. Since the 1920s, southern politicians
and boosters had touted successful southern college football teams in their
ceaseless campaign to improve the South's negative image. "Well, the Alabama football team showed the world, the whole wide world what our men
could do. I doubt if we could have gotten half of the publicity or advertisement that you and your great team gave us had we spent a million dollars."
While an earlier generation of boosters saw the public relations value of football primarily in terms of economic development, Boykin had larger political issues in mind. He saw the Crimson Tide as a natural rallying point for
the embattled white South as it engaged in the escalating political battle over
civil rights. "There was so much joy, there was so much pleasure that you gave
all of the home folks and people all over the South and people all over this
Nation that want us to keep some part of our way of life," he gushed.[2]

Bryant and his championship team had become a potent symbol of pride
and cultural vitality to white southerners in the midst of a profound social
transformation. The "southern way of life" was a well-known euphemism
for legally sanctioned white supremacy, and Boykin and many other southern political leaders were then engaged in an increasingly desperate effort to
stave off its demise. By 1961, massive resistance was collapsing under the combined weight of federal pressure and grassroots agitation by southern blacks.
By the end of 1961, Alabama and Mississippi were the only states yet to desegregate a single public school. Boykin and his peers were hoping to effect
a miraculous defeat of the second Reconstruction by reviving the "Right
Fork" alliance with conservative northerners that had thwarted the first Reconstruction. Boykin's naive faith that the Crimson Tide's prowess could
somehow convince the rest of the nation of the decency and viability of the
dying racial caste system is a testament to the talismanic power the southerners ascribed to college football.[3]

The protracted death throes of Jim Crow produced a profound sense of social
dislocation among the millions of southern whites who believed that segregation was the cornerstone of their civilization. Yet the civil rights revolution
proceeded in tandem with the less dramatic but nonetheless highly significant
"Bulldozer Revolution." The unprecedented post–World War II economic
boom was finally lifting the South from a century of underdevelopment. Ag-
gregate personal income in Alabama rose by a phenomenal 554 percent between
1939 and 1959. During the same period, per capita income rose from a dismal
47 percent of the national average to a more respectable 65 percent.[4]

This economic transformation created new problems as it alleviated others. The disruption of family and community bonds and the ascendancy of

a consumer culture that fostered a worldview alien to traditional southern norms partially negated the satisfaction that came from a rising standard of living. A Thanksgiving Day 1959 editorial in the *Birmingham News* entitled "Thanks—For What?" expressed the malaise and disillusionment that fitfully coexisted with the steady drumbeat of optimistic boosterism. "The future is seemingly more vague than ever has been the case before," it observed. A "society of industrialism and big government" threatened to erode the southern character and lead ultimately to the loss of individual freedoms. The *News* welcomed Alabama's impressive economic growth, yet decried the soulless materialism symbolized by "Yankee Christmas parades."[5]

The postwar economic boom had a devastating impact on once-vibrant rural communities. Fully two-thirds of those rural-born Alabamians who came of age in the immediate postwar era abandoned the countryside. This flight from the soil was proportionately as great as the outmigrations that occurred as a result of the enclosure of the English countryside during the seventeenth century and the Irish Potato Famine of the 1840s. A staggering one-third of all Alabama farmers quit farming between 1954 and 1959. With the exception of the Mississippi Delta and parts of East Texas, the Cotton South had ceased to exist—the irrigated deserts of the Southwest had, by the early 1960s, become the center of U.S. cotton production. A young woman from New Mexico was even named the national Maid of Cotton in 1962. William Faulkner lamented the decline of the agricultural roots that had nourished the rich and distinctive culture of the South. "We no longer farm in Mississippi cotton fields," he stated. "We farm now in Washington corridors and committee rooms." The endemic rural poverty of the South was diminishing, but the agrarian society of traditional work rhythms, family stability, and unifying religious values was disappearing along with it.[6]

The postwar increase in material wealth also failed to erase the moral stigma that the region had borne since the Civil War. The South lost its Depression-era designation as the nation's number one economic problem just in time to acquire the status of national pariah during the era of the black freedom struggle. A nation that had yet to confront fully the hard realities of racial injustice still comfortably assumed that bigotry was strictly a southern problem. The growing ostracism of the South in the years after the *Brown* decision had dashed the southern progressive nostrum that economic growth would mitigate the South's status as the villain in the American morality play. White southerners, especially the urban middle class, desperately wished to convince the rest of the nation that they were members of the republic of virtue, and they reacted with both anguish and anger when this recognition was not forthcoming.

Millions of southerners, including many fans of other southern football programs, looked to Paul Bryant and his national champions to soothe the anguish and give expression to the anger. The Crimson Tide was simultaneously a proud symbol of the southern virtues the rest of the nation refused to recognize and a defiant statement that southerners could command respect if it were not freely granted. Reeling under the weight of social change, embattled white Alabamians embraced Bryant and the Crimson Tide with the passion of true believers. A national football championship spoke for itself; it was undeniable proof of achievement and legitimacy for a state that historically led the nation only in adult illiteracy and infant mortality.

The iconic image of Paul Bryant and his teams during the early 1960s embodied the complex and often radically contradictory impulses of this divided southern mind. Bryant repeatedly paid sincere homage to the simpler values of the agrarian South of his boyhood. He grew up in extreme poverty in Moro Bottom, Arkansas, and often spoke in reverential tones about how his mother's piety and inner strength enabled the family to persevere. His early teams at Alabama were comprised mostly of undersized boys from rural areas and small towns. Like their coach during his playing days at Alabama in the 1930s, they excelled more by dint of superior endurance and willpower than natural athletic gifts. The starters on his 1961 team averaged a scant 199 pounds, and he proudly referred to them as his "little bitty boys." Bryant modestly refused to claim credit for the stellar performance of his players, instead praising the parents, preachers, teachers, and high school coaches who had produced such fine young men. He lauded the "mamas and papas" of his players so frequently that the phrase became a buzzword throughout the state. Alabamians who had left their childhood homes in the countryside for growing cities and suburbs and their relatives who remained in rural communities saw Bryant and his teams as proof that bedrock values could survive in a changing world.[7]

Benny Marshall, the sports editor of the *Birmingham News,* noted that "boys from large places no longer dominate the Alabama football scene as they once did." Only six players on the 1961 roster were natives of the state's only three metropolitan areas of Birmingham, Montgomery, or Mobile. White Alabamians confronted with social, economic, and racial transformations saw the traditional rural virtues of hard work and social unity writ large on the Alabama football team. "Paul Bryant often speaks of his boys' raising and I applaud him," Marshall observed in 1960. "Upbringing does count." Three years later, he asserted that Bryant's players represented the "old, true values." Alabamians anointed their football champions as symbols of southern cultural vitality just as Americans frenetically lionized the Mercury astronauts as a symbols of American strength at the height of the cold war.[8]

The quarterback, Pat Trammell, was the heart and soul of the 1961 team and a made-to-order hero for white Alabamians as they crashed headlong into the social turbulence of the 1960s. He was the quintessential Everyman who lacked great natural athletic ability but performed the most heroic of deeds through hard work and the intangible qualities of audacity and perseverance. Trammell was a scrappy fighter who possessed the same competitive fires and passionate will to win that had propelled his coach from the Arkansas cotton fields to the national spotlight. He possessed the southern variant of Tom Wolfe's "Right Stuff." He was an uncanny extension of Bryant, a kindred spirit who shared a deep bond with his coach. In his autobiography, Bryant said simply, "Pat Trammell was the favorite person of my entire life."[9]

After his 1962 graduation, Trammell followed his father and brother into the medical profession, married the daughter of one of Bryant's friends, and settled his young family in Birmingham. This fairy tale story changed abruptly in 1968, when he was stricken with cancer. Bryant accompanied him to New York for surgery to allay his fears of "going up there and letting those goddam Yankees work on me." The coach and his favorite player shared a bottle of Jack Daniel's bourbon the night before surgery.[10]

The cancer recurred in the fall of 1968, and Trammell stoically faced his impending death. "'It's in the hands of the good Lord, now,'" he said. "'However it comes out, I'm not going to do a lot of crying about it.'" The entire state seemed to rally to him as his life ebbed. The University of Alabama created a "Pat Trammell Award" to be given annually to the student athlete who best exemplified the heroic qualities that he had embodied. Governor Albert Brewer presented the inaugural award to Tramell himself in October 1968. Trammell grimaced in pain as he held the hand of his six-year-old son on the sideline at the Alabama-Auburn game in November of that year. The Alabama team captain presented Trammell with the game ball; he, in turn, gave it to his son. He died in Birmingham eleven days later.[11]

His death generated an outpouring of emotion in the state. Newspaper editorials mourned his passing and praised him as proof that the vast majority of Alabama's young people were not like the long-haired, foul-mouthed radicals who appeared on television screens. The University of Alabama's president, Frank Rose, a Methodist minister, preached the sermon at his funeral. In his autobiography, Bryant said, "Pat Trammell was everything known to man. Everybody loved him. He was twenty-eight years old when he died. I still miss him."[12]

Lee Roy Jordan anchored the defense as a linebacker and, in the era of single-platoon football, played offensive center as well. Another of the "little bitty boys" at 205 pounds, he worked his way up the depth chart by demonstrating game-day ferocity on the practice field. A teammate recalled that Jordan "was the only man who ever practiced too hard for Coach Bryant." He instinctively took to heart Bryant's dictum, "Every play is a personal challenge." During his junior and senior seasons, the defense that he led never gave up more than seven points in a game. Before his final game at Alabama, Bryant said, "Jordan is the kind of kid—heck, he's a grown man—that you'd want your son to be. . . . The Lord was sure smiling on us when we got Jordan."[13]

Jordan came from Excel, Alabama, a town of 313 people in the piney woods region of south central Alabama. Excel has never been known for anything else before or since, but it became a symbol of the bygone rural world to millions of Alabamians after Jordan made it famous. Newspapers and sportscasters referred to him as "The Pride of Excel" or by the somewhat more formal title of "Lee Roy Jordan from Excel, Alabama." With a wink and a nod, the Birmingham News grandly proclaimed that he had made Excel "one of the biggest towns in the USA." Alabamians vicariously celebrated the shared traditions of their rural past by lionizing the farm boy from the town with the funny name that few had ever heard of. The youngest of four sons, Jordan helped run the family farm while still in high school. Like his coach, he used Alabama football as a means of transcending a modest rural background. "Yep, Lee Roy and I have a lot in common," said Bryant one day in the fall of 1960 after the two discussed that year's peanut crop. "We can talk."[14]

Billy Neighbors, a 225-pound senior tackle on the 1961 team, was not one of the "little bitty boys." He had, however, lost twenty-five pounds from his high school playing weight in order to fit into Bryant's speed-oriented system. If his size and talent were incompatible with the "average boy" image of that team, his humble demeanor and adherence to the southern code of good manners were reassuring to a society becoming acquainted with the concept of juvenile delinquency. The Birmingham News lauded him as "a soft voiced boy who says 'Yes sir' and 'No sir' like he was brought up to." A native of Northport, an industrial town across the Black Warrior River from Tuscaloosa, Neighbors was a hometown boy who embodied rootedness in an increasingly rootless world. He bragged that Tuscaloosa and Northport were the "best cities in world" and was proud to claim each as home. "'The people, that's what makes a city,'" he said. "'Mighty nice people there.'" An avid hunter, Neighbors once admitted that he preferred to hunt birds in Georgia, and then apologized for this minor display of disloyalty to his home state.[15]

Look named Neighbors to its 1961 All-American team, and he accepted the award at a banquet in New York City. Benny Marshall of the Birmingham News accompanied him there to cover the story, and he contrasted the virtue of a small-town boy like Neighbors with the numbing anonymity of New York. "Northport, Alabama, is a small place where everybody knows everybody,"

Marshall averred, while "Manhattan is a large place, where nobody wants to know anybody. . . . New York and Northport are 10 million miles apart." Marshall concluded that while New York had been exciting for Neighbors, "anyone from Northport, Alabama, knows that home is a great deal better."[16]

Yet this homiletic deference to the simple values of a moribund rural world may obscure how Bryant and his teams also symbolized the new society rising to take its place. Bryant's life was a classic American success story. His keen intelligence, driving ambition, and obsessive desire to outwork his opponents enabled him to rise to the pinnacle of the meritocratic and highly competitive world of commercialized sport. His 1960 book, *Building a Championship Football Team,* is a primer on the application of modern management techniques to the coaching profession. Bryant was also a millionaire businessman whose business ventures ranged from real estate, banking, and insurance to a meatpacking plant and a car dealership. He was also an inveterate player in the stock and commodities markets and was constantly on the phone with his broker. He may have reminisced fondly about plowing furrows behind a mule in Arkansas and recruited players who came from similar backgrounds, but the desire to make that world a distant memory drove him to excel. Many urban and suburban southerners one or two generations removed from rural poverty saw in Bryant the embodiment of the best of the old and the best of the new. Any coach who won as consistently as Bryant could be assured of tremendous popularity, but his mythic status in southern culture rested in large measure on the eagerness of southerners to view him as an affirmation of their own values and virtues.

Bryant and his players thus embodied a reconciliation of both the optimism and the misgivings that white southerners held regarding the social changes associated with the Bulldozer Revolution. While he maintained a cautious silence on the far more volatile race issue, this did not prevent many of his fans from regarding the success of his all-white teams as symbolic of the viability of white supremacy. Football, like virtually every other aspect of southern life in the early 1960s, was interpreted through the lens of racial politics. Bryant himself was a racial moderate who quietly aligned himself with the businessmen working for a peaceful end to legal segregation. He and Frank Rose brokered a deal with Alabama's race-baiting governor, John Patterson, that allowed the Crimson Tide to break the "unwritten law" and compete against a racially integrated Penn State team in the 1959 Liberty Bowl. Rose even obtained a sub rosa assurance from the leader of the Tuscaloosa County Citizens' Council that the latter would not instigate any protests against this unprecedented breach in the color line. Yet Bryant's white players, like the segregated university they represented, took on a symbolic value that overshadowed the subtleties of Bryant's own moderate position on the continuum of southern racial politics. Like Frank Boykin, many southerners viewed the Crimson Tide's success as a vindication of the "southern way of life" and loved Bryant all the more for it. Yet an influential segment of non-southerners judged Bryant harshly precisely because the cultural text that southern football fans helped to shape defied the evolving national consensus in support of black civil rights.[17]

Bryant, his team, and millions of southern football fans suffered a devastating disappointment in 1961 as a result of the growing national outrage over southern racial policies. The Crimson Tide's strong showing in 1961 had attracted the attention of the Rose Bowl Committee, and the serendipitous possibility of a New Year's Day appearance in Pasadena seemed likely. The Rose Bowl had held a talismanic power in Alabama since the Crimson Tide had established the legitimacy of southern football with its upset victory over the University of Washington there in 1926. Alabama's governor, William W. Brandon, had proudly declared then that the victory demonstrated that, contrary to popular belief, Alabama was not a provincial backwater populated by lazy white trash stricken with malaria, hookworm, and pellagra. The reclamation of the Rose Bowl tradition in an undefeated, national championship season would be something akin to magic to the Alabama faithful. The aura of the Crimson Tide's first three Rose Bowl appearances had influenced Bryant's decision to attend Alabama, and he had played on Alabama's fourth Rose Bowl team in 1935. His passion to return there as a coach led him to forsake the customary coyness that coaches generally observe when reporters question them about possible bowl matchups. When asked about the prospect of a return to the Rose Bowl at a postgame press conference in early November 1961, Bryant's normally taciturn visage melted into an enormous grin. "'I would just about walk out there for the chance to play in it,'" he said, "'and I believe my players would too.'"[18]

Bryant and Rose assured the Rose Bowl Committee that they would not object to playing an integrated UCLA team in the Rose Bowl. Alabama had competed against an integrated Penn State team in the 1959 Liberty Bowl, and Bryant and Rose planned once again to draw on the immense prestige and popularity of the Alabama football program to mute any political opposition to the game within the state. As he did in 1959, Governor Patterson, an Alabama alumnus and strong football booster, approved the Tide's participation in an interracial athletic contest. The sacrosanct status of Alabama football allowed its interests to take precedence over an absolute adherence to white supremacy. The 1961 Rose Bowl illustrated the internal contradictions of the southern racial system. Alabama's political power structure gave

permission to the Crimson Tide to play a football game against black players before nearly a hundred thousand people and a national television audience while it simultaneously defended the infamous Birmingham ordinance
that prohibited an interracial game of checkers at home. The epiphany of a
national championship season capped by a triumphant return to the Rose
Bowl appeared to be a reality. Delighted Alabama fans began making plans
to spend the New Year's holiday in southern California.[19]

The dream began to unravel when Alabama's rumored Rose Bowl invitation ignited a controversy on the West Coast. Three days before the Alabama–
Georgia Tech game, a black student group in Los Angeles announced that it
would organize demonstrations and a boycott of the game by black players if
Alabama were invited. Mel Durslag, a columnist for the *Los Angeles Examiner,*
declared that extending a Rose Bowl invitation to a segregated southern university with an all-white team "'would be a scandalous affront to Southern
California . . . it would be sheer lunacy for people who believe in integrated
athletics to mess with a school whose leaders hold firmly to segregation.'"[20]

The Rose Bowl Committee, the Southern California Football Writers Association, and the sports editors of the *Los Angeles Times* and the *Pasadena
Star-Telegram* had all supported the Alabama invitation, and all sought to
downplay the controversy. These senior members of the West Coast athletic
fraternity tried to keep the divisive race issue from entering the heretofore
conservative and self-contained world of sports. Paul Zimmerman, the sports
editor of the *Los Angeles Times,* declared, "It is a tragic thing that racial prejudice should become a big bugaboo this year in the selection of the Rose Bowl
team." He noted that USC and UCLA had played regular-season games over
the past decade against teams from segregated southern universities. "So why
all the uproar now over Alabama?" he pleaded.[21]

The uproar was a harbinger of the increasing politicization of sports. Younger sportswriters like Durslag and Jim Murray of the *Los Angeles Times* believed
that the political consciousness of their generation should be applied to the
athletic world. Durslag spoke favorably of the nascent "sociological revolution" and the role that integrated athletics could play in it. Murray traveled
to Alabama for the Alabama–Georgia Tech game and wrote, "I came down
to Birmingham not to find social injustice but to cover a football game. But
the crosscurrents of our time are such that the two are interrelated."[22] Murray, Durslag, and their peers explicitly repudiated the genial familiarity that
sports journalists had customarily displayed toward the men and institutions
they covered. They refused to accept the comfortable role of cheerleader for
the home team. They sought instead to explore the larger social and political
issues that arose in the sporting world. Murray published five columns about

the Rose Bowl controversy, fanning the flames of opposition to Alabama's participation in the game. He admitted that denying the Alabama players the opportunity to play in the Rose Bowl was unjust, but he asserted that an Alabama appearance in Pasadena on New Year's Day would implicitly legitimate the far greater injustices of southern society. He called Birmingham the "show place of the Deep South, gateway to the Ku Klux Klan . . . the place where when they say 'Evening Dress,' they mean a bed sheet with eyeholes." Murray declared that Alabama's number one ranking in the wire service polls was "as meaningless as a baby's gurgle, an affront to the disciples of desegregation. An all-white team has no business being No. 1."[23]

This display of outrage in California reflected the emerging transformation in national attitudes toward the southern racial caste system. The live-and-let-live stance that most non-southerners had held toward the southern system of white supremacy since the late nineteenth century was rapidly disappearing. The 1960 platforms of both major parties contained fairly strong civil rights planks. The direct action tactics of the lunch counter sit-ins of 1960 and the Freedom Rides of the following year had a profound effect on the national consciousness. The televised images of white mobs taunting and beating earnest black and white students wearing conservative suits or dresses reverberated through the nation. Stirred by the activist image and oratorical eloquence of John F. Kennedy, moved by the gross injustices inflicted upon southern blacks, and outraged by the brutality that television news now brought into their living rooms, a critical mass of Americans had become convinced that the evils of racial injustice must be eliminated. Many Americans now believed that the toleration of racial injustice was morally wrong. With the northern ghetto riots still several years in the future, non-southerners allowed themselves the luxury of viewing racial bigotry as a uniquely southern problem, and an emerging majority began to view the white South as an insult to the democratic ideals of the nation.

Alabama in particular bore the stigma of this rising national scorn and indignation. E. Culpeper Clark states, "Alabama was to the civil rights movement what Virginia was to the Civil War, its significance lending itself to enlargement in the public mind because the most memorable engagements occurred on its soil." One of the most politically progressive southern states in the two decades prior to the *Brown* decision, Alabama had fallen into the mire of demagoguery and officially sanctioned terrorist violence during the era of massive resistance. The white leadership of Montgomery had met the 1955–56 bus boycott with flagrantly discriminatory prosecutions, and Ku Klux Klansmen bombed the homes of Martin Luther King Jr. and other boycott leaders. The University of Alabama itself was the scene of several days of ri-

oting in February 1956, when a black woman named Autherine Lucy unsuccessfully attempted to enroll there under a court order. Birmingham was
notorious as the most rigidly segregated major city in the nation, and to call
Birmingham's public safety commissioner Eugene "Bull" Connor brutal
cheapened the word. The city had earned the nickname "Bombingham" due
to the forty racially motivated bombings that had occurred there between
1955 and 1961. Birmingham police turned a blind eye toward the bombings,
and policemen actually participated in several of them. Prosecutorial laxity
ensured that no one was convicted of any of the bombings until the 1970s.[24]

Alabama solidified its position as a national pariah in May 1961, when
CORE and SNCC members tested compliance with recent Supreme Court
and Interstate Commerce Commission decisions banning segregated accommodations in interstate travel. The Freedom Riders met little resistance in
Virginia, the Carolinas, and Georgia but experienced a hellish orgy of violence shortly after crossing the Alabama line. A mob of whites in Anniston
beat the Freedom Riders and burned their bus. Another bus with CORE
volunteers ran the gauntlet in Anniston only to be greeted at the Birmingham Trailways station by a vigilante mob wielding baseball bats, lead pipes,
and blackjacks. Bull Connor had ordered his police to stay away from the
station to allow the Klansmen a free reign, and later explained the absence
of police with a disingenuous declaration that his department had been
short-staffed because of Mother's Day. Six days later an even larger riot greeted the Freedom Riders in Montgomery. John Siegenthaler, an assistant to
Attorney General Robert Kennedy, was among those beaten badly enough
to require hospitalization. Governor Patterson reacted to this terrorism by
blaming the victims and absolving the mobs. "The citizens of this state are
so enraged that I cannot guarantee protection to this bunch of rabble rous-
ers," he declared.[25]

These enormities were etched into the minds of the Californians who protested Alabama's appearance in the nation's most prestigious and lucrative
bowl game. Citing accusations that Bryant's teams played with unnecessary
brutality, Jim Murray portrayed the Crimson Tide as an aggregation of violent ruffians little different from the white mobs who wore the black hats in
the real-life drama unfolding in the South. Bryant and the Crimson Tide
became identified with the ugly face of segregation that had been exposed
to the nation by the assaults on the Freedom Riders.

The Rose Bowl Committee's trial balloon lay in tatters, and Alabama's Rose
Bowl dreams were dead. Neither the Rose Bowl sponsors nor University of
Alabama officials were eager to charge blindly forward into this looming
debacle. A hasty retreat was more palatable to each than a maelstrom of

boycotts and demonstrations. Alabama settled for a more prosaic bowl matchup, agreeing to meet Arkansas in the Sugar Bowl. Bryant, his players, and the Alabama faithful were devastated. The Rose Bowl had been dangled before them and then cruelly snatched away. Jim Murray noted that the collapse of the Rose Bowl dream "hit this southern city as hard as if Fort Sumter had suddenly returned fire after all these years." A crestfallen Frank Rose personally delivered the news to the team, explaining that Alabama could not accept a Rose Bowl bid even if it were offered because the political risk was too great.[26]

The Rose Bowl controversy marked the beginning of the most trying period in Bryant's career. He came to embody the worst northern fears of the South as a land of irrationality and violence. A 1961 *Time* profile labeled Bryant "a relentless and brutal taskmaster. He drinks Salty Dogs, runs up scores, browbeats sportswriters, cusses his players, and believes in corporal punishment—usually a size 12-D shoe applied to the seat of the pants." *Sports Illustrated* lauded the achievements of the national champions but seemed uneasy about the team and its coach. It noted that the Alabama defense hit "with the viciousness of a pack of sharks" and added, "Bryant's image outside of Alabama . . . is that of a tyrant, a slave driver on the practice field, a recruiter without scruples, a ruthless opponent."[27] Alabama journalists and politicians angrily dismissed the *Time* and *Sports Illustrated* articles as scurrilous attacks on a genuine southern hero by the biased northeastern media. In a press release entitled "Statement for *Time* Magazine," Frank Rose defended Bryant as "one of the finest men I have ever known." The sisters of the University of Alabama chapter of the Kappa Kappa Gamma sorority registered their dissent by hanging an effigy of *Time* at a campus pep rally.[28]

The Pavlovian defensiveness of most Alabamians to the attacks on Bryant demonstrated the bitter sectional hostilities engendered by the second Reconstruction. But a controversial incident in the 1961 Georgia Tech–Alabama game revealed political divisions within the white South that would play a key role in the eventual southern acceptance of desegregation. Darwin Holt, an Alabama linebacker, illegally struck the Georgia Tech halfback Chick Graning in the face with his elbow, breaking his jaw and knocking out several teeth. Holt and Bryant quickly apologized for the incident, but a swirling firestorm erupted nonetheless. Georgia Tech's head coach, Bobby Dodd, wrote Bryant, "knowing you as I do, Bear, if Graning were your son and in the condition he is now in at the hospital, you would personally be searching out Holt in order to get revenge." Atlanta's mayor, William B. Hartsfield, advised Frank Rose that "it would be unwise for the Alabama team to appear on the Tech Campus next year."[29] These private recriminations appear

Paul Bryant was a master at crafting his own public image. This publicity photograph from the early 1960s demonstrates the image of unrelenting toughness that he sought to create during that phase of his career. (Paul W. Bryant Museum, University of Alabama)

civil when compared to the bitter war of words that erupted between the Birmingham and Atlanta newspapers. Furman Bisher, the sports editor of the *Atlanta Journal,* called Holt "bestial," asserting, "It is virtually a requirement that any young man who plays football for a Bryant team behave in a most violent manner." Bisher issued a blanket indictment of Alabama itself, declaring that Holt's behavior "represents the character of the sportsmanship of the state."[30]

The Birmingham newspapers accepted the challenge. "I'm Ashamed of Atlanta's Vicious Orgy," screamed a *Birmingham News* headline, as if the entire city of Atlanta had conspired to defame Alabama's hero. Benny Marshall, the sports editor of the *Birmingham News,* denounced the "propaganda machine in Atlanta . . . hammering away long after good newspapering or duty demanded." He claimed that the *Journal* was guilty of "yellow journalism at its rankest. . . . Men with jaws a-drool, hungry for a kill" published material that was "infamous, disgraceful, indecent, [and] unworthy of the newspaper profession."[31]

This angry invective was partly a natural response to the devastating injury suffered by popular player and partly a reflection of a highly charged football rivalry. But two similar incidents in 1960 involving cheap shots that had inflicted serious injury on Southeastern Conference (SEC) players had not ignited anything approaching a comparable level of controversy. The long-standing urban rivalry between Birmingham and Atlanta and the two cities' antithetical visions of southern racial politics intensified the Holt-Graning controversy. Since the late nineteenth century, Atlanta and Birmingham had been bitter competitors for economic primacy in the Southeast. They were roughly the same size as late as 1940, but by 1961 metropolitan Atlanta had grown to nearly twice the size of Birmingham. Racial politics was the key factor in Atlanta's postwar growth and Birmingham's stagnation.[32]

A progressive-minded business and political elite dismantled legal segregation in Atlanta with an eye toward creating a favorable national image; Birmingham fought to the bitter end, becoming an international symbol of oppression and racist violence. Atlanta peacefully desegregated its public schools and downtown stores by 1961; Birmingham turned police dogs and fire hoses on peaceful demonstrators two years later in a last-ditch effort to preserve white supremacy. Atlanta wooed the national media with a skillfully orchestrated public relations campaign; Birmingham police placed the *New York Times* reporter Harrison Salisbury under surveillance, and an Alabama grand jury indicted him for criminal libel after he published an article that portrayed Birmingham negatively. Atlanta promoted itself as the "City Too Busy to Hate"; Birmingham was darkly referred to as "Bombingham." Atlanta's elite and its increasingly affluent and cosmopolitan middle class saw their city as an oasis of enlightenment amid a miasma of southern violence and backwardness. They were also annoyingly eager to trumpet this assertion to the world. Many white southerners bitterly resented Atlantans' economic success, their condescending air of superiority, and their unseemly eagerness to court Yankee approval and investment capital.[33]

Southerners committed to a bitter-end defense of white supremacy reviled the memory of the scalawags who had sold out their southern heritage for political and economic advancement during Reconstruction. Likewise, many of their descendents saw Atlanta's acquiescence in desegregation and its carefully polished image of racial tolerance as a repetition of this shameful episode of southern history. A *Birmingham News* editorial greeted the 1961 victory of the racially moderate Ivan Allen over the arch segregationist Lester Maddox in that year's Atlanta mayoral race by observing that Allen "Would make Atlanta a mayor they would be proud of in Washington, New York, and Ghana." This statement emanated from a newspaper considered one of the more temperate public voices in the city dubbed the "Johannesburg of North America."[34]

Paul Bryant and Bobby Dodd served as dramatic foils of one another because their respective public images presented the same stark contrast as did Birmingham and Atlanta. Dodd had crafted an image of himself as an urbane coach at an academically demanding school whose wile and finesse enabled him to outwit less enlightened coaches who relied on mere brawn. In his 1954 book, *Bobby Dodd on Football,* he repeatedly stressed that football was only a game and should not be treated as a matter of life and death. Dodd denounced the atmosphere of "drudgery" that most college coaches inflicted on their players and advocated "free and easy practice sessions."[35]

Bryant, at least in the first two decades of his coaching career, was an unabashed authoritarian who stressed a "winning is everything" philosophy, and his infamous preseason practice regimen was the collegiate equivalent of the Bataan Death March. *Time,* which had recently skewered Bryant as the "relentless and brutal taskmaster," had previously published two flattering profiles of Dodd, lauding him as "The Happy Coach" who gave players "a maximum of attention and a minimum of tough talk."[36]

The lingering bitterness over the Holt-Graning incident erupted into a renewal of overt hostilities the following October. In a *Saturday Evening Post* article entitled "College Football Is Going Berserk," Furman Bisher denounced the increasing violence in college football and singled out Bryant as the worst offender. Alabamians accustomed to George Wallace's rhetoric about "carpetbaggin', scalawaggin' federal judges" were quick to see this latest chapter in the war with Atlanta as an unholy alliance of a renegade southerner and the perfidious Yankee press. Bryant sued Bisher and the *Post* for libel, but a *Birmingham News* columnist lamented that Bryant could not dispense with the courts and deal with his tormentors in the time-honored manner of the southern gentleman: "In Andrew Jackson's good days, the 'or else' might have implied pistols at dawn, or somebody might have reached for a convenient horsewhip, but in Bryant's case, the challenge meant the courts. . . . Bryant, who one hundred years ago would have ridden to Horseshoe Bend with Andrew Jackson, might personally have preferred the former, but . . . life is more complicated."[37]

In March 1963 the *Post* published "The Story of a College Football Fix," which accused the University of Georgia's athletic director, Wally Butts, of passing secret information to Bryant eight days prior to the 1961 Alabama–Georgia Tech game. The hated Bisher had again teamed up with biased Yankees to attack Bryant. Once again, the vast majority of white Alabamians rallied instantly and unquestioningly to Bryant's defense. Governor George

Wallace called the *Post* the "sorriest authority on truth." Frank Rose and the Alabama board of trustees each publicly affirmed their support of Bryant, and the state legislature passed a resolution condemning the *Post* for its "unfair" attack. The *Birmingham News* intoned, "Bryant has been under increasing vitriolic attack by national publications as his success has soared." An Auburn fan in Montgomery wrote Bryant that the article was the most "ridiculous pack of lies I have ever seen." The article, she asserted, "is as much of a crime as murder."[38]

Bryant and Butts each filed multimillion-dollar lawsuits against the *Post*. The Butts case came to trial in August 1963, in U.S. District Court in Atlanta. The jury found the *Post* guilty of libel and awarded Butts over three million dollars in compensatory and punitive damages. A judge later reduced the award to four hundred thousand dollars, but Butts and Bryant had been dramatically vindicated. Bryant settled both this suit and the one he had filed over Bisher's football violence article out of court for $320,000. Bryant angrily concluded his testimony at the Butts trial with the assertion, "Taking their money is not good enough. Somebody ought to go to jail." While neither the *Post* editors nor the hated Bisher went to jail, Bryant stood as a genuine southern hero, righteously triumphing over his foes. Three years after the trial, Frank Boykin was still angry over what he regarded as Bryant's undeserved persecution. "They tried to ruin you," he asserted, "but you came out right square on top of the heap. . . . Those people that tried to frame you surely must be so ashamed they will tuck their tails between their legs and silently slip away."[39]

Bryant's personal vindication occurred simultaneously with Alabama's descent into what Howell Raines calls "the midnight of its humiliation." The press accounts of the Butts trial competed for media attention with accounts of Wallace's infamous stand in the schoolhouse door at the University of Alabama. Three months earlier, the televised images of Bull Connor's fire hoses and police dogs had shocked the nation and the world. The nadir of this cycle of violence and hatred came in September 1963, when four black girls were killed by a bomb blast at the Sixteenth Street Baptist Church in Birmingham.[40]

The nation seethed with righteous anger at Alabama's endless parade of horrors, and, as the mythic hero of white Alabamians, Bryant once again became a lightning rod for criticism. The Crimson Tide won another national championship in 1964, but Jim Murray protested that Bryant's team did not deserve it because neither Alabama nor any of its 1964 opponents scheduled games with racially integrated teams. "So Alabama is the 'National Champion,' is it?" sneered Murray. "Hah! 'National' Champion of what? The Confederacy? This team hasn't poked its head above the Mason-Dixon Line since Appomattox." He suggested that Alabama might qualify for the "Front-of-the-Bus championship," because, like all Deep South universities, Alabama didn't want "any you-know-what in there cluttering up the color scheme." Murray also linked Bryant's team with the southern penchant for violence, a topical subject, given that the day before his column was published the FBI had arrested Sheriff Lawrence Rainey and twenty other white residents of Neshoba County, Mississippi, for the murders of three civil rights workers. Murray declared, "Football recruiters in the South don't go out looking for Robert E. Lee types anymore. 'They go out and hunt till they find a boy kicking a sleeping dog,' an Atlanta newsman once confided to me. 'Him, they take.'" The unnamed Atlantan, who was generally assumed to be Furman Bisher, blamed the increasing level of violence in college football on Bear Bryant.[41]

Many outraged southerners once again rallied reflexively and vociferously to Bryant's defense. An Alabama fan in Lexington, Kentucky, wrote Bryant, "I think Jim Murray is full of b.s. I don't think the SEC has to take a back seat to any d-m Yankee football or basketball team. Tell your players we Kentuckians are rooting for Alabama to give an old-fashioned country licking to Nebraska" in the upcoming 1965 Orange Bowl. He requested a picture of Bryant and the Alabama team as a perfect expression of southern pride. "I want some Yankees working around me to see a real coach and a *real football team,*" he declared. An Alabama alumnus living in Alexandria, Virginia, complained in a letter to Bryant that Murray "must be sick to make such statements. . . . I wish someone could shut him up. Personally I would like to jam the entire newspaper down his throat."[42]

Vincent Johnson, the sports editor of the *Mobile Press-Register,* commented on the mounting frenzy in his city. "Alabama football fans, reacting like so many toros, are pawing the ground in helpless anger and snorting words of flaming hate in the direction of the Los Angeles toreador." Johnson dismissed "Murray's frothings" as an attempt to curry favor with a "reading audience in Los Angeles [that] is comprised of a large slice of the country's Negro population." Benny Marshall of the *Birmingham News* passed Murray off as "a sort of a Mack the Knife, who never lets facts stand in the way of a good slashing." He took note of the cultural gulf that divided Alabama and California, calling Los Angeles "the kook capital of the world." A Birmingham television sports anchor elaborated on this theme, suggesting that Alabamians send care packages of razor blades, soap, and deodorant to Murray for distribution to his long-haired, unwashed fellow Californians.[43]

While Jim Murray became the bête noir of the moment, the editors of the *New York Times* had never been on the Christmas card lists of many Alabam-

ians. The unflinching editorial support the *Times* gave the civil rights movement outraged the sensibilities of the vast majority of white southerners.
Alabamians particularly resented the *Times* for Harrison Salisbury's 1961
article, "Fear and Hatred Grip Birmingham." Salisbury offered a brutally
frank portrayal of the violence and racial animosity that pervaded the city,
and he asserted that the level of repression there was comparable to that of
Eastern Europe. The *Times* reporter Calvin Trillin was stopped by Birmingham police for a minor traffic infraction while covering the 1963 civil disobedience campaign led by Martin Luther King Jr. and was taken to jail after the
policeman learned the identity of his employer. The Montgomery Police
Commissioner, L. B. Sullivan, won a huge libel judgment against the *Times*
in an Alabama court due to minor factual errors in a 1961 advertisement
denouncing the lack of police protection given to Freedom Riders by Montgomery city officials. The *Times* escaped the wrath of the Alabama legal system when the Supreme Court absolved it of any legal culpability in the landmark *New York Times v. Sullivan* decision in 1964.[44]

The 1964 Alabama-Auburn game gave the editors of the *Birmingham News*
what they considered absolute proof of the *Times'* bias. In an editorial entitled "We Had a Game, Too," the *News* claimed that the *Times* intentionally
trivialized the Alabama-Auburn game by burying a brief story about it on
the last page of the sports section, alongside a report on the NYU-Harvard
fencing match. The *News* concluded, "Alabamians have felt slighted or mis-
treated at the hands of the good, grey *Times* before, and in connection with
much more momentous matters, and have survived and prospered. Everybody but the *New York Times* knows where the 1965 football season really
climaxed."[45]

The only problem with this impassioned defense of Alabama football
honor was that the *News* based its editorial on an early edition of the *Times*.
The *Times* had indeed included a small article about the Alabama-Auburn
game in its first edition, but six later editions contained lengthy accounts on
page one of the sports section. James Roach, the sports editor of the *Times*,
complained in a letter sheepishly published by the *News* that the editorial
"dedicated itself to the proposition that I was either an incompetent dimwit
or an addlebrain with anti-Alabama prejudice." Roach suggested that an
apology would be in order and added, "I am astonished at your lack of knowledge of the mechanics of the newspaper business." The editors of the *News*
took their football seriously indeed, and they gave voice to an opinion held
by many white Alabamians, namely, that politically motivated Yankees were
conspiring to rob Bryant and his teams of their due for political reasons.[46]

The football conspiracy theorists could not complain about the 1965 wire service polls, which named Alabama the national champions for the third time in five years, but the 1966 polls provoked strong controversy. The defending national champion Crimson Tide finished third in the final wire service polls in 1966 despite finishing the regular season with a perfect 10-0 record. Notre Dame won the national title despite its controversial 10-10 tie with Michigan State, in which Notre Dame's coach, Ara Parseghian, chose to run out the clock rather than try for a game-winning score. The wanton police brutality inflicted on voting rights marchers in Selma and George Wallace's evasion of the constitutional prohibition of gubernatorial succession by running his cancer-stricken wife Lurleen as a stand-in may have influenced even the ordinarily apolitical sportswriters and coaches who voted in the polls. Bud Collins of the *Boston Globe* believed this to be the case. "It is unfashionable to say anything nice about Alabama and Coach Bear Bryant because they are segregationists," he declared. "Nevertheless, they are winning them all in that cutthroat area where anything goes." Collins believed that the University of Alabama had been deprived of the national championship that it had earned on the field because of Alabama's horrible reputation. "Poor Alabama. It has Selma to live down, as well as Lureen [*sic*] and George, and Sheriff Bull O'Connor's [*sic*] police dogs. Surely there's something worthwhile down there. Yes—it has the best football team," he asserted.[47]

Like Collins, suspicious southerners were also convinced that the football pollsters had made a political scapegoat out of the Crimson Tide. Bull Connor commiserated with Bryant in a letter written the day after the release of the final 1966 football polls. "Thousands of others in this State and country know that Alabama is Number 1," asserted Connor. "Any team that has not been beat [*sic*] should be No 1. What the heck do you have to do to be No. 1?" J. N. Lipscomb, a member of the board of trustees of the University of Mississippi, wrote a letter to Bryant that made Frank Boykin's look like a beacon of logical and rhetorical clarity. He informed Bryant that he was "hotter than a six shooter about the way the boys of superior complex ignored Alabama's great football team in the number one placement honors." He was outraged by what he regarded as a transparent Yankee plot to deny Bryant and his team their due. "Some great Americans seem to think that any thing coming out of the South is inferior," he grumbled, "unless it bears the stamp (and color) of Martin Luther [King] and a few of our white Pulitzer Prize winners." Lipscomb expressed confidence that Alabama would defend the honor of the South against Nebraska in the upcoming 1967 Sugar Bowl, and he assured Bryant that the SEC rivalry between Alabama and Ole Miss would not prevent Mississippians from rooting for Alabama. While he regretfully informed Bryant that he would not be able to attend the game, Lipscomb promised to "chain my bird dog to her bed, lay down my automatic, and glue my vindictive eyes to the television set. In the words of Light Horse Harry Truman, GIVE 'EM HELL."[48]

A Hollywood producer who needed to cast the role of a fire-eating, unreconstructed southerner who was itching to lead a charge against some damn Yankees could do no better than Lipscomb. Yet while southerners have long manifested a defensive and often xenophobic sectionalism, this impulse has coexisted with a powerful strain of intense nationalism. Since the antebellum era, southerners have generally sought to maintain loyalty to both region and nation. These often contradictory impulses have been manifested in their varying responses to the outside criticism directed at Bryant and his teams. While many southern whites reacted with anger and outrage, many were genuinely hurt by the nation's failure to recognize the patriotism, work ethic, and human decency of Bryant and his players. This desire to defend the basic moral goodness of the South, what Fred Hobson calls "the southern rage to explain," is a common thread uniting twentieth-century progressives, postbellum New South boosters, antebellum proslavery theologians, and generations of southern writers.[49]

Alma Christine Todd, an Alabama native living in Papillion, Nebraska, wrote an anguished letter of protest to the University of Nebraska's coach, Bob Devaney, after she heard him tell an off-color joke about Bryant and the Alabama quarterback Joe Namath at a high school football banquet. She alternately scolded and pleaded with Devaney: "When we hear leading citizens giving this type of degrading view to the leaders of tomorrow we have no need to wonder why we as adults have to take so much abuse concerning our background. Please Mr. DeVaney [sic], we are good people. We love this country but why is it necessary to degrade us as you do?"[50] Todd sent a copy of this letter to Bryant along with a personal note expressing her distress over the demonization of the South. Devaney's jibe had been bad enough, she informed Bryant, but that very morning, her own minister had harshly condemned southern whites for their racial bigotry. His sermon specifically singled out Alabama as the most despicable state in a benighted region. "You'd think the South was another continent the way we are disected [sic] from the United States and condemned by its leaders," she lamented.[51]

Todd's heartfelt, confessional letter to Paul Bryant testifies to his iconic status among white southerners. Bryant successfully mediated the conflicting ideals of unhesitating patriotism and deep loyalty to his southern roots. He also projected the image of a powerful patriarch with the ability to defend the honor of a persecuted but virtuous people. George Wallace employed the slogan "Stand Up for Alabama" in the mid-1960s, and the most memorable line of Lurleen Wallace's 1967 inaugural address was her declaration, "I am proud to be an Alabamian." These words, which were inscribed on the base of a marble bust of her in the capitol rotunda, possessed a poignant emptiness that Alabamians knew all too well. George Wallace attracted headlines and stirred deep emotions, but he invariably lost his quixotic battles. Alabamians who had been given so few reasons to feel pride in their native state saw Paul Bryant as a warrior who turned those mere slogans into tangible, flesh-and-blood reality. In a 1966 letter to Bryant, an Alabama native who had recently moved to Atlanta extended his "sincere congratulations and deep felt gratitude" for everything that Bryant had done for Alabama. "Each day," he declared, "I'm more and more proud of being from Alabama. One reason is because of U of A and you."[52]

George Wallace thrived on abuse by outsiders, but Paul Bryant realized that Alabama's status as national pariah diminished the stature of his football program. A hard line on race and a condemnation of the "pointy-headed Yankee intellectuals" who needed a "barbed wire enema" was good politics for the governor, but the coach was far better served by a moderate stance. Shortly after the 1966 football poll debacle, Bryant attempted a bit of damage control. "A few years ago, we had segregation problems. But now, we'd like to ask the help of you fellows up above us in the North, who have been our critics, to help us get games with the Big Ten, the Big Eight, the Pacific Coast." Jim Murray howled in delight at Bryant's extension of an olive branch to the Yankees. "Dust off the courthouse at Appomattox! Get ready for a new era of Reconstruction! Bear Bryant and the sovereign state of Alabama have handed over the swords!"[53]

Murray's sarcasm contained a nugget of truth. Alabama's 1966 and 1967 bowl games against integrated teams from the University of Nebraska were a significant racial milestone in Alabama. Moderate Alabamians breathed a collective sigh of relief when both games passed without a replay of the Holt-Graning incident with racial overtones in front of a national television audience. In fact, Bryant's players displayed an exaggerated and somewhat disingenuous form of southern chivalry to the Nebraska players, including the blacks, while administering a 34-7 drubbing to the Cornhuskers in the 1967 Sugar Bowl, repeatedly helping Nebraska players to their feet after knocking them down. While Nebraska players complained after the game that they regarded this unwanted assistance as condescension, the press and public gushed over this wonderful display of good sportsmanship. The many Americans conditioned to view white southerners as congenitally violent thugs were probably mildly surprised that the Alabama players did not commit unspeakable mayhem against the black Nebraska players. Moderate southerners desperate for any type of good public relations were pleased by this show of racial amity.[54]

Howell Raines believes that Alabamians understood that Bryant did this "to show the national sports audience that the state's football team was more civilized than its governor." The Alabama business leaders who desperately sought an end to the persistent cycle of racial confrontation and violence were especially grateful that Bryant had enhanced the reputation of the state. Winton Blount, a millionaire Montgomery businessman and close associate of Bryant's who later served in the Nixon cabinet, was a leading figure in the effort to reach a racial accommodation that would facilitate economic growth. Blount was pleased that Bryant and his team had generated a rare bit of favorable publicity for Alabama. "The sportsmanship that everybody exhibited was so marked and with 40 million people watching I don't know how we could have done anything more effective in this area which so badly needs help," he wrote Bryant.[55]

During the late 1960s, Bryant cautiously inched toward the more liberal end of the skewed spectrum of southern racial politics. In July 1966, he participated in a ceremony prior to a baseball game between the Atlanta Braves and the San Francisco Giants honoring the Alabama natives Henry Aaron, Willie Mays, and Willie McCovey. Since George Wallace would sooner have presided over a satanic Black Mass in the rotunda of the state capitol than attend a ceremony honoring black athletes, Bryant agreed to serve as Alabama's unofficial representative. The Braves' sales director, Eddie Glennon, believed that Bryant's actions helped put white southerners at ease with the idea of integrated athletics. "I personally believe your visit will do more to ease the racial tension than anything . . . as we know your influence will carry a lot of weight in the Southeastern area." Bryant also began inviting black high school coaches to his summer coaching clinic on the Tuscaloosa campus in 1967. These seemingly unremarkable actions were reasonably significant breaches in racial protocol in the polarized racial atmosphere that permeated Alabama during the mid-1960s. This record of racial moderation and his strong popular support attracted the attention of business and political leaders seeking to thwart George Wallace's plan to run his wife Lurleen for governor in 1966. When State Senator Ryan DeGraffenreid, the leading anti-Wallace candidate, was killed in a plane crash, his backers unsuccessfully attempted to persuade Bryant to run for governor against Lurleen Wallace.[56]

Byrant did not hesitate to offer behind-the-scenes support to the business leaders who well understood that racial polarization hindered economic growth. Still, he moved with glacial speed when it came to the recruitment of black players at Alabama. In his autobiography, he recalls that in 1967 he recommended that a black player attend another school because "we were still two or three years away." In that same year, Bryant informed Frank Rose that he had no intention of signing any black athletes in the foreseeable future. "We have not actively attempted to recruit any colored athletes in the State because we have none that we felt qualified both academically and athletically," stated Bryant. Alabama gave an athletic scholarship in 1972 to a football recruit who recorded the abysmally low score of eleven on the ACT, rendering his stated adherence to high academic standards more than a bit disingenuous. Bryant clearly was proceeding with extreme caution in racial matters.[57]

In 1966, Don McGlamery, a sociology professor at the University of Alabama and a member of the school's Faculty Athletic Committee, suggested that Bryant begin to recruit black athletes. In response, McGlamery was unceremoniously dumped from the committee eighteen months prior to the expiration of his term. Later that year he sought reappointment to the committee, assuring Jeff Bennett, Frank Rose's executive assistant, that he would not repeat his earlier breach of racial protocol. "I also promise I'll never vote 'No' or mention recruiting of Negro athletes," McGlamery vowed. His supplications notwithstanding, McGlamery was not reappointed. In 1968, leaders of the University of Alabama Afro-American Association met with Bryant and the chairman of the Faculty Athletic Committee, Willard F. Gray, to demand that Alabama recruit black athletes. While Bryant was already planning to do exactly that, albeit on his own cautious timetable, he would sooner resign than allow a student group to successfully pressure him on such a sensitive subject. Gray, a close ally of Bryant's, chortled that "Coach Bryant was on the offensive throughout the conversation, and the meeting resulted in a rather one-sided score." The Afro-American Association and the NAACP Legal Defense Fund filed a lawsuit in federal court the following year that sought to force Alabama to sign black football players, although the case was quickly dismissed.[58]

Bryant was clearly the most powerful figure on the Alabama campus and could safely ignore occasional complaints from professors or students. But he had obviously known for some time that desegregation was inevitable, and three trends coming to fruition in the late 1960s convinced him that he could safely recruit black players. First, by the summer of 1969, six of the ten SEC football programs had signed black recruits. Bryant found a second inducement to recruit black athletes amid the declining fortunes of his football program in the late 1960s. His teams lost as many games in 1969 and 1970 as it had in the previous eight years combined. Black athletes provided the Alabama program with a needed infusion of talent and allowed it to remain competitive with the other SEC schools that were by then recruiting black players. Third, overwhelming pressure from the federal government and grassroots action by southern blacks had finally broken the back of massive resistance in the Deep South. Thus, by 1970 desegregation of the Alabama football team no longer carried significant political risks.[59]

By the late 1960s, virtually all of Alabama's public schools had undergone at least token desegregation, and full-scale school integration took place under a federal court order in September 1970. Alabama's racially segregated state high school athletic organizations were combined in 1969, and that year's state high school basketball tournament featured interracial competition for the first time. Whites in the Deep South were finally acquiescing, albeit belatedly and grudgingly, in the demise of de jure segregation. By 1970 Bryant could desegregate the Alabama football program without moving faster than southern society as a whole. When the stunningly rapid shift of southern racial conventions occurred in the late 1960s and early 1970s, Bryant was perfectly positioned to make the transition. In the spring of 1970, Wilbur Jackson of Ozark, Alabama, became the first black athlete to sign a football scholarship at Alabama. In September 1971, he and a junior college transfer, John Mitchell, became the first blacks to play for the Alabama varsity.

Most southerners badly wanted Bryant's move to succeed. A majority of whites had become exhausted by the nonstop orgy of confrontation, violence, and impotent demagoguery that had prevailed since the *Brown* decision. They had come to understand that civilization as they knew it would not come to an end if the rigid barriers of de jure segregation were eliminated. The election of such progressive, racially moderate governors as Jimmy Carter of Georgia, Reuben Askew of Florida, and Dale Bumpers of Arkansas in 1970 offered evidence that a desegregated, economically prosperous, and orderly society could indeed exist in the South. Even George Wallace did a political about-face and began eagerly to seek black support in the early 1970s. A critical mass of southerners constructed a new racial paradigm around what Stephen Smith calls the "rhetorical reality" of "the new myth of racial harmony." The symbolic importance of southern football made it the perfect venue to display the viability of this new construction of race relations. The desegregation of the Alabama football program went smoothly, in contrast to the simmering racial conflict that beset some other southern college football programs in the early 1970s, notably those of Auburn and Ole Miss. Bryant's heroic stature also contributed to the lack of overt racial conflict on his team. John David Crow, a former assistant coach at Alabama, recalls that players regarded Bryant with such intense feelings of respect, awe, and fear that they would never violate a dictum that was so obviously important to their coach. When Bryant made it clear that he would tolerate no racial conflict on his team, his players followed that command as if it were inscribed on stone tablets.[60]

Bryant's racially integrated teams became a symbol of the new racial paradigm of partial assimilation. The symbolic potency of these teams was enhanced by their success. The Crimson Tide emerged from its slump of the late 1960s to become the preeminent team in the nation during the next decade. Alabama compiled an astonishing record of 116-15-1 between 1971 and 1981, winning eight SEC championships and three national titles during that span. Southerners lionized Bryant as an icon of this latest incarnation of the New South. Eager to construct a usable past compatible with their newly desegregated society, they embraced Bryant as a hero who embodied the proud traditions of the southern past without possessing the taint of racial bigotry. Charles Reagan Wilson states that Bryant "embodies the hope for a biracial South, in which southern blacks and whites, working together, will achieve great things off the football field as well as on it." In a similarly abrupt reversal, the national media, which in the early 1960s had demonized Bryant for representing the dark side of the southern tradition, were by the mid-1970s portraying him as an authentic American folk hero. *Time,* which had viewed him with suspicion and hostility in 1961, gave him the ultimate popular culture encomium in 1980, when his avuncular visage adorned its cover and a laudatory feature article sang his praises. The dramatic alteration of Bryant's image at both the national and sectional levels reflects the perennial societal need for heroes who give form to cherished dominant values.[61]

Paul Bryant never sought the role of defender of white supremacy or martyr to the cause of states' rights. He was accorded that status by white southerners eager for a symbol of victory and perseverance amid the repeated failures of massive resistance and by a northern press that was not sensitive to the subtleties of the southern racial continuum. Bryant, unlike George Wallace, achieved his iconic stature without employing the inflammatory racist rhetoric that was the sine qua non of political leadership in the Deep South during the late 1950s and early 1960s. Yet neither was he a courageous apostle of desegregation. His policy of cautious moderation was predicated on two dicta: take no major political risks, and do nothing that will not advance the fortunes of the Alabama football program. It is perhaps unfair to wish that Paul Bryant had done more than he did to hasten the end of institutionalized white supremacy. His primary responsibility was to win football games, not to promote social justice. Yet the tantalizing possibilities remain. Bryant possessed a huge reservoir of affection and respect among white Alabamians and could have used that to effect positive social change. He could have desegregated his team in the mid-1960s, thus repudiating George Wallace's cheap demagoguery. This action would have been a monument to courage and justice. He asserted in his autobiography that he wanted to recruit black players for the Kentucky football team when he was head coach there in the late 1940s. Bryant recalled that he told Kentucky's president, Herman Donovan, that the latter would be remembered as the Branch Rickey of the SEC if he would permit black players there, but Donovan refused. Paul Bryant could have become the Branch Rickey of the SEC in the mid-1960s. It is a pity that he chose not to do so.[62]

Notes

This chapter previously appeared as "Bear Bryant: Symbol for an Embattled South" and is reprinted, with minor editorial changes, from *The Colby Quarterly* 32 (March 1996): 72–86, with the permission of the journal's editor.

1. Frank Boykin to Paul Bryant, January 2, 1962, Rose Papers, 6-83A7680-21, William Stanley Hoole Special Collections (hereafter HSC), University of Alabama Library, Tuscaloosa.

2. Ibid.

3. Numan V. Bartley discusses the desperate and destructive efforts of southern politicians to defend legal segregation in *The Rise of Massive Resistance: Race and Politics during the 1950s* (Baton Rouge: Louisiana State University Press, 1969).

4. Alabama Business Research Council, *Transition in Alabama* (University: University of Alabama Press, 1962), 5, 12. C. Vann Woodward discusses the mixed blessings of the Bulldozer Revolution in "The Search for Southern Identity," *Virginia Quarterly Review* 34 (1958): 321–38. See also Bruce J. Schulman, *From Cotton Belt to Sun Belt: Federal Policy, Economic Development, and the Transformation of the South, 1938–1980* (New York: Oxford University Press, 1991).

5. *Birmingham News*, November 26, 1959, 10.

6. William Faulkner, "On Fear," in *Essays, Speeches, and Public Letters by William Faulkner*, ed. James Merriweather (New York: Random House, 1965), 98. Seventy percent of Alabama's population lived in rural areas in 1940; a mere twenty years later, this figure had declined to 45 percent. In rural Alabama, the only age cohorts to grow in size between 1940 and 1960 were those of persons older than forty-four. The outmigration of young people in those years was far greater than that of the decade between 1930 and 1940, as the generally rising level of prosperity in urban areas offered a previously unavailable level of economic opportunity. *U.S. Census of Population: 1960*, vol. 1, pt. 2 (Washington, D.C.: U.S. Government Printing Office, 1963), 2–28; *U.S. Census of Population, 1940*, vol. 1, pt. 2 (Washington, D.C.: U.S. Government Printing Office, 1942), 211–12. For the comparison of the depopulation of the southern countryside with the enclosure process and the Potato Famine, see Jack Temple Kirby, *Rural Worlds Lost: The American South, 1920–1960* (Baton Rouge: Louisiana State University Press, 1987), 276.

7. For Bryant's account of his childhood, see Paul Bryant and John Underwood, *Bear:*

The Hard Life and Good Times of Alabama's Coach Bryant (New York: Little, Brown, 1974), 17–45. Geoffrey Norman explores the intense attachment that Alabamians formed for Bryant during the early 1960s in *Alabama Showdown: The Football Rivalry between Alabama and Auburn* (New York: Henry Holt, 1986), 72–113.

8. *Birmingham News,* November 16, 1960, 44, January 11, 1963, 18.

9. Norman, *Alabama Showdown,* 88; Bryant and Underwood, *Bear,* 184.

10. Bryant and Underwood, *Bear,* 186–87.

11. *Birmingham News,* December 10, 1968, 1, 10.

12. *Birmingham News,* December 10, 1968, 1, 10, December 11, 1968, 62; Bryant and Underwood, *Bear,* 189.

13. Norman, *Alabama Showdown,* 88; Paul Bryant, *Building a Championship Football Team* (Englewood Cliffs, N.J.: Prentice-Hall, 1960), 26; *Miami Herald,* December 4, 1961, C-1.

14. *Birmingham News,* January 1, 1963, 22; Norman, *Alabama Showdown,* 88; *Birmingham News,* September 30, 1960, 15.

15. *Birmingham News,* December 10, 1961, C-1; *Montgomery Advertiser,* September 16, 1962, C-3.

16. *Birmingham News,* December 10, 1961, C-1.

17. Charles Martin, "The Integration of Southeastern Conference Athletics," paper presented at the Southern Historical Association, November 1990, New Orleans; E. Culpeper Clark, *The Schoolhouse Door: Segregation's Last Stand at the University of Alabama* (New York: Oxford University Press, 1993), 161.

18. *Atlanta Journal,* November 7, 1961, 19.

19. *Montgomery Advertiser,* November 14, 1961, A-11, November 19, 1961, 1, November 20, 1961, B-5.

20. *Montgomery Adviser,* November 19, 1961, 1; Durslag quoted in *Atlanta Constitution,* November 15, 1961, 31.

21. *Los Angeles Times,* November 22, 1961, IV-3.

22. *Atlanta Constitution,* November 15, 1961, 31; *Los Angeles Times,* November 20, 1961, IV-1.

23. *Los Angeles Times,* November 19, 1961, VIII-1, November 20, 1961, IV-1.

24. E. Culpeper Clark discusses the Autherine Lucy case in *Schoolhouse Door,* 53–133 (quote on xi). Racial politics in Alabama during the 1950s and 1960s are explored in Dan T. Carter, *The Politics of Rage: George Wallace, the Origins of the New Conservatism, and the Transformation of American Politics* (New York: Simon and Schuster, 1995); and Robert J. Norrell, *Reaping the Whirlwind: The Civil Rights Movement in Tuskegee* (New York: Alfred A. Knopf, 1985). William Nunnelly, *Bull Connor* (Tuscaloosa: University of Alabama Press, 1990); and Frank Sikora, *Till Justice Comes Down* (Tuscaloosa: University of Alabama Press, 1990), discuss the wave of Ku Klux Klan violence that terrorized Alabama in this period.

25. *New York Times,* May 15, 1961, 30. For an account of the Freedom Rider episode, see Taylor Branch, *Parting the Waters: America in the King Years, 1954–63* (New York: Simon and Schuster, 1988), 412–50.

26. *Los Angeles Times,* November 20, 1961, IV-1; author's interview with Tim Davis, August 29, 1991.

27. "A Bear at 'Bama," *Time* 78 (November 17, 1961): 72; Roy Terrell, "The Bear and Alabama Come Out on Top," *Sports Illustrated* 15 (December 11, 1961): 20, 87.

28. *Birmingham News*, December 1, 1961, 10.

29. Bobby Dodd to Bryant, November 22, 1961, and William B. Hartsfield to Frank Rose, November 25, 1961, Rose Papers, 6-80A3021-13, Special Subject File: "Alabama–Georgia Tech Football Game," HSC.

30. *Atlanta Journal,* November 20, 1961, 31, November 21, 1961, 11, 29.

31. *Atlanta Journal,* November 20, 1961, 31, November 21, 1961, 11, 29; *Birmingham News,* November 23, 1961, 35, November 24, 1961, 13.

32. For details of the two similar incidents of football violence, see *Birmingham News,* November 21, 1960, 32.

33. *Birmingham News,* September 14, 1961, 11, August 18, 1961, 6. The *Atlanta Constitution* and its liberal editor, Ralph McGill, continually heaped scorn on Birmingham and Alabama as the epitome of backwardness and bigotry during the late 1950s and early 1960s. See *Atlanta Constitution,* July 11, 1962, 4, September 6, 1963, 4, September 17, 1963, 1.

34. *Birmingham News,* September 3, 1961, A-10.

35. Robert L. Dodd, *Bobby Dodd on Football* (New York: Prentice-Hall, 1954), 10–11.

36. *Time* published two profiles of Dodd during the 1950s that celebrated him as a coach who eschewed the dictatorial tactics of the run-of-the-mill football coach but still managed to win. See "Football for Fun," *Time* 60 (November 24, 1952): 66, and "The Happy Coach," *Time* 68 (November 12, 1956): 83–84. *Sports Illustrated* noted in 1969 that "Dodd's training regimen is notoriously lax" in "A New Slant on an Old Game in Atlanta," *Sports Illustrated* 31 (September 1, 1969): 40.

37. *Birmingham News,* October 17, 1962, 17.

38. Frank Graham Jr., "The Story of a College Football Fix," *Saturday Evening Post* 235 (March 23, 1963): 80–87; *Birmingham News,* March 16, 1961, 1, March 22, 1963, 34, August 12, 1963, 1, August 31, 1963, 11; Inge Hill to Bryant, March 21, 1963, 0039-02, Bryant Museum Archives, University of Alabama, Tuscaloosa (hereafter BMA).

39. James Kirby, *Fumble: Bear Bryant, Wally Butts, and the Great College Football Scandal* (New York: Harcourt Brace Jovanovich, 1986), 34–35, 147–48, 165; *Birmingham News,* August 12, 1963, 1; Frank Boykin to Bryant, January 6, 1966, A-0009-2, BMA. Kirby concludes that while there was no strong evidence that the game was fixed and that the *Post* article contained several crucial misstatements of fact, there was compelling evidence that Butts and Bryant did indeed improperly exchange information prior to the game. Their pretrial statements were often at variance with their trial testimony, and there were several crucial inconsistencies between the testimony of Bryant and that of Frank Rose. Kirby expresses his "deep chagrin that Butts and Bryant [enjoyed] undeserved vindication in the public eye." Kirby, *Fumble,* 222.

40. Howell Raines, "Goodbye to the Bear," *New Republic* 188 (January 24, 1983): 11. On the racial violence in Birmingham during the early 1960s, see Carter, *Politics of Rage;* Nunnelly, *Bull Connor;* and Sikora, *Till Justice Comes Down.*

41. *Los Angeles Times,* December 4, 1964, III-1.

42. William Harrington to Bryant, December 14, 1965, A-0002-05, Louis H. Anderson to Bryant, undated (likely January 1966), A-0009-5, BMA.

43. *Mobile Press-Register,* December 13, 1964, D-2; *Birmingham News,* December 9, 1964, 63, December 11, 1964, 20.

44. Harrison E. Salisbury, "Fear and Hatred Grip Birmingham," *New York Times,* April 12, 1960, 1; Carter, *Politics of Rage,* 114–15, 229; Branch, *Parting the Waters,* 295–96, 270–71.

45. *Birmingham News,* December 2, 1965, 15.

46. *Birmingham News,* December 15, 1965, 14.

47. *Boston Globe,* November 22, 1966, 43.

48. Eugene "Bull" Connor to Bryant, December 6, 1966, A-0009-22, J. N. Lipscomb to Bryant, December 17, 1966, A-0010-15, BMA.

49. Fred Hobson asserts that "the radical need of the Southerner to explain and interpret the South is an old and prevalent condition" in *Tell about the South: The Southern Rage to Explain* (Baton Rouge: Louisiana State University Press, 1983), 3.

50. Alma Christine Todd to Bob Devaney, April 26, 1965, A003-03, BMA.

51. Todd to Bryant, April 26, 1965, A003-03, BMA.

52. Frank David Brizendine to Bryant, November 1, 1966, A0009-11, BMA. For a discussion of George Wallace's exploitation of Alabamians' intense desire to feel pride in their state, see Carter, *Politics of Rage,* esp. chap. 9.

53. *Los Angeles Times,* December 8, 1966, III-1.

54. *Birmingham News,* January 3, 1967, 14.

55. *Montgomery Advertiser,* January 27, 1983, A-9; Winton Blount to Bryant, January 5, 1967, A0009-09, BMA.

56. Eddie Glennon to Bryant, August 2, 1966, A0010-01, BMA.

57. Bryant and Underwood, *Bear,* 319; Bryant to Frank Rose, March 20, 1967, Rose Papers, 6-80A3921-2, HSC; "ACT Raw Scores, 1972 Football Scholarship List," Matthews Papers, box 18, file 17, HSC.

58. Don McGlamery to Jeff Bennett, August 10, 1966, Rose Papers, 121-84A6411-5, HSC; Willard F. Gray to David Matthews, August 19, 1968, Matthews Papers, box 18, file 2, HSC; *Crimson-White,* 7 July 1969, 1.

59. Joan Paul, Richard McGhee, and Helen Fast, "The Arrival and Ascendance of Black Athletes in the Southeastern Conference, 1966–1980," *Phylon* 44 (Fall 1984): 287.

60. Steven A. Smith, *Myth, Media, and the Southern Mind* (Fayetteville: University of Arkansas Press, 1985), 63–89, 136–37; author's interview with John David Crow, October 22, 1991.

61. Charles Reagan Wilson, "Bear Bryant," in *Encyclopedia of Southern Culture,* ed. Charles Reagan Wilson and William Ferris (Chapel Hill: University of North Carolina Press, 1989), 1252; "Football's Supercoach," *Time* 116 (September 29, 1980): 70–77.

62. Bryant and Underwood, *Bear,* 316–17.

11. "The Tennessee Test of Manhood": Professional Wrestling and Southern Cultural Stereotypes

LOUIS M. KYRIAKOUDES AND
PETER A. COCLANIS

IN HIS *Georgia Scenes,* Augustus Baldwin Longstreet describes a fight between two early nineteenth-century backcountry brawlers, Billy Stallions and Bob Durham. Each fighter was reputed to be the toughest in his locality, although their friendship had heretofore kept the issue of county champion unresolved. One day, however, after an exchange of insults between their wives, honor now aggrieved, Billy and Bob agreed to settle the matter in "'a fair fight; catch as catch can, rough and tumble.'" It being market day in the county seat, word of the coming battle spread quickly through town, and a large crowd gathered, forming a ring in anticipation of the contest. Each combatant's supporters boasted of their man's impending victory:

> "What's Bob Durham going to do when Billy lets that arm loose upon him?"
> "God bless your soul, he'll think thunder and lightning a mint julep to it."
> "Oh, look here, men, go take Bill Stallions out o' that ring, and bring in Phil Johnson's stud horse, so that Durham may have some chance!"

The spectators appealed to Squire Tommy Loggin—"a man . . . who had never failed to predict the issue of a fight in all his life"—for insight into the outcome, and his inscrutable gaze encouraged both parties that victory would be theirs.[1]

The fight began when Bob "dashed at his antagonist at full speed," grasping Billy in an "'all under-hold'" that put Billy's "'feet where his head ought to be.'" The struggle continued. Bob "entirely lost his left ear, and a large piece from his left cheek," while Billy lost "about a third of his nose," which was "bit off," and his "face [was] so swelled and bruised that it was difficult to discover in it anything of the human visage." Less one finger and upon having "dirt and sand" ground into his eyes, Billy ended the battle with a cry of "'ENOUGH!'" The audience erupted in "shouts, oaths, frantic gestures, taunts, replies, and little fights."[2]

Present-day professional wrestling owes much to the type of fighting described by Longstreet. When examining the role of sport in southern culture, one inevitably must come to terms with these local contests. Nineteenth-century visitors to the southern backcountry noted the frequency of bloody brawls and the large crowds they attracted. So prevalent was such fighting, one might consider it, along with horse racing, the South's first spectator sport, albeit on an amateur level.[3] By the 1990s professional wrestling's core American audience was southern, with some estimates placing 60 percent of the attendance at live matches in the South. Southern athletes also make up a disproportionate share of professional wrestlers. The sport's two leading impresarios also have deep southern roots. Ted Turner, the Atlanta-based media mogul, owns World Championship Wrestling (WCW). Vince McMahon, who presides over the World Wrestling Federation (WWF) from its Connecticut headquarters, had a hardscrabble childhood in rural eastern North Carolina.[4]

The catch-as-catch-can style of backcountry fighting, a free-for-all constrained by few meaningful rules, persists in creative combat in modern professional wrestling. Consider this description of a match between Crusher Blackwell, a "huge wrestler from the Georgia hills," and Bruiser Brody, a Texan. Upon their meeting in the ring, "kicks, punches, and gouging [became] the general order of the day." The two wrestlers carried their fight over the ropes to the floor below. "Blackwell rammed Brody's head into the iron post [and] Brody responded in kind . . . ripping a huge gash in the Crusher's forehead." The combatants turned to whatever was at hand to pummel each other, and the match "soon became an epic feat of arms, legs, cowboy boots, and even folding chairs." The match ended with the combatants "all saturated with somebody's blood, [and] the entire ring area looked like a Red Cross donors' bank."[5]

More than unbridled violence connects the fight in the Georgia backcountry with present-day professional wrestling. Backcountry fighting and modern wrestling both are embedded in cultural contexts that draw audience and combatants—spectators and spectacle—together to create a larger competitive narrative. The Stallions-Durham contest was held before an audience that was keenly attuned to the drama of the fight and needed to consult an expert evaluation of the action in the opinions of Squire Logan. Like Longstreet's backcountry grapplers, present-day wrestlers arrive with their attendants, promoters, and "managers" who, like Stallions's and Durham's seconds, boast of their man's prowess and certain victory, and who don't always stay out of the fray. The spectators at the Stallions-Durham brawl invested the fight with meaning that went beyond the immediate contest. Because each combatant represented his section of the county, the affair was riven with overtones of local pride, honor, and bragging rights.

Contemporary professional wrestling similarly involves its fans in the spectacle by recreating loyalties and antagonisms not unlike those in the Stallions-Durham brawl. Wrestling does so by drawing upon racial, ethnic, and regional stereotypes, shamelessly scavenged from popular culture, to create stylized personas that will attract and hold fans' interest. Wrestlers' personas drive the theatrical narrative, which pits hero against villain and creates the dramatic tension that intensifies the conflict in the ring. In a famous essay written over forty years ago, the French critic Roland Barthes suggested that wrestling depicts a "purely moral concept: that of justice." The wrestling promoter Dick Steinborn expressed the same idea more forthrightly by pointing out that wrestling is about "good overcoming evil." While wrestling's dramatic conflicts occur within this morality-play framework, every wrestling match does not end in the defeat of evil. Villainous characters pack the venues, and a skillful wrestling promoter will stage a rivalry between two wrestlers that can last a season or more and is only ended in a well-attended "grudge match." Wrestlers' personas can move between good and evil, and it is not uncommon to wrestle as a villain in one regional territory and as a hero in another.[6]

The sport's popularity in the South has meant that many individual wrestlers have drawn upon southern social types in formulating their personas, and southern cultural stereotypes have become an important element in professional wrestling.[7] The sport has been replete with hillbillies, rednecks, and good ol' boys, and the appeal of these characters has risen and fallen in relation to broader national views about the South and its place in the nation. Thus, the role of southern cultural stereotypes in wrestling tells us not only a great deal about sport in the South but also about how southern identity has been constructed in American popular culture.

To be sure, some may object to calling professional wrestling a sport. Certainly, if a truly competitive outcome is the sine qua non of sport, wrestling does not qualify. In professional wrestling contests, "the outcome is generally known." Professional wrestling organizations carefully note that they provide "sport entertainment" rather than truly competitive contests. Matches are scripted, moves are choreographed, and punches are pulled. As one WWF official pointed out, their contests are "'entertainment no different than when the circus comes to town.'"[8] An unnamed wrestling fan expressed a similar view: "'I say the wrestling is like a good fiction book; it may be fake but it's very exciting.'"[9]

Nonetheless, professional wrestling is not without its dangers; injuries are common, and sometimes the blood is real. A recent example resembles Longstreet's backcountry fighters all too well. Michael Foley, who at the time wrestled under the name "Cactus Jack," had his right ear torn off after a botched attempt at performing the "Hangman" maneuver, in which his head and neck were to appear to be entwined in the middle and top ropes of the ring. Foley had successfully performed the maneuver some seventy-five times, but on this attempt the ropes were too taut, and his ear was ripped off as he tried to free himself during the match. Surgeons were unsuccessful in completely reattaching Foley's severed ear, and he now wrestles with a leather mask under the new name "Mankind."[10] Despite these occasional injuries, however, truly competitive professional wrestling is as much fiction as Longstreet's description of the fight.

The lack of a competitive outcome should not exclude wrestling from the world of sport. To most who ponder the role of sport in American life, the competitive element of the contest holds the least interest; such concerns are the province of collectors of statistics and play-by-play antiquarians. It is the social and cultural elements in modern spectator sports that draw scholars to study the phenomenon. Modern sport is an entertainment that draws fans into an emotional involvement with individual sports figures and teams. Spectator sports have become narratives in which conflict is ritualistically reenacted. All modern sport is spectacle, a struggle between good and evil, between one's "team" and its despised rival.

Taken in this light, professional wrestling's scripted matches and predetermined outcomes make it no less a sport than any other bona fide sporting endeavor. Professional wrestling's formal theatrical conventions, or as Barthes put it, the "iconography" of wrestling, make "reading" its symbols a straightforward affair.[11] Like true theater, professional wrestling broadcasts its cultural and symbolic meanings with greater clarity than sports constrained by binding rules and truly competitive outcomes. Moreover, the mutability and elusiveness of wrestlers' identities, their self-conscious irony, and their willingness to flout, or "transgress," cultural and moral conventions make the sport especially well-suited to these postmodern times.

Origins of Professional Wrestling in the South

While professional wrestling has been popular in the South at least since the end of World War II, its American roots reach back to the frontier tradition of itinerant wrestlers who would travel alone or accompany touring minstrel shows and fairs, challenging all comers. Mark Twain drew the prototype in *Life on the Mississippi* in the fighter named "Sudden Death and General Desolation," whose boasting was nearly as effective as his strength in defeating his opponents. After the turn of the century, wrestling moved to northern cities and became a popular spectator sport. Early notable wrestling matches pitted Frank Gotch, an Iowa-born grappler, against George Hackenschmidt, the Russian Lion. The appeal of legitimate contests with paying spectators, however, was unpredictable. These truly contested matches could be long affairs, dominated by slow, defensive maneuvering that failed to hold fan interest, or they could end quickly in defeat. After a number of notable matches, including a 1909 Gotch-Hackenschmidt rematch in Chicago that attracted some forty thousand spectators, legitimate wrestling went into decline as a professional sport.[12]

In its place rose the modern variety of wrestling characterized by exaggerated violence, theatrical conflicts, and outrageous characters. Early professional wrestlers sought to appeal to the urban immigrant working class of northern cities that comprised the sport's base. Leading wrestlers of the 1920s included Irish Dan Mahoney, Turkish-born Ali Baba, and Stan Zbyszko. Jim Londos (Christos Theophilou), the Golden Greek, reigned as the leading wrestler of the 1930s. After World War II, Killer Kowalski, Bruno Sammartino, and Antonio "Argentine" Rocca, who billed himself as both Hispanic and Italian by virtue of his Italian and Argentine heritage, continued the tradition of ethnic wrestlers.[13]

The spread of television did much to broaden professional wrestling's appeal. Wrestling was a staple of early television broadcasts, especially for smaller stations seeking cheap programming that could appeal to family audiences. In the early 1950s, Chicago stood as the center of professional wrestling, hosting nationally broadcast wrestling cards on Wednesday and Saturday nights over the ABC and the now-defunct Du Mont television networks.[14]

Wrestling's burlesque antics, invisible on radio, were well-suited to the new visual medium, and television promoted the stylized violence and outrageous characters that have come to dominate the sport. The 1950s saw masked wrestlers such as Zuma, Man from Mars, and the Hooded Phantom; super patriots such as Mr. America and the thinly disguised homoerotic antics of "Gorgeous George" Wagner, who bleached his hair and disinfected the ring with perfume; and "Nature Boy" Buddy Rogers, who inspired the 1980s and 1990s wrestler Ric Flair. Midget and women wrestlers were also very popular. German and Japanese wrestlers enraged a public still seething with resentments from World War II, while Soviet wrestlers provided the new cold war villains.[15]

As professional wrestling's popularity grew with the television boom in the early 1950s, it also moved South. The sport initially migrated below the Mason-Dixon line in the 1930s, when wrestlers like the German-born Milo Steinborn toured the region's leading cities, becoming especially popular in the Southeast.[16] In the 1950s regional promotions such as Jim Crockett's Charlotte-based National Wrestling Alliance (NWA) attracted ever larger audiences and gave the "Mid-Atlantic" Carolinas-Virginia circuit the reputation as "the hotbed of professional wrestling."[17] Gulf Coast Championship Wrestling, operated by Dick Steinborn, the son of Milo Steinborn, promoted wrestling in Alabama and Florida.[18] Other leading promotions centered around western Tennessee, especially Memphis, and Texas. By the early 1960s professional wrestling's popularity had declined in the North as more respectable mainstream sports, notably professional football, gained larger followings.[19] Conversely, wrestling's popularity increased in the South, which still lacked a base of major-league professional franchises. Since that time, the sport has thrived on southern soil and has enjoyed a dedicated regional following.[20]

Like other loosely organized itinerant entertainment industries such as circuses and carnivals, the wrestling business has been a close-knit, family-organized affair. A remarkable number of wrestlers and promoters are the second or third generation in the business. Take, for example, Edward Welch, a wrestler and promoter who died at the age of seventy-one in 1996. The son and nephew of pioneering southern wrestlers and promoters, Welch wrestled and later promoted in the South under the name Buddy Fuller. His sons, Robert and Ronald, continue the family business. Robert Welch is better known as Colonel Rob Parker, a manager who adopts the persona of a southern gentleman. Welch's nephew also wrestles under the name Bunkhouse Buck. Father-son combinations abound, such as Jerry and Jeff Jarrett and Dusty and Dustin Rhodes. Sibling combinations are common, too: Jake "The Snake" Roberts and Sam Houston are brothers; their sister wrestles under the name Rockin Robin. Similarly, Lanny Poffo and "Macho Man" Randy Savage are brothers and are the sons of a wrestler, Angelo Poffo.[21]

The 1980s saw wrestling enjoy increasing national exposure for the first time since the early 1950s. Bolstered by the popularity of superstars such as Terry Bollea, an ex-bodybuilder and failed rock musician from Florida who wrestles as Hulk Hogan, professional wrestling rose to unprecedented levels of popularity. Hogan appeared in films and on television, and he even graced the cover of *Sports Illustrated*. Celebrities like the rock musician Cyndi Lauper and the comedian Andy Kaufman embraced the sport for its naive extravagance and stylized artifice, qualities the critic Susan Sontag has described as part of the essence of "camp." In 1985 professional wrestling returned to network television for the first time since 1955 with the airing of *Saturday Night's Main Event* on NBC. The series of wrestling extravaganzas known as WrestleMania became national sporting events. WrestleMania III, for example, drew seventy-eight thousand spectators to Michigan's Pontiac Silverdome.[22]

The growth of new cable television outlets for the sport sparked a consolidation in the industry in the 1980s. Like the networks in the 1950s, cable TV programmers were attracted to wrestling as an inexpensive way to fill air time. Seeing opportunities for growth in the sport on the new cable medium, the wrestling impresario Vince McMahon, a second-generation wrestling promoter, expanded his World Wrestling Federation out of its traditional base in the Northeast. The WWF's roster of stars, including Hulk Hogan, and its popular and profitable WrestleMania and TV pay-per-view programs allowed McMahon to buy or drive out of business most of the smaller regional wrestling organizations. In 1984 McMahon moved his WWF into the South, purchasing a time slot on Ted Turner's Atlanta-based cable "superstation" WTBS. Personality conflicts between Turner and McMahon, as well as programming disagreements, prompted McMahon to sell his slot to Jim Crockett's NWA. The smaller NWA, however, was poorly prepared to compete with the WWF and was near bankruptcy by 1988. Turner, who needed programming to fill the airtime of his growing cable empire, purchased the NWA, renaming it World Championship Wrestling.[23]

Turner's Atlanta-based WCW and McMahon's WWF emerged as the reigning powers in wrestling. The stakes are high, and competition between the two is intense and bitter. In 1995 the WWF and WCW grossed $58.4 million and $48.1 million, respectively, on cable television pay-per-view programs alone. In 1999, retail sales of WWF merchandise alone exceeded $400 million.[24]

Professional wrestling targets males, aged eighteen to fifty-four, although just over one-fifth of the sport's audience is under eighteen. While wrestling promoters are fond of pointing out that the sport appeals to a wide range of education and income groups, three-quarters of the sport's television viewership has earned only a high school education or less, and nearly 70 percent have household incomes under forty thousand dollars. Males may be wrestling's target group, but as any spectator at a wrestling match would know, women have long comprised a substantial portion of the sport's audience. The chief sponsors of early televised wrestling were household appliance dealers who sought to reach an adult female audience. Today, 36 percent of wrestling's television audience is female. Something of the sport's appeal to women, particularly southern women, might be gathered from the fact that

Lillian Carter, in her capacity as First Mother, once invited the masked wrestler Mr. Wrestling II to her Plains, Georgia, home for a visit.[25]

Southern Wrestlers

While wrestling has not been a strictly southern phenomenon, southern wrestlers have been central to the sport, dominating the ranks of wrestlers and supplying an important source of characters for the theatricality of wrestling. A 1995 listing of leading professional wrestlers revealed that 70 percent were from the United States. Of those American-born wrestlers, nearly half—49 percent—hailed from the South, and Texas, Tennessee, and Florida were three of the five leading states of origin for wrestlers. Texas and Tennessee, the two leading sources of wrestlers, contributed 14 and 10 percent, respectively, of the wrestlers in the listing. Like country music, wrestling draws its performers from the southern periphery; both count Texas and Tennessee as the two leading sources of their performers.[26]

Given this southern-dominated roster, it is not surprising that individual wrestlers have heavily mined the popular images of southerners for the raw materials from which they construct their stylized wrestling personas. Identifiably southern characters in wrestling began to appear in significant numbers in the 1960s, when the sport took on an increasingly southern cast. Early southern stereotypes tended toward either the *Tobacco Road* and *Deliverance* view of the white South as home to a class of degenerate subnormals capable of horrific violence or the popular romantic primitivism of the hillbilly uncorrupted by modern civilization best depicted in 1960s television programs like *Hee Haw* and *The Beverly Hillbillies.* Haystacks Calhoun, a 601-pound "mammoth super heavyweight" from Morgan's Corner, Arkansas, who wrestled in knee-length overalls, was a crowd favorite in Virginia and the Carolinas in the 1960s. Crusher Blackwell, who weighed in at a mere four hundred pounds, and Bruiser Brody, a Texan, also illustrated this stereotype.[27]

Crusher Blackwell is a good example of how wrestling integrates southern themes into its drama. Blackwell had largely wrestled as a villain, but in the 1970s, wrestling in Knoxville, Tennessee, he became involved in a plot line that cast him in the role of innocent victim. Blackwell was managed by Boris Malenko, a wrestling promoter skilled at building villainous characters that could inflame wrestling audiences. In the mid-1960s Malenko, himself the patriarch of an illustrious wrestling family, built his career posing as a pro-Soviet wrestler in the Cuban-dominated areas of South Florida. Casting Blackwell as a "reserved and kind man" who only wrestled because Malenko held the mortgage to his family's farm, the manager made it clear to audiences that he would foreclose on the farm if Blackwell did not use his strength to "destroy his opponents" in the ring. The climax to this drama came when the local hero, Ronnie Garvin, jumped into the ring, paid off the "mortgage," and thus released Blackwell from Malenko's clutches. Blackwell then turned his fury on his former master, to the delight of the audience. Blackwell thus became a reluctant warrior entering the ring only to prevent a decline into dependency that must have been all too familiar to a wrestling audience only one or two generations off the farm.[28]

The 1970s saw more positive images of southerners appear in wrestling. Dusty Rhodes (née Virgil Runnels Jr.), perhaps the most popular wrestler before Hulk Hogan's reign began in the mid-1980s, embodied this trend. Obese, with eyes that seemed perpetually swollen shut, Rhodes seemed every inch the common man he billed himself to be. Rhodes boasted of his working-class roots—he claimed to be a Texas plumber's son—and he

Dusty Rhodes. (World Championship Wrestling)

bragged that he began his own working career at the age of eight digging ditches. Taking "The American Dream" as his epigraph, Rhodes wrestled as an "all around good guy, fighting for the American way of life."[29]

Rhodes's rivals were those who threatened the way of life he sought to defend. Chief among them was Kevin Sullivan, "a deranged madman" from Boston who claimed connections to devil worship and the occult. At one point the two met in a "Loser Leaves Florida" cage match in which the wrestling ring was enclosed by a chain-link fence and victory was had by clambering out over the top. Sullivan won, but only by concealing an unidentified "lethal weapon," which he used to "pound the great Dusty into a bloody American mess." Disguised as the Midnight Rider, Rhodes returned later that season and dedicated himself to ridding "the Florida rings of scum and vermin like Sullivan." Later, the two grappled again, and Rhodes again lost when Sullivan called to his aid an LSD-inspired sidekick known as Purple Haze.[30]

Rhodes represented a new type of southern wrestler persona: urban and blue-collar, a southern "embodiment" of the silent majority yet clearly still within the "good ol' boy" mold of regional stereotypes. Rhodes, however, also represented a broader trend in the 1970s. Tied to Jimmy Carter's election to the presidency and to the popularity of films like *Smokey and the Bandit,* this trend identified white southerners with mainstream American values. Sullivan's godless persona and its clear association with the 1960s drug culture and satanism was a perfect foil to Rhodes's traditional values of love of God and country. That Sullivan was a Yankee only heightened the struggle between good and evil in the minds of southern audiences.

The association of southerners with patriotism can also be seen in the character Sergeant Slaughter. A Parris Island marine drill instructor who was billed as having been discharged from the marines for "excessive cruelty to his troops in boot camp," Slaughter initially wrestled as a villain in the post-Vietnam 1970s.[31] The Iranian hostage crisis presented Slaughter with the opportunity to transform himself into a heroic figure, and he became a superpatriot, standing for "love of God and country." Slaughter's "intense hatred for America's enemies and detractors made him one of the most respected men in wrestling." Through most of the 1980s, Slaughter's chief rival was the Iron Sheik, the "Madman from Iran." The Sheik would incite the crowd by waving a large Iranian flag, and Slaughter would promise that upon his defeat, the villain would "'kiss my combat boots.'"[32]

By the 1980s black southern wrestlers could also fit the mold of superpatriot. Tony Atlas, Mr. USA, an African American bodybuilder from Roanoke, Virginia, showed skill equal to Slaughter's in creating dramatic opportunity out of international crisis. Atlas's target was Ivan Koloff, a "Russian" wrestler by way of Charlotte, North Carolina. Atlas took Koloff's "insults against the United States as a personal insult." When Soviet fighters shot down a Korean Airliner that strayed into Soviet airspace, Atlas "made Koloff his personal target for revenge." Koloff soon joined forces with the hated Iron Sheik, and the two vowed to "stamp out all American snakes." Atlas, however, teamed up with an unlikely ally, Captain Redneck, and the two were able to defeat the "two double-dealers in villainy." The black southerner and the redneck, too busy to hate, crossed the racial divide to join forces against a common foreign threat.[33]

The African American superpatriot theme continued into the late 1980s with Ranger Ross. A former airborne ranger from Fort Bragg, North Carolina, who fought in the Grenada mission, Ross would pose in his service beret and jacket, saluting and carrying a large American flag. The latest manifestation of the type is Sergeant Craig "Pitbull" Pittman, who wrestles in camouflage pants, marine boots, and a T-shirt emblazoned with "Semper Fidelis."[34]

Wrestling personas have sometimes reflected the harder edge of the modern South. Such was the case with the trio of wrestlers known as "The Fabulous Freebirds" in the early 1980s. Adopting the reactionary white southern populism of the ill-fated rock group Lynyrd Skynyrd, the Freebirds also gave expression to white working-class resentments during a time of high inflation and unemployment. Billing themselves as the "fearsome threesome," the Freebirds were famous for pulling off their cowboy boots and using them as weapons against their opponents. The Freebirds even recorded a rock song in the style of their inspiration entitled "Badstreet USA."[35]

Nonetheless, by the mid-1980s there were fewer and fewer mainstream southern wrestling personas in the mold of Dusty Rhodes, Tony Atlas, or Sergeant Slaughter. By then, interest in the South as a reservoir of an authentic Americanism had waned. Working-class America identified less and less with hard-bitten blue-collar personas as a wave of Republican optimism and prosperity swept the country. Carter had exited the presidential stage in defeat while Reagan began his ascendancy with the resolution of the Iranian hostage crisis. Southern voters had bought in to the Reagan vision. Carter's South was clearly out, the glamour and glitz of Reagan's California was in, and professional wrestling responded in kind.

Wrestlers who did adopt explicitly southern personas wrestled as fools or villains, atavistically drawing upon those elements in southern culture that had crystallized into larger-than-life icons of American pop culture, creating, in essence, parodies of existing parodies of the region. The Memphis-based Elvis impersonator Wayne Ferris wrestled as the Honky Tonk Man in

Honky Tonk Man. (World Wrestling Federation)

the late 1980s and early 1990s. Nearly always cast as a villain, Honky Tonk Man entered the ring dressed in the large-collar, rhinestone-studded jump suits favored by the original "King" and would often perform tunes such as "Hunka Honky Love." Honky Tonk's signature wrestling move was the "shake, rattle, and roll," and he briefly headed up a tag-team called the "Rhythm and Blues." He would often beat his opponents about the head with a guitar and then gyrate his hips, Elvis-style.[36]

Also patterning his persona upon a notable southern rock-and-roll musician was the wrestler Johnny B. Badd. The Macon, Georgia, native cast himself as a Little Richard look-alike, complete with pencil-thin mustache and bouffant. Like Honky Tonk Man, Johnny B. Badd generally wrestled as a villain. He also played on the sexual ambiguities of the real Little Richard, dressing in "matching pretty-in-pink outfits" and wearing "more makeup than senior citizens at a Florida condominium."[37]

The wrestling manager Colonel Robert Parker combined the image of the southern gentleman with allusions to Colonel Harlan Sanders and Elvis Presley's manager, Colonel Tom Parker, to create a composite of stereotypes. Dressed in a white wide-brimmed hat and white jacket, Parker was known for his shady dealings and willingness to break wrestling rules. When he wrestled on his own, his opponents were women, and even then he was known for cheating, much to the delighted outrage of wrestling audiences. Parker often faced another manager, Jimmy "The Mouth of the South" Hart. A Memphis native, Hart combined the look of a slick Nashville country-music producer with that of a used-car salesman who is pushy and loud, yet identifiably southern.

Southern religiosity has been mocked in wrestling, too. Brother Love, a mid-1990s wrestler turned manager and announcer, based his character explicitly upon the disgraced evangelist Jimmy Swaggart. Dressed in a white suit, red shirt, and white satin tie with gold rings on each finger, Brother Love covered his face and neck with red makeup "to look like a redneck." Brother Love preached "I love you" to the crowds, who knew that this was just a "smokescreen to hide his selfish greed."[38]

This said, it should be noted that the real thing also exists among professional wrestlers. George South, a wrestler and promoter from Concord, North Carolina, wrestled with "John 3:16" airbrushed on the back of his tights. Tully Blanchard, one of a long line of West Texas State football players to wrestle professionally, was born again when "he met God in the person of Jesus Christ in a personal way Nov. 13, 1989," at his home in Charlotte. Blanchard went on to direct "Ring of Truth Ministries" and serve as the minister of evangelism at Central Church of God in Charlotte.[39]

Wrestling Today

By the end of the 1990s, wrestling had come full-circle to the hillbilly images that were so prevalent in the 1960s and early 1970s. The most popular wrestlers to adopt a southern persona today are the "cousins" Henry O. Godwinn (HOG) and Phinneas I. Godwinn (PIG), who were managed by the 1980s wrestling standout Hillbilly Jim. The two members of this tag-team billed themselves as pig farmers from Bitters, Arkansas. Overall-clad, they often entered the ring with their pigs, Priscilla and Potbelly. Their "finishing" wrestling move was the Slop Drop, where they unloaded the contents of a slop bucket onto the heads of their opponents.

A "pig pen" match between Henry Godwinn and Hunter Hearst-Helmsley, the "scion of a patrician Greenwich, Connecticut, clan," revived sectional tensions while reinforcing the Godwinns' populist appeal. By tossing Hearst-Helmsley into a mud-filled pig sty, Godwinn recapitulated the victory of a more notable "good ol' boy" from Hope, Arkansas, who also defeated a Connecticut patrician. Like Bill Clinton, as well, the Godwinns' weakness for the fairer sex can be their undoing. They lost a championship match at Wrestle-

The Godwinns with Hill-billy Jim. (World Wrestling Federation)

Mania XII when the opposing team's "manager," Sunny, a shapely blond version of *Li'l Abner*'s Stupefyin' Jones, distracted Phinneas by posing suggestively before him. "'I never saw anything like that down on the farm,'" was his explanation.[40]

HOG and PIG notwithstanding, southern personas have been less popular in professional wrestling. The career of Ray Trayler, who once wrestled as the Big Boss Man, is instructive. Touting his home as Cobb County, Georgia, Boss Man was variously a southern prison guard or a violent police officer, complete with nightstick, who would rough up his opponents in the ring. Failing to succeed with that persona, Trayler then wrestled as Big Bubba, tattooing a Confederate flag on his arm. Just as Cobb County, increasingly dominated by Atlanta suburbanites, has become less "southern," Trayler abandoned his regional character for his latest moniker, the vaguely New York–sounding Guardian Angel.[41]

Southern wrestling personas seem to be losing their appeal as sports-minded southerners increasingly transfer their fan loyalty to the rising number of professional football, basketball, and, yes, even hockey teams now burgeoning in major southern cities. Perhaps as the South becomes more like the rest of the country—or the rest of the country more like the South, as the argument sometimes goes—the fascination with regional distinctiveness is relegated from the realm of the popular imagination to the arena of museums and preservation societies.

Moreover, the decline in popularity of regionally specific wrestling personas may also be the result of the internationalization of the pro wrestling business. Both Turner's WCW and McMahon's WWF have been looking to overseas markets, expanding into Europe, Asia, and Latin America. Overseas business accounted for 15 percent of the WWF's earnings in 1995, and the organization distributes programming to Rupert Murdoch's BSkyB and Star TV, which reach Asian markets. The WWF also appears on German, Italian, French, and Spanish television, and Turner beams WCW into Latin America on TNT International.[42]

While it is unclear if American professional wrestlers will soon hear Ross Perot's "great sucking sound," the internationalization of the sport has helped to bring about a shift away from regionally specific cultural stereotypes. Wrestling's chief inspiration seems to come from the developing global media culture. An example is the wrestler Galaxy, based upon the international cartoon superheroes the Power Rangers. In the late 1990s the sport's reigning stars such as Sting, Diesel, and the Giant were comic-book heroes that could appeal to many nationalities and cultures and required no specific cultural referent.

Wrestling, alas, has not been immune to broader postmodern cultural and intellectual trends. A case in point is Goldust, the former Dustin Rhodes and son of Dusty, "The American Dream." Having failed as a cleaner-cut, upscale version of his father, Goldust/Dustin Rhodes saw opportunity in America's postmodernist tendency to render casual the distinctions between genders. His character was a transgendered, sexually ambiguous, and rapacious cross dresser. Goldust entered the ring in gold pancake makeup, sporting fishnet stockings, garter belt, and bustier beneath a silver and gold lamé uniform, making provocative sexual overtures to opponents, fans, and himself alike. Initially a villian, Goldust became one of the more popular "good guys" in the WWF. Yet even Dustin Runnels eventually returned to his southern roots. In 1998 he dropped the Goldust persona, claiming a born-again experience. As Goldust, Runnels performed "vile and reprehensible acts." Now saved, Runnels "loudly praises the Lord around his peers" and preaches that "the love of God will soon flush the evil out" of the fans who heckle him.[43]

So the southern elements of professional wrestling still live on, even in the face of postmodernity and the alleged Americanization, or even internation-

Goldust. (World Wrestling
Federation)

alization, of Dixie.[44] On a cold winter night in 1997 at a Butner, North Carolina, National Guard armory, the wrestlers of Southern Championship Wrestling, one of many small-town, minor-league promotions, did their stuff. The
highlight of the evening came when two wrestlers went at each other in the
"Tennessee Test of Manhood," an obviously painful ordeal that involved
"swift kicks and private parts." Longstreet's "Fight" lives on.[45]

Notes

This chapter is reprinted, with minor editorial changes, from *Southern Cultures* 3:3 (Fall
1997): 8–27. © 1997 by the University of North Carolina Center for the Study of the American South. Used by permission of the publisher.

1. Augustus Baldwin Longstreet, "The Fight," from *Georgia Scenes, Characters, Incidents,
etc., in the First Half Century of the Republic, by a Native Georgian,* reprinted in *The Literary South,* comp. and ed. Louis D. Rubin Jr. (Baton Rouge: Louisiana State University Press,
1979), 230, 228, 229.

2. Ibid., 230–31.

3. Elliott J. Gorn, "'Gouge and Bite, Pull Hair and Scratch': The Social Significance of
Fighting in the Southern Backcountry," *American Historical Review* 90 (February 1985):

18–43; Timothy H. Breen, "Horses and Gentlemen: The Cultural Significance of Gambling among the Gentry of Virginia," *William and Mary Quarterly* 34 (April 1977): 239–57.

4. Randall Williams, "Tonight: The Hulk vs. Ox Baker," *Southern Exposure* 7 (Fall 1979): 30; "WCW: Where the Big Boys Play," media brochure (Atlanta, Ga.: WCW Media Relations Office, n.d.); John Leland, "Why America's Hooked on Wrestling" *Newsweek,* February 7, 2000, 46–54.

5. Bert Randolph Sugar and George Napolitano, *Wrestling's Great Grudge Matches: "Battles and Feuds"* (New York: Gallery Books, 1985), 44–47; Roberta Morgan, *Main Event: The World of Professional Wrestling* (New York: Dial Press, 1979), 204.

6. Roland Barthes, "The World of Wrestling," in *Mythologies,* trans. Annette Lavers (1957; reprint, New York: Hill and Wang, 1972), 21; *Richmond Times Dispatch,* June 13, 1996, D-4. See also Gerald W. Morton and George M. O'Brien, *Wrestling to Rasslin: Ancient Sport to American Spectacle* (Bowling Green, Ohio: Bowling Green State University Popular Press, 1985), 103–25, which places professional wresting in the morality-play tradition.

7. John Shelton Reed, *Southern Folk, Plain and Fancy: Native White Social Types* (Athens: University of Georgia Press, 1986).

8. Jim Tillman, a lobbyist for the WWF, commenting on the federation's successful effort to defeat proposed legislation regulating professional wrestling as a competitive sport in Florida, *Atlanta Journal and Constitution,* February 8, 1992, D-2.

9. Quoted in Thomas Hendricks, "Professional Wrestling as Moral Order," *Sociological Inquiry* 44:3 (1974): 177.

10. *Atlanta Journal and Constitution,* March 2, 1996, D-3.

11. Barthes, "World of Wrestling," 20.

12. Mark Twain, *Life on the Mississippi* (Boston: James R. Osgood and Co., 1883), 44–47; "Pro-Wrestling Illustrated," in *The 1996 Wrestling Almanac and Book of Facts* (Ambler, Pa.: London Publishing Co., 1996), 99; Michael R. Ball, *Professional Wrestling as Ritual Drama in American Popular Culture* (Lewiston, N.Y.: Edwin Mellen Press, 1990), 42–43.

13. Hendricks, "Professional Wrestling as Moral Order," 178, 181.

14. Ball, *Professional Wrestling as Ritual Drama,* 54–55.

15. "It Pays to Sponsor Television Corn," *Business Week,* October 7, 1950, 25–26; Jane Stern and Michael Stern, "Professional Wrestling," in *The Encyclopedia of Bad Taste* (New York: HarperCollins, 1990), 258–59.

16. Williams, "Tonight," 31.

17. *Charleston Post and Courier,* June 4, 1995, B-10; Larry Bonko, "Stomping at the Greensboro Coliseum," *Esquire* 70 (November 1968): 116–17.

18. Williams, "Tonight," 34.

19. Benjamin G. Rader, *American Sports: From the Age of Folk Games to the Age of Televised Sports,* 3d ed. (Englewood Cliffs, N.J.: Prentice Hall, 1996), 250–53.

20. See Joe Jares, *Whatever Happened to Gorgeous George?* (Englewood Cliffs, N.J.: Prentice-Hall, 1974), 1–10, for an excellent description of touring the 1950s southern wrestling circuit.

21. *Charleston Post and Courier,* March 31, 1996, C-24; George Napolitano, *The New Pictorial History of Wrestling* (New York: Gallery Books, 1990), 71, 76, 95.

22. "Mat Mania: Hulk Hogan, Pro Wrestling's Top Banana," *Sports Illustrated,* April 29,

1985, cover; *Tampa Tribune,* July 7, 1996, Business and Finance, 1; Susan Sontag, "Notes on 'Camp,'" *A Susan Sontag Reader* (New York: Farrar, Straus and Giroux, 1982), 105–19.

23. *Tampa Tribune,* July 7, 1996, Business and Finance, 1.

24. Ibid.; Leland, "Why America's Hooked on Wrestling," 46–54.

25. "WCW: Where the Big Boys Play"; Morgan, *Main Event,* 134.

26. Calculated from a listing of currently active wrestlers (*n* = 389) in "Pro-Wrestling Illustrated," 74–83. George O. Carey, "T for Texas, T for Tennessee: The Origins of American Country Music Notables," *Journal of Geography* 78 (November 1979): 221. The South is defined here as the eleven states of the former Confederacy plus Kentucky and Oklahoma.

27. Morgan, *Main Event,* 204–5; Sugar and Napolitano, *Wrestling's Great Grudge Matches,* 44–47.

28. Morton and O'Brien, *Wrestling to Rasslin,* 136.

29. Napolitano, *New Pictorial History of Wrestling,* 22.

30. Sugar and Napolitano, *Wrestling's Great Grudge Matches,* 156–57.

31. George Napolitano, *Wrestling Heroes and Villains,* quoted in Ball, *Professional Wrestling as Ritual Drama,* 106.

32. Bert Sugar and George Napolitano, *Pictorial History of Wrestling: The Good, the Bad, and the Ugly* (New York: Gallery Books, 1984), 35, 75; Sugar and Napolitano, *Wrestling's Great Grudge Matches,* 140.

33. Sugar and Napolitano, *Pictorial History of Wrestling,* 14.

34. Napolitano, *New Pictorial History of Wrestling,* 101; *WCW Magazine,* November 1996, 40–41.

35. Sugar and Napolitano, *Pictorial History of Wrestling,* 104; Sugar and Napolitano, *Wrestling's Great Grudge Matches,* 69.

36. Ball, *Professional Wrestling as Ritual Drama,* 128; Napolitano, *New Pictorial History of Wrestling,* 75.

37. "Pro-Wrestling Illustrated," 25.

38. Napolitano, *New Pictorial History of Wrestling,* 64; *World Wrestling Federation Magazine* 14 (March 1996): 6.

39. *Charleston Post and Courier,* December 15, 1996, C-14; June 23, 1996, C-12; *Chattanooga Free Press,* November 1, 1996.

40. *World Wrestling Federation Magazine,* September 1996, 34; Vince Russo, ed., *Showdown! Settling the Score . . . the Hard Way* (Stamford, Conn.: World Wrestling Federation, 1996), 49.

41. Napolitano, *New Pictorial History of Wrestling,* 46; *Charleston Post and Courier,* December 25, 1994, C-12.

42. *Financial World,* February 14, 1995, 112.

43. Bill Banks, "Touched by the Light," *World Wrestling Federation Magazine,* October 1998, 48–51.

44. John Egerton, *The Americanization of Dixie: The Southernization of America* (New York: Harper's Magazine Press, 1974); Peter Applebome, *Dixie Rising: How the South Is Shaping American Values, Politics, and Culture* (New York: Times Books, 1996).

45. *Raleigh News and Observer,* February 26, 1997, E-4.

12. The King, the Young Prince, and the Last Confederate Soldier: NASCAR on the Cusp

KARYN CHARLES RYBACKI AND
DONALD JAY RYBACKI

AMERICANS HAVE been racing their automobiles almost from the day the second one was built. America's first stock[1] car race was held on Thanksgiving Day in 1895. The *Chicago Times Herald* laid out a fifty-two-mile course from Chicago to Waukegan along Lake Michigan's shore. Eighty drivers entered their cars, but on that cold snowy day only six were able to start the race. The winner, J. F. Duryea, driving a car bearing his family name, blazed across the finish line after racing for ten hours and twenty-three minutes at an average speed of slightly more than five miles per hour.[2] Stock car racing had begun in America.

Racing was used as a means of drawing public attention to this new means for traveling across the nation's vastness. Americans soon became worshipers at the altar of automobilia. Early racing took place above the Mason-Dixon line, but the lore of stock car racing does not acknowledge these "Yankee" origins. Stock car racing has been described by B. C. Hall and C. T. Wood as "the true blood sport" of the South, the "unbridled passion of the Dixie way of life." With millions of viewers around the world and a hundred thousand fans at the racetrack, where the crowd roars "at every turn, lapping it up and praying for a ten car crash with fire and blood, wanting it and not wanting it at the same time," stock car racing is one of the South's "anomalous" contributions to sport. "It's shivering, it's soul stirring, it's bewildering, it's intoxicating, it's concupiscent."[3]

The National Association of Stock Car Automobile Racing (NASCAR) evolved from the dirt tracks of the Piedmont and drivers who outran the law on southern back roads as they delivered cargoes of moonshine. From these origins, NASCAR has become a sport of super speedways and corporate sponsorship for multimillion-dollar racing teams. From its southern cradle, NASCAR today is the fastest growing American sport in terms of gate receipts, television coverage, fan organizations, and sales of licensed merchandise. Long perceived as the sport of the lower-income southern "redneck," NASCAR is on the cusp of becoming an international phenomenon.[4]

Mark D. Howell's cultural history of Winston Cup racing credits the popularity of the sport to its appeal on a mythic as well as a tangible level. To a considerable extent, NASCAR attracts those who seek the quantitative analysis of the data that fill press releases and on which sponsorship deals are made. It is a sport of numbers and statistics—laps led, races won, engine revolutions per minute turned, gear ratios used, seconds needed per pit stop, prize money earned, and championship points awarded. Less tangibly, though perhaps just as vital to its increasing popularity, NASCAR has a stronger cultural mythology than any other sport for Americans, Yankees and southerners alike. It derives from a widely shared romanticism of the frontier spirit and the nobility of the outlaw challenging officialdom. According to Howell, the romantic myth of NASCAR resides in "the outlaw nature of folks forced to break the law in order to put food on their tables."[5]

NASCAR's southern roots have imbued the sport with elements of the mythic Old South. As scholars of historical "memory" have ably demonstrated, the losers in "The War between the States" coped by reinventing themselves as a chivalric society of gallant knights-errant, fair ladies, and stately manors with a steadfast belief in a code of honor. Despite the inherent falseness of that image, it remains a potent myth for many.

The late Dale Earnhardt, a seven-time NASCAR champion, represented NASCAR's traditional image. An aging driver from North Carolina who had not won a race in over a year until his 1998 win at the Daytona 500, Earnhardt went on to win five more races before dying in a crash on the last turn of the last lap of the 2001 Daytona 500, typically—his fans would say—running hard to the very end. Among the NASCAR faithful, Earnhardt was called the Last Confederate Soldier, the embodiment of the Old South—an individualist, defying authority, never giving up in the face of adversity. Accompanying those images was another, no less significant. Earnhardt was also known for his unflagging personal code of honor.

Juxtaposed with Earnhardt was NASCAR's "young prince," Jeff Gordon, who won more races than anyone from 1995 to 2000. While Earnhardt continued to garner coverage, Gordon, the kid from California who grew up in Indiana, appeared everywhere—on David Letterman, on the cover of *TV Guide,* in television ads for Pepsi, and wearing a "milk mustache" in magazine ads. The differences between Earnhardt and Gordon are symbolic of the tension between the old and new in NASCAR. While the "young prince" may someday match the accomplishments of the man still regarded as "the King," Richard Petty, those shaping NASCAR's future must recognize the danger in abandoning their sport's heritage, especially now that one of the last links to its early history is gone. Much of the basis for NASCAR's growing popularity derives from its southern roots, particularly the chivalric tradition of the myth of the Old South. To forsake these cultural roots for the mass-marketing techniques of stick-and-ball sports will diminish NASCAR's essence.

The Old South and the Origins of NASCAR

The myth of the Old South that most commonly comes to mind is that of a gracious, romantic society, predicated on the medieval code of chivalry, mediated for antebellum southerners by the works of Sir Walter Scott. According to John Fraser, Scott's novels and epic poetry packaged medieval life in a way that southerners believed mirrored their own culture. Both before the Civil War and after, white southerners conveniently embraced "the Saxons in *Ivanhoe* (1820), the culture of a supposedly primitive but in fact proud, sturdy, and morally admirable slave-owning people who rightly refused to acknowledge any inferiority to the ostensibly more sophisticated Normans who shared the country with them and were seeking to dominate them."[6] As suggested by John Shelton Reed and Dale Volberg Reed, Robert E. Lee was the embodiment of Scott's gallant Saxon knight, "the chivalrous warrior of Christ, the knight who loves God and country, honors and protects pure womanhood, practices courtesy and magnanimity of spirit and prefers self-respect to ill-gotten wealth." Scott's chivalry placed individual honor above all else, and Lee epitomized this code when he declined to lead the Union forces, saying: "I wish to live under no other government and there is no other sacrifice I am not ready to make for the preservation of the Union save that of honor."[7] This myth of the Old South with its chivalric code of honor rested, of course, on the "peculiar institution" of slavery.

But there is another aspect to the myth of the Old South: the core value of the autonomy of the individual to do what he or she thinks is right, which grounded Lee's willingness to leave the Union. This is a very personal "individual determinism," commonly articulated in the myth of the Rugged Individual or the American Frontier Spirit. It is fundamental to Americans, whether their ancestors came over on the *Mayflower*, in the holds of slave ships, or in third-class steerage aboard ocean liners in the early twentieth century. The myth of the Rugged Individual is predicated on the belief that an American has a natural right to use ingenuity, chicanery, and personal grit to make ends meet, whether it suits some faraway government or not. In his classic work *The Mind of the South,* W. J. Cash calls this "intense individualism" a dominant trait in the southern psyche. "Everywhere and invariably his fundamental attitude is purely personal—and purely self-asserting. . . . the frontier had loosened his bonds as completely as it is possible to imagine them being loosed for a man in a social state."[8]

What is today the geographic South was the first American frontier, settled by those who found the growing closeness of the northern colonies too constricting for their liking. In moving south and west, they left behind all but the most necessary elements of formal social structure. Thomas Jefferson described the transmutation of these frontiersmen into southern characters that were " 'fiery, voluptuary, indolent, unsteady, independent, jealous for their own liberties, but trampling on those of others, generous, candid, without attachment or pretensions to any religion but that of the heart.' "[9] What the South came to value as more important than one's lineage or wealth was the independence of one's spirit. Cash describes this as "great personal courage, unusual physical powers, the ability to drink a quart of whiskey or to lose the whole of one's capital on the turn of a card without the quiver of a muscle." Such a mentality led to a sort of Jeffersonian democracy in which no man was better than another and a southern man who "would knock hell out of whoever dared to cross him," whether he ever said so or not.[10]

Cash says this individualism and its concomitant code of personal honor "reached its ultimate incarnation in the Confederate soldier." The rank-and-file Confederate soldier was an "independent cuss" who would go home for the spring planting if a battle was not in the offing. He addressed officers with a most unmilitary familiarity as "Cap'n" or "Gin'ral." But when the chips were down, in Cash's words, "by the virtue of precisely these unsoldierly qualities . . . the thing that sent him swinging up the slopes at Gettysburg on that celebrated, gallant afternoon was before all else nothing more or less than the thing which elsewhere accounted for his violence—was nothing more or less than his conviction, the conviction of every farmer among what was essentially only a band of farmers, that nothing living could cross him and get away with it."[11]

Reconstruction attempted to imbue white southerners with the supposed virtues of the victorious North—"diligence, austerity, frugality, and the gospel of work." According to C. Vann Woodward, southerners were admonished to put behind them the frailties of the irrational and "outmoded notions of honor, chivalry, paternalism, pride of status, and noblesse oblige." Proponents of the New South, such as Henry Grady, attempted to remold the South into a quasi Yankeedom of business interests and industrialism. White southerners responded with the invention of "the Lost Cause," Woodward suggests, and this was a substitute "more defiantly proclaimed, articulately defended, and punctiliously observed than the genuine article had been."[12] The myth of the Lost Cause reified and magnified the code of honor of Robert E. Lee. "Against the forces most formidable, the southerner pitted himself, his small fortune, his Lilliputian industry, his life, and his girded honor," Frank Vandiver has written. "He lost, but lost magnificently. He lost wholly, utterly, but out of the ashes of his homes, his cities, his broken generation, he salvaged his sacred honor."[13]

The myth of the Lost Cause contained two thematic elements, according to Stephen Smith. First, "the gentleman planter had served as an officer in gray, most likely with the rank of general or colonel and always in the cavalry." In its second element, the South attempted to disassociate itself from slavery, claiming that the Civil War had really been about states' rights. "Soldiers fighting instead for liberty, constitutional principles, and protection of the agrarian splendor, had been martyred on the field of battle by the overwhelming numbers of the industrial North."[14] The persona of the Confederate soldier, the yeoman-everyman, resides in this second mythical element.

After World War II, particularly during the civil rights movement, the nobility associated with the Lost Cause faded as millions of Americans watched the inhumanity perpetrated on nonviolent demonstrators. But as William Faulkner tells us, the South is a place where "'the past is never dead, it isn't even [the] past.'"[15] There was a place in the American South where some vestiges of the Confederate soldier's "intense individualism" remained —the dirt tracks and new super speedways of NASCAR.

Stock car racing became popular in the South as a result of geography. Jobs became plentiful after World War II as the pent-up demand for consumer goods and the baby boom fueled the nation's economy. Californians did not invent the commute; it began in the South. To get to their postwar jobs, most people had to drive.

Baseball was still "as American as apple pie," and football, played primarily by college teams, was an obsession for southerners, but stock car racing was something different. "Here," according to Tom Wolfe, "was a sport not using any abstract devices, any *bat* and *ball,* but the same automobile that was changing a man's own life, his symbol of liberation," and furthermore, "it didn't require size, strength and all that, all it required was a taste for speed, and the guts."[16]

There was another factor in the popularity of stock car racing for many southerners, one more closely connected to the veneration of the nobility of the Confederate soldier, the outlaw ethos of the "moonshine tripper." The repeal of prohibition had not diminished the market for moonshine. The late Tim Flock, a racer whose family was heavily involved in the moonshine trade, recalled that "'people would rather have the bootleg liquor 'cause they could buy so much of it for not very much money.'"[17] An additional factor was that much of the South continued to be "dry" on a county-by-county basis.

For southern men, the right to drink, make, and sell moonshine was a God-given right, and no federal agent bent on collecting a tax was going to stop the production of moonshine. Moonshine had to be delivered to the customer, something federal revenue agents were determined to prevent. The local law was seldom a problem. County sheriffs, who had to stand for election and most likely had a relative in the 'shine business, were loath to impede something as fundamental to male southern culture as the right to a drop of whiskey now and then. According to Paul Hemphill, the transport system consisted of "the nearest wild hare of a boy whose souped-up car, the first one he had ever owned, was his love, his life, his passion, his passport out of there. He was afraid of nothing—a daredevil who would rather die violently in his car than of boredom" working in a factory.[18]

These young daredevils were the lineal descendants of the poor whites who had filled the ranks of the Confederate army a few generations earlier. They had the same disdain for any authority that tried to tell them how to live their lives as their grandfathers had in 1861 when they went off to fight Yankee officialdom. Something new, however, had been added to the equation—the automobile. As Hemphill indicates, the 'shine runner was honoring "the same tradition that had brought the untameable Scots-Irish settlers to the isolated Appalachian outback in the first place." Their cars were "the family jewels, the proof of their manhood, the pride of their life, and it seemed inevitable that soon they would race them."[19] Tim Flock, recalling one of these impromptu races run in a Georgia cow pasture in the mid-1930s, asserted that "'We didn't have no tickets, no safety equipment, no fences, no nothing. Just a bunch of these bootleggers who'd been arguing all week about who had the fastest car. . . . These guys would run and bet against their own cars, betting who had the fastest car. That night they'd be hauling liquor in the same car.'"[20]

While federal agents do not seem to have had rivalries over which had the best "revenooer" car, they drew upon the talents of local race shops to improve their cars. Ralph Moody of the Holman-Moody race shop worked both sides of the street in the late 1950s. He recalls, "'we worked a lot of revenue cars that chased them cats, and we worked on a lot of whiskey runners' cars too. We'd hop up their cars, soup them up, improve their suspensions.'"[21]

Junior Johnson, immortalized as the quintessential moonshine tripper-racer by Tom Wolfe, had a career as a 'shine tripper, a NASCAR champion, and a team owner. Johnson maintained that he "'never saw a better race car than what we built for haulin' whiskey.'" He took pride in pointing out that while he was arrested, "'I got caught at the still . . . I never got caught on the road. . . . They never could have outrun me.'"[22] He served time (a point of honor among moonshiners was that if you got caught, you did your time) and was pardoned long after the fact by Ronald Reagan. Although NASCAR makes every effort to minimize its roots in 'shine tripping, the outlaw spirit lives on in every Winston Cup team. According to Hemphill, "Even now, in the glitzy world of Winston Cup racing at the end of the twentieth century, a season never passed without one of those uniformed mechanics, born-again Christian or otherwise, being nailed at the on-track NASCAR inspection stall for trying to slip past with a 'refinement' that would make a tripper smile."[23]

Before and after World War II, stock cars had raced at small tracks throughout the Northeast and the South. As early as 1902, attempts to set land-speed records took place on the hard-packed sand beaches of Daytona, Florida. Little effort had been made to create a national circuit for stock car racing until William Henry Getty "Big Bill" France gathered promoters together in a popular Daytona bar in December 1947. France had begun promoting races on Daytona Beach and at other venues in the 1930s. According to Mike Hembree, Daytona had attracted "men who drove wild and free in races on a course carved from the sand along the beachfront and the parallel asphalt of adjacent Highway A1A."[24]

France believed that postwar America was ready to embrace the sport of stock car racing. Prior to the 1947 meeting, there were many different "sanctioning" bodies for stock car racing, each with its own rules, leading to assertions by several drivers that they were "national champion" in a given year. France wanted to bring uniformity and parity to the sport. NASCAR, the organization he founded, succeeded because Big Bill appealed to the economic interests of backers and the safety concerns of drivers. He convinced track owners accustomed to making their own rules that joining together would be mutually beneficial and that stock racing had a future in postwar America. The AAA (American Automobile Association), the occasional sanctioning body for some prewar races, had declined participation, claiming that the concept of stock car racing was a dying fad.[25] Big Bill understood the essential nature of those to whom he planned to sell race tickets and concession-stand hot dogs and beer. "Winston Cup fans were famously ornery and downright close-minded about their racing preferences," Paul Hemphill writes. "If a car didn't at least *look* like something they could drive away from a dealership, wasn't big and loud and fast, hadn't been built in an American plant and retooled by some salt-of-the-earth mechanic named Pete, or Mike, or

Harry, wasn't driven by someone who had come up the hard way (better a Southerner named Bubba), and went around the track any way other than in a counter-clockwise circle . . . well, it hardly counted."[26]

The Indianapolis 500, the self-proclaimed Greatest Spectacle in Racing, garnered more media coverage, and sports writers were attracted to grand prix racing because it had the "tone" of European nobility even though it was "the least popular form of racing in the United States," according to Wolfe.[27] A farmer from a small town in South Carolina, Harold Brasington, had been to the Indy 500 in the 1930s and was impressed that so many people paid "good money" to see a race when money was so scarce. He came home determined that the South should have a 500 of its own, built Darlington Raceway, and "changed the face and future of NASCAR racing." The South got its own five-hundred-mile race—the Southern 500, held in blistering summer heat on "the track too tough to tame."[28]

Not to be outdone by Brasington's 1.366-mile track, France had his own dream for a two-and-one-half-mile speedway at Daytona. In 1959 he moved the Daytona race from the beach-highway track to his own "super" speedway—a palace built for racing. Since France was the driving force behind NASCAR, the Daytona race had the honor of being the first race of the season. France's new track was designed with high banked turns and a sweeping "tri-oval" configuration that would allow every ticket holder a view of the entire track from his or her seat.[29] The Daytona 500 became the Super Bowl of racing, "the Great American Race." Winning at Daytona has taken on the same cachet as winning the Indy 500. Even Indy-car and Formula One drivers have tested their mettle on the high banks of Daytona. Although the smaller tracks such as Darlington still have a place on the NASCAR schedule, the "super-speedway" track design and modern facilities that offer fans a variety of amenities have come to dominate NASCAR racing.

Presently, Daytona also offers Daytona USA, the "ultimate motorsports attraction," a themed experience on the history of NASCAR and the France family's creation of the super speedway. Fans can see Jeff Gordon's race car vertically deconstructed so they can inspect the inner workings of today's stock cars. They can participate in a "pit crew" experience and race against the clock to change tires and fuel a car. Interactive video-game-style activities allow fans to "qualify for a pole position," play sportscaster and "call a race" as a video is screened, and test their knowledge of racing at Daytona. Fans may also take in an IMax-style film of Daytona 500 highlights accompanied by the thundering effects of a magnificently, deafeningly accurate soundtrack. Such themed attractions are planned for other speedways in the near future.

Daytona USA bills itself as "the ultimate motorsports attraction." Its interactive and static displays span more than eighty years of motorsports activity, beginning with speed trials on Daytona Beach but emphasizing NASCAR and the two-and-one-half-mile super speedway. (Donald and Karyn Rybacki)

Dale Jarrett's 1996 500-winning Ford Thunderbird had a place of honor at Daytona USA for fifty-two weeks. The week after this picture was taken, Jeff Gordon's 1997-winning Chevrolet replaced it under the spotlights. (Donald and Karyn Rybacki)

Twenty years after Big Bill's track opened, another significant change took place—CBS television covered the 1979 Daytona 500 live, from flag to flag. CBS and other networks had previously covered NASCAR on a tape-delayed, edited basis. The announcer Ken Squier convinced CBS that televising the race live would draw viewers, and CBS got far more than they expected. The Northeast was hit by severe blizzard conditions, forcing many people to stay home. There were few options for sports fans on television that Sunday, other than a stock car race in Florida. In that race, Cale Yarborough and Donnie Allison were on the last lap, racing for the checkered flag. Donnie's brother Bobby Allison was in front of them on the track but was not a contender since he was two laps behind. As Bobby told the story almost two decades later, "'my crew came on the radio and said, "Donnie and Cale are coming up on you. Make sure you give them plenty of room." . . . I said, "I'll be in the grass if I have to be." And with that, I looked up and they were about a half a mile behind me, wrecking.'" Cale Yarborough had tried to use the slipstream created by Donnie Allison's car to "slingshot" past him to take the lead. Donnie eased his car to the left to try and hold off Yarborough, and suddenly both cars were careening out of control. The two cars came together in the infield, and Cale and Donnie were out of their cars. Bobby drove back around the racetrack to see if his brother "needed a ride back to the garage" and was pulled into the fray. According to him, "'Cale began yelling at me, saying I had caused the wreck. He ran at me, saying I had caused the wreck. . . . I think I probably questioned his ancestry. . . . I was sitting in the car, but I had the window net down, and the next thing I knew, he had hit me in the face with his helmet.'"[30]

Cale Yarborough's version of the last lap of the 1979 Daytona 500 was a little different, suggesting that Bobby Allison was engaged in the time-honored strategy of blocking for a teammate or, in this case, a brother: "It doesn't always go like you plan; that's racing," Yarborough asserts. "I decided to pass him coming down the back straightaway on the last lap, rather than wait until I got to four, because I saw Bobby way up there, slowing down. He was two or three laps down, so I knew he had to be slowing down so he could block for Donnie when we got to three. It would have kept me from getting past. I told Junior [Johnson] on the radio: 'I'm gonna have a problem up there, so I'm makin' my move now.' 'Stand on it,' Junior said." As Cale and Donnie's cars skidded, spun, and collided into the infield, Richard Petty cruised by to take the checkered flag for a record-setting sixth Daytona 500 win. Cale says he was too mad at that point to care about Petty. "Bobby pulled his race car into the grass. He was running back to see if his brother was all right. I flew out of that car and decked Bobby. And then I went over and punched Donnie."[31] Petty was in Victory Lane celebrating his win, but the television cameras were focused on Cale and the Allison boys duking it out in the infield. According to Thomas Pope, all across the country viewers watched in fascination—"Speed, crashes, and brawls . . . a life-and-death game that had it all, and a previously underexposed sport had just gotten the biggest publicity boost it had ever known."[32]

By the end of the 1996 season, NASCAR's television audience had grown to 112 million. With the advent of cable television and the appearance of networks exclusively devoted to sports, notably ESPN and ESPN2, along with The Nashville Network (TNN), NASCAR viewership is second only to professional football. Playoffs and championship events in basketball, football, and hockey continue to draw viewers. Fans realize that there is only one Super Bowl to a season. NASCAR offers a "championship" event with each race. There is but one race to see each week, whereas fans have several games to choose from in other sports. NASCAR's value is in offering a quality product in limited supply against the proliferation of other sports' product. Each race pits the best against the best, while mismatches in many basketball, football, and hockey games make the outcome a foregone conclusion.[33] NASCAR has experienced significant changes from the early 1960s, as the days of the drinking, brawling, hard-driving, unkempt roughneck have given way to the driver-as-public-relations-representative of a corporate sponsor.[34] NASCAR fans have always been a loyal bunch, each fiercely devoted to a particular driver. Nurturing this ongoing sense of driver-fan kinship that gives NASCAR its uniqueness involves striking a careful balance between the sport's chivalric, individualistic mythos and its increasingly buttoned-down, corporate ethos.

NASCAR Driver Mythos

The NASCAR driver is the embodiment of the frontier hero. According to Howell, the driver is considered "fearless, intuitive, physically adroit, and emotionally cool. . . . There is little difference between dodging bullets along a trail in Wyoming and dodging concrete walls along a straightaway at Daytona." While most of us "climb into" our cars for the day's errands or drive to work, "the Winston Cup driver climbs into his car to try and defy principles of physics and engineering." The uniqueness of the NASCAR driver is that he (and sometimes she) uses frontier individualism to seize civilization's technology and use it to serve his purpose. "This is not unlike the frontiersman who gained acclaim for his abilities to shoot, hunt, track game, and ride."[35]

The sheer mastery of man over machine makes the NASCAR driver inherently larger than life. The legendary drivers of stock car racing's early days—Lloyd Seay, Curtis Turner, Joe Weatherly, Banjo Mathews, the Flock brothers (Tim, Fonty, and Bob), and Junior Johnson—were men whose intense expression of individualism was initially a response to the economic failure of civilization. As Peter Golenbock observes, "the Depression created a class of fierce, competitive men who without formal educations dragged themselves up by their bootstraps and who, even after they attained success, never lost that hard inner drive." In the southern manifestation of the frontier spirit, that "hard inner drive" was something more potent than a mere work ethic. According to Ralph Moody, these were "'real country boys. . . . Ain't nothing gonna hurt them, they figured.'"[36]

The fearlessness of NASCAR's pioneer drivers took many forms. As a personal-promotional stunt, Tim Flock raced for part of one season with a monkey, "Jocko Flocko," tied to a perch in his car. The monkey wore a suit and helmet like Flock's. Jocko was "retired" after a race at Raleigh, North Carolina. "Everything was going along just fine, Tim was leading the race, and Jocko was having a fine time, but another car spun into Tim and it knocked Jocko onto the floorboard, right over the exhaust pipe." Jocko suffered a slight burn and ran amok in the race car. An unscheduled pit stop to drop off his simian partner cost Tim the lead and ended Jocko's brief career.[37]

The racing exploits of Fonty and Bob Flock also demonstrate the individualism and casual disdain for rules characteristic of NASCAR's early drivers. Fonty once drove the Southern 500 wearing shorts, a T-shirt, and sneakers, to stave off the summer heat. Bob's opposition to arbitrary rules was even more memorable. Atlanta's Lakewood Speedway banned convicted felons from its races in an abortive attempt to bring respectability to the sport. Many of the top drivers at that time had run 'shine, and more than a few had been convicted and served their time. Lakewood officials anticipated that the lure of a race would attract some of the banned drivers and strategically positioned a few of the local constabulary to warn them off. Bob Flock had not allowed federal revenue agents to prevent him from running 'shine, so he certainly wasn't going to allow the Atlanta police to keep him from racing. As Richard Petty tells it, "he waited outside the track until the race had started, and then he just entered the track from the gate on the back straightaway." Bob's only mistake was that he was too good a driver, so he quickly moved to the front of the pack. "The cops got in their cars and took after him. Right on the track. Here came the race cars and right behind them, were two police cruisers, lights flashing and everything. It was like the Keystone Kops." Bob, the police, and the other drivers made several laps before his pit crew was able to open the gate so he could make his escape. He ran out of gas in downtown Atlanta and was arrested. Bob wasn't hauling 'shine, and the municipal code of Atlanta did not extend to Lakewood's ban on convicted felons racing, so the police could only charge him with speeding on a city street.[38]

Off the track, a NASCAR driver's life was also a reflection of the frontier spirit, southern-style. A majority of white settlers in the South were of Scots-Irish, Celtic heritage. White southerners maintained some of their ancestral ways, such as drinking to fuel their courage.[39] Curtis Turner upheld the code, fueling his fearlessness with alcohol. His racing philosophy was that if you had a bad enough hangover when the green flag dropped, nothing that happened on the track could hurt you. Turner—and his partner in mischief "Little" Joe Weatherly, the "clown prince" of stock car racing—were legendary party men. Turner would throw parties that lasted for a week. His only rule was that everybody had to get drunk. If you stayed sober, you weren't invited again.[40]

Practical jokes, pranks, and creative larceny were as much a part of the driver persona as the amount of alcohol he could hold. Weatherly was fond of practical jokes. He had a stuffed mongoose that he would pop out in a driver's face, like a jack-in-the-box, and a rubber snake that he would toss through the open window into a driver's lap. Weatherly especially enjoyed pulling this stunt on Cale Yarborough. He knew that Cale had been struck by a rattlesnake as a teenager. In retaliation, Cale caught a real rattler, defanged it, and dropped into Weatherly's lap at Darlington. "He was white as a ghost," Yarborough recalls. "As soon as he stopped shaking he turned red. . . . Everybody was falling on the ground laughing. Joe ran over to his tool box, got a ball peen hammer, and took off after me. He chased me clear out of the pits, and I'll tell you, . . . he would have killed me if he had caught me."[41]

Fighting was another legacy of the southern Celtic heritage. Along with drinking and gambling as a means of military preparedness, the Celts fought each other when they had no one else to fight. According to Bertram Wyatt-Brown, "a cultivation of ferocity meant that when attacked from without, men could trust each other, almost as brothers."[42] Tales of mayhem on the racetrack, fist fights in the pits, and drivers pummeling each other in the garages are legion. Buck Clardy, who raced in the 1940s and 1950s, recalls, "'You kind of made up the rules as you went back then. . . . I've seen 26 drivers fighting in the infield at Greenwood [S.C.] at one time, and 24 of them didn't know what they were fighting for.'"[43]

Although grudges were certainly carried (even in recent times two of the Bodine brothers didn't speak to each other for over a year over an incident), the southern proclivity for and love of a good fight meant that once the fight was over, so was the anger that provoked it. A week after their fight at the 1979 Daytona 500, Cale Yarborough and the Allison brothers were "friends" again.

Tiny Lund's wife recalls thinking "back then" that all the drivers were crazy. They'd help each other out, share everything from parts to motel rooms, "'but on that track they were bitter enemies.'"[44] Bobby Allison would fight anyone he thought got in his way on the track. More recently, he talked about these fights with a tinge of embarrassment. At some point, "'fighting is beyond what the sport will accept. That . . . and knowing you want to be in the sport for several years, serve as deterrents.'" Allison said NASCAR is a different kind of sport than baseball, football, and basketball, where most players are only around for a few seasons. "'We care more about our sport than other athletes in the world care about theirs,'" he said. "'That makes a difference. We'll fight for the sport, but not each other, at least not for long.'"[45] The depth of Allison's feeling for racing reflects the southern chivalric sense of honor, which, according to Wyatt-Brown, was "a state of grace linking mind, body, blood, hand, voice, eyes, and even genitalia."[46]

NASCAR has its own permutation of the southern code of chivalry. Honor resides in bond of driver, team, and fans. Drivers use the collective "we" to denote driver, crew, sponsor, and fans. A driver never speaks of "his" victory; it is always the team's victory supported by the loyalty of the fans. When a driver makes a mistake and causes a wreck, he takes the responsibility personally. As Shaun Assael notes, "if you cause a wreck, you're expected to own up to it quickly and decisively. Nothing's worse than being known as someone who can't admit mistakes."[47]

In the evolution of the driver persona, honor also meant being resourceful in outwitting those who make the rules—NASCAR's authority as a sanctioning body. As Richard Petty puts it, "cheating had always been a way of life with racers, but it had also been the main reason cars had gotten any better." Cotton Owens and the case of the "too-fast" Dodge represents the chicanery drivers and mechanics use in pursuit of the honor of having the fastest car on the track. Owens had a race-prepped Dodge that went faster and farther on a load of fuel than any other driver's Dodge. NASCAR officials repeatedly called it in, inspected it, and then checked it again. Nothing seemed to be different from any other Dodge. As Cale Yarlborough remembered the incident: "In desperation they hauled out the templates, which were full scale forms—gauges built from stock-bodied production cars." Templates were used to ensure that the body of a race car was exactly the same size and shape as a production car body, as NASCAR rules required. When they applied the template to Owens' car they discovered he had built a perfect seven-eighths scale reproduction of a stock Dodge. It was smaller and lighter, and that's why it went faster.[48]

Even the stern Lee Petty, described by Golenbock as "a family man and too serious about winning races to party late into the night," had his outlaw side. Petty had a reputation of doing anything to win. "Petty put wing nuts and armor plating on the side of his Oldsmobile, so that anytime his car brushed against the side of another car, he'd shred the opponent's sheet metal."[49]

One incident demonstrates the strong bonds of friendship among men who would do anything on the racetrack to beat each other to the checkered flag. Whenever drivers reminisce about what makes NASCAR great, they inevitably recall the story of Ned Jarrett's bad check. In 1957 the automakers withdrew their sponsorship from NASCAR. Many drivers, including Ned Jarrett, were struggling from race to race to stay in the sport. In 1959, after a season of "scrounging around trying to find a ride," Jarrett decided to buy his own race car. He found one for two thousand dollars, but he had less than a hundred dollars in his bank account. Jarrett knowingly wrote a bad check to the owner on Friday, giving it to him after the banks had closed. The plan was to win one race at Myrtle Beach on Saturday with a thousand-dollar purse and then go on to Charlotte for a Sunday race with the same purse. He could then take the winnings to the bank when it opened on Monday in time to cover the check. If all went according to the plan, Ned Jarrett would own his own race car. He won the race on Saturday, but the grand plan nearly came undone. In the 1950s drivers wore almost no safety equipment, and taping was standard practice to keep their bare hands from slipping off the steering wheel. The steering wheel in the car Jarrett bought was wrapped in electrical tape, but whoever did the wrapping had it on sticky-side up. By the end of the Saturday race, Ned recalls, "'I was bleeding so bad . . . I had to have a tourniquet put on my arms to stop the blood flow. I could see the bone in my thumbs.'" Ned started the race but had to rely on Joe Weatherly and Junior Johnson as relief drivers. He still remembers their generosity in saving his racing career. "'Somehow, word had got out among the other drivers and crews about that bad check. . . . Neither Joe nor Junior would take any money for driving in relief. They knew if they did I wouldn't have enough to cover the check.'"[50]

The mythos of the NASCAR driver persona resides in the outlaw spirit of the 'shine trippers, the tricks and skullduggery to gain a competitive edge, the fearlessness it takes to drive a stock car, and the bonds of friendship among opponents. For NASCAR fans, their favorite driver is the embodiment of the frontier hero, that rugged individual long celebrated in American popular culture and whom twentieth-century mass media parade before them as the essence of America. Fans are constrained by the obligations of civilized society, as are most Americans, but their driver-hero can transcend those obligations for a few hours on Sunday in the greatest thrill ride of all. Signifiers of a fan's favorite driver are all-important in identification with their hero. By wearing his colors and his car number, the fan identifies with and becomes one with that driver persona. Everyone has to have a favorite driver or at least be devoted to an automobile manufacturer. Robert Hagstrom advises that if you are attending a race for the first time, "you'd be smart to stop by a trailer and adopt a stock car driver for the race. The simple act of allegiance will save you from having to answer for the next three hours, the same question . . . Who's your favorite driver?"[51] NASCAR fans venerate their favorite drivers with the same passion and outward displays of identification that medieval penitents showed for their patron saints. So powerful is the attachment that fans will engage in some seemingly odd behavior.

We attended the Inaugural Las Vegas 400 in 1998 with a travel service, Grand Prix Tours. On Saturday morning, we were waiting for Grand Prix Tours' busses to load, standing by the door of the second of three busses. An older couple approached, wearing Dale Earnhardt shirts and caps and carrying a tote bag—all in black, emblazoned with Earnhardt's number three—and started to board. Don told them they had the wrong bus, this was the "number two," the "Rusty Wallace" (whose car number is two) bus. The couple moved down to the third bus in line. On Sunday morning they passed by the first two busses in line to get on the third one.

The veneration of the fan's favorite driver does not stop with track attire and tote bags. The bus trip from our hotel in Orlando to the Daytona Speedway for the 1997 Daytona 500 gave us a chance to visit with other Earnhardt fans. One woman had a catalog of Earnhardt's licensed merchandise. She showed us the things she'd already purchased—sheets, rugs, and towels, all in Earnhardt's colors (black and red)—and pointed out the cotton throw she planned to order next. The custodian who takes care of our offices is a devoted Earnhardt fan, and we've never seen him without his black cap with the red number three on it until the weeks following the tragic end of the 2001 Daytona 500. Earnhardt's fans are not the only ones who proudly wear their favorite driver's colors, it just seemed that way.

Whoever a fan's favorite driver might be, those knowledgeable of the history of stock car racing will argue passionately about who the greatest drivers have been. On the occasion of NASCAR's fifty-year anniversary, *Sports Illustrated* named Junior Johnson "the greatest race car driver in NASCAR history." Johnson received the accolade of "greatest" on the basis of "the way he drove—with a cerebral yet relentless style a generation ahead of its time."[52] Although Junior Johnson may well deserve *Sports Illustrated's* homage, he has never been called "the King."

The King

A Petty has been involved in NASCAR racing since the organization was founded in 1948. At age eleven, Richard Petty attended "NASCAR's very first official strictly stock car race, a 200-lap event in Charlotte on June 19, 1949, to watch his dad, Lee, pilot a '46 Buick Roadmaster to a 17th-place finish." At age twelve he was Lee's "crew chief," and by age seventeen he was racing himself. Richard Petty so dominated NASCAR that even when he wasn't winning, he was still a headliner. Petty tells the story of a fan who sent him an article from a Canadian newspaper, a short story with the headline, "Petty Runs Second." What is it about Richard Petty that earned him the sobriquet "the King"? For decades, Petty "ministered" to his followers. As Ed Hinton has noted, "he is of them and among them. One by one, hour by hour, day by day, since 1958, he has not only shaken hands and signed [autographs] . . . he has also 'talked to me just like I was *somebody*.'" Petty achieved two hundred career wins and seven national championships. In the process of creating his legend, Petty also helped make NASCAR.[53]

NASCAR could not have invented a better persona as its first superstar as that of Richard Petty. Athletes in other sports emerged during the same era as aloof, arrogant, opportunistic, and often hostile to the fans who made them superstars. In NASCAR Petty set the tone that created the intense emotional bond between fans and their favorite drivers. Petty has said "one of the first lessons my daddy . . . taught me was, Don't get above your upbringing." He has carefully cultivated a down-home, not-overly-educated image. He connects with fans on their own level, no pretensions of grandeur.[54]

Although he was unquestionably a great driver, Richard Petty became the King through his sense of noblesse oblige to his fans. Championship drivers do not charge fans for their autographs (as do stars in other sports), but they are frequently paid for public appearances or hold fan appreciation sessions "on orders from a corporate sponsor." Younger drivers may "hand out machine-printed autographs," but not Richard Petty. According to Golenbock, he "decided early on that he owed the fans and the press, rather than the other way around. No matter how many wins he had, if a fan wanted an autograph, Richard Petty would oblige, repaying his legion of fans for their loyalty by allowing them easy access." Petty has explained why he has always been accessible to his fans: "'I will never turn away a fan who wants an autograph. The deal is that no racetrack has ever paid me a penny. NASCAR has never paid me a penny. STP has never paid me a penny, and no car company has ever paid me a penny, in the sense that it is the fans who bought the products, bought the tickets, bought STP or Pontiac, and that money goes through those people and then comes to me. So without the fans, the tracks or NASCAR or STP or Pontiac wouldn't be here, and I wouldn't be here.'"[55]

Richard Petty became King Richard by doing what kings do today—going out among his subjects and being visible, accepting their adoration. Petty's kingship may well have cost him his competitive edge on the track. According to Hinton, "his public image may have helped to hasten his downfall, for he was simply too busy with the public to spend time with his mechanics improving the team's race cars." Although he did not retire from racing until 1992, Petty's last victory, his two hundredth, came on the Fourth of July, 1984, at the Daytona Firecracker 400, with President Ronald Reagan in attendance.[56]

The willingness of Petty fans to buy merchandise with his name on it was evident during his 1992 year-long Fan Appreciation Tour, which, according to Assael, "would become the single largest marketing bonanza in NASCAR." Dubbed "baublepalooza" by some, or the year Richard Petty's wallet got *fat*, fans bought everything from the traditional hats and T-shirts to the "official skewered poultry, Richard Petty Chicken on a Stick." Merchandisers took note of the NASCAR fan's willingness to buy almost anything with a favorite driver's name or number on it, observing, according to Bechtel, "Petty might as well have been printing money."[57]

Richard Petty's contribution to the NASCAR driver persona was his devotion to the fans, his ability to connect with them on a personal level. Humpy Wheeler explained the significance of this element. "It's been proven rather conclusively that if you can meet an athlete, and feel like you know him a little bit from having shaken his hand or maybe gotten an autograph, you're going to be much more interested in the sport he's in." Jeff Gordon may surpass Petty's records, but according to Bechtel, he "will never match Richard Petty simply because he was the first one to possess the regal aura, the first one to be larger than life and just one of the guys at the same time."[58]

The Young Prince

Jeff Gordon—"Men envy him. Women love him. Children idolize him. Rival fans hate him," says Ben White. More than any other driver, past or present, Jeff Gordon has made NASCAR a national phenomenon. He appears alone and with big-name sports stars like Shaquille O'Neal and Deion Sanders in Pepsi commercials. The week after his win at Daytona in 1997, he was wearing a "milk mustache" in mainstream magazines. He and his Hendrick Motorsports teammate Terry LaBonte appear on Kellogg's cereal boxes. Gordon and his wife, Brooke, smile out from boxes of Close Up toothpaste. These are but a few of the marketing tie-ins that take NASCAR drivers beyond the stereotypical image of the rednecked, illiterate good ol' boy. Jeff Gordon represents a major change. Not so long ago, a NASCAR driver just drove the car. As Richard Huff observes, drivers "didn't worry much about the business aspects, because there wasn't much business to worry about." Things are different today, and Gordon's clean-cut image appeals to corporate America. Ken Squier and CBS may claim some of the credit for making Richard Petty "king," but the king-as-common-man metaphor no longer fits the younger, larger-than-life stars such as Jeff Gordon.[59]

Jeff Gordon seems to be almost too good to be true, as the journalist Liz Clark describes him: "born for this moment in stock car racing history, cultivated like a hothouse flower and groomed like a thoroughbred race horse." Gordon is handsome, trim, young, has a beautiful wife, and has the squeaky-clean image beloved by corporate sponsors. In an age where highly paid sports figures punch out fans and officials, sport tattoos and oddly colored hair, spit on people, use drugs, or are in rehab-programs, Jeff Gordon stands out as the boy next door, Barbie's dream date. Gordon has never tried to remake himself in the image of the good ol' boy or claim ties to NASCAR's past that he does not possess. Gordon's public persona was that of a young adult of the 1990s who loved *Seinfeld,* played video games, water skied, read *People* magazine, and praised the Lord for his good fortune. Gordon was able to appeal to sponsors and fans alike. According to Hemphill, he moved as "easily among DuPont executives twice his age as with goggle-eyed young fans who finally had a driver they could relate to, and could bubble like a teenager ('cool man, awesome') after going door-to-door with the gnarly Earnhardt for three hours at hairy speeds."[60]

Gordon also changed the sport for the next generation of drivers. As Bones Bourcier observes, "he was not a son of the South, not a product of the old stock car pipeline, not someone who rose gradually through the ranks." In six seasons, Gordon won two Winston Cup Championships, the Inaugural Brickyard 400, the Daytona 500, the Winston Million four times in four years, and a host of other honors. Gordon seems to have burst on the NASCAR scene fully formed and ready to race. Such is not the case. Much like Tiger Woods in golf, Jeff Gordon had the natural talent and the desire to race and was carefully guided in developing his talents by his stepfather, John Bickford. Racing since he was five years old, Gordon describes what he does as "fun." On his way up, Gordon raced and won in go-karts, sprint cars, and the Busch Grand National series (one level below Winston Cup). Before he was old enough to get a driver's license, Gordon had a room full of trophies for his success on the racetrack. As he describes it, "I just love what I do."[61]

Jeff Gordon is also widely booed when he takes the ceremonial pre-race ride around the track. Fans cheer when he is involved in an accident or a mechanical problem forces him out of a race. The letters section of *Stock Car Racing, Winston Cup NASCAR Illustrated,* and *Richard Petty's Stock Car Magazine* have been filled with "hate Jeff" screeds. The anti-Gordon faction has claimed that: 1) he must be getting away with rule infractions because his Chevy is faster than any other Chevy (usually the one driven by Dale Earnhardt), 2) he intentionally causes other drivers to wreck, 3) he has never had to work hard, and 4) he gets too much media attention. There are Web sites entirely devoted to Gordon-bashing,[62] though he also has his supporters who respond to the "hate Jeff" contingent with the rejoinder that he's well spoken and always gives God credit for his talent.

Booing a winner or a new guy who seems to be getting "too much, too soon" is a time-honored tradition among NASCAR fans. Bourcier acknowledges they are "a fickle breed whose most rabid element is able to find something to hate in almost anybody who wins." Fans may "boo one guy because he drives a Ford, boo the next because he drives a Chevrolet," and just boo because booing is fun. "They boo Earnhardt because they think he drives too hard, boo Rusty Wallace because they think he talks too much, boo Jeff Gordon because they think he's too damn young."[63]

Significantly, Brooke Gordon is almost as well known as her husband. Drivers' wives engage in a host of NASCAR-related activities but are seldom in the public eye as much as Brooke. The camera loves an attractive young woman, and Jeff and Brooke look cute together as they walk toward Jeff's rainbow-painted race car. According to Karsen Palmer Price, Brooke Gordon is the "one woman in the male-monopolized sport who's gained the name recognition generally reserved for the sport's actual players." The boos, anti-Gordon Web sites, and letters do not single out Brooke for any particular invective, but "Brooke is unknowingly a victim of the 'let's-hate-the-prom-queen' syndrome: She's got the hair, the clothes and all the attention, and her husband is the most sought after guy in school."[64]

Fans perceive Jeff Gordon to be reluctant to connect with them. Richard Petty's constant courting of fans with handshakes, autographs, and conversation created a model against which all other drivers' behavior is measured. A fan in our Las Vegas group was showing off the autograph "Rusty [Wallace] gave me in the breakfast line." For her, Wallace was both a hero and a real person who had been friendly to her. She said she didn't think much of Jeff Gordon. She'd seen him the day before, "hiding in the parking garage" at the Mirage hotel. "He got into a Cadillac and drove away by himself." It did not matter to her that Gordon may well have just spent the preceding few hours at a sponsor's "meet and greet" session or was on his way to such an event. There was Jeff Gordon at the Mirage hotel with hundreds of fans, and, unlike other drivers, he wouldn't talk to them or sign a few autographs.

Jeff Gordon's opposite, at least in the eyes of his fans, was Dale Earnhardt, who called him "Wonder Boy" and "the kid." As Earnhardt put it, "'We just don't like the same things. I like to hunt and fish. He likes those video toys.'"[65] Earnhardt's disdain may have been based upon more than a generational difference. Just as Earnhardt appeared certain to break Richard Petty's record of seven national championships, along came Gordon to claim the Winston Cup in 1995, 1997, and 1998.

The Last Confederate Soldier

Dale Earnhardt was the son of a no-holds-barred dirt track racer. Bourcier described him "as a kid [who] had little patience for teachers and less for the stuff they taught." He dropped out of school after the ninth grade, married his first wife at seventeen, and worked at a variety of jobs, including as a mechanic for his father Ralph. By the time he began driving at age twenty-four, he was married a second time and had three children. Jeff Gordon may be racing for fun, but Earnhardt said that at Gordon's age he "wasn't racing for fun . . . he was racing to buy groceries for his family." Richard Petty, as befitted a "king," was a conservative driver who, according to Hinton, "won by calculation, finesse and superior financing." Petty did not charge to the front as soon as the green flag dropped. He bided his time, "waited for attrition, then made his move in the final few miles." Earnhardt was the Last Confederate Soldier, come to challenge the authority of the King.[66]

In the 1980s Earnhardt was a "predator" who built his reputation on the wrecks he had with other drivers. They complained about Earnhardt's unrestrained driving style, "trading paint" and shoving his way through traffic to get to the front. Mark Zeske asserts that "Earnhardt shrugged it off, proud of his slew of nicknames. . . . 'I don't care what they call me as long as I get to the bank on Monday,' he said." Earnhardt called the complaining drivers crybabies. "'They ain't ever seen the kind of rough racing I've had to do in my own life. . . . They don't want to mess with this ol' boy.'" Earnhardt was *attitude* personified. According to Zeske, he drove like a throwback to "a time when the car was more of an extension of the driver and his personality and less a complicated, high-tech tool."[67]

It may be difficult to fathom why fans were drawn to Dale Earnhardt. He had "anything but a warm, cuddly, and inviting personality." Compared to Jeff Gordon, Mark Martin, and John Andretti, drivers who look like they should be jockeying a horse instead of horsepower, Earnhardt looked like a "gunslinger . . . looking for some action: angular, scowling through mirrored sunglasses, a mischievous crinkly half-grin flashing through a brushy mustache that slashed across a face wrinkled and burned by the sun and hard knocks . . . he seemed to enjoy his reputation as one tough hombre."[68]

Dale Earnhardt commanded the loyalty of many racing fans, and they seemed to increase in number, even as his career waned and suddenly ended. His fans still engage in an Earnhardt shopping frenzy as part of their race-day experience. At Las Vegas in 1998 and again in 2001 two weeks after his death we toured the "trailers," rows of cargo haulers designed to open up on one side, souvenir shops on wheels. A trailer is painted in the same color scheme as the car of the driver whose merchandise is sold there. Like the drivers and their race cars, the trailers move from track to track for each race of the season. Each driver's merchandise is available at, at least, one trailer. The more popular drivers may have several, dispersed among the rows of trailers (a scene that resembles a crowded bazaar in some ancient city with narrow streets). There were three Earnhardt trailers at the 1998 Las Vegas race, and fans were stacked three deep, early in the morning, waiting to buy a piece of the Man in Black's attitude. Later in the day it was impossible to get anywhere near the Earnhardt trailers. All three trailers were back in Las Vegas in 2001, and the crowds were even bigger as fans came to write a final message to their fallen hero on the sides of his merchandise trailers. Variations of "Dale, you were the best" and "Dale, we'll miss you" were written with felt tips on every exterior surface.

Jeff Gordon is one of those drivers who has multiple merchandise trailers. Early in the morning a Gordon fan can stroll up to the counter without having to elbow anyone out of the way to check out the souvenirs or make a purchase. The same is true at the trailers of many other drivers, but the Earnhardt fans have always had to emulate the man himself and push through the crowd to get to the front. We have never found Earnhardt fans becoming surly in these circumstances. They remain good-natured and polite while caught up in the crush of people waiting to make a purchase, although their conversations were more subdued in 2001 than they had been in previous years, and they were careful to leave room for those who had come to inscribe a reminiscence rather than buy a keepsake.

Humpy Wheeler, who is said to be one of the best analysts of the psyche of both the hardcore and casual NASCAR fan, thinks that more and more Americans identified with Earnhardt out of their frustration with the nation's highway system. According to Wheeler, urban road rage makes us hate traffic with a passion. "Earnhardt drives through traffic too. And he won't put up with anything. He's going to get through. And that's what *they* want to do—

Souvenir truck, Las Vegas Motor Speedway. Most teams bring a truckload of T-shirts, hats, bumper stickers, and other memorabilia to every stop on the thirty-one-race Winston Cup circuit. Popular drivers such as Jeff Gordon and Dale Earnhardt have two or three trucks to shorten the lines of fans waiting to buy merchandise. (Donald and Karyn Rybacki)

but they can't. So Earnhardt is playing out their fantasies." In important symbolic ways, Dale Earnhardt was widely believed to challenge the authority that governs our lives. Wheeler has said that "Earnhardt will stand his ground and say, 'I'm not going to do that.' And the people who love him are the people who are told, every day, what to do and what not to do, and they've got all those rules and regulations to go by." For example, he did not want his field of vision obstructed and so was one of the last to wear an open-face helmet. At age forty-nine, Dale Earnhardt possessed the same determination to do things his way that he had had at twenty-four. Picked by *Inside NASCAR's* panel of experts as the greatest driver of all time, Earnhardt was not ready to retire. "'The will to win hasn't diminished. . . . There's one thing on my mind when the race starts: How am I going to get to the front?'"[69]

Tellingly, Earnhardt saved his most intimidating off-track thrusts for his young nemesis, Jeff Gordon. Gordon won the inaugural Brickyard 400 in 1994, the first stock car race ever held at the Indianapolis Motor Speedway. David Letterman, a racing fan and former Hoosier himself, has had several drivers on his show. Earnhardt was a guest after his own win at Indy, claiming to be the first man to win a NASCAR race at the speedway. Letterman observed that Gordon had won the first race. Earnhardt's rejoinder, "No, I said I was the first *man*," got a hearty response from the audience. Taunting Gordon about his youth when he won his first Winston Cup Championship in 1995 at age twenty-three, Earnhardt announced that they'd probably be serving milk instead of champagne at the banquet that year. Demonstrating that he could be a good sport, Gordon had milk delivered in a champagne bucket, poured himself a flute, and toasted Earnhardt. Gordon seemed to regard Earnhardt's jibes as good-natured ribbing that is part of the sport.

Earnhardt's off-track verbal jabs also revealed how he earned his Ironhead image. Jeff Gordon was dating Brooke Sealy (now his wife) at the time she was Miss Winston. The Miss Winston women are not allowed to date drivers, so the two were keeping their budding romance quiet. Since Gordon would show up without a date for NASCAR events, Earnhardt went up to him at a party and pointedly asked him if he were gay.

Curiously enough, Dale Earnhardt was even more standoffish with the fans than Jeff Gordon seemed to be, but the fans seem to like him all the more for it. Ed Clark, the general manager of the Atlanta Motor Speedway, had a small cocktail party for Earnhardt in 1993. Clark described the Earnhardt-fan encounter. "Earnhardt sat on one side of the room and the fans sat on the other. . . . Even the ones bold enough to go over and get their pictures taken with Earnhardt would pose with him quickly and then move on—as if they were all afraid he was going to punch them." Humpy Wheeler asserts that "Earnhardt's testy reluctance" to mingle with his fans is part of his image as the Last Confederate Soldier. He may have been rich and married to a pretty, young wife (his third), but Dale Earnhardt had had a hard life. He had stood his ground, and he had suffered just as much as any ordinary person.[70] Similar behavior from Jeff Gordon would earn him the title of "spoiled brat," but Earnhardt's surliness enhanced his popularity. To many observers, Earnhardt was the last remnant of that Jeffersonian democracy in which a man has a natural right to "knock the hell out of anyone who dared to cross him."

We overheard one fan's explanation of the ups and downs of Earnhardt's marital relationships that affirmed the belief that fans were drawn to him because his life connected with theirs. One woman told another about how "good" Earnhardt's third wife, Theresa, had been for him. Like so many young people, Dale couldn't wait to get married, and it didn't work out because he was too young. His second wife just didn't understand why racing was so important to him. But Theresa knows what racing means, and she was right there; she supported Dale. We later learned that this fan had never met Earnhardt personally. Still, she felt so connected to him that she spoke about him using his first name, as though he were a family member or a close friend.

There were signs in the last years of his life that even the gruff Dale Earnhardt had been softened somewhat by the hard knocks he had suffered. In 1996 he experienced the worst crash of his career so far. He was winless in 1997 and suffered from a bizarre loss of consciousness at the start of the Southern 500 at Darlington. Nineteen ninety-eight began on a positive note, as he finally won the race that had eluded him all those years, the Daytona 500. After the win, Earnhardt sounded more like Jeff Gordon than the Intimidator. "'You get the teary eyes. [Earnhardt had criticized Jeff Gordon two months earlier for getting teary-eyed at the 1997 Winston Cup banquet]. . . . This was one of the most awesome races I've ever won.'"[71]

NASCAR offers fans a fascinating "stew of personalities." Earnhardt came from the "old school of roughriders from the dirt track days." Jeff Gordon is of the "yuppies-for-Jesus crowd." For the free-spirited liberal there is Kyle Petty, who collects (and reads) first editions. For "the smokers and the red-meat-eaters" there is the "blustery overweight" Jimmy Spencer, "Mr. Excitement," the man most likely to be in the middle of the big pile-up coming out of a turn. Whatever his background, a driver who hopes to hang onto his fans "must be able to imply, with a tug of the ear and an endearing grin, *I might be rich, but it ain't changed me none.*"[72]

NASCAR on the Cusp

NASCAR celebrated its fiftieth anniversary in 1998 on the cusp of a major change. In the 1990s stock car racing transcended its southern origins. NASCAR fans are now found in every geographic region in the United States, and they are clamoring for races closer to home. There are also fans in Europe and Asia who would like to see NASCAR go international. Although some Confederate flags are still seen waving in the infield, guys with beer-bellies found, and southern accents heard, NASCAR fans and drivers are as likely to come from Des Moines, Iowa, Bakersfield, California, and Seattle, Washington, as they are from Hueytown, Alabama, or Dawsonville, Georgia. While NASCAR need not teach new drivers to "talk southern" or encourage them to discover a 'shine tripper hiding somewhere in their family trees, if NASCAR is to continue to draw new fans and retain the old ones there is one fundamental principle to remember: Fans identify with drivers, first and foremost. They identify with the sponsor of a favorite driver only indirectly. If Kellogg's sponsors their favorite driver, they buy a Kellogg's product at the supermarket. But if the driver changes sponsors, loyalty to Kellogg's may waver. It's a long-held principle in NASCAR, first stated in the days when the auto industry openly sponsored teams: Win on Sunday, Sell on Monday.

Fans identify with a driver not on the basis of who sponsors him (or sometimes her) but on the basis of what kind of person the driver is. NASCAR has promoted itself with the claim that "our athletes don't go out on strike" or sulk as "free agents" demanding more money. When they need more money, "they go out and race for it." Even though top NASCAR drivers make a great deal of money, there is a strong perception that they work for it. Unique to NASCAR is the firm belief that a fan will have the opportunity to meet that favorite driver, even if he or she never takes advantage of it. Humpy Wheeler has identified this accessibility as the biggest challenge NASCAR faces going into the next century. "If they [the drivers] stop being accessible, this sport will start going downhill."[73]

NASCAR on the cusp represents another kind of change, a movement away from its white southern heritage, though not away from the essential principle of "intense individualism" that undergirds that heritage. NASCAR offers the potential for an ethnic, racial, and sexual equality found in no other sport. The ranks of young drivers in the early stages of career development portend greater diversity for the next generations of NASCAR Winston Cup drivers. Minority-owned teams, minority drivers, teams owned by women, and women drivers are changing the face of NASCAR but not the core values of the sport.

The only African American–owned team in NASCAR's history was Wendall Scott's, twenty-five years ago. When southern racism was overt, Scott was "accepted" because he didn't win much. The NBA legend Julius Erving and the NFL veteran Joe Washington formed Washington Erving Motorsports for the express purpose of increasing minority participation in NASCAR on the track and in the stands. Ozzie "the Wizard" Smith of the St. Louis Cardinals co-owns Wizard Motorsports, which has a car in the Busch series. Joe Washington believes that "'it's only a matter of time before NASCAR has a significant minority presence.'"[74]

About half of those attending any race are women. For the most part, women are not at a race because they tagged along with a husband or boyfriend. They are there to see the race and are into it every bit as much as any man at the racetrack. NASCAR holds another appeal for the female fan—women race too, and they race against men, on the same track, under the same rules. There are only a few active women drivers, and none at the Winston Cup level since Janet Guthrie (better known for being the first woman to race in the Indy 500) tried her luck in the 1970s. Patty Moise ran in the lower-division Busch series, Tammy Jo Kirk was successful in the Craftsman Truck series, and Shauna Robinson made her first Winston Cup start in 2001. Companies hawking "women's products," such as Lovable undergarments, see the advantage of sponsoring women drivers. Even though Moise was bringing up the rear of the pack in the Busch race at Las Vegas on February 28, 1998, the women around us in the stands were cheering her on, and the men were watching to see how she would finish.

There is one final element of NASCAR on the cusp that suggests the importance of the sport over the next decades. NASCAR is poised to replace "the Greatest Spectacle in Racing" as the centerpiece of American motor sports. Once the premier motor sports event in the United States, the Indy 500 has become less important with the schism in open-wheel racing. Joyce Stanbridge has reflected: "How ironic it is that some of the arrogant open wheelers who sneered that taxi cabs would never run at Indy are now on the outside with their noses pressed up to the glass." Mario Andretti showed up for the Daytona 500 (and won it) just to prove he could do it. For the most part, the open-wheel drivers tended to look down on NASCAR as some lesser breed of sport. In 1997, car owner Felix Sabates had some advice for his new driver Robby Gordon, who came from the ranks of Indy-car (and is no longer with Sabates), about the difference between how Indy-car drivers and NASCAR drivers treat their fans: "This is not a putdown of Indy drivers, but a lot of these Indy drivers think their poo-poo don't stink when it comes to the fans. . . . I've been around enough of them [to know] that they think they are God's gift to the world. I told Robby, 'Robby, when a fan stops to get an autograph, I don't care if you have an ulcer attack, you stop and sign.'"[75]

NASCAR is on the cusp of a change from the era of Richard Petty's cultivation of his personal kingdom to the era of the driver as a part of some sponsor's marketing plan. Today, instead of sitting on the pit wall signing autographs and chatting with the fans, a driver is whisked by limo from one gathering to another, to meet the top brass, pose for pictures with the Employee of the Year, and mingle with those who won awards for selling the most widgets. NASCAR fans are passionate about the sport, and its continued success depends upon keeping those who are loyal and enticing new fans.

Afterword

The breadth and depth of that passion was poignantly demonstrated in the reaction of NASCAR fans to the death of Dale Earnhardt on the last lap of the 2001 Daytona 500. Tens of thousands of messages were posted on Web sites as fans bonded in a mutual sharing of grief and disbelief that Earnhardt was not immortal after all. Earnhardt devotees often expressed the sentiment that they would "pull for" Dale Junior or one of the Dale Earnhardt Inc. (DEI) teams, "but just not yet." Others avowed they were not Earnhardt fans, but they respected the man and his talent. Poems, songs, prayers, pleas, and every imaginable expression of comfort to the Earnhardt family filled sites on the Web.

The spontaneous memorializing began at Daytona in the hours after the announcement of Earnhardt's death. At first, only a few candles and flowers were placed at the track. By Monday, the floral mounds and tributes began to resemble those placed in memory of Princess Diana. Impromptu shrines began popping up at racetracks, Chevy dealerships, shops that specialized in racing items, and just about any place that race fans might gather. On the Sunday following Daytona, the NASCAR family of teams, sponsors, and fans gathered at Rockingham for the season's second race. The spirit of Dale Earnhardt seemed to hover over the place.

On a gray, overcast day, military aircraft flew a "missing man formation" over the racetrack. In the parade lap, the pole sitter, Jeff Gordon, dropped back from his front-row starting position to perform NASCAR's own version of the "missing man." The Fox broadcast team began the race by indicating that for 2001 they would fall silent for the third lap of every race in memory of Earnhardt. The most eerie aspect of NASCAR's first race without the Man in Black occurred on the first lap. Dale Earnhardt Jr. crashed into the wall at the same angle that had killed his father just days before, in an accident that looked frighteningly similar. Dale Junior was shaken but uninjured. Shortly thereafter the rain came, and the race was postponed until Monday. Steve Park, one of three DEI drivers, went on to win Rockingham.

Earnhardt's presence seemed to be everywhere as a curious numerology pervaded the early part of the NASCAR season. In the three races following Daytona, accidents caused the third lap of each race to be run under a caution flag. Kevin Harvick, who replaced Earnhardt on the Richard Childress team (but driving a white car, number 29), won at Atlanta in only his third race as a Winston Cup Driver. His win resembled Earnhardt's final win at Atlanta in 2000—a photo finish racing with Jeff Gordon (Earnhardt had won against Bobby Labonte, the 2000 Winston Cup champion, in similar fashion). Harvick had won the fourth race of the season, driving car number 29, starting fifth, and finishing first. In sequence, those numbers become 4/29/51, the date of Dale Earnhardt's birth.

Dale Earnhardt Sr. was to NASCAR what Michael Jordan was to basketball and Tiger Woods is to golf. A Harris poll taken in January 2000 found that 90 percent of Americans knew who he was, and he ranked third in popularity as a sports "team" behind the New York Yankees and the Dallas Cowboys. His death took from NASCAR one of its last links to its past. At NASCAR's urging, fans stood during the third lap of each race in 2001 with three fingers held high in memory of his passing. For many, love him or hate him, Earnhardt was the last vestige of the American dream. He came from a poor background and was a ninth-grade dropout who became a successful businessman. He went from having nothing to having it all by doing the one thing he loved and was good at—racing a car. Dale Earnhardt was the Last Confederate Soldier and the best at what he did.

Notes

1. The term "stock" refers to a car that is not specially built for the purpose of racing, as is the case with the open-wheel cars of Indianapolis-style racing. The earliest automobiles were not "stock" in the sense we think of the term because they were built by hand. They were "stock" in the larger sense that they were built for public consumption, as were the cars raced through the 1970s. Today's racing stock cars have bodies built to resemble those of cars you would see at a new car dealership, but everything under their sheet-metal skins is purpose-built for racing.

2. See David K. Wright, *America's 100-Year Love Affair with the Automobile and the Snap-on Tools That Keep Them Running* (Osceola, Wis.: Motorbooks International, 1995), 21.

3. B. C. Hall and C. T. Wood, *The South* (New York: Scribner's, 1995), 91.

4. NASCAR sanctions approximately two thousand races a year in twelve separate divisions. Winston Cup is the top division. For a complete list of the divisions of NASCAR, see Robert G. Hagstrom, *The NASCAR Way: The Business That Drives the Sport* (New York: John Wiley and Sons, 1998), 31–34.

5. Mark D. Howell, *From Moonshine to Madison Avenue: A Cultural History of the NASCAR Winston Cup Series* (Bowling Green, Ohio: Bowling Green State University Press, 1997), 5.

6. John Fraser, *America and the Patterns of Chivalry* (Cambridge: Cambridge University Press, 1982), 7.

7. John Shelton Reed and Dale Volberg Reed, *1001 Things Everyone Should Know about the South* (New York: Doubleday, 1996), 98–99 (Lee quote on 273).

8. W. J. Cash, *The Mind of the South* (1941; reprinted, New York: Vintage Books, 1991), 38.

9. Jefferson quoted in Reed and Reed, *1001 Things Everyone Should Know about the South,* 272.

10. Cash, *Mind of the South,* 38, 43.

11. Ibid., 43, 44.

12. C. Vann Woodward, "The Southern Ethic in a Puritan World," in *Myth and Southern History,* ed. Patrick Gerster and Nicholas Cords (Urbana: University of Illinois Press, 1989), 63, 65.

13. Frank E. Vandiver, "The Confederate Myth," in *Myth and Southern History,* ed. Patrick Gerster and Nicholas Cords (Urbana: University of Illinois Press, 1989), 148.

14. Stephen A. Smith, *Myth, Media, and the Southern Mind* (Fayetteville: University of Arkansas Press, 1985), 148.

15. Faulkner quoted in Peter Applebome, *Dixie Rising* (New York: Times Books, 1996), 14.

16. Tom Wolfe, "The Last American Hero," in *A Collection of Classic Southern Humor II,* ed. George W. Koon (Atlanta: Peachtree Press, 1986), 44.

17. Quoted in Peter Golenbock, *The Last Lap* (New York: Macmillan, 1998), 14.

18. Paul Hemphill, *Wheels* (New York: Simon and Schuster, 1997), 84.

19. Ibid., 84–85.

20. Quoted in Peter Golenbock, *American Zoom* (New York: Macmillan, 1993), 17.

21. Quoted in ibid., 29.

22. Quoted in Monte Dutton, "The Growing Years," *Inside NASCAR Presents: NASCAR's 50 Greatest Moments* (Winter 1998): 77.

23. Hemphill, *Wheels*, 12.

24. Mike Hembree, "The Early Years," *Inside NASCAR Presents: NASCAR's 50 Greatest Moments* (Winter 1998): 48.

25. Hagstrom, *NASCAR Way*, 27.

26. Hemphill, *Wheels*, 38–39.

27. Wolfe, "Last American Hero," 45.

28. Hembree, "Early Years," 54.

29. Our first visit to the Daytona super speedway was for the 1997 Daytona 500. We discovered a peculiarity of NASCAR fans that defeats the brilliance of France's design. Fans do not sit during the race, they stand. We had "good" seats, relatively high up in the stands, but all we could see was a small part of the track.

30. Quoted in Thomas Pope, "The Glory Years," *Inside NASCAR Presents: NASCAR's 50 Greatest Moments* (Winter 1998): 102, 104

31. Cale Yarborough, *Cale: The Life and Times of the World's Greatest Stock Car Driver* (New York: Times Books/Random House, 1986), 216.

32. Pope, "Glory Years," 105.

33. Hagstrom, *NASCAR Way*, 83.

34. Golenbock, *Last Lap*, 173.

35. Howell, *From Moonshine to Madison Avenue*, 110.

36. Golenbock, *American Zoom*, 23–25 (Moody quote on 29).

37. Richard Petty with William Neely, *King Richard I: The Autobiography of America's Greatest Auto Racer* (New York: Macmillan, 1986), 100.

38. Ibid., 45.

39. Bertram Wyatt-Brown, *Southern Honor: Ethics and Behavior in the Old South* (New York: Oxford University Press, 1982), 41.

40. The exploits of the "wild bunch" of the early NASCAR era is narrated in Golenbock, *American Zoom*, 23–35; and Golenbock, *Last Lap*, 20–23, 45–49.

41. Yarborough, *Cale*, 168.

42. Bertram Wyatt-Brown, *Southern Honor: Ethics and Behavior in the Old South* (New York: Oxford University Press, 1982), 39.

43. Quoted in Hembree, "Early Years," 60.

44. Quoted in Golenbock, *Last Lap*, 264–65.

45. Allison quoted in Benny Phillips, "Push Comes to Shove," *Stock Car Racing* 32 (June 1997): 111; Wyatt-Brown, *Southern Honor*, 49.

46. Wyatt-Brown, *Southern Honor*, 49.

47. Shaun Assael, *Wide Open: Days and Nights on the NASCAR Tour* (New York: Ballantine Books, 1998), 187.

48. Petty, *King Richard*, 192; Yarborough, *Cale*, 221.

49. Golenbock, *American Zoom,* 28.

50. Quoted in Tom Higgins, "The Gentleman's Gamble," *NASCAR Winston Cup Illustrated* 16 (September 1997): 68–69. Stock car racing began with both driver-owners, who scraped together whatever resources they could to support their efforts, and teams sponsored by local car dealers or garages, which often provided nothing more than a car or a place to work on it in exchange for their name on the door. When race winners called the automakers' attention to the publicity gained from racing, more direct factory support began. That support ranged from financing the team's racing budget at one extreme, to selling parts at discounted prices to the driver-owners.

51. Hagstrom, *NASCAR Way,* 9.

52. "The 12 Greatest Drivers," *Sports Illustrated Presents 50 Years of NASCAR, 1948–1998* (special issue 1998), 86.

53. Mark Bechtel, "The King," *Sports Illustrated Presents 50 Years of NASCAR, 1948–1998* (Special issue 1998), 82, 83; Ed Hinton, "The King," *Sports Illustrated* 77 (October 19, 1992): 70.

54. Hagstrom, *NASCAR Way,* 152–54; Hinton, "King," 70; Bechtel, "King," 83.

55. Golenbock, *American Zoom,* 91, 100.

56. Hinton, "King," 68.

57. Assael, *Wide Open,* 39; Bechtel, "King," 82.

58. Bones Bourcier, "What Humpy Thinks . . . about Everything," *Stock Car Racing* 32 (July 1997): 57; Bechtel, "King," 85.

59. Ben White, "Interview: Jeff Gordon," *Winston Cup NASCAR Illustrated* 16 (August 1997): 23–24; Richard Huff, "On the Fast Track," *Inside NASCAR* 1 (June/July 1997): 22; Scott Burton, "Total Coverage," *Richard Petty's Stock Car Magazine* 2 (April 1998): 70.

60. Liz Clark, "The Boy King," *Richard Petty's Stock Car Magazine* 1 (1997): 26; Hemphill, *Wheels,* 168.

61. Bones Bourcier, "The Next Jeff Gordon (Is Not Your Kid!)," *Stock Car Racing* 32 (July 1997): 12; White, "Interview," 26.

62. Mark Bechtel, "Jeff Gordon," *Sports Illustrated Presents 50 Years of NASCAR, 1948–1998* (special issue 1998), 100.

63. Bones Bourcier, "Winning Attitude," *Stock Car Racing* 32 (June 1997): 20.

64. Karsen Palmer Price, "NASCAR's Most-Watched Woman Savors Stardom without Losing Herself," *NASCAR Winston Cup Illustrated* 16 (September 1997): 43.

65. Quoted in Bechtel, "Jeff Gordon," 100.

66. Bones Bourcier, "Larger Than Life," *Stock Car Racing* 16 (March 1997): 24; Mark Bechtel, "Dale Earnhardt," *Sports Illustrated Presents 50 Years of NASCAR, 1948–1998* (special issue 1998), 96; Ed Hinton, "Attitude for Sale," *Sports Illustrated* 82 (February 6, 1995): 72–73.

67. Mark Zeske, "Expansion Years," *Inside NASCAR Presents: NASCAR's 50 Greatest Moments* (Winter 1998): 129; Hinton, "Attitude for Sale," 72–73.

68. Hemphill, *Wheels,* 22.

69. Wheeler quoted in Hinton, "Attitude for Sale," 71–72; Earnhardt quoted in "Is Earnhardt the Greatest Driver Ever?" *Inside NASCAR* 1 (January/February 1997): 32.

70. Clark and Wheeler quoted in Hinton, "Attitude for Sale," 71–72.

71. ESPN SportsZone, "Conversation with Dale Earnhardt," February 16, 1998, <http://espnet.sportszone.com>.

72. Hemphill, *Wheels,* 42.

73. Hagstrom, *NASCAR Way,* 152–54; Wheeler quoted in Bourcier, "What Humpy Thinks," 58.

74. "It's a Jock Thing," *Sports Illustrated* (Special issue 1997: "Winston Cup"), 9.

75. Joyce Standridge, "Echoes from the Past," *Stock Car Racing* 16 (November 1997): 18; Sabates quoted in Angelique S. Chengelis, "What, Another Gordon?" *Richard Petty's Stock Car Magazine* 1 (1997): 50.

13. Manhood, Memory, and White Men's Sports in the American South

TED OWNBY

In the 1960s, Paul Dietzel, the football coach at Louisiana State University and later the University of South Carolina, loved to read his own poem when he spoke at athletic banquets. He called it "Sissy."

> Is it a sissy to be the first guy on the practice field.
> Is it a sissy to be the most vicious tackle on the squad.
> Is it a sissy to *knock* your opponent on his butt.
>> Pick him up, and say, "get braced, Buddie, cause
>> That's how our team does things!"
> Is it a sissy to say NO when your buddies ask you to join them in abusing
> your body by dissipation
> And your only excuse that you can say is, "I don't think that'll help me to be
> a National Champion."
> A sissy to teach a Sunday School class like Jerry Stovall, or
> A sissy to believe in God.
> Yes, it takes a real sissy to be the toughest guy on the field and not a *tough* in
> the classroom,
> A sissy to wear short hair rather than a mop-cut like the rest of the girls,
> A sissy believes that the *team* always comes first before any personal
> glorification,
> And only a sissy has courage enough to be a *member* of a team rather than
> one of the creeps
>> whom every bartender in the area calls by first name.
> He's definitely a *sissy* if he respects Mom and Dad and honors their wishes,
> And he's not only a sissy, but a stupid one too if he "guts it out" even if he
> doesn't get to play too
>> much rather than joining the *ever growing ranks* of quitters.

And of those who get to play, you'll note that the sissies'll lay it on the line
    any time the team asks.
If that's being a sissy
    Thank God for sissies
        I'm hunting for sissies
Because sissies, Gentlemen, are the timber
    From which CHAMPIONS are fashioned.[1]

Perhaps the most remarkable thing about this poem is that Dietzel felt that he needed to defend football players from charges of being sissies. Believing that some people considered his players less than manly, Dietzel hoped that irony could show the positive and manly values of football.

Few images of the contemporary American South seem to say as much about the region as the beloved college football coach, the stock car driver, or the lonely deer hunter. This essay offers an interpretation of the relationship between sports, white male identity, and regional memory. Does it mean anything significant to be southern, white, and male after all of the changes that have challenged the traditional meanings of manhood in the American South since the 1940s? And do the meanings of being white and male and southern have any connection to older meanings rooted in southern history? Why would a football coach in the American South have to defend his players against charges of being sissies?

There was a time when sports had little to do with southern identity. Sports hardly appear at all in the classic works from the 1930s through the 1950s in which one white male southern writer after another tried to define what it meant to be southern. Most clearly, in *I'll Take My Stand*, published in 1930, the Vanderbilt Agrarians mentioned sports primarily to say southern culture was better off without them. The Agrarians valued leisure and thought southern history offered modern America an example of a culture given over not to strenuous work and acquisitiveness but to noncompetitive pleasures enjoyed in a community setting. Donald Davidson complained that in industrial society, "The furious pace of our working hours is carried over into our leisure hours, which are feverish and energetic," and he claimed that most modern forms of play are "undertaken as a nervous relief." In his introduction to the volume, John Crowe Ransom included only one sport when he asserted that the best habits of the region's people were the "social arts of dress, conversation, manners, the table, the hunt, politics, oratory, the pulpit. These were the arts of living and not the arts of escape; they were also community arts, in which every class of society could participate after its kind. The South took life easy, which is itself a tolerably comprehensive art."[2]

Eleven years later, in another aggressive attempt to define what it meant to be white, male, and southern, W. J. Cash analyzed the leisure and hunting of southern white men not as part of long communal traditions but as one of the new and defining features of antebellum southern culture. Most white men, separated by slavery, fertile land, and fat hogs from the need to work very hard, felt free to enjoy the pleasures of the frontier. Cash claimed that most antebellum white men hunted not as a continuation of English tradition or within an agrarian sense of identity but out of a hedonistic pursuit of intense, individualistic excitement. When the typical southern white farmer hunted, "It was simply and primarily for the same reason that, in his youth and often into late manhood, he ran spontaneous and unpremeditated foot-races, wrestled, drank Gargantuan quantities of raw whisky, let off wild yells, and hunted the possum; because the thing was already in his mores when he emerged from the backwoods, because on the frontier, it was the obvious thing to do, because he was a hot, stout fellow, full of blood and reared to outdoor activity, because of a primitive and naive zest for the pursuit in hand."[3] Thus, Cash's sportsman is not the Agrarians' hunter who understood his pleasures as part of a folk community; nor, certainly, was he the sportsman of the Teddy Roosevelt age, who sought especially physical pleasures because his work and education allowed him no excitement or exertion. Instead, this was a sportsman with no boundaries and no limits.[4] For both Cash and the Agrarians, hunting was the only sport that mattered in thinking about southern identity, and it was part of a complex of activities not related to sport. Writing at the same time, William Faulkner was creating the most exhaustive portrait of southern life, and he had the same relative inattention to all sports except hunting. He wrote at length about hunting, but his only character who played a modern sport did so outside the knowledge and respect of the various communities of Faulkner's men. In *The Hamlet,* published in 1940, Roy Labove, a teacher and University of Mississippi student, played football, but he had to explain the game to a planter who had never seen it and showed no particular interest in it. The game also held no interest for his own family, who only cared that he brought them back shoes, or even for the students he was teaching, or their parents.[5]

Beyond those books, it becomes almost ridiculous to think about sports as playing a significant role in the works that analyzed southern identity at mid-century. William Alexander Percy's *Lanterns on the Levee,* published in 1941, is the classic statement of what upper-class manhood meant to someone who felt his generation could not live up to that standard. He had a chapter entitled "A Small Boy's Heroes," which if written today almost certainly would include some sports figures. His heroes were men his father knew—

amateur philosophers, accomplished talkers. The only sport he mentioned was, again, hunting, which he associated with the self-assurance of his father. But Will Percy himself considered hunting a sport that was "lacerating to the spirit."[6] The other major work of 1941 was *Let Us Now Praise Famous Men*, by James Agee and Walker Evans. The book says not a word about sport, and it is almost impossible to imagine the tenant farmer men of the Ricketts, Woods, and Gudger families as fans of spectator sports—almost as impossible as it is to imagine their contemporary male descendants *not* following sports of some kind.[7]

The final work in that body of literature that searched so hard for the identity of southern white men was C. Vann Woodward's essay "The Search for Southern Identity," published in 1958. Interested less in the values of white southerners than their defining experiences, Woodward said that what made people southern was their shared experience with military defeat, agricultural poverty, and racial conflict and guilt. In a fourth point, Woodward wrote that southerners, black and white, male and female, had learned the importance of the past and a sense of limits in thinking about the future.[8] There was little in those points that one could even try to attach to sports. The experience of limits and the understanding gained from defeat offer little help in understanding contemporary spectator sports, with their emphasis on money, publicity, and devotion to winning.

The belabored point is that when white male writers at mid-century tried to figure out what made white men think of themselves as southerners, they thought of no organized sports and of no sports at all except hunting. They wrote about government and politics, economics and work, certainly race and the Civil War, probably religion, but they did not write about sports. For comparison, one needs only to think of all of the people who have chosen over the years to theorize about why baseball helped define American culture. Up to mid-century, no sport attracted much attention from people trying to define southern culture. In fact, the first writer in that genre who wrote about team sports, Thomas Clark in *The Emerging South*, published in 1961, interpreted them as a sign of how much the South was changing. Discussing high school and college football and basketball, he wrote, "Today most southern communities have developed a local mania over their athletic teams. Even hardened old rednecks who have wandered in from the cotton fields have caught the fever. Fifty years ago they would have regarded these sports as either effeminate or juvenile."[9]

If a similar body of literature in the late 1990s tried to explain what it means to be a southerner, sports would seem far more significant.[10] If no one thought John Heisman helped to define southern identity for white men in his day, many people think Bear Bryant and Richard Petty have helped them define what it means to be a southerner. This should not be surprising. Scholars of southern identity have been saying for some time that as the objective features of southern distinctiveness decline—a concentration on farming, poverty, state-supported racial segregation, a single-party political system—people in the South, especially white people, have been looking to culture for definitions of regional identity.[11] The most celebrated of these scholars, John Shelton Reed, argues that a southern middle class has developed a particular desire for consumer products like magazines, books, T-shirts, and food that can offer an identity in the midst of the seeming placelessness and timelessness of mass culture.[12]

Have modern sports offered part of that identity?[13] If so, have they offered any connections to traditional meanings of manhood in the South? Historians have described at least five definitions of manhood that southern white men once claimed as their own.[14] First was the goal of personal independence. To many southern white men, working for someone else or depending on someone else for one's livelihood seemed to resemble the position of slaves or women, or men with no character.[15] Second was the concept of honor. Men whose sense of esteem came not from themselves but from their communities had an extraordinary sensitivity to challenge and insult and a corresponding desire to prove themselves publicly.[16] A third meaning involved racism—especially the desire white men had long showed for physical power over African American men.[17] Fourth was the notion of paternalism. That meaning defined fatherly control as the best model for all of society and tended to celebrate the rule and special character of an old upper class.[18] A final meaning, one especially important in discussing sports, is the "helluvafella," a term W. J. Cash used to describe the hedonistic man cut off from past social institutions. According to Cash, the primary interest of the helluvafella was "To stand on his head in a bar, to toss down a pint of raw whiskey in a gulp, to fiddle and dance all night, to bite off the nose or gouge out the eye of a favorite enemy, to fight harder and love harder than the next man."[19] The rest of this essay asks what modern hunting, stock car racing, and college football have come to express about the identities of southern white men and if they continue any of those five traditional meanings of manhood.

Hunting is the one sport with roots deep in southern history. Many people who do not hunt have little idea of how dramatically hunting practices have changed in the past fifty to seventy-five years, but it seems fair to argue that hunting has changed in that period more than it has stayed the same.

In the late 1800s and early 1900s, with large numbers of people living on farmland either as owners or laborers, hunting operated both as a sport and a supplement to family diets.[20] Men pursued a broad range of small animals—squirrels and rabbits most of all, raccoons and opossums, foxes, doves, quail—all of which could help feed the family. Large game such as deer did not thrive in an agricultural system that spread farm people widely on the land; deer lived primarily on uncleared areas around rivers, and the bears and panthers that once roamed substantial parts of the South fared even worse.

Two realities helped encourage the helluvafella pursuit that W. J. Cash described. First, hunters often took small game in large numbers and thus could delight in a kind of binge-killing.[21] Second, general access to land that almost everyone treated as common encouraged most hunters to feel free to pursue and kill any game they found. This freedom encouraged the widespread use of dogs in most forms of hunting, and hunting with dogs encouraged a rushed kind of attack on game. (The important exception to this access to common land were African Americans. Large landowners had tried to restrict their access to hunting since shortly after emancipation, largely because they did not want potential laborers to be able to feed themselves.)[22] But most white hunters had access to most game on most land. To return to my list of definitions of manhood, white men in the late nineteenth and early twentieth century could hunt in ways that combined the notion of personal independence, in putting food on the table, with the notion of the helluvafella, in the freedom to run like crazy over fields and through woods with few worries about limits of any kind.

The best scholarly work on hunting in the modern South, Wiley Prewitt's M.A. thesis on Mississippi, concludes that "Just as slipping out the back gate for a mess of quail symbolized hunting" in the earlier period, "so the drive from town to the rural deer camp symbolized the chase after agricultural mechanization, demographic reorganization and organized wildlife conservation."[23] The most significant change involves the dramatic decline in the number of people who make their living from farming. Most of those people and their descendants now live in towns and in cities, and they do not step out the back gate to help feed their families. Closely connected to that change is the revolution in land use, with the rise of large-scale commercial farming and the dramatic growth of the timber industry. Owners of large expanses of profitable rural land have severely restricted any access hunters may have to it.

With those changes, hunting land is simply not available to many people, or at least not easily accessible or affordable. There is public hunting land, available to anyone with a license and a brightly colored vest, and on certain Saturdays in November public lands are full of orange-clad men with guns. But most people in the South gain access to hunting land either by leasing it, sometimes from timber companies, or by joining all-male hunting clubs for several hundred dollars a year. As hunting becomes a commodity, the poor—increasingly urban and with access to land blocked out by fences, prominently posted "no hunting" signs, and their own lack of income—are more than ever left out of the sport. For most hunters or would-be hunters, the sport has little to do with gaining personal independence.

With the changes in land use, the animals hunted have also changed. Deer thrive in areas with low human populations, so with rural depopulation and with help from state game policy, they have returned in extraordinary numbers. In Mississippi, where deer were rare early in the century outside a few areas of the state, deer and deer hunters thrive in every county. Turkeys, which also need a great deal of space, have likewise increased in number and in popularity as game birds. On the contrary, quail numbers have declined in many parts of the South, and today they thrive primarily on quail preserves kept largely for wealthy hunters and their high-priced dogs. Rabbit hunting and squirrel hunting survive, but certainly not with the popularity they once had.[24]

Hunting with dogs has declined, and with it the helluvafella frontal assault on game has declined as well. Hunting with dogs only made sense when land was treated as common, because of course dogs do not respect property rights. Many hunting clubs have passed rules against hunting with dogs, and some hunting groups are trying to make it illegal. Dogs remain essential in fox hunts and quail hunts, both of which have become primarily upper-class sports on land preserved just for the purpose, and in coon hunting.[25]

Perhaps the greatest change of all is the extraordinary complexity of the rules. Southern legislatures first created game and fish commissions in the early twentieth century, but the complexity and enforcement of the rules has grown dramatically in recent decades. Once the hunter has found a place to hunt, he must think about the season, the number of game, the size, the age, and sometimes the sex of the game, and the legality of his own weapon before proceeding with his sport. Once he hunts, he must then report frequently to a state official to prove he is not breaking the rules.

Most hunters recognize the need for game conservation and in one way or another have led movements for it. However, the larger point is that the modern experience of hunting is an extremely limiting sport. It has limits on space, with the hunting camp as a fenced area beyond which hunting is not acceptable. Men no longer hunt in the natural world, they hunt in what are essentially special sporting arenas with special rules.[26] It has limits on time, both in the seasons in which certain hunting is legal and the time hunters must find away from their nonagricultural employment. It has limits enforced by state officials. And it has limits based on the ability to pay. With all of those limits, hunting is becoming very much like a modern sport—a commodity for the middle and upper classes, enjoyed primarily on weekends, at special places and times, with arcane rules determined by a distant governing body.

There are, to be sure, traditional sides of hunting. Men still take pleasure in escaping everyday behavior into a male world in a natural environment. Young men still learn from older men. Gun ownership and marksmanship are still parts of the definitions of freedom. Nonetheless, the changes are significant enough that it seems fair to conclude that hunting offers few connections to traditional definitions of manhood. Modern hunting does not help men gain independence; it simply represents freedom from the job. Hunting is rarely part of being a helluvafella; with the many limits on hunting, the sense of limitless freedom is a distant memory.

Stock car racing is one of the few professional sports with unmistakable southern origins. As an organized sport, it began in the 1930s in the South, most of the races are held in the South, and virtually all of the drivers and most of the team members and owners are white southerners. The sport's best drivers are some of the most durable and most recognizable white southern heroes—especially working-class heroes—and the striking number of recent drivers who are the sons of older drivers suggests that fans can follow a racing family for their entire lives.

Significantly, stock car racing is one of the few mass sporting events in which white people make up virtually all of the spectators and participants. Perhaps stock racing offers lower-class whites the connection to a regional past that hunting does not allow. Stock car racing seems the clearest example in sport of what bluegrass represents in southern music; that is, something new that seems old and seems to offer connection to the past.[27] In fact, racing has numerous connections with the music of white southerners. Racing figures have drawn the comparisons themselves,[28] and today one can turn on the radio on Saturdays and hear the AC-Delco NASCAR Country Countdown, which calls itself "the fastest two hours on radio."

One could easily construct an argument that would depict stock car racing as a white man's paradise. Even more than hunting, it is an almost exclusively male sport. One prominent mechanic made the point that " 'If you get mad at the car and you want to cuss because the damn thing won't run, you shouldn't have to turn around and apologize to some woman.' "[29] With few exceptions, the women of significance in the sport are waiting in Victory Lane with champagne, kisses, and corporate logos. It is well known—probably too well known—that some of the earliest racers learned to drive fast by bootlegging whiskey in the hills of North Carolina. The term "good ol' boy" was coined to describe the early driving hero Junior Johnson in a mem-

orable article by Tom Wolfe, a starry-eyed New York writer looking for someone who combined folk traditions and resistance to authority.[30] The scholar
inclined to think of the sport as a carrier of traditional male identities could
make a case that begins with the helluvafella who lives for immediate, hedonistic pleasures like speed, then connects that to the legacy Junior Johnson
represented in trying to maintain independence by selling a corn product,
and then ties it all together with the southern white man's traditional resistance to the federal government. In those ways, the sport, despite its recent
origins, would seem a thoroughly traditional union of the goal of independence with the pleasures of the helluvafella.

But there are serious problems with drawing a straight line from traditional
meanings of southern manhood to Winston Cup racing. Writers about stock
car racing have almost certainly overstated the significance of the bootlegging origins of the sport.[31] As an organized sport, it began not in the mountains but in Daytona Beach, Florida, a relatively new place, a tourist place, a
place for new money, people, and technology. And the sport has numerous
corporate elements that have either helped or forced redefinitions of old
concepts of manhood.

It seems fair to speculate that stock car racing is particularly appealing to
working-class southern white men who are undergoing one of the most
significant changes in the region's economic life. Most southern industry has
been the kind that moves into a town that offers a package of tax breaks, puts
up an inexpensive building, hires some nonunion workers, and then moves
on to another town or another part of the world.[32] Workers in those insecure
jobs can choose to move repeatedly, but many choose to live in the same place
and drive a lot. For workers who drive substantial distances five or six days a
week, the time on the road is probably a significant part of the meaning of
freedom. It is time away from an unsatisfying job and contemporary uncer-
tainties about family life. When they are on the road, they want to drive fast,
and they can for a time feel free from anyone—boss, government, parent, or
wife—trying to tell them what to do. In that definition of freedom, they seem
connected less to country music, where the road always leads either safely
home to a good woman or to sin and sadness,[33] than to the message of 1970s
southern rock music that portrayed life on the road as a constant reality and
the only place for any real pleasure. It was Lynyrd Skynyrd who sang, "The
only time I'm satisfied is when I'm on the road."[34] For people who identify
with such a sentiment, stock car racing—driving with no ultimate destina-
tion—represents a significant part of the definition of freedom.

By identifying freedom with life on the road, fans of stock car racing also
identify themselves with at least part of the corporate side of stock car rac-

ing. More important to the experience of racing and race-watching than the corporate sponsors—Tide and Mountain Dew and Spam and the rest—are the ways the cars themselves connect the sport and the fans to Detroit automakers. Two myths about the cars tell democratic stories. One asserts that the cars are, in appearance at least, essentially the same as the cars anyone can buy. As the former driver and owner Bud Moore from Spartanburg, South Carolina, said, "'we're running the kind of cars that Mr. Tom, Dick and Harry can go down and buy. I mean a replica of that car. . . . This is really what brought stock car racing along, because we raced the cars that the American public drives.'"[35] The former driver and announcer Ned Jarrett made the same point. "'You see cars raced in stock car racing that look like your own car.'" The second myth is that fans root for stock cars of the same brand as the cars they drive themselves. As Richard Petty said of race fans, "'if they drove a Pontiac, they pulled for Pontiac. If they drove a Ford they pulled for Ford.'" Bud Moore agreed, "'If you drive a Ford, you love that Ford to death and you want to see it win.'"[36]

These are myths. The cars we drive do not go 190 miles per hour, and we do not drive them on specially constructed speedways that allow us to take turns at full speed. But like other myths in sport, these myths help reveal some of the attraction of the sport. The idea that an important part of freedom is the ability to select among consumer choices has a short history in the South. Whereas white men traditionally tied freedom to control over production, this freedom suggests pleasure and identity in consumption—in buying a favorite car.

Thus, the notion of personal independence embodied in stock car racing has taken the old notion of freedom from being controlled and celebrates the relatively few moments that allow that kind of freedom. Obviously, stock car racing, as a mass spectator sport, merely represents and celebrates that freedom for people who feel they do not have much of it in the rest of their lives. If the modern southern white man believes freedom comes with mobility, he is celebrating in stock car racing a form of mobility that goes nowhere except around and around and around.

The ideal of the helluvafella also lives in stock car racing. The sheer emphasis on speed, on barely escaping injury, on running as fast as possible, sounds as much as any modern sport like something W. J. Cash would have recognized. One of the biggest reasons for the popularity of Dale Earnhardt, nicknamed The Intimidator, is that his racing style risked his own safety and the good will of other drivers by trying to drive without limits, most obviously by bumping drivers who got in his way. Richard Petty claimed that such an attitude fueled the early popularity of the sport in the South. When stock car racing was "about as unrespectable as a sport could be," he remembered that "Nobody would give an inch, and if one guy didn't get out of the way, they would run right over him."[37]

But there are complications with trying to see the stock car driver as a helluvafella. Stock car racing, even more than hunting, is an extremely complex sport, with numerous rules that change every year both to protect the drivers and to offer the illusion that the cars do indeed have some qualities of the stock that anyone can buy. Stock car racing is a sport for cheaters—a sport for understanding the limits of what one can do to one's car and going beyond them only slightly. It says something about the sport that the first race sanctioned by NASCAR, at Charlotte in 1949, involved a substantial amount of money (a six-thousand-dollar winner's prize), attracted a surprising crowd (thirteen thousand people), and saw its winner disqualified for cheating.[38] Perhaps part of the appeal lies in feeling that the stock car racer can be a helluvafella within a system dominated by rules and officials. Thus it may be that stock car racing offers dramatizations of the helluvafella and a very limited dramatization of the ideal of personal independence in a spectator sport dominated by technology and corporate power. He is not free from rules; he gains freedom by breaking the rules.

The only sport to rival stock car racing in popularity in the South is college football. College football was a growing sport in the early 1900s, but it did not dominate newspapers, normal conversation, and life on Saturdays on campuses and in campus towns until the post–World War II period. The early proponents of football at southern colleges, as Patrick Miller and Andrew Doyle have shown, tried hard to link the game to regional symbols and to derive regional pride from it,[39] but it took a long time before football came to work in the opposite direction and helped define what it meant to be southern.

Just as changes in hunting illustrate cultural shifts related to changes in agriculture and stock car racing dramatizes changes in how lower-class whites make their living, college football only makes sense in light of changes in the South's upper and middle classes. The most important precondition for the growing popularity of college football lies in the dramatic increase in the number of people in the South who attend colleges and universities. Throughout most of southern history, higher education was reserved for the wealthy. The number of students was on the rise with the building of agricultural and teachers' colleges in the late 1800s and early 1900s, but by far the most dramatic increase has come since World War II. In 1950, 565,000 people in the southern states attended college of some kind. By 1992 there were 4.2 million—a rate of expansion far surpassing the national rate.[40]

In his 1971 autobiography, the University of Mississippi coach Johnny Vaught recalled that football seemed irrelevant to most people in northern Mississippi when he started coaching in the 1940s. The farmers who went to the town square on Saturdays, he said, were not interested in football. "[T]he university had to face the fact that a lot of farmers didn't know or care that 15,000 people were yelling their lungs out a mile away from the square. I suppose many of those who heard the cheers wondered 'what in tarnation' was going on. But times change. Today, they and their children are sitting in the stands at kickoff time."[41] What happened is that the number of those farmers declined dramatically, and the number of people whose livelihoods connected them to the university system increased almost as sharply. The farmers did not have a change of heart and start going to the games; more importantly, their children started going to colleges and universities and developed closer ties to university social life.

Connections between the nature of modern football and college education are clear. Football has become an enormously complicated sport with complexities that mirror the technical, scientific, and especially professional language and expertise demanded by the economic changes of the modern South. Football probably has the fattest rulebook of any sport, and that book changes every year. The sport has a large number of officials on the field to enforce those rules. Not only is the rule book long and complex, the playbook is longer than many university textbooks. Football forces its players to learn a complex technical language that combines a numerical system with idiosyncratic jargon. And players do not simply learn their own language; every week they learn the language of the other team. Football requires considerable memorization in dealing with plays and scouting reports, and it requires constant close scrutiny in dealing with games on film. During the season, some coaches give tests, some of them more than once a week, to make sure players keep up with their own plays, new plays, and plays run by opposing teams.

In his book *Bobby Dodd on Football,* the Georgia Tech coach made a point in 1954 that coaches probably say about each new generation of players. Because of innovations in the game, he wrote, "A player had to be thinking all the time to play at any position on a modern football team and the days of sheer brawn were gone forever." In the first sentence of that book, Dodd celebrated the increasing complexity of the sport, saying, "the game of football has advanced from the roughest of beginnings to one of the most scientific and interesting of all athletic events."[42] With its emphasis on technical language and specialized knowledge, football represented the sport of a society undergoing the kind of professionalization that characterized the northeastern United States much earlier in the twentieth century.[43]

But when football fans, players, and coaches talk about their sport, they rarely emphasize specialized knowledge, idiosyncratic language, and numerical systems. The long-time University of Alabama coach Bear Bryant said he asked parents of potential players, "Listen, does your boy know how to work? Try to teach him to work, to sacrifice, to *fight*."[44] He and most coaches claim that football embodies and teaches essential character traits. Are any of those traits, like the willingness to fight, part of the traditional southern meanings of manhood? There is no sense of the traditional meaning of personal independence in football. Players learn to work within their coach's system, or they do not play. Likewise, there may be some degree of the helluvafella in the headhunting linebacker, but football places so many limits on what players can and cannot do that Cash's ideal type has little role on the team either. Most of the violence within football is carefully coached, and it has little to do with the limitless hedonism Cash imagined.

If football continues any of the traditional definitions of manhood, it would seem to be the old language of honor. Bear Bryant, in a section of his autobiography in which he condemned quitters, recalled, "I've laid it on the line to a lot of boys. I've grabbed 'em, kicked 'em, and embarrassed them in front of the squad. I've got down in the dirt with them, and if they didn't give as well as they took I'd tell them they were insults to their upbringing, and I've cleaned out their lockers for them and piled their clothes out in the hall, thinking I'd make them prove what they had in their veins, blood or spit, one way or the other, and praying they would come through."[45] Bryant's statement brings together several features Bertram Wyatt-Brown described as part of the antebellum concept of honor—the overpowering fear of being shamed within the male community, the need to protect the family name, and the centrality of violence. The notion that a man either had character or did not—either had blood or spit in his veins—also sounds a great deal like the old notion of upholding one's own honor from any challenge.[46]

Bryant's assertion that football echoed an old code of ethics returns to Paul Dietzel and his sissies. Football players, Dietzel said, could not be countercultural figures. They do not drink or enjoy "dissipation" and thus could not be a helluvafella. Nor could football players believe strongly in personal independence; they had to think of the team before themselves and be willing to "lay it on the line any time the team asks." Thus, honor came to mean fighting for one's team and, ultimately, serving one's college.

To conclude, none of these three sports offers a direct line to any of the traditional definitions of southern white manhood. Modern hunting offers a faint resemblance of the experience of personal independence, but only in a postagricultural South. Stock car racing offers a drama about the independence of mobility and a vision of the helluvafella in a corporate and consumer age. And college football offers violence within the language of group honor, but in a university setting that stresses technical language, complicated planning, and the crucial significance of the team. People thinking and writing about sports should be wary of making simplistic assertions about regional stereotypes as if any of these sports were part of ages-old folk cultures. In all three sports, the traditional southern meanings of manhood have undergone dramatic redefinition to fit contemporary needs.

Men playing and watching modern sports may be expressing other, newer notions of manhood and newer southern identities. Only new questions can sort out how the racial desegregation of team sports, the growing importance of women's athletics, and the rapid expansion of professional sports may offer new definitions of region and gender. There is no reason to believe that the concept of the South has become meaningless in discussions of sports, but it seems clear that modern sports offer white southern men a sense of regional identity that has little to do with southern history.

Notes

This chapter is reprinted, with minor editorial changes, from *International Journal of the History of Sport* 15 (August 1998): 103–18, with the permission of the editor, J. A. Mangan, and Frank Cass Publishers.

1. Paul F. Dietzel, "Sissy," in *Coaching Football* (New York: Ronald Press, 1971), 7–8.

2. Donald Davidson, "A Mirror for Artists," and John Crowe Ransom, "Reconstructed but Unregenerate," in *I'll Take My Stand: The South and the Agrarian Tradition,* by Twelve Southerners (Baton Rouge: Louisiana State University Press, 1958), 34.

3. W. J. Cash, *The Mind of the South* (New York: Alfred A. Knopf, 1941), 31–32.

4. On physicality and sports among Victorian men, see Steven A. Riess, "Sport and the Redefinition of American Middle-Class Masculinity," *International Journal of the History of Sport* 8 (1991): 5–27.

5. William Faulkner, *The Hamlet* (New York: Random House, 1940), 103–13.

6. William Alexander Percy, *Lanterns on the Levee: Recollections of a Planter's Son* (Baton Rouge: Louisiana State University Press, 1941), 58.

7. James Agee and Walker Evans, *Let Us Now Praise Famous Men* (Boston: Houghton Mifflin, 1941).

8. C. Vann Woodward, "The Search for Southern Identity," *Virginia Quarterly Review* 34 (1958): 321–28.

9. Thomas D. Clark, *The Emerging South* (New York: Oxford University Press, 1961), 162.

10. Near the conclusion of his interpretation of the twentieth-century South, Pete Daniel describes football as very significant, but not as a part of regional identity. A growing middle class, he writes, "laughed at the sitcoms, told racist jokes, belched through

football games, sent their children to soccer practice, worried about drugs, read *Southern Living* and *Sports Illustrated,* attended a nearby church (or watched one of the evangelists on television), and lived or died by the victories and defeats of their college alma maters. In other words, they were thoroughly American." Pete Daniel, *Standing at the Crossroads: Southern Life since 1900* (New York: Hill and Wang, 1986), 230.

11. The most prolific proponent of this point is John Shelton Reed. See his works such as *The Enduring South: Subcultural Persistence in Mass Society* (Chapel Hill: University of North Carolina Press, 1972); *One South: An Ethnic Approach to Regional Culture* (Baton Rouge: Louisiana State University Press, 1982); and *"My Tears Spoiled My Aim" and Other Reflections on Southern Culture* (Columbia: University Press of Missouri, 1993).

12. Reed, *One South,* 119–38.

13. For a characterization of modern sports, see Allen Guttmann, *A Whole New Ball Game: An Interpretation of American Sports* (Chapel Hill: University of North Carolina Press, 1988).

14. I have described these meanings in more detail in "Freedom, Manhood, and Male Tradition in 1970s Southern Rock Music," in *Haunted Bodies: Gender and Southern Texts,* ed. Anne Goodwyn Jones and Susan V. Donaldson (Charlottesville: University Press of Virginia, 1998), 369–88, esp. 371.

15. Among the many works discussing the significance of personal independence for men are Lacy K. Ford Jr., *Origins of Southern Radicalism: The South Carolina Upcountry, 1800–1860* (New York: Oxford University Press, 1988); Steven A. Hahn, *The Roots of Southern Populism: Yeoman Farmers and the Transformation of the Georgia Upcountry, 1850–1890* (New York: Oxford University Press, 1983); Joan E. Cashin, *A Family Venture: Men and Women on the Southern Frontier* (New York: Oxford University Press, 1991); and Stephanie McCurry, *Masters of Small Worlds: Yeoman Households, Gender Relations, and the Political Culture of the Antebellum South Carolina Low Country* (New York: Oxford University Press, 1995).

16. Bertram Wyatt-Brown, *Southern Honor: Ethics and Behavior in the Old South* (New York: Oxford University Press, 1982); Steven M. Stowe, *Intimacy and Power in the Old South: Ritual in the Lives of the Planters* (Baltimore: Johns Hopkins University Press, 1987); Edward L. Ayers, *Vengeance and Justice: Crime and Punishment in the Nineteenth-Century American South* (New York: Oxford University Press, 1984); Kenneth S. Greenberg, *Masters and Statesmen: The Political Culture of American Slavery* (Baltimore: Johns Hopkins University Press, 1985); Kenneth S. Greenberg, *Honor and Slavery: Lies, Duels, Noses, Masks, Dressing as a Woman, Gifts, Strangers, Humanitarianism, Death, Slave Rebellions, the Proslavery Argument, Baseball, Hunting, and Gambling in the Old South* (Princeton, N.J.: Princeton University Press, 1996).

17. See, for example, Winthrop D. Jordan, *White over Black: American Attitudes toward the Negro, 1550–1812* (Chapel Hill: University of North Carolina Press, 1968); and Joel Williamson, *The Crucible of Race: Black-White Relations in the American South since Emancipation* (New York: Oxford University Press, 1984).

18. The principal theorist on the significance of paternalism is Eugene D. Genovese. See especially *Roll, Jordan, Roll: The World the Slaves Made* (New York: Vintage Books, 1976). See also Elizabeth Fox-Genovese, *Within the Plantation Household: Black and White Women of the Old South* (Chapel Hill: University of North Carolina Press, 1988).

19. Cash, *Mind of the South,* 52. See also Elliott J. Gorn, "'Gouge and Bite, Pull Hair and

Scratch': The Social Significance of Fighting in the Southern Backcountry," *American Historical Review* 90 (February 1985): 18–43; Ted Ownby, *Subduing Satan: Religion, Recreation, and Manhood in the Rural South, 1865–1920* (Chapel Hill: University of North Carolina Press, 1990).

20. The following paragraphs on hunting draw on Wiley Charles Prewitt Jr., "The Best of All Breathing: Hunting and Environmental Change in Mississippi, 1900–1980" (M.A. thesis, University of Mississippi, 1991). The conclusions about the cultural distance of modern from earlier hunting are my own.

21. Ownby, *Subduing Satan*, 21–37.

22. Hahn, *Roots of Southern Populism;* Charles Flynn Jr., *White Land, Black Labor: Caste and Class in Late Nineteenth-Century Georgia* (Baton Rouge: Louisiana State University Press, 1983).

23. Prewitt, "Best of All Breathing," 131.

24. Ibid., 131–53.

25. On fox hunting, see Stuart A. Marks, *Southern Hunting in Black and White: Nature, History, and Ritual in a Carolina Community* (Princeton, N.J.: Princeton University Press, 1991), 93–134; and Wiley Charles Prewitt Jr., "Going Inside: Transformation of Fox Hunting in Mississippi," *Mississippi Folklife* 28 (1995): 26–32. On coon hunting, see Marks, *Southern Hunting in Black and White*, 231–62.

26. On space and modern sport, see John Bale, *Landscapes of Modern Sport* (Leicester: Leicester University Press, 1994).

27. On the ancient image of a relatively new form of music, see Robert Cantwell, *Bluegrass Breakdown: The Making of the Old Southern Sound* (New York: Da Capo Press, 1992).

28. Ned Jarrett compared stock car drivers to country music figures like Dolly Parton because both hailed from poor backgrounds but remained "down to earth" after they achieved wealth and fame. Sylvia Wilkinson, *Dirt Tracks to Glory: The Early Days of Stock Car Racing as Told by the Participants* (Chapel Hill, N.C.: Algonquin, 1983), 154.

29. Quoted in ibid., 81.

30. Tom Wolfe, "Junior Johnson Is the Last American Hero Yes!" *Esquire* 80 (October 1973): 211.

31. Arguing that previous writers, especially for Hollywood, have placed too much emphasis on bootlegging is Allan Girdler, *Stock Car Racers: The History and Folklore of NASCAR's Premier Series—"Tail Straight Out and Belly to the Ground"* (Osceola, Wis.: Motorbooks Illustrated, 1988), 13.

32. See James C. Cobb, *The Selling of the South: The Southern Crusade for Industrial Development, 1936–1990*, 2d ed. (Urbana: University of Illinois Press, 1993); Linda Flowers, *Throwed Away: Failures of Progress in Eastern North Carolina* (Knoxville: University of Tennessee Press, 1990).

33. Cecilia Tichi, *High Lonesome: The American Culture of Country Music* (Chapel Hill: University of North Carolina Press, 1994).

34. Lynyrd Skynyrd, "Whiskey Rock-a-Roller," *Gold and Platinum*, MCA (MCAD2-6898).

35. Wilkinson, *Dirt Tracks to Glory*, 74, 54. See also Richard Petty with William Neely, *King Richard I: The Autobiography of America's Greatest Auto Racer* (Toronto: Paperjacks, 1986), 64.

36. Girdler, *Stock Car Racers*, 42; Wilkinson, *Dirt Tracks to Glory*, 71. See also Petty, *King Richard I*, 26.

37. Petty, *King Richard I*, 40–41.

38. Girdler, *Stock Car Racers*, 28.

39. Andrew Doyle, "'Causes Won, Not Lost': College Football and the Modernization of the American South," *International Journal of the History of Sport* 11 (August 1994): 231–51; Patrick B. Miller, "The Manly, the Moral, and the Proficient: College Sport in the New South," in this volume.

40. See E. F. Schietinger, *Fact Book on Higher Education in the South, 1965* (Atlanta: Southern Regional Education Board, 1965), 18, for the figures on 1950. See National Center for Education Statistics, *Digest of Education Statistics* (Washington, D.C.: U.S. Department of Health, Education, and Welfare, 1994), 191, for the figures on 1992. On the southern rate of expansion, compared to the national rate, see Michael M. Myers, *Fact Book on Higher Education in the South, 1981 and 1982* (Atlanta: Southern Regional Education Board, 1982), 16.

41. John Vaught, *Rebel Coach: My Football Family* (Memphis: Memphis State University Press, 1971), 36.

42. Robert L. Dodd, *Bobby Dodd on Football* (New York: Prentice-Hall, 1954), 8, 1.

43. Still one of the major works on professionalization is Robert Wiebe, *The Search for Order, 1877–1920* (New York: Hill and Wang, 1967).

44. Paul W. Bryant and John Underwood, *Bear: The Hard Life and Good Times of Alabama's Coach Bryant* (Boston: Little, Brown, 1974), 10. The emphasis on fight is Bryant's.

45. Ibid., 11.

46. Wyatt-Brown, *Southern Honor*.

Contributors

PETER A. COCLANIS is the George and Alice Welsh Professor and chair of the Department of History at the University of North Carolina at Chapel Hill. He is the author of many works in economic, social, and business history, including *The Shadow of a Dream: Economic Life and Death in the South Carolina Low Country, 1670–1920* (1989), which won the Allan Nevins Prize of the Society of American Historians.

JACK E. DAVIS teaches history at the University of Alabama at Birmingham, where he directs the Environmental Studies Program. He is the author of *Race against Time: Culture and Separation in Natchez, Mississippi, since 1930* (2001) and the editor of *The Civil Rights Movement* (2000).

PAMELA DEAN is the archivist at the Northeast Archive of Folklore and Oral History at the University of Maine. She is the author of *Women on the Hill: A History of Women at the University of North Carolina* (1997) and a coauthor, with Petra Munroe and Toby Daspit, of *Talking Gumbo: A Teacher's Guide to Using Oral History in the Classroom* (1998).

ANDREW DOYLE is an assistant professor of history at Winthrop University. He has published articles on athletics and regional culture in a number of journals, including the *Journal of Sport History* (1997), and is working on a book tentatively titled *"Causes Won, Not Lost": A Cultural History of Southern College Football from the 1890s through the 1920s.*

ROBERT GUDMESTAD is an assistant professor of history at Southwest Baptist University in Bolivar, Missouri. His current research and writing concerns antebellum history and includes a book manuscript entitled "A Troublesome

Commerce: Southern Perceptions of the Interstate Slave Trade, 1815–1837." The essay reprinted here received the *Virginia Magazine of History and Biography*'s C. Coleman McGhee Award for best article by a graduate student.

RUSSELL J. HENDERSON is a doctoral candidate at the University of Mississippi and teaches at Maryville University in St. Louis, Missouri, and St. Charles County (Mo.) Community College. His dissertation will examine the social and legal history of the Twenty-sixth Amendment, which lowered the national voting age to eighteen, as part of his ongoing research in the history of American adolescence.

LOUIS M. KYRIAKOUDES is an assistant professor of history at the University of Southern Mississippi, where he specializes in nineteenth- and twentieth-century southern social and economic history. He is the author of *The Social Origins of the Urban South: Nashville, Tennessee, 1890–1930* (forthcoming) and articles in *Agricultural History, Social Science History,* and *Southern Cultures.*

RITA LIBERTI is an assistant professor in the Department of Kinesiology and Physical Education at California State University at Hayward. Her current research on women's competitive basketball at black colleges in the South prior to integration is an extension of her doctoral dissertation, "'We Were Ladies, We Just Played Basketball Like Boys': A Study of Women's Basketball at Historically Black Colleges and Universities in North Carolina, 1925–1945."

CHARLES H. MARTIN is an associate professor of history at the University of Texas at El Paso. His articles on sports history, race relations, and labor history have appeared in the *Journal of Southern History, Journal of Sport History, Journal of Negro History, Georgia Historical Quarterly,* and other historical reviews. Martin is currently completing a book manuscript on the color line in intercollegiate sports between 1890 and 1980. He is also the author of *The Angelo Herndon Case and Southern Justice.*

PATRICK B. MILLER is an associate professor of history at Northeastern Illinois University in Chicago. He is the author of *The Playing Fields of American Culture: Athletics and Higher Education, 1850–1945* (forthcoming) and the coauthor, with David K. Wiggins, of *The Unlevel Playing Field: A Documentary History of the African-American Experience in Sport* (forthcoming). He is also the coeditor, with Elisabeth Schäfer-Wünsche and Therese Frey Steffen, of *The Civil Rights Movement Revisited: Critical Perspectives on the Struggle for Equality in the United States* (2001) and has published articles in *The Journal of Sport History, Olympika, American Studies,* and the *History of Education Quarterly,* among other journals.

TED OWNBY is an associate professor of history and southern studies at the University of Mississippi. He is the author of *Subduing Satan: Religion, Recreation, and Manhood in the Rural South, 1865–1920* (1990) and *American Dreams in Mississippi: Consumers, Poverty, and Culture, 1830–1998* (1999) and the editor of *Black and White: Cultural Interaction in the Antebellum South* (1993).

DONALD JAY RYBACKI is chair of the Department of Communication and Performance Studies at Northern Michigan University and an associate dean of the College of Arts and Sciences. He is the coauthor, with Karyn Rybacki, of *Advocacy and Opposition: An Introduction to Argumentation* (1986) and *Communication Criticism: Approaches and Genres* (1991).

KARYN CHARLES RYBACKI is a professor of speech communication and public relations at Northern Michigan University. She is the coauthor, with Donald Rybacki, of *Advocacy and Opposition: An Introduction to Argumentation* (1986) and *Communication Criticism: Approaches and Genres* (1991).

Index

Sport and Society

A Sporting Time: New York City and the Rise of Modern Athletics, 1820–70
  Melvin L. Adelman
Sandlot Seasons: Sport in Black Pittsburgh   *Rob Ruck*
West Ham United: The Making of a Football Club   *Charles Korr*
Beyond the Ring: The Role of Boxing in American Society   *Jeffrey T. Sammons*
John L. Sullivan and His America   *Michael T. Isenberg*
Television and National Sport: The United States and Britain   *Joan M. Chandler*
The Creation of American Team Sports: Baseball and Cricket, 1838–72
  George B. Kirsch
City Games: The Evolution of American Urban Society and the Rise of Sports
  Steven A. Riess
The Brawn Drain: Foreign Student-Athletes in American Universities   *John Bale*
The Business of Professional Sports   *Edited by Paul D. Staudohar and*
  James A. Mangan
Fritz Pollard: Pioneer in Racial Advancement   *John M. Carroll*
Go Big Red! The Story of a Nebraska Football Player   *George Mills*
Sport and Exercise Science: Essays in the History of Sports Medicine   *Edited by*
  Jack W. Berryman and Roberta J. Park
Minor League Baseball and Local Economic Development   *Arthur T. Johnson*
Harry Hooper: An American Baseball Life   *Paul J. Zingg*
Cowgirls of the Rodeo: Pioneer Professional Athletes   *Mary Lou LeCompte*
Sandow the Magnificent: Eugen Sandow and the Beginnings of Bodybuilding
  David Chapman
Big-Time Football at Harvard, 1905: The Diary of Coach Bill Reid   *Edited by*
  Ronald A. Smith
Leftist Theories of Sport: A Critique and Reconstruction   *William J. Morgan*
Babe: The Life and Legend of Babe Didrikson Zaharias   *Susan E. Cayleff*
Stagg's University: The Rise, Decline, and Fall of Big-Time Football at Chicago
  Robin Lester
Muhammad Ali, the People's Champ   *Edited by Elliott J. Gorn*
People of Prowess: Sport, Leisure, and Labor in Early Anglo-America
  Nancy L. Struna
The New American Sport History: Recent Approaches and Perspectives   *Edited by*
  S. W. Pope
Making the Team: The Cultural Work of Baseball Fiction   *Timothy Morris*
Making the American Team: Sport, Culture, and the Olympic Experience
  Mark Dyreson
Viva Baseball! Latin Major Leaguers and Their Special Hunger   *Samuel O. Regalado*
Touching Base: Professional Baseball and American Culture in the
  Progressive Era (rev. ed.)   *Steven A. Riess*
Red Grange and the Rise of Modern Football   *John M. Carroll*
Golf and the American Country Club   *Richard J. Moss*

Extra Innings: Writing on Baseball   *Richard Peterson*
Global Games   *Maarten Van Bottenburg*
The Sporting World of the Modern South   *Edited by Patrick B. Miller*

Reprint Editions

The Nazi Olympics   *Richard D. Mandell*
Sports in the Western World (2d ed.)   *William J. Baker*

The University of Illinois Press
is a founding member of the
Association of American University Presses.

Composed in 10.5/13 Minion
with Minion display
by Jim Proefrock
at the University of Illinois Press
Manufactured by Thomson-Shore, Inc.

University of Illinois Press
1325 South Oak Street
Champaign, IL 61820-6903
www.press.uillinois.edu